INTERNATIONAL BANKING

INTERNATIONAL BANKING

Principles and Practices

edited by
Emmanuel N. Roussakis

PRAEGER SPECIAL STUDIES • PRAEGER SCIENTIFIC

Library of Congress Cataloging in Publication Data

Main entry under title:
International banking.

  Bibliography: p.
  Includes index.
  1. Banks and banking, International—Addresses,
essays, lectures.   2. Banks, and banking, American—
Addresses, essays, lectures.   I. Roussakis, Emmanuel N.
HG3881.I57516   1983   332.1'5   82-16660
ISBN 0-03-062387-1

Published in 1983 by Praeger Publishers
CBS Educational and Professional Publishing
a Division of CBS Inc.

© 1983 Praeger Publishers.

 456789   052   98765432

Printed in the United States of America

PREFACE

The unprecedented expansion in international trade and investment that the world economy has experienced since World War II has contributed to a phenomenal growth in the internationalization of banking activity. New types of international banking services have evolved; the volume of international services has expanded; and the number of banks offering these services has increased. As these changes have been taking place, there has also been a gradual shift from official to private sources of funding for international transactions.

The growing emphasis on private over government financing will continue for two reasons: legislative support for official government aid programs is declining, and international banking institutions are exhibiting an increasing capability to meet the international demand for credit. These important developments in international financing have occurred so rapidly that the existing literature has yet to match the significance of this change. This book has been undertaken in an effort to help narrow the gap in the literature.

More than a synopsis of the progress made to date in international banking, this book is a synthesis of the thinking of some of the best experts in the field. International banking involves so many areas of expertise that, in order to give proper treatment to each area, experts were drawn from the law, academe, and international banking. The objective of *International Banking: Principles and Practices* is to provide important insights into, and a frame of reference for understanding, the various aspects of international banking, with special emphasis on international lending policies, procedures, and considerations. Thus, it is hoped that the book will be of value to students, career-oriented individuals in international banking, customers of banks, lawyers involved in international banking, and academicians interested in how bankers manage their international business.

This book is designed to provide the principal materials on international banking and to expose the reader to the many issues involved. Those interested in the practical problems of international banking may find it useful to follow the reading of this book with another publication developed by the same editor, *International Lending by U.S. Commercial Banks: A Casebook* (New York:

Praeger, 1981). The combination of the two books should serve two major purposes: to stimulate the reader's thinking in dealing with related issues raised in these cases, and to help the reader develop (or improve) some basic analytical skills by using financial techniques in reaching sensible decisions for action.

Although practitioners will probably read selected chapters related to their interests, academicians may wish to utilize a variety of teaching approaches. The sequence of reading assignments will be based on the emphasis of the course. Those interested in a general overview can eliminate the more specialized lending chapters—7, 14, 15, 16, and 17—whereas those emphasizing credit analysis and lending would utilize those chapters but possibly eliminate the introductory chapters and those discussing the international banking function and structure. In order to accommodate the different selective approaches to reading the book, the editor has attempted to preserve the independence of each chapter. However, those utilizing the entire book may find minor overlap, and some differences of opinion, between the chapters. In such a dynamic, evolving atmosphere, differences of opinion are not only expected, but healthy and stimulating.

In developing this book I received important help and advice from several individuals. I am particularly indebted to Dean Constantine Kalogeras of the Ancell School of Business at Western Connecticut State College, Danbury, for his encouragement in the initial stages of this book, and subsequently for his helpful comments and suggestions on specific points in the manuscript. Special debt is also due to Richard Schwartz, assistant professor of English at Florida International University, Miami, for his valuable editorial assistance. Thanks are also in order to Melville Brown, vice-president, Mellon Bank, for valuable suggestions, and to Sofian Zakkout for performing the tedious task of indexing.

Special recognition should be given to the individual authors, without whom this book would not have been possible. Working with such a diverse group and so many exceptionally capable individuals was a challenging and stimulating experience.

Finally, my deep appreciation to my wife, Sophie, for her understanding and patient support; and to our daughter, Marina, and sons, Nicholas and George, for giving me the time to work on this book.

CONTENTS

LIST OF TABLES AND FIGURES

TABLES   Page

FIGURES

Part I

INTRODUCTION

1 EVOLUTION OF INTERNATIONAL BANKING AND ITS U.S. DEVELOPMENT
Emmanuel N. Roussakis

Perhaps the most remarkable development that the financial industry has experienced since the end of World War II has been the internationalization of banking. This development, which signals the beginning of a new era in international finance, was commenced by the major commericial banking institutions, located principally in Western Europe and the western hemisphere. The banks that took the lead and embarked on multinational banking were individual institutions from such foreign-banking-oriented countries as Canada, France, Germany, Switzerland, the United Kingdom, and the United States. To these countries one may also add Japan, whose banking institutions, though latecomers in the world financial arena, have played an increasingly important role in the development of international financing. Unhampered by geographical restrictions, these banks embarked upon the creation of worldwide networks of outlets and became actively engaged in international operations. The international expansion of these banks has brought about the effective linkage of national financial markets and the increasing integration of worldwide banking systems. Despite apparent differences in the patterns of their international expansion, these banks have become a truly multinational set of competing financial institutions.

Though collectively these various banks have been instrumental for the momentum generated in the internationalization of financial markets, on a national basis it is U.S. commercial banks that have been most active in these markets, and hence have come to dominate multinational banking. By and large they have exhibited a high degree of aggressiveness and flexibility, devising new ideas or copying foreign techniques, and adapting the structure and operations of their global networks to cope with new developments and changing situations. This leadership by U.S. banks represents the most recent phase in the history of international banking.

THE BEGINNING

Although commercial banking is one of the oldest industries in the United States (the first U.S. bank was organized in 1782, before the adoption of the Constitution), the growth of international activities of U.S. commercial banks has been only a recent development. As far back as the Middle Ages and through a good part of the twentieth century, international banking was the preserve of European financial houses. From the twelfth through the fifteenth centuries, banks in Italy were supreme in international finance. In some instances this development was the outcome of the maritime ties of coastal Italian cities with the Byzantine Empire and the growing Islamic countries. These ties contributed to the emergence of these cities as important conduits for trade with the European interior.

In other instances international finance developed from the regional emergence of important agricultural and manufacturing centers that grew to become hubs of a commercial and financial network covering every major European city. The activities of the Italian banking houses were essentially of a merchant banking nature, and included, in addition to accepting deposits, financing foreign trade, making a market in foreign exchange, meeting the short- and medium-term credit needs of enterpreneurs, rulers, noblemen, and the clergy, and investing in industrial and commercial ventures. These services were extended, through branches, to the major centers of Europe. The most important banking house of its time was the Medici Bank, which was headquartered in Florence and had branches in Rome, Venice, Avignon, Lyons, Catalonia, Geneva, Bruges, and London.

During the sixteenth century German banks assumed the lead in international finance. The initial momentum in the rise of German banking houses came from the southern part of the country, specifically from the cities of Augsburg and Nuremberg. The remarkable prosperity of this region propelled these cities into a position of prominence and placed them in the midst of a commercial and financial network that extended to the great European centers of production and consumption. It was not, however, until the discovery of the trading routes to the Indies and the opening of the markets of southern Asia that German banks rose to a position of eminence in international finance. The discovery and exploitation of these routes by the Portuguese brought about a significant shift in the trading activities from the Mediterranean to the Atlantic seaboard. This shift in European trading patterns changed the fate of the Low Countries and contributed to the development and growth of Antwerp into a sophisticated international money market. German banks continued to dominate international banking by moving the center of their activities to this city. The most prominent of the German banking houses was that of the Fugger family. Some of their most influential clients included the Tudors of England and the Hapsburgs, whose credit needs the Fuggers financed for a century and a half.

The history of international trade reveals that the center of commerce has never stayed long in one place, but has moved about with the winds of economic prosperity. Thus, by 1600, Amsterdam, which had experienced the benefits of the great maritime commerce of its traders as early as the fourteenth century, had become the economic center of the world. As a consequence Dutch banks dominated international finance.

In the early eighteenth century Great Britain, which had begun to flourish as a result of the growth of large-scale industry and capitalistic enterprise, started challenging Holland's economic leadership of the world. The gap between the two narrowed steadily, and at some point during the second half of that century, British banks assumed the leadership in international finance, which they maintained until the period between the two world wars. A significant factor contributing to the continued prominence of British banks during this period was no doubt the spread of Britain's dominion overseas. This dominion, by providing an important outlet for the banks' expansion, helped sustain their position of leadership through the twentieth century.

THE FORMATIVE YEARS OF
U.S. INTERNATIONAL BANKING

Unlike their European counterparts, banks in the United States had a late start in international finance. Indeed, as late as the pre-

World War I era, the financing of international trade by U.S. banks was quite negligible for a variety of reasons. In the first place, U.S. exports during this era represented only a small proportion of total production. The private sector was so busy developing the country's resources and satisfying the needs of an immense domestic market that the tapping of the export market, except as an outlet for abundant products, was generally neglected. Hence, it was natural for banks to gear their financing to domestic activity rather than to foreign trade. Also, the great majority of U.S. banks suffered from lack of capital, a development that undermined their ability to expand the scope of their operations. Last but not least, U.S. national banks were prohibited from branching abroad or accepting drafts arising from international transactions (bankers' acceptances), a prohibition that automatically excluded a large segment of the banking system from financing international trade. Unaffected by this regulatory prohibition were state-chartered banks and private unincorporated banks whose international banking activity was not of any great importance.

As the United States began to emerge as a major industrial power, there was a significant change in regulatory attitudes toward international banking. Thus, with the passage of the Federal Reserve Act in 1913, national banks were permitted to finance foreign trade through bankers' acceptances. Also, national banks with $1 million in capital and surplus were permitted to establish branches in foreign countries, subject to the approval of the Board of Governors of the Federal Reserve. Section 25 of the Federal Reserve Act makes the intent of this provision very clear: "for the furtherance of the foreign commerce of the United States."

Although these provisions opened the door for U.S. banks to engage in international banking, its development was slow. Indeed, over the next three years the volume of acceptance financing increased insignificantly, and only one national bank took advantage of the new authority and established branches abroad.

An additional inducement to the expansion of the international activities of American banks was the amendment in 1916 of Section 25 of the Federal Reserve Act, to permit national banks with capital of $1 million or more to invest, individually or jointly, up to 10 percent of their capital and surplus in state-chartered corporations for the sole purpose of conducting international banking business. This authority required that such corporations enter into an agreement with the Federal Reserve Board to operate and be governed by its regulation. Because of this requirement these institutions became known as *agreement corporations.*

In 1919, in a further effort to encourage the development of international banking, the U.S. Congress again amended the Federal Reserve Act to allow the Federal Reserve Board to charter corporations to engage in international banking. This amendment, which became Section 25(a) of the Federal Reserve Act, is also referred to as the Edge Act, after its sponsor, Senator Walter Edge of New Jersey. Corporations chartered under this amendment have come to be known as *Edge Act corporations.*

Although both types of corporations—Edge Act and agreement—enabled national banks to take advantage of the existing provisions governing international banking, in time the Edge Act corporation emerged as the preferred alternative, because of the benefits it entailed. From a regulatory perspective a bank's choice of either alternative was essentially a matter of the supervisory exposure desired—that is, whether a bank would be willing to subject its international operations to the dual supervision (state and federal) associated with agreement corporations rather than the single supervision (federal) associated with Edge Act corporations. State supervision was seen as superfluous, since in either case a bank's international activities would be regulated by the Federal Reserve Board. Another important factor in favor of the Edge Act corporation was the position and prestige that the federal chartering of these corporations projected overseas. Indeed, many banks felt that their image abroad was greatly enhanced by association with the U.S. government.

The emergence of the Edge Act subsidiaries as the more popular vehicle occurred despite the more liberal terms of the agreement corporation charter, which has no minimum capitalization requirement (unlike a $2 million minimum capital requirement for Edge Act corporations), and has no restrictions on the nationalities of its owners or directors (as Edge Act corporations had until recently).

As this legislative framework for the development of international banking was being laid, the American economy was undergoing important changes. The United States entered World War I as a debtor nation, and emerged as a creditor. This war turned the tide in the country's economic development. The growing needs of the Allies and neutral nations generated the necessary momentum for the growth of exports. At the same time this war stimulated the influx of flight capital from Europe, and thus contributed to the rise of New York as an international financial center.

In the postwar period the United States experienced greater demand for its manufactured products, increased its investments abroad, and generally witnessed its transformation into an industrial and financial power. In fact, by 1929 it was the world's outstanding manufacturing power, its largest creditor, and its second largest trader after Great Britain. A natural consequence was that the dollar began to replace the pound sterling as world currency, and New York rivaled London as the center of international finance. The international rise of the United States ended suddenly with the outbreak of the Great Depression, which eventually engulfed the world economy and triggered a wave of protectionism and economic nationalism that dominated all channels of international trade and payments. The introduction of exchange controls and currency inconvertibility over a rather large area of the world set in motion the tendency toward the bilateral channeling of trade—that is, seeking markets for exports and sources of imports by means of bilateral trading arrangements. These conditions prevailed until the outbreak of World War II, which caused a further reduction in the international activities of U.S. banks and severely disrupted the functioning of an already badly weakened world economy.

Even after the end of the war, the growth of the international activities of U.S. banks was moderate. The United States had come out of World War II with its productive capacity expanded and modernized, and its dollar the world's strongest and most wanted currency. By contrast, West European countries emerged from this war with their economies shattered and with shortages of all kinds, particularly of hard currency. This state of affairs led the governments of these countries to revert to controls and protectionism to spur the reconstruction of their economies. As a result, currency inconvertibility was once again widespread, along with controls on foreign exchange transactions. Bilateral trading arrangements were again the vehicle adopted by many countries to ensure minimum essential imports.

The United States came to play a very active role in the postwar reconstruction efforts of Western Europe. American assistance came essentially in two ways. The most visible one was financial aid, which the United States extended to war-torn countries to assist them in rebuilding their economies. Between 1945 and 1950, U.S. aid to these countries rose to $9.3 billion and was delivered through such programs as the Marshall Plan for Western Europe, Point Four for Greece and Turkey, lend-lease for the bilateral settlement of claims between the United States and receiving nations, and multilateral assistance against starvation, disease, and economic collapse implemented through the United Nations Relief and Rehabilitation Administration. Foreign aid continued in subsequent years (1951–60), but was essentially directed to developing countries and aimed at sustaining a reasonable development effort in agriculture and industry.

The less visible but perhaps more important way that the United States helped in the postwar reconstruction efforts was by opening its markets to foreign goods and simultaneously exporting a great deal of long-term capital in the form of direct investment by its multinational corporations. The combined effect of the U.S. contribution in the postwar reconstruction process was quite decisive. This process lasted less than a decade, yet by 1958 the principal West European countries were strong enough to introduce the convertibility of their currencies and to embark upon the formation of the European Economic Community. These developments combined with other forces to bring about an environment conducive to the international expansion of U.S. banks and their rise to a position of world leadership. These forces were the phenomenal recovery of the Japanese economy, the rapid economic growth of other countries, the independence of former colonies, and the general worldwide reduction in tariffs and other barriers to trade and international payments.

INTERNATIONALIZATION OF U.S. BANKING

Concurrently with the aforedescribed developments in the broader international environment, important forces on the domestic scene gave significant impetus to the internationalization of U.S. commercial banks. These forces, essentially legal and regulatory, were responsible for shaping the channels through which U.S. banks responded to the challenge of a changing international environment. To understand the current international orientation of U.S. banks, one must review the domestic forces responsible for the current dimension of U.S. foreign banking and the channels through which it was effected.

As large U.S. corporations began to establish international networks and develop global operations during the 1950s and 1960s, they created a natural incentive for expanding the foreign activities of U.S. commercial banks. The lead in the international expansion of bank services was taken by some of the larger U.S. banks when they sought to service the foreign credit requirements of their multinational clients through direct loans from their home offices, using domestic funds. At the same time, however, with long-term funds more expensive abroad than in the United States, nonresident borrowers increasingly began to use the U.S. financial markets as cheaper and more convenient sources of long-term funds. The effect of these developments was that international transactions were withdrawing substantial sums of funds from financial markets in the United States. Since these dollar outflows contributed to deficits in the U.S. balance of payments, they were subjected to important government controls that had a strong influence on the evolution of the international operations of U.S. banks. Specifically, the capital controls introduced by the U.S. government consisted of three interrelated measures: the Foreign Direct Investment Program (FDIP), the Interest Equalization Tax (IET), and the Voluntary Foreign Credit Restraint (VFCR) Program.

The FDIP, introduced as a voluntary program in 1964, was made mandatory in 1968.[1] Until its termination in 1974, it was administered by the Department of Commerce and aimed at limiting foreign direct investment by U.S. corporations. Important limitations were placed on the amount of funds that U.S. corporations could transfer to their affiliates abroad, as well as on the amount of foreign earnings that these affiliates could reinvest abroad.

The IET, enacted in 1964, imposed a tax on the security issues of nonresidents who borrowed long term in the United States from July 1963 on.[2] The imposition of this tax reduced the effective yield of such securities, and hence rendered it more difficult for nonresident concerns—including the foreign affiliates of U.S. companies—to finance their capital needs in the American market. As the foreign demand for financing shifted from the U.S. securities markets to American banks, the IET was extended to the longer-term loans of banks. The influence of this measure lasted until 1974, when the Nixon administration terminated the capital control program.

The VFCR Program, instituted in 1965, was designed to curb the foreign lending capacity of the head offices of U.S. commercial banks. The Federal Reserve Board, which administered this program until its termination in 1974, sought to attain this goal by limiting foreign lending to ceilings that reflected the banks' historical foreign-credit levels.[3] It was not until later (November 1971) that U.S. banks were offered the option of adopting a ceiling that reflected their size.[4]

The combined effect of these measures was to divert U.S. corporations to foreign markets in order to finance their growing investments overseas. These circumstances led banks with established foreign business to open branches abroad and to finance the needs of their multinational clients by tapping foreign sources of funds. Thus, between 1965 and 1970 there was a significant increase in the number of U.S. branches operating abroad. It is of course true that some of the major U.S. commercial banks headquartered in coastal centers (such as New York and San Francisco) had branches abroad that dated from the period prior to World War II or immediately after it. What is interesting about the foreign branch increase of 1965–70 is that it included banks located in such inland regional money centers as Chicago, Detroit, and Pittsburgh.

The foreign branch increase generated by the government's capital control program was accentuated further as the 1960s drew to a close. The new impetus came as a result of another regulatory barrier that originated in the banking reforms of the Depression era and that has become known as Federal Reserve Regulation Q. This regulation imposed a ceiling on the rate of interest that banks were allowed to pay on time and savings deposits. The effects of this regulation were felt by domestic banks in the second half of the 1960s, and then only because of the financial pressures of the Vietnam war upon the U.S. economy and the consequent monetary policy pursued during that period. Specifically, the booming state of the economy and the increasingly tight monetary policy that prevailed during these years gave rise to drastic increases in interest rates in 1966, but most importantly in 1969–70.

As market rates began to rise above the ceiling rates that banks could pay on deposits, banks found themselves at a competitive disadvantage in attracting funds from traditional sources. To supplement these sources, many banks found it expedient to open branches abroad in order to compete effectively for funds. These branches, exempted from Regulation Q and from reserve requirements, were able to offer a very attractive investment vehicle to foreigners—the Eurodollar certificate of deposit. In essence, this was a dollar-denominated deposit issued by the overseas branch of a U.S. bank, although such a deposit could be also issued for funds placed with any bank located outside the United States. As a result of this activity, foreign branches proved very instrumental in raising dollar deposits (Eurodollars) in the external dollar market. These were then diverted to their home offices for lending in the internal dollar market at the prevailing higher domestic rates.

A peak was reached in November 1969, when Eurodollar borrowings rose to $15 billion.[5] The Federal Reserve's response to this situation was increased regulation—imposition of a 10 percent margin reserve requirement on the Eurodollar borrowings of U.S. head offices from their foreign branches.[6] This measure, by increasing the cost of Eurodollars for domestic banks, moderated the further use of this source of funds, and hence affected the incentive to establish branches abroad for the purpose of securing such funds.[7]

The foreign branching movement of the 1960s gained new impetus in 1970–73, when the Federal Reserve Board sought to further the foreign commercial interests of the United States by promoting competition among U.S. banks in international markets. Recognizing the competitive advantage enjoyed in these markets by some of the country's larger banks, the board, to encourage the participation of a greater number of U.S. banks, provided for the establishment of offshore, limited-service facilities or "shell" branches.[8] As a result of this development, a number of U.S. banks were permitted to establish such facilities and conduct international activity from a Caribbean base—Nassau, the Bahamas, or the Cayman Islands. Despite their location, these branches have been functioning as adjuncts of, or conduits to, the Eurocurrency market (the market for currencies held as deposits and loaned outside the country of which they are the domestic currency—that is, a dollar, a deutsche mark, or a Swiss franc deposit in a London-based bank would be a Eurocurrency).

Establishing a shell branch has been an attractive alternative, especially for the smaller inland banks with no adequate resources to support a full-service branch overseas.[9] For such banks, shell branching offers the opportunity for interbank money market placements and participations in syndicated loans. For large multinational banks a shell branch offers, in addition, the opportunity to finance loans generated within the organization. The large majority of shell branches are associated with banks that have no other branch facility abroad. At the end of 1980, about two-thirds of the banks with branches abroad had but a single shell branch located either in Nassau, the Bahamas, or in Georgetown, Cayman Islands.

More recently the Federal Reserve has given U.S. banks a new option to implement their international business, the international banking facility (IBF). Effective December 3, 1981, U.S. banks, with Federal Reserve Board approval, can establish IBFs to conduct offshore banking operations from their domestic offices. Specifically, through these facilities U.S. banks can accept time deposits of $100,000 or more from nonresident individuals and businesses (including the overseas subsidiaries of U.S. corporations) and make loans to nonresidents, free from reserve requirements and interest rate ceilings. Clearly the IBF will operate as a record-keeping entity similar to an offshore shell branch. In this regard it may be established by initially identifying and segregating existing assets and liabilities that qualify under the Federal Reserve regulation applicable to IBFs.

The objective of the IBF option is to encourage American banks to bring into the United States some of the Eurodollar business that they conduct through other financial centers. It is anticipated that the IBF will partially substitute for purely offshore booking offices— that is, transactions currently placed on a bank's offshore shell branch books will be placed instead on its IBF books. Indeed, 20 days after the effective date for IBF establishment (December 23, 1981), the assets of the IBFs amounted to $47.2 billion. Of this sum 50.8 percent was held by the IBFs of U.S. banks and 49.2 percent by the IBFs of U.S.-based branches and agencies of foreign banks.[10]

TYPES OF INTERNATIONAL BANKING OFFICES

The first step a bank can take in providing international services is to establish a department in the bank's head office for the handling of international transactions. The size and organization of this department should be tailored to the specific needs of the bank. Until the volume of foreign business grows significantly, international collections, bookkeeping, credit information, and business development should be handled by the bank's domestic organization. However, once the volume of business builds up appreciably, performance of these functions by specific sections of the international department becomes essential. For example, increases in the volume of foreign deposits—from nonresident businesses and individuals—and the need to carry accounts with banks abroad will lead to the establishment of a bookkeeping section within the international department. By the same token, growth in foreign receipts and payments will call for maintaining a collection section. Expansion of loans to domestic and foreign concerns will justify credit information and business development sections.

Thus, at some point growth in the volume of business will make it essential for the international department to operate virtually as a miniature bank in itself. That is, the international department will find itself handling every basic operation performed at the domestic level in order to extend all types of services to its customers for the successful implementation of their foreign business. The variety of the services offered and performed will be unavoidable due to prevailing intercountry differences in monetary systems, business practices, and language.

As the activities of the international department increase, the need arises for new vehicles for expansion. Although several forms of organization for international expansion have been available to U.S. banks, selection of the best form usually depends upon such variables as the laws of each host country, the U.S. parent bank's goals for each location, and the desired size of investment. As the laws, goals, and desired investment change, so does the legal form of organization. Large banks use a combination of vehicles for conducting their international business. An aggregate picture of the various vehicles through which U.S. banks have conducted their international banking activities is shown in Table 1.1.

As can be seen in Table 1.1, the international assets of U.S. banks and bank holding companies at the end of 1980 amounted to $432 billion, with foreign branches accounting for 67.8 percent of these assets. Following in importance, by a significant margin, were the international assets of foreign subsidiaries (14.8 percent), domestic offices (14.3 percent), and Edge Act corporations (3.1 percent). It is worth noting the overriding importance of branches compared with their head offices. This development reflected the effects of the U.S. capital control program, which, though repealed in 1974, was instrumental in reversing the relative importance of head offices and branches, and played a substantial role in transforming the structures or operations within U.S. international banking.

Table 1.1 provides an overall picture of the foreign assets of U.S.

TABLE 1.1. Foreign Assets of U.S. Insured Commercial Banks and Bank Holding Companies, by Type of Office, as of December 31, 1980

Type of Office	Total Assets[a] (billions of dollars)	Percent of Total
Domestic office[b]	$ 61.7	14.3
Foreign branch	292.7	67.8
Edge Act corporation[c]	13.6	3.1
Foreign subsidiary	64.0	14.8
Total	$432.0	100.0

[a]Amounts are adjusted to eliminate "interfamily" transactions, and assets of U.S. branches and agencies of foreign banks. The figures for foreign subsidiaries reflect controlled companies, and include assets of certain companies of which the U.S. bank is not majority owner.
[b]Represents amount of credit extended by domestic offices of U.S. banks to foreign parties, plus the amount of international trade financing indicated by customer's liability on acceptances outstanding.
[c]Includes banking Edge Act corporations only.
Source: James V. Houpt, senior financial analyst, Federal Reserve Board, based on Federal Reserve data for 1980.

banks and of the vehicles through which these banks have effected their international operations. Though important, the above picture is too general to identify the entire range of alternative organizational forms open to each individual bank in the conduct of its international banking activities.

A bank desiring to expand its international banking services has several avenues from which to choose:

1. Establish representative offices abroad on a selective basis
2. Develop a network of foreign correspondent bank affiliations
3. Establish foreign branches
4. Acquire complete or partial interests in foreign banks or related financial institutions, thereby establishing foreign subsidiaries or affiliates
5. Participate with other domestic and foreign banks in the equity ownership of specialized financial consortia
6. Establish an Edge Act corporation in the United States.

IBFs are omitted from the list of alternatives because they fall within the framework of the head office's international banking business and/or that of the bank's Edge Act corporation.

Any one, or any combination, of the vehicles listed above might be selected by a bank wishing to expand its international activity. The following discussion reviews each of these vehicles.

Representative Offices

Some banks establish representative offices as an interim step prior to direct establishment of a full-fledged branch. These offices are also utilized for entry into countries where the presence of foreign commercial banks is either limited (Japan) or prohibited (Saudi Arabia and India). A representative office is usually staffed by three or four nationals who have been given a short orientation course on the U.S. bank's operations. The establishment of such an office provides the business clients of the U.S. bank with introductions and contacts to local authorities, businessmen, and government officials. In addition, it gives the parent bank's clients credit analysis and economic and political intelligence on local firms and the country. On the other hand, the representative office is expected to answer local inquiries about the parent bank's services.

While the representative office is slightly less expensive than a branch, it can not provide full banking services, such as accepting deposits, making loans or committing the parent bank to a loan, or issuing letters of credit, drafts, or traveler's checks. Because of the limited capabilities of the representative office, in conjunction with its significant expense, some banks prefer the correspondent bank alternative.

Correspondent Banks

Most banks engaging in international business rely on a network of correspondent banks abroad to handle their foreign transactions. Under this arrangement a U.S. bank, for example, may have a prior agreement with a foreign bank to the effect that each will function as the agent of the other in their respective countries. The banks may carry deposit accounts with one another and refer business on a reciprocal basis.

A good correspondent bank abroad can do everything for a U.S. bank that a representative office can, and at lower cost—that is, it entails no investment, no salaries for staff, or any other related expenses. Also, some foreign correspondents are necessary in order to assist customers dealing in imports and exports via letters of credit, which representative offices cannot issue. Correspondents can also collect and remit funds and documents, or buy and sell securities for the account of the U.S. bank or its customers.

The major disadvantage of the correspondent relationship is in loans—most correspondents place a higher priority on their local clients' needs than on credits for another bank's customers. Because of this limitation some U.S. banks have opted for a full branch, where the law permits.

Branches

A foreign branch is a banking office owned by a U.S. bank, and therefore does not constitute a separate legal entity. This means that the foreign branch's assets and liabilities, corporate charter, and policies are those of the parent bank. They are subject to two sets of regulations—those of the home country and those of the host country. Branching abroad places a bank in a position to offer more personalized services than through a representative office or a correspondent relationship. Thus, it can provide full banking services, including large loans based on the size of the parent bank's capital. Deposits are a legal obligation of (guaranteed by) the parent bank, not the branch. From the customer's viewpoint, the branch organization is the safest and most accommodating: safest because the branch represents the direct extension of the home office abroad, and most accommodating because branch services are based on the worldwide value of the customer relationship rather than on the relationship to any specific office. The branch gives the parent everything that a correspondent can, plus more control and a place to train its officers (rather than have them simply visit correspondents).

The disadvantages of the branch structure are to the parent, not to the customer. The parent must invest large sums (several hundred thousand dollars) for land, building, staff, equipment, and communications in order to establish a branch. The parent can be sued locally and can be taxed in the United States on the branch's profits. This

TABLE 1.2. Overseas Branches of U.S. Member Banks, 1965–81 (as of January 1)

Country of Location	1965	1968	1970	1971	1972	1973	1974	1975	1976	1977	1978	1979	1980	1981
Belgium-Luxembourg	2	8	11	11	8	8	15	15	17	15	15	17	13	12
France	4	6	11	12	15	17	15	17	19	19	18	17	13	12
Germany	3	9	17	21	22	27	30	30	30	27	28	27	27	27
Greece	1	2	8	9	13	14	16	18	18	18	18	17	16	16
Italy	1	2	3	4	6	7	8	10	10	11	13	14	14	14
Netherlands	3	3	7	7	7	6	6	6	6	6	6	6	6	6
Switzerland	1	3	6	7	8	8	9	9	9	9	9	9	9	9
United Kingdom	17	24	37	41	45	49	52	55	54	58	60	60	60	57
Total Europe[a]	32	59	103	116	128	142	157	167	172	173	177	177	172	169
Bahamas	2	3	32	60	73	94	91	80	80	77	74	75	77	75
Cayman Islands	–	–	–	–	–	2	32	44	49	52	58	67	73	79
Total Caribbean[b]	5	10	53	89	107	131	164	164	170	167	168	175	175	174
Argentina	16	25	38	38	38	38	38	37	37	32	32	33	41	45
Brazil	15	15	15	16	19	21	21	19	19	19	19	19	20	19
Colombia	5	8	23	26	28	28	32	36	37	7	–	–	–	–
Panama	10	19	26	29	29	32	33	33	33	33	33	31	32	31
Total Latin America[c]	72	123	182	191	195	190	195	198	200	164	157	162	176	180
Taiwan	–	2	2	2	2	3	5	7	7	7	7	7	7	10
Hong Kong	6	10	13	13	15	19	23	24	25	27	30	32	46	44

India	5	8	11	11	11	11	11	11	11	11	10	10	10	10
Indonesia	–	–	6	6	6	6	6	6	6	6	5	5	5	5
Japan	13	14	15	15	17	21	25	31	31	31	31	29	29	29
Lebanon	3	3	3	3	3	3	3	3	3	3	3	4	4	4
Persian Gulf[d]	2	3	3	8	11	10	10	11	17	21	20	22	22	20
Singapore	–	8	9	11	11	11	14	18	22	23	21	22	22	23
Total Asia[e]	45	69	83	91	98	112	126	143	149	159	165	176	190	192
Total Africa[f]	3	3	1	2	2	2	2	5	8	10	15	18	20	20
Overseas areas and trust territories of U.S.	23	31	38	43	47	50	55	55	63	58	56	55	56	52
Grand Total	180	295	460	532	577	627	699	732	762	731	738	763	789	787
U.S. member banks with overseas branches	11	15	53	79	91	107	125	125	126	126	130	137	139	152

[a] Also includes Austria, Denmark, Ireland, Monaco, Romania, and Spain.
[b] Also includes Barbados, Haiti, Jamaica, Netherlands Antilles, Trinidad-Tobago, British Virgin Islands, and other West Indies.
[c] Also includes Bolivia, Chile, Dominican Republic, Ecuador, El Salvador, Guatemala, Guyana, Honduras, Mexico, Nicaragua, Paraguay, Peru, Uruguay, and Venezuela.
[d] Includes Bahrain, Oman, Qatar, Saudi Arabia, United Arab Emirates, and Yemen Arab Republic.
[e] Also includes Brunei, Fiji Islands, Israel,* Jordan, Korea, Malaysia, Pakistan, Philippines, Seychelles, Sri Lanka, Thailand, and Vietnam.*
[f] Includes Egypt, Gabon, Ivory Coast, Kenya, Liberia, Mauritius, Nigeria,* Senegal, Sudan, Tunisia.
*No resident U.S. branches as of January 1, 1978.
Source: For 1965-75, Federal Reserve Bank of Chicago; subsequent years from Board of Governors, Federal Reserve System, *Annual Report.*

latter point can become an advantage during the formative years of the branch, when it is usually losing money.

The magnitude of U.S. branching activity abroad is shown in Table 1.2. The number of U.S. banks with foreign branches rose from 11 at the end of 1964 to 152 at the end of 1980. During this same period the number of U.S. branches abroad increased dramatically, from 180 to 787. These branches were located in 76 foreign countries and overseas areas and trust territories of the United States.

The largest concentration of U.S. branches is in Asia, obviously because of the paramount importance of two financial centers—Hong Kong and Singapore. Both of these cities have a natural advantage in capturing business from such eastern commercial centers as Tokyo, Sydney, Manila, and Kuala Lumpur. Apart from these two cities, U.S. bank presence in Asia has been enhanced in recent years by both the absolute increase in the number of U.S. branches and their increased dispersion among Asian countries.

Following in importance is Latin America, long a site of U.S. banking presence. Trailing Latin America is the Caribbean basin, which has attained international stature largely in the 1970s, primarily in response to the Federal Reserve's encouragement of shell branches. Next in importance is Europe, with the United Kingdom enjoying the largest concentration of U.S. branches because of London's prominent position as an international financial center. Of minor importance is the number of American branches in the U.S. overseas areas and territories, and in Africa.

The total number of U.S. branches abroad will be affected by the introduction of IBFs. The ease with which IBFs can be formed and maintained should greatly enhance their popularity at the expense of shell branches. Specifically, the impact of the IBFs will be felt in the Caribbean basin with respect to both the number and the size of U.S. branches there.

The geographic distribution of U.S. foreign branches does not in any way reflect the relative financial importance of the various geographic areas. Table 1.3 identifies the magnitude of U.S. foreign branch activity by geographic area for the years 1978-80. A general overview of this data suggests that the bulk of U.S. branch assets are concentrated in developed countries—and, more specifically, in financial centers of international rather than national stature. At the end of 1980, U.S. branches in the United Kingdom alone held 33.4 per-

TABLE 1.3. Geographic Distribution of Assets of Overseas
Branches of U.S. Banks, 1978–80
(in percent, end of year, net of intrafamily claims)

Geographic Area	1978	1979	1980
United Kingdom and Ireland	32.6	32.8	33.4
Continental Europe	14.0	13.0	12.0
Bahamas and Cayman Islands	29.5	30.0	30.4
Latin America	4.8	5.1	5.2
Far East	13.1	13.6	14.6
Near East and Africa	4.2	3.7	2.6
U.S. overseas areas and trust territories	1.8	1.8	1.8
Total	100.0	100.0	100.0

Source: Board of Governors, Federal Reserve System, *Annual Press Release on Assets and Liabilities of Overseas Branches of Member Banks*, various issues.

cent of all U.S. foreign branch assets, which boosted the share of European branches to 45.4 percent of the total. This represents the largest portion of U.S. branch holdings, obviously because of London's international banking eminence. London has been the leading banking center of the world, exhibiting the largest concentration of banking vehicles—representative offices, bank branches, subsidiaries, and affiliates.[11] This concentration of banking institutions has made London the principal center of the Eurocurrency interbank market, with U.S. branches constituting an integral part of this market. U.S. branches lend their funds to many banking institutions in the interbank market, to nonbank or private foreign borrowers, and to foreign governments and official institutions.

London branches have held the largest share of foreign branch holdings since the U.S. branching momentum of the mid-1960s. Their holdings reached a peak in 1969, when these branches functioned as important suppliers of Eurodollars to their parent banks for use in domestic operations. In subsequent years London branch holdings declined steadily as Caribbean shell-branching activity started gaining momentum. By the end of 1980, Caribbean branch holdings accounted for 30.4 percent of all branch assets. Just like their London counterparts, Caribbean branches have been lending their resources in the interbank market as well as in the private and public foreign markets. Though Federal Reserve policy proved instrumental in encouraging the development of Caribbean branches, the effect of Caribbean tax incentives has been no less important. Indeed, while London branches are subject to British taxation on income earned in Great Britain, Caribbean-based branches are legally exempted from such taxation by local authorities. This preferential tax treatment has led U.S. banks to funnel much of their lending through their Caribbean outlets, thereby reducing their overall foreign tax exposure.

Far East branch asset holdings accounted for 14.6 percent of the aggregate, basically reflecting the increased activity of U.S. branches in such international financial centers as Hong Kong and Singapore. Latin American branches held 5.2 percent of total assets, and this reflected primarily the activity of U.S. branches in Panama. In fact, many U.S. banks employ their Panama branches as their centers for lending to customers in Latin America. Branch holdings in the Near East and Africa have been declining, reflecting the limited presence and activities of U.S. multinationals in these markets. The holdings of branches in U.S. overseas areas and territories have been of minor importance because of the evolving sophistication of other international markets.

Though branching abroad has been a preferred form of overseas operation, some countries provide for the conduct of foreign banking through a related form of operation, the establishment of an agency. This type of arrangement is similar to a branch bank except that host country legislation limits the range of services performed. For example, unlike branches, agencies are prohibited from accepting deposits from the local public; otherwise, they may provide the same nondepository services offered by branches, and especially those associated with international transactions—for example, issuing letters of credit, accepting drafts, making collections, extending foreign-trade-related loans, and engaging in foreign exchange.

Subsidiaries and Affiliates

Branching is an aggressive vehicle for conducting bank business abroad, and has been utilized extensively by banks interested in penetrating and extending their presence in the international banking community. Since the scope of U.S. branch activity abroad is limited by domestic regulations covering the activities permitted the parent bank, expansion abroad is generally sought through an alternative vehicle, bank subsidiaries or affiliates. In fact, in some countries (such as Colombia) these vehicles may be the only means legally open to U.S. and other foreign banks for participation in the domestic banking business.

The term "subsidiary" refers to a foreign bank or related financial institution that is owned entirely or in major part by an American parent (that is, ownership of more than 50 percent of the voting stock). If the American parent has a minority interest (from as little as 10 percent to as much as 50 percent of the voting stock), the foreign institution is referred to as affiliate. In essence, then, the difference lies only in the size of equity investment in—and, hence, extent of control of—the foreign institution, which otherwise operates with its original name, charter, and personnel.

Equity investments in foreign institutions can be effected by U.S. banks either directly or indirectly, through an Edge Act corporation. The latter approach offers a U.S. bank important advantages over the former: wider scope of equity investments—that is, investments in virtually any foreign company, provided it does not do business in the United States; centralization of international operations and more effective control over foreign investments; and protection for the parent bank, since any losses sustained by the foreign subsidiaries or affiliates can be limited to the amount of the Edge Act corporation's capital. These advantages have propelled Edge Act corporations into a position of primacy as a medium for overseas equity investments.

Because of the greater investment flexibility of Edge Act corporations, the foreign equity investments of U.S. banks spread over a wide range of activities. Specifically, U.S. investment holdings overseas are intertwined with foreign banking institutions, nonbank financial institutions, and business firms.[12] These investment holdings, though prohibited in the United States, are permissible in other countries.

Table 1.4 identifies the number and asset sizes of the foreign subsidiaries of U.S. banks and Edge Act corporations by country at the end of 1980. With bank investments in foreign affiliates ignored, the table is a very conservative measure of the overall size of foreign investment holdings by U.S. banks. At the end of 1980, U.S. bank subsidiaries abroad numbered 943 and had total assets of $64 billion. The largest concentration in assets (about 53 percent) is in Europe,

TABLE 1.4. Geographic Distribution and Asset Size of Foreign
Subsidiaries of U.S. Banks, Bank Holding Companies, and
Edge Act and Agreement Corporations as of December 31, 1980

Area and Country	Number of Subsidiaries	Total Assets[a] (billions of dollars)
Europe	345	$33.7
Austria	7	.6
Belgium	16	3.2
France	23	2.8
Italy	8	3.8
Switzerland	25	.7
United Kingdom	191	14.5
West Germany	21	6.8
Other countries	54	1.3
Latin America	152	3.4
Argentina, Colombia, Mexico	23	1.0
Brazil	61	2.1
Other countries	68	.3
Africa	42	1.1
Australia	47	3.1
Other Areas	357	22.8
Middle East	9	2.6
Hong Kong	59	3.3
Canada	73	8.2
Offshore banking centers[b]	143	6.4
All other countries	73	2.3
Total	943	$64.0

Note: Details do not add to total due to rounding.
[a]Net of intrafamily claims.
[b]Includes Bahamas, Cayman Islands, Channel Islands, Luxembourg, Netherlands Antilles, Panama, Bermuda, and Singapore.
Source: Estimates by James V. Houpt, senior financial analyst, Federal Reserve Board, based on Federal Reserve data for 1980.

with the remainder widely scattered. Many of the European subsidiaries of U.S. banks are large, consumer-oriented banks and merchant banks. The latter offer U.S. banks a stake in the Eurobond market and—to a much lesser extent—the Euroequity market. In addition to commercial and merchant banking activities, European subsidiaries engage in other financial services and commercial enterprises. Other geographic areas attractive to U.S. subsidiary activity are characterized by one or more of the following factors: presence of important financial centers, growing economies that encourage foreign investment, a favorable tax climate.

Overall, the data of Table 1.4 reveal a phenomenal growth of U.S. subsidiaries abroad. In the early 1970s the assets of the foreign subsidiaries of U.S. banks were less than $6 billion, compared with $64 billion at the end of 1980. This tenfold expansion in less than a decade underlines the importance of subsidiaries.

It follows from the preceding that purchase of complete or partial interests in foreign institutions has been an important avenue in the international activities of U.S. banks. In general, as vehicles for implementing an international banking program, subsidiaries and affiliates provide the parent bank with an entry into foreign markets with only minimal demands on its manpower resources while adding international expertise to the domestic experience of the nationals managing the subsidiary or affiliate. The major advantage for the parent bank, however, is that the potential for developing new business and fruitful connections in the foreign country is far greater than might be possible through the establishment of a branch or the *de novo* formation of a banking institution.

The major disadvantage of this organizational form is the conflict that can result between its owners in the setting of goals and the formulation of appropriate policy. To avoid this disadvantage, some banks have formed joint ventures or consortia with respect to very specific goals or markets.

Banking Consortia

A group of banks, not necessarily of the same nationality, may jointly establish a separate venture known as a consortium bank. Each of the participating banks contributes a prorated portion of the capital and has a proportionate representation on the board of the consortium bank. The consortium bank has its own name, and functions as an independent corporate entity in the framework of the policies developed by its shareholding banks represented on the board of directors.

The consortium movement started in the 1960s, and is of European origin. Three factors were especially important in the development of this vehicle: the U.S. capital control program, which adversely affected the availability of long-term funds to foreigners in U.S. financial markets; the introduction of medium-term loans in the European markets by the branches of U.S. banks, and the receptiveness of Continental markets to this type of credit; and the growing demand of large corporations for multicurrency credits and the need to accommodate such demand. These conditions led to the emergence of consortium banks as the vehicle for medium- and long-term credits that they finance primarily through the purchase of deposits from the Eurocurrency market. In fact, the projects that they finance often are so large as to go beyond the lending or risk limits of any one of their owners. Other activities typical of consortium banking are facilitating corporate mergers and acquisitions, taking equity participations, and performing underwriting or private placements of public and private issues. Many of the consortium bank customers are referrals from the parent institutions, while others are a product of the bank's own business development program.

At the end of 1980, there were 27 consortium banks in London, and more than 100 such institutions in other cities around the world.[13] Though some of the participants in these ventures are small banks seeking a presence in foreign markets, a great many of them are major international banks, several of which have interests in more than one consortium institution. In some of the consortia, participating banks come from the same country—as is the case, for example, with the United Bank of Kuwait and the Associated Japanese Bank. In most cases, however, the participating banks come from different geographical areas and are a mixture of American, Canadian, European, and Japanese banks. An example of such a multinational consortium is the Orion Bank, which is owned by the National Westminster Bank (Britain), the Royal Bank of Canada (Canada), the Chase Manhattan Corporation (United States), the Credito Italiano (Italy), the Mitsubishi Bank (Japan), and the Westdeutsche Landesbank Girozentrale (Germany).

The multinational nature of the consortium banks places these institutions beyond the reach of the central banking system of any one country, and hence above its control over a wholly owned subsidiary or a branch. In other words, a multinational consortium operating abroad and including U.S. banks among its participants would be beyond the authority of the Federal Reserve. Banking consortia thus offer U.S. banks the opportunity to participate abroad in activities they are prohibited by law from conducting at home (for instance, investment banking business in corporate securities).

Despite their important merits, consortium banks have had their share of problems. During periods of financial strain, they encounter funding problems because they do not relate to any one country or central banking institution that otherwise could be responsible for back-up support. Such was the case, for example, in 1974–75, when consortium banks enjoyed less than prime stature in the Eurocurrency markets.

Another sensitive issue affecting the performance of a consortium bank is the way that parent banks perceive their relationships with and responsibilities to this institution. For a consortium bank to be successful, it must have a strong and effective managerial leadership, supplemented by the dedication and support of all participating shareholders. The implication of this is twofold. First, that the senior management of the consortium bank should enjoy sustained independence in decision making; otherwise, conflicts of interest will arise with the parent banks that will undermine the consortium bank's very existence. Second, the participating banks should give the consortium bank their cooperation and assistance rather than show their antagonism.

Edge Act Corporations

Despite the early enactment of legislation pertaining to Edge Act corporations (or simply Edges), the interest of U.S. banks in this vehicle dates basically from the late 1950s, coinciding with the postwar dismantling of exchange controls and increased international flow of private capital. Banks interested in establishing an Edge subsidiary initially had a choice of two distinct types of corporations: the investment (or financing) Edge, which was empowered to make portfolio-type investments in foreign corporations other than banks, but was prohibited from accepting deposits; and the banking Edge, which was authorized to engage in the deposit banking business—that is, to accept deposits and to invest in the equity of foreign banking corporations. To avoid confusion over the logic governing these two types of Edges, in 1963 the Federal Reserve Board revised the regulatory provisions covering these corporations (Regulation K) to permit the integration of both types of activities. Despite the merger of functions into one corporation, most banks chose to maintain the separation of activities.

One outstanding feature of the Edge legislation was that it permitted banks to establish multiple Edge subsidiaries—separately incorporated and capitalized—in various parts of the country. This feature made the Edge vehicle a unique channel for the conduct of international banking, since it exempted it from the interstate restrictions of the McFadden Act of 1927. Thus, during the 1960s a number of regional and large state banks took advantage of this feature and established Edge subsidiaries in New York City to better serve the international banking needs of their customers. In the 1970s this trend was directed toward other financial centers, such as Chicago, Houston, Los Angeles, Miami, New Orleans, and San Francisco.

The attractiveness of Edges for interstate operations was increased by a 1979 amendment of Regulation K permitting branching. Amendment of Regulation K resulted from provisions of the International Banking Act of 1978, which directed the Federal Reserve Board to revise its regulations in order to improve the competitiveness and efficiency of Edges in providing international banking and financial services. In June 1979 the new Regulation K provided for the interstate branching of Edges in the United States, authorized their financing the production of U.S. goods and services for export, simplified the procedures governing their foreign investment activity and establishment of branches abroad, broadened the domestic sources and uses of their funds, reduced their reserve requirements on deposit liabilities to correspond to those for commercial banks, and permitted their ownership by foreign banking institutions.

The interest of U.S. banks in Edges for the conduct of their internationally related business can be sensed from the following data. Between 1957 and 1979 the number of Edges rose from 4 to 127 (while agreement corporations increased, during the same period, from 3 to only 5). By the end of 1980, and as a result of domestic Edge-branching activity, there were 165 Edge offices throughout the country. Of these offices, 103 were banking Edges and 62 were investment Edges. Far more impressive, however, was the asset size of banking Edges vis-à-vis investment Edges. At the end of 1980, banking had total assets, net of intrafamily claims, of $13.6 billion, compared with only $0.7 billion for all investment Edges. In other words, banking Edges accounted for 95 percent of the total Edge assets.

The geographic distribution and asset size of banking Edges are shown in Table 1.5. At the end of 1980, New York City had the largest concentration of banking Edge offices and of their assets. Another interesting observation is Miami's phenomenal emergence as a major center of Edge activity, which placed it next in importance only to New York City, and ahead of such financial centers as San Francisco, Los Angeles, Houston, and Chicago.[14]

As might be expected, the main thrust of banking Edges has been making foreign loans and financing international trade—that is, exports and imports, as well as trade activity between foreign countries. Another important function has been to provide a means of processing international clearings for their parent banks. This is especially true for Edges located in New York, where clearing activity is para-

TABLE 1.5. Number and Asset Size of Banking Edge Offices, U.S. City, at End of 1980

City	Number of Offices	Assets* Amount (millions of dollars)	Assets* Percent of Total
New York	26	$ 7,382	54.2
Miami	23	1,499	11.0
San Francisco	6	1,071	7.9
Los Angeles	11	717	5.3
Houston	11	479	3.5
Chicago	11	306	2.2
All other U.S. cities	10	48	.3
Foreign countries	5	2,130	15.6
Total	103	$13,632	100.0

*Net of intrafamily claims.
Source: Board of Governors, Federal Reserve System.

mount. The bulk of Edge assets has been financed through foreign demand and time deposits.

INTERNATIONAL SERVICES OF U.S. BANKS

Continued growth of the international economy in the postwar years has contributed to an ever-increasing demand for international financial services. Responding to this demand, U.S. banks have focused not only upon developing an extensive network of international banking facilities but also upon expanding the different types of international services offered and increasing the volume of these services. U.S. banks offer some of these services directly, while others are offered indirectly through subsidiaries and affiliates operating abroad. In the latter instance, as indicated earlier, the wider scope of activities permitted local banks abroad has induced U.S. banks to acquire equity interests in foreign banks and other financial institutions, and to offer a variety of ancillary services to meet the needs of their multinational clientele.

Of the international services that U.S. banks offer directly, some are an extension of those they provide in the domestic market (such as transfer of funds and acceptance of deposits), while others are unique to international banking (such as purchase and sale of foreign exchange, and letter of credit financing). Because of the variety of services that U.S. banks extend to their customers—both American and foreign—discussion here will be limited to the more important ones. These include transfer of funds, deposit and loan activities, purchase and sale of foreign exchange, and collections.

Transfer of Funds

One of the basic services offered by banks engaging in international banking is the transfer of funds between parties residing or traveling in different countries. This transfer can be effected in any of three ways: airmail remittance, cable remittance, or foreign drafts. A customer wishing to transfer funds via air mail to a party in another country would pay the bank, in cash or by a check drawn on his account, the stated amount plus a fee covering the expenses of the transaction. The bank then would send an airmail letter to its correspondent bank in the country where the beneficiary resides, specifying the amount of payment, the name and address of the beneficiary, the name of the sender, and authorized signatures. Upon receipt of these instructions, the foreign bank would verify the authenticity of the signatures and contact the beneficiary. After payment of the funds (in local currency), the account of the instructing bank would be charged for the amount of the payment.

If speed is important, the transfer can be effected by cable or by telephone. The process will be the same, except that the message is cabled or telephoned to the correspondent bank. The authenticity of the instruction is verified by code or test key arrangement. Clearly, the code or key issued would be prearranged, and would change daily for purposes of security.

Unlike the airmail and cable remittances, which are bank-to-bank instructions, a foreign draft is a negotiable instrument drawn by a bank on its foreign correspondent bank. A draft is issued when a client wants to have an actual instrument to mail to the beneficiary abroad. In such a case it is customary for the issuing bank to send its foreign correspondent a nonnegotiable copy of the draft, or a letter of advice that includes all the necessary details, as a protection against fraud.

One of the most widely known and used forms of transferring funds abroad has been traveler's checks, a negotiable instrument of worldwide acceptability. Though few banks issue these checks, virtually every bank maintains a large inventory to accommodate the needs of its traveling customers. Traveler's checks have generally come to be accepted by tourists as a safe and easy instrument for the transfer of funds from one country to another.

Foreign Deposit-Taking and Lending

Internationally, as domestically, the major function of banks is to intermediate—that is, to obtain deposits and to make loans. In performing this traditional function, banks always strive to acquire deposits at a minimal cost and to lend these funds out to relatively low-risk customers. The objective, of course, is to obtain a reasonable spread. Lending policies pertaining to major domestic corporate customers are usually determined at the bank's home office. This is less frequently the case when the bank is dealing with international loans. In such instances more reliance is placed on the foreign branch or vehicle located abroad.

As in domestic activity, the largest source of income from international operations is lending. Most active in international lending are usually the banks that maintain branches abroad or other types of vehicles that ensure a presence in foreign markets. Banks that have only international departments generally limit themselves to lending funds or giving credit to their domestic customers, thereby helping to finance international trade by making possible both the production of goods for export and the import of goods for domestic use. In the latter case these shipments are financed through bankers' acceptances, drawn under letters of credit. Unlike domestic trade, where shipments are usually made on an open account basis and bank financing of accounts receivable is a generally accepted practice, in foreign trade this is hardly practical for an exporter because of the problems that it entails. Specifically, it calls for credit-checking across international boundaries to ensure the creditworthiness of the foreign buyer; and once the sale is made, the exporter has no negotiable instrument evidencing the obligation of the foreign buyer. To circumvent these and other problems, the banker's acceptance mechanism has been developed. Under this arrangement the importer's bank will substitute its own credit standing for that of its customer, accepting a time draft for the price of the goods. Upon maturity of this draft, the customer pays the bank in full. This procedure works as a short-term loan, with the difference that no funds are actually advanced. In place of interest, the bank charges its customer a fee for the use of the bank's credit standing.

Foreign-trade financing is but one type of international lending, and obviously the one with the longest history. In recent decades, and specifically since the late 1960s, the international lending activity of U.S. banks has been essentially in the form of cross-border loans. Initially the main borrowers were the foreign subsidiaries of U.S. corporations. By the mid-1970s, following the dramatic rise in oil prices and the recession of 1974, government agencies in Europe and in developing nations replaced in importance the overseas affiliates of U.S. firms as the major recipients of loans from U.S. commercial banks.

Foreign loans are of different types, each requiring various credit skills. Yet foreign credits share some characteristics with the domestic. In general, foreign credits may be broadly classified in three distinct types: loans or placements to foreign banks or foreign branches of U.S. banks (interbank lending), loans to governments and official institutions, and loans to businesses. The latter category exhibits significant variation: loans to foreign companies, partnerships, and proprietorships; loans to corporations or their foreign branches, subsidiaries, or affiliates with parent company guarantee or other form of support; project loans for developing natural resources; and other types. New and specialized patterns continue to emerge, of course, but the above general categories still apply. (A detailed discussion of each of these loan categories is undertaken in chapters 12–17.)

Foreign Exchange Trading

One activity conducted by a bank's international department that has no domestic parallel is foreign exchange trading. No matter what the nature of an international business transaction, as long as it involves foreign payment, it will entail the exchange of one currency for another. Since there is no one central marketplace for this exchange (equivalent to the New York Stock Exchange for bonds and stocks), trading depends upon direct communications among the parties involved. The market is thus very informal, with no official setting of rates or trading rules, and is generally guided by a code of ethics that has evolved over time. In essence, this market is not a place, but a mechanism that brings together buyers and sellers of foreign exchange. The function of making and maintaining a market is limited to a small group of large domestic and foreign banks and a few dealers. (Trading in foreign exchange and the assumption of risk are discussed in greater detail in chapter 10.)

Collections

Collection, the presenting of an item for payment, is essentially the same internationally as domestically. The major difference is the absence of an international clearinghouse for checks and other negotiable items drawn on the banks of one country and deposited in the banks of another. Correspondent relationships are therefore established between commercial banks that also serve as agents, collecting negotiable items for exporters.

These collections may be either *clean* (without documents attached) or *documentary* (with documents attached). Clean items are usually checks, traveler's checks, and money orders, which, drawn on banks in the currency of one country, are exchanged for local currency in another country. American tourists abroad using traveler's checks to pay for services received or goods purchased, represent an example of clean collections. Recipients of these checks turn them over to their local banks for settlement. These foreign banks collect by sending the clean items, usually by airmail, to their correspondent American banks, either for immediate credit or as a collection, with the amount of the item to be credited only after payment is made by the maker's bank. Clean items are thus presented for collection in exactly the same manner internationally as they are domestically.

More complicated and, at this time, more important to international trade are documentary collections. The basis of such a collection is that banks act only as agents, and must exercise care to protect the collection documents from any loss or damage. The customer gives the bank precise instructions pertaining to presentation of the collection for payment, the party that will pay the fees, the method for transferring payment, and the steps to be taken if the collection is not made. Any deviation from the explicit instructions of the foreign bank and any action initiated by the collecting bank are at the risk of the latter.

The principal international clearing center in the United States is New York. In the mid-1960s a committee composed from the New York Clearing House banks was given the task of designing a system, acquiring the equipment, obtaining subscribers, and putting in place a computerized communications network to handle the clearing of interbank money transfers and to facilitate the clearing of Eurodollar transactions. The result was the Clearing House Interbank Payments System (CHIPS), which, introduced in April 1970, is the conduit for settlement of more than 90 percent of the world's foreign exchange business and the leading settlement mechanism for Eurodollar markets and other international trade transactions, such as letter of credit payments, collections, and bank-to-bank reimbursements. On October 1, 1981, CHIPS changed its operating procedures to provide settlement within the same day in federal funds (deposit balances held with Federal Reserve banks). To date, the volume record was set on November 28, 1980, when the system processed a staggering $289 billion of interbank funds (compared with a mere $4 billion a day in 1971).

FUTURE PROSPECTS

The future role and importance of U.S. international banking will depend upon the continued growth of the international economy and the state of the political environment. Barring any major political disturbances, which could restrict the free international movement of capital and undermine the functioning of the international credit markets, world economic expansion will sustain the further growth and development of international banking. Indeed, because of growing domestic opportunities in less-developed countries and the expansion of local business activities into the international sphere in other countries, the demand for international banking services will continue to grow. As the international market grows and encompasses a multinational clientele with more diverse and complicated financial needs, individual lending institutions—both American and foreign banks—will find themselves forced to create increasingly distinctive and attractive financial service packages in order to acquire and maintain a share of the market.

As international banking opportunities expand, the overseas involvement of the U.S. money market and regional banks will broaden further. Factoring, leasing, investment banking (merchant banking), and medium-term financing are some of the services offered by U.S. banks abroad. This range of activity goes beyond traditional U.S. banking standards, and may be justified in the light of prevailing competition in international financial markets.

The increased interrelationship between domestic and international markets is causing the domestic banking system to adopt international banking practices. Proposed legislation supported by the Reagan administration seems to recognize the trend to greater liberalization in U.S. international banking activities. Specifically, two bills currently considered in the U.S. Congress (S 144 in the Senate and HR 1321 in the House of Representatives) provide for the formation of export trading companies by U.S. banks, bank holding companies, and international banking corporations. Clearly, the objective of both bills is to boost U.S. export activity. The rationale behind bank ownership of, or participation in, trading ventures is that U.S. banks are already in the business of researching foreign markets, evaluating risks, and understanding the subtleties of international finance. Though bank ownership of export companies would be unprecedented in the United States, it is a reality in other developed countries, such as France and Japan. Congressional approval of the proposed trading company bills will add an important dimension to the role of U.S. banks in international banking activities.

Looking ahead into the 1980s, it is clear that U.S. international banking will be confronted with a number of challenging problems—some altogether new, others a variation of those encountered in the past. The types of problems to be encountered seem to be related, for example, to the maintenance internationally of sound principles and credit standards, to coping with changes in the political and economic environments of host countries, to acquiring a favorable share of the international banking market, and to further adaptation of the methods and organizational forms used in the conduct of international banking in order to cope both with foreign competition and the needs of an ever-evolving world economy.

Judging from the reaction of international bankers to challenging problems in the past, we can feel confident of their ability to respond positively and competitively in the future.

NOTES

1. On its introduction on a voluntary basis, see the letter describing the program, sent by the secretary of commerce to the major U.S. corporations in December 1965, reproduced in *International Legal Materials* 5 (1966): 30-34; on its becoming mandatory, see the president's executive order issued on January 1, 1968, reproduced in *International Legal Materials* 7 (1968): 53-54.

2. Interest Equalization Tax Act, Public Law 88-563, September 2, 1964, *United States Code*, Title 26, sec. 4911-31.

3. See "Guidelines for Banks," *Federal Reserve Bulletin* 51 (March 1965): 371-75. These guidelines eventually instituted a new legal mechanism of direct controls on commercial banks that could hardly qualify as voluntary. See revised "Guidelines for Banks," *Federal Reserve Bulletin* 54 (January 1968): 64-68. Provisions for nonbank financial institutions also were issued by the Federal Reserve Board of Governors, and constituted a separate section of the above guidelines.

4. Revised guidelines, "Banks," *Federal Reserve Bulletin*, 57 (November 1971): 907-11.

5. *Federal Reserve Bulletin*, 56 (July 1970): A86.

6. Ibid. 55 (August 1969): 657.

7. In January 1971 the reserve requirement against Eurodollar borrowings (Regulation M) was increased to 20 percent in response to renewed home office borrowing from foreign branches. *Federal Reserve Bulletin* 56 (December 1970): 1941-42. In subsequent years this requirement was adjusted by the Federal

Reserve Board on more than one occasion, as warranted by prevailing conditions. These adjustments were 8 percent in June 1973, 4 percent in May 1975, 1 percent in December 1977, 0 in August 1978, and 3 percent in November 1980.

8. In the words of Arthur Burns, then chairman of the Board of Governors of the Federal Reserve, "The public interest of furthering the foreign commerce of the United States is best served by permitting competitive alternatives among U.S. banks abroad, rather than confining branch facilities to the few very large U.S. banks who have long had foreign branches." Response of Arthur Burns to questions submitted by Honorable Wright Patman, *Economic Report of the President*, Hearings Before the Joint Economic Committee, 93rd Cong., 1st Sess., pt. 2 (February 20, 1973), p. 434.

9. Such facilities have no contact with the local public, and transactions can be directed by the branch's parent bank or other foreign branches. Books are kept by contract parties, and are usually duplicates of those kept at the home office. In essence such a facility may consist of no more than a mailing address. See Stuart G. Hoffman, "U.S. Banks Expand Offshore Banking in Caribbean Basin," Federal Reserve Bank of Atlanta, *Economic Review*, July–August 1980, pp. 22–25.

10. Federal Reserve Bank of Chicago, *International Letter*, January 1, 1982, p. 1.

11. In January 1979 there were 425 banking vehicles in London, ranging from representative offices to banking consortia; this was more than twice the number of vehicles in New York (202) or Hong Kong (199). Steven I. Davis, *The Euro-Bank: Its Origins, Management and Outlook*, 2nd ed. (New York: John Wiley and Sons, 1980), p. 33.

12. U.S. holdings in foreign banking institutions cover commercial, merchant, and investment banks, and trust companies. Holdings in nonbank financial institutions consist essentially of investments in finance companies, leasing companies, and other companies involved in lending. Holdings in business firms refer to investments in companies that are not in the business of lending money: investment advisory companies; data processing companies; premises holding companies; industrial, commercial, and real estate firms; and even mines, farms, and hotels.

13. Michael Blanden, "Joint Venture and Consortium Banks," *The Banker* 131, no. 661 (March 1981): 93.

14. On Miami's emergence as a full-service specialized Latin American banking center, see E. N. Roussakis, *Miami's International Banking Community: Foreign Banks, Edge Act Corporations and Local Banks* (Miami: Peat, Marwick, Mitchell and Co., 1981).

SUGGESTED REFERENCES

Angelini, Anthony, Maximo Eng, and Francis A. Lees. *International Lending, Risk and the Euromarkets.* New York: John Wiley and Sons, 1979.

Baker, James C., and M. Gerald Bradford. *American Banks Abroad: Edge Act Companies and Multinational Banking.* New York: Praeger, 1974.

Center for Medieval and Renaissance Studies, U.C.L.A. *The Dawn of Modern Banking.* New Haven, Conn.: Yale University Press, 1979.

Davis, Steven I. *The Management Function in International Banking.* New York: John Wiley and Sons, 1979.

Department of the Treasury. "Report to Congress on Foreign Government Treatment of U.S. Commercial Banking Organizations," September 17, 1979. (Typed manuscript.)

Donaldson, T. H. *Lending in International Commercial Banking.* New York: John Wiley and Sons, 1979.

Houpt, James V. *Performance and Characteristics of Edge Corporations.* Washington, D.C.: Board of Governors, Federal Reserve System, 1981.

Khoury, Sarkis J. *Dynamics of International Banking.* New York: Praeger, 1980.

Lees, Francis A. *International Banking and Finance.* New York: John Wiley and Sons, 1974.

Mathis, F. John, ed. *Offshore Lending by U.S. Commercial Banks.* 2nd ed. Washington, D.C., and Philadelphia: Bankers' Association for Foreign Trade and Robert Morris Associates, 1981.

Oppenheim, Peter J. *International Banking.* 3rd ed. Washington, D.C.: American Bankers Association, 1978.

Richards, R. D. *The Early History of Banking in England.* London: Frank Cass and Co. Ltd., 1958.

Roussakis, Emmanuel N. "The Internationalization of U.S. Commercial Banks." *Bank Administration* 55, nos. 10-12 (1979); 56, nos. 1-2 (1980).

Steuber, Ursel. *International Banking.* Leiden: A. W. Sijthoff, 1976.

2 INTERNATIONAL BANKING: A FUNCTIONAL OVERVIEW

Kaj Areskoug

Commercial banking can be said to be "international" in some sense whenever the bank's customer—whether a depositor or a borrower—or a party to its security trading resides abroad. The transaction can be conducted from the bank's headquarters, or from branches or other offices in its home country. Or it can be conducted from facilities abroad—either in the customer's home country or, occasionally, in a third country. In the latter case the bank is effectively a multinational enterprise.

International banking, so characterized, obviously entails several types of financial and economic transactions among nations. Some are flows of funds or services to or from customers, others are transfers of financial or nonfinancial resources within the global banking enterprise itself. International banking is therefore directly interdependent with financial-economic conditions in several groups of countries: the bank's home country, the host countries of its foreign facilities, and the home countries of its customers.

This chapter provides a broad overview of the distinguishing functions of international banking and a brief analysis of its significance for financial markets, saving, investment, and global economic development. It views the internationally active bank as a special kind of firm, structured on one of several alternative organizational models and pursuing certain corporate goals. The bank operates in several national or international financial markets, each of which has its distinct regulations and practices, and is subject to various local and global demand and supply forces. In turn, international banking influences conditions in these markets, especially interest rates. These influences may occasionally facilitate, and occasionally hinder, the success of government economic policies in the countries involved. Yet, on balance, they tend to reduce the segmentation and fragmentation of the global financial system and to help to promote the integration of national money and credit markets.

The perspective in this chapter is partly microeconomic, partly macroeconomic. The underlying theoretical concepts are those traditionally used in analyses of domestic banking, financial markets, and international monetary economics. The overall thesis is that international banking can best be understood as a geographic extension of domestic financial intermediation and through analogies with international trade and investments by firms in other, nonfinancial industries.

ORGANIZATIONAL STRUCTURE

Industrial organization theory describes how a firm in a given line of business seeks to determine the geographic and functional structure that best suits its overall corporate goals. Essentially, it tries to balance the relative advantages and disadvantages of locational concentration and functional integration, on the one hand, and locational dispersion and functional differentiation, on the other. The former, centralized strategy normally permits a sharing of various overhead facilities, swift communication, close coordination and control, and related scale economies. The latter, decentralized strategy tends to promote better customer contacts, easier access to information about market developments, and greater flexibility in responding both to shifting market conditions and to changing pressures from tax and regulatory authorities. The optimal structure will reflect the nature of the firm's inputs and outputs, its technology, transportation costs, and the relative attractiveness and stability of the business climates in the relevant locations.

This is the background against which the organization of international banking should be analyzed.[1] The range of options is wide, and no single operational mode has proved to be superior. In fact, most large banks, including those in the United States, pursue a combination of different organizational strategies.[2]

At one extreme is the bank that carries out its international activities from its domestic headquarters, ordinarily through an *inter-*

national department that is closely corrdinated with its domestic departments but that has correspondent relationships with banks abroad. It typically concentrates on providing export and import credits, extended to foreign as well as domestic parties; it may also, if the regulatory authorities permit, engage in the purchase and sale of foreign securities or the taking of foreign deposits.[3]

This type of bank is basically in the business of exporting and importing. Via trade finance it "exports" funds, or credit, and related services, such as those connected with the verification and processing of shipping documents or the settlement of export- or import-related claims. It may, in addition, "export" or "import" funds through security purchases or sales, or through the withdrawal or taking of deposits, whenever the other parties reside in foreign countries. Like a firm trading, say, agricultural products, it deals in well-known, relatively standardized "commodities" on a long-distance basis. Unlike the agricultural trader, however, its transportation costs are minimal; and there are usually no outright customs tariffs or quotas (although taxes and foreign exchange controls can sometimes entail similar "barriers to trade").

At the other extreme is a bank with a network of full-service branches or affiliates (wholly or partially owned subsidiaries) in foreign countries. Normally, each of these facilities engages both in international banking—mostly in cooperation with the bank's home-country headquarters—and in local banking in the host country; but from the home-country perspective, all these activities can be regarded as international. The appropriate analogy for this situation is with a manufacturing firm that has producing units (divisions) in foreign countries, and conducts buying and selling transactions with parties situated both in the home and in the host countries—and, possibly, in third countries; in addition, the different units of the firm itself may be trading with one another.

A bank's headquarters may thus engage in "exports" and "imports" even while it has transferred some of these functions to its foreign branches or affiliates. The latter in turn act as "marketing" and "distribution" centers for host-country transactions initiated at headquarters. And when the customers are located in third countries, the foreign facilities may obviously be "exporting" or "importing" in their own right.

At the same time the relationship between the head office and the various foreign facilities can be looked upon as a mixture of "trade" and "investment." When foreign facilities are established, acquired, or physically expanded, there may be an outward international movement of equity capital (and, perhaps, labor and technology). This capital tends, over time, to yield returns (net income) that may be immediately put at the disposal of the head office or plowed back into assets under the primary control of the branch or affiliate. (In the case of branches, the funds and the recorded assets will legally belong to the home-country corporation, whereas affiliates have their own capital.) In addition to these "factor movements," there is typically a steady back-and-forth flow of funds between the bank's head office and its foreign facilities, connected with international trade credits, loans to customers, or adjustments of liquid reserves. These are rather like intracorporate shipments of final or intermediate products, for ultimate disposal in either the home or the host market.

Between these extremes are several intermediate arrangements for partial centralization. The head-office approach can, as far as the United States is concerned, be supplemented by the use of special domestic subsidiaries devoted to international banking—so-called Edge Act and agreement corporations. They derive their existence from the general U.S. prohibition on interstate banking, which otherwise limits the parent bank's ability to accommodate international corporate customers that need banking services in different parts of the country. They might be likened to the special international trading companies that exist in certain countries (such as Japan).[4]

Two other major organizational vehicles for international banking are *foreign representative offices* and *consortium banks*. The former offers a somewhat more active involvement in foreign credit markets than does a correspondent relationship, because the representative—somewhat like a sales agent—can directly negotiate loan agreements on behalf of the home office; such an office involves at least a small foreign investment of real resources. The consortium bank is essentially a variant of the foreign affiliate. It is established in cooperation with foreign financial institutions, but does not give any one bank a controlling interest. On the one hand, this is a highly decentralized approach to international banking. On the other, such a joint venture can be viewed as a partial step toward the creation of an even broader multicountry banking empire, under multicorporate control and with opportunities for a sharing of market access, real resources, and risks.

Except in regard to consortium banks and other minority interests in foreign banking institutions, an international network of jointly owned bank facilities is effectively a single enterprise. It has a common set of financial objectives; it achieves at least a partial pooling of resources; and it normally takes a consolidated approach to strategic planning. After all, every unit of the enterprise is ultimately responsible to the parent bank's stockholders, in accordance with the head office's interpretation of their interests. The activities of a foreign branch or affiliate, or of an Edge Act corporation, thus may not make complete sense unless they are put in the context of the consolidated multicountry enterprise.

INPUTS, OUTPUTS, AND ARBITRAGE

Privately owned commercial banks are a special kind of profit- and wealth-maximizing firm, devoted to various types of trading in financial markets and to the provision of certain specialized services. As with other financial intermediaries, their basic function can be described in two alternative ways: as purchases of "inputs" that are somehow "processed" and transformed into salable, higher-priced "outputs," or as buying and reselling of a limited range of "commodities" that happen to be differently priced in different segments of the markets. The former perspective is akin to manufacturing; the latter, to distribution and retailing, or to commodity and security arbitrage.

The relevant international financial inputs into banking are the funds obtained from foreign depositors or otherwise borrowed from foreign parties (through the issue of notes or bonds, or through interbank loans). If there are foreign stockholders, equity funds will represent another (normally quite small) category of "imported" inputs. These inputs are, for the most part, purchased in short-term foreign credit markets. Their prices are determined partly in these markets, partly in the broader international markets.

When the funds are denominated in the bank's home currency (as when U.S. banks take dollar deposits from foreign corporations or government agencies), the price variable is simply the interest rate, i_D, payable on these deposits or other bank-issued instruments. By contrast, if the funds are denominated in a foreign currency (for instance, the local currency of the host country of a foreign branch), the price variable, $i_D{}^*$, becomes more complex. Apart from the interest rate, it will, from the bank's consolidated standpoint, include the expected (positive or negative) change in the pertinent exchange rate, $E(\Delta ER/ER)$, between the home currency and the currency of denomination:

$$i_D{}^* = i_D + E(\Delta ER/ER).$$

The total price may thus exceed, or be lower than, the nominal interest rate, depending on whether the denomination currency is anticipated to appreciate or depreciate.

Since any estimate of future exchange-rate changes is subject to uncertainty, there is in principle also a risk factor, which could introduce an additional implicit cost element. Yet whether the bank, in estimating its likely costs of funds, needs to make such a risk adjustment (via a cost "premium" on the interest rate payable on these deposits) depends on the overall balance-sheet situation of the bank, and thus cannot be determined in this general context.

The major international financial output categories are the funds supplied to foreign private or government borrowers in the form of trade credits, other types of loans, or purchases of debt (or, in some foreign banking systems, equity) securities on foreign financial markets. The recipients of the funds are either the foreign borrowers or the previous foreign holders of the purchased securities.

The prices obtained on the implicit sales transactions ("exports" of funds) are the pertinent interest rates, i_L, plus (minus) the expected currency appreciation (depreciation):

$$i_L{}^* = i_L + E(\Delta ER/ER).$$

In this case the bank may need to make a downward adjustment of its estimated interest receipts to compensate for any addition to its overall riskiness; and certain foreign-currency loans may then not be worthwhile unless the implicit price "discount" can be offset through additional nominal interest charges.

Banks with foreign branches or affiliates will normally have to place some funds into reserves with foreign central banks or in low-yield foreign government securities. These may be characterized as special output categories sold, under regulatory pressure, at low or zero prices to privileged official borrowers. Or they may be likened to inventories that have to be held as cushions against unforeseeable, unfavorable shifts in input availability (deposit inflows) or sales opportunities (loan demand).

The "production" that transforms the bank's financial inputs into its financial outputs lies primarily in the resulting change in the funds' average maturities, because funds on the input side are generally of shorter maturities than those on the output side.[5] Accordingly, international banking can effect a transformation of short-term foreign funds into longer-term domestic or foreign funds, depending on whether the funds so obtained are placed in the domestic or foreign financial markets. And it can transform short-term domestic funds into longer-term foreign funds, via international lending financed through domestic deposits or borrowings. For these transformations to be profitable, $i_L{}^*$ must exceed $i_D{}^*$. That is, there must be a positive markup, or spread, between output and input prices.

The input-output structure of a multinational bank is reflected in its consolidated balance sheet, as illustrated—for a hypothetical U.S.-based bank—in Table 2.1. Its assets and liabilities have been grouped in accordance with the location of the bank facilities where the underlying transactions originated—home-country offices or foreign branches or affiliates—and, within the former category, according to the domestic or foreign residence of the respective customers. The main foreign inputs are funds recorded under liability categories VI and VII (especially VIB, which includes Eurodollar borrowings, and VIIA, which includes Eurodollar deposits at foreign branches). The main foreign outputs are those reflected in asset categories IIB and IIC (mostly head-office trade credits and loans to foreign governments, banks, and corporations) and IIIB and IIIC (various loans and security purchases booked at foreign branches and affiliates).

International banking can sometimes entail a transformation of the currency, as well as the maturity, characteristics of the traded funds. Banks operating in the Eurocurrency markets are especially in a position to finance some home-currency lending with foreign-currency funds, and vice versa, normally for the purpose of widening the interest-rate markups they enjoy. This might seem too risky to be feasible on a large scale, but forward market contracts (which do not in themselves involve any commitments of funds) provide convenient offsets to such risks.

TABLE 2.1. Consolidated Balance Sheet of a U.S.-Based Multinational Bank

Assets	Liabilities and Capital
I. Acquired via home-country offices in home country	V. Incurred via home-country offices in home country
A. Cash (domestic vault cash, balances at domestic central bank, due from domestic banks) B. Securities (domestic bills, notes, and bonds) C. Loans (to domestic firms and individuals)	A. Deposits (due domestic firms, individuals, and financial institutions) B. Borrowings (from domestic central bank, financial institutions, and corporations)
II. Acquired via home-country offices in foreign countries	VI. Incurred via home-country offices in foreign countries
A. Cash (due from foreign banks) B. Securities (acceptances) C. Loans (to foreign governments and corporations)	A. Deposits (due foreign banks, corporations, and affiliates of domestic corporations) B. Borrowings (from foreign banks)
III. Acquired via foreign facilities in local or third countries	VII. Incurred via foreign facilities in local or third countries
A. Cash (local vault cash, balances at local central banks, due from foreign banks) B. Securities (foreign bills, notes, bonds, and acceptances) C. Loans (to foreign governments, firms, and individuals)	A. Deposits (due foreign firms, individuals, governments, and affiliates of domestic corporations) B. Borrowings (from local central bank and financial institutions)
IV. Real assets (in home and host countries)	VIII. Equity (due domestic and foreign stockholders)

Note: Items I, II, V, and VI are denominated entirely in U.S. dollars; items III and VII are denominated, in part, in the local foreign currencies (unless they constitute Eurodollar assets or liabilities).

Source: Authors' data.

In Table 2.1 foreign-currency items on the liability side appear under category VII (local-currency deposits and borrowings at foreign facilities); on the asset side foreign-currency items are included under III (local-currency loans, securities, and cash balances acquired at foreign facilities). Should the former (liability) items exceed the latter (assets), the bank would be transforming U.S. dollar assets (on its own books) into foreign-currency assets (on the books of its depositors and creditors). In the opposite case it would be transforming some of its foreign-currency assets into publicly held dollar assets.

International banking thus produces changes in the nature of the funds available to the international nonbank public (and also among the banks themselves). In the absence of international banking, many saver-depositors would not have as attractive short-term outlets for their funds. Nor would, in many cases, borrowers have as attractive longer-term sources of funds. For performing this job the profitable bank enjoys a price markup that is sufficient to cover its operational expenses (the costs of nonfinancial inputs) and to provide adequate returns to its owners.

Under the alternative view, one can characterize international banking as a special kind of international security trading. All debt (and equity) instruments, including deposits, fall under the broad term "securities," and banks specialize in the profitable trading of certain types of securities. Some of these are issued by the banks themselves; they are "secondary"—that is, intended to raise funds for relending. Others are issued by private or public borrowers, mostly to finance spending ("primary" securities). International banking therefore consists, in part, of secondary-security sales to foreigners (security exports, coupled with funds imports); this occurs through the taking of foreign-owned deposits and receipts of interbank funds from abroad. It also consists of security imports (coupled with funds exports) via direct foreign loans, acceptance financing, treasury bill purchases in foreign money markets (all typical primary-security acquisitions), and loans to unaffiliated foreign financial institutions. Reexports of previously imported securities occur through sales or redemptions of foreign money-market instruments.

The buying and selling of essentially similar "commodities" (securities with varying maturity and risk features) across national borders can be construed as a form of international arbitrage activity. It permits the banks to take advantage of international differences in security prices (including those implicitly associated with deposits).

From a broader perspective such activity tends to promote the equalization of prices (of securities and of funds, in given maturity and risk classes)—the normal outcome of all arbitrage.

INTERMEDIATION AND RESOURCE ALLOCATION

Through their international activities, banks become international middlemen between parties with different financial needs. They find borrowers for their foreign depositor-lenders, and lender-depositors for their foreign borrowers. They do so by acquiring the debt instrument of one party ("primary" security) while issuing their own debt instrument ("secondary" security) to the other. This is the essence of indirect finance—in this case, indirect international finance, in which banks play the major, though not exclusive, role. (In contrast, consider direct international finance, via the placement of corporate or government debt instruments on foreign capital markets. And consider nonbank international intermediaries, which, in the private sphere, include insurance companies, pension funds, investment banks, and other firms with major foreign security holdings.)

By establishing its own asset-liability relationships to its two groups of customers, the bank can more easily satisfy their respective financial needs. Their individual funds, supplies, and demands need not match, in either amounts or maturities. Since funds are both perfectly divisible and fungible, internationally obtained funds can be divided up, or combined, so as to provide financing for a different number of domestic or foreign funds seekers; and short-term funds normally can easily be replaced so as to meet the bank borrowers' longer-term needs. Therefore, a bank may borrow short internationally to finance long domestically or internationally. Or it may borrow short domestically and lend long internationally.

Generally, funds represent immediately available purchasing power that can be obtained through income or securities sales, and can be allocated through securities or real-asset purchases (or extinguished through depreciation or consumption). International banking enhances the public's opportunities to increase its current spending and to acquire additional income-producing assets, via additional funds sources. It also broadens the public's opportunities for short-term financial asset accumulation (typically with better returns or greater liquidity than available domestically) via additional funds outlets. International banking thereby may stimulate saving; and even if this effect should be minor, it will undoubtedly improve the real income and wealth positions of depositors, as well as of borrowers.

This is nothing more than an elaboration of the conventional theory of domestic financial intermediation, with a few additional, international wrinkles.[6] Under ideal circumstances such intermediation draws surplus funds from savers (and, occasionally, other intermediaries) with low preferences for immediate spending (generally because of poor real investment opportunities relative to current incomes). It relends them to deficit units (and, occasionally, to other intermediaries) with high preferences for immediate spending (generally because of ample real-investment opportunities relative to current incomes). Both groups can then be said to be better off. The same applies internationally—that is, to international saver-depositors and borrower-spenders in different countries.

From a macro perspective, bank intermediation is believed to increase the allocational efficiency of the economies involved. Funds will be rechanneled from less productive to more productive spenders or uses. The spending shift will permit a better use of physical and human resources, for the benefit of overall social productivity.[7] This assumes that market participants have easy access to accurate information about relative costs and returns, and that there are no serious anticompetitive distortions of the banks' behavior and no distortive government interventions. The real world does not, of course, conform fully to this picture, either domestically or internationally. Many international funds flows through banks may, in fact, be predicated on rate or risk distortions in foreign-exchange markets, on attempts to avoid useful regulations on domestic banking, or on politically motivated relations among governments.

Even so, it seems reasonable to believe that international banking contributes to a better, more productive allocation of funds among nations, especially by helping to finance worthwhile investment projects in funds-scarce countries. And it may contribute to improved resource allocation within nations, by channeling funds to other sectors within the same countries (for instance, via the Euromarkets). This is especially likely to occur when the indigenous banking systems and financial markets are underdeveloped and inefficient.

The macroeconomic effects of international banking are essentially a matter of integration—of building bridges between national money and credit markets and pushing rates of interest and return toward greater international equality. Indeed, banking is a major vehicle for international economic integration. Among the main actual beneficiaries of this fact are developing countries that are using foreign bank funds for financing a large part of their real capital formation. They also include governments that have obtained bank loans to finance part of their oil-induced trade deficits in the 1970s. And they include the oil-exporting countries in the Middle East, which, via international banks, have found dependable outlets for their surplus funds.

PORTFOLIO ASPECTS

International banking expands the menu of bank deposit instruments (and other claims on banks) available to financial managers, both private and official. It improves the return-risk tradeoffs available for the short-term employment of their excess funds, for the benefit of efficient portfolio management.

In particular, the financial investor can, because of international banking, shop around among a larger number of deposit-taking banks that offer different interest rates and currency denominations, along with different degrees of assurance that withdrawal will always be possible and repayments promptly made. On the one hand, foreign banks may offer deposit opportunities with higher returns and greater liquidity than those at home. On the other hand, even if they do not, the very broadening of available deposit types creates further possibilities for diversification. For example, the multinational firm may, because of international banking, be able to place its liquid funds in deposits in an expanded range of currencies (partly via the Euromarkets), and thereby better cushion itself against unforeseen changes in import costs or export receipts connected with fluctuating currency values.

Banking, whether domestic or international, also affects the liability side of the nonbank public's balance sheet. By and large, commercial banks permit corporations and other deficit units to obtain somewhat longer-term financing than would otherwise have been possible by seeking funds directly, on the open market, from surplus units. Many multinationals and some government agencies—especially those in developing countries and in countries severely hurt by the oil-price crises—have surely borrowed more, and at more attractive terms (lower costs and/or longer maturities), than would have been available in the absence of international banking. And, from a cost-risk perspective, they may thereby have managed to link some of their actual or potential foreign-currency assets to bank loans denominated in the same currencies—an example of balance-sheet hedging against exchange risks.

In all, international banking facilitates income- and wealth-producing changes in the portfolios and balance sheets of large international firms, nonbank international financial institutions, and nations with balance-of-payments problems or urgent development projects.

POLICY IMPLICATIONS

The volume, pervasiveness, and transnational character of modern-day international banking suggest that it must have major consequences for the conduct of national economic policies, and also for supranational financial cooperation. On the one hand, international banking seems to promote global competition for credit and international resource mobility; this ought to stimulate a more productive pattern of real investment, easier absorption of unemployed labor, and an expansion of international trade in accordance with comparative-advantage principles. On the other, international banking may occasionally obstruct the pursuit of specific national policies, in particular when they are aimed at insulating a national economy from adverse or unpredictable changes in world markets.

Unavoidably, international banking will affect the potential for independent national monetary and credit policies. Through their activities in the local financial markets of their host countries, international banking facilities, like indigenous banks, act as conduits for the implementation of local monetary, credit, and interest-rate controls. But through their links with home-country and third-country financial markets, they can siphon off some of the pressures that national credit policies are meant to generate, and thus undermine the policies' effectiveness. Specifically, the Eurocurrency markets permit large corporations to substitute international for local bank loans, and vice versa, sometimes in contravention of the policy makers' intentions; this can hinder efforts to reduce inflation or to stimulate economic activity.

Also, international banking can, via deposit shifts, lending, or open-market security transactions, lead to capital flows that complicate attempts to maintain external balance. If the exchange rate is pegged—as is now the case among most of the EEC countries—bank-intermediated capital outflows can, at times, produce balance-of-payments deficits and undesired international reserve losses. Under different circumstances capital inflows can lead to reserve buildups that pose similar problems for, and threats of counteractions by, major trading partners. If, by contrast, the exchange rate is floating relatively freely (as are the U.S. dollar, the British pound, and the Japanese yen), the policy implications will be somewhat different: There may result a sudden exchange-rate change (depreciation or appreciation) that undercuts an anti-inflation program or weakens the competitive position of key export industries on world markets.

On the global plane, international banking undoubtedly is making a positive contribution to the gradual integration of financial markets and a better allocation of investable funds among surplus and deficit nations, sectors, and firms. It is a vehicle for the ongoing transfer of resources to the developing world, complementing the lending activities of the World Bank and the International Monetary Fund. It promotes international trade and investment, both by supplying finance and by providing operational facilities for funds transfers, foreign-exchange transactions, and other services. Finally, international banking is adding to the supply of international liquidity through additional deposit instruments denominated in a variety of internationally acceptable currencies, thereby accommodating market needs while potentially stimulating global inflation.

NOTES

1. Professor Aliber considers industrial organization theory to be one of the main alternative approaches (along with neoclassical trade theory) to the analysis of international banking. R. Z. Aliber, "Toward a Theory of International Banking," Federal Reserve Bank of San Francisco, *Economic Review*, Spring 1976, pp. 5–8.

2. For a more detailed description of the characteristics and relative advantages of different organizational methods, see F. Lees, *International Banking and Finance* (London: Macmillan, 1974), ch. 2. For data on the organization of international banking in developing countries, see United Nations, Centre on Transnational Corporations, *Transnational Banks: Operations, Strategies and Their Effects in Developing Countries* (New York: United Nations, 1981).

3. In the United States the regulatory authorities do not, as a rule, permit banks to engage in foreign-currency lending, security transactions, or deposit taking. This rule sharply curtails the international activities of the banks' home offices.

4. Additional opportunities for U.S.-based international banking will arise when U.S. banks start to take advantage of the newly adopted legislation on "international banking facilities," exempt from reserve requirements and interest-rate restrictions, within U.S. borders. The law is intended to permit U.S. banks, via the resulting "free-trade zones," to compete on more equal terms with banks operating in the essentially unregulated Eurocurrency markets. For a summary and evaluation of the new law, see E. D. Short, "Free-Trade Zone International Banking Facilities: A New Option for U.S.-Based Banks," Cato Institute, *Policy Report*, October 1981, pp. 4-9.

5. This aspect of banking, and the underlying financial-theoretic framework, are developed in B. Moore, *An Introduction to the Theory of Finance* (New York: Free Press, 1968), chs. 4, 6.

6. Ibid.

7. This argument is further elaborated in J. Van Horne, *Financial Market Rates and Flows* (Englewood Cliffs, N.J.: Prentice-Hall, 1978), chs. 1, 9.

SUGGESTED REFERENCES

Federal Reserve Bank of San Francisco. *Economic Review*, Fall 1977. Symposium "Banking in the World Economy."

Grubel, H. "A Theory of Multinational Banking." Banca Nazionale del Lavoro, *Quarterly Review*, December 1977, pp. 349-63.

Weston, R. *Domestic and Multinational Banking.* New York: Columbia University Press, 1980.

Part II

INTERNATIONAL BANKING: FUNCTION AND STRUCTURE

3 INTERNATIONAL CAPITAL MARKETS

David K. Eiteman

Any market is a meeting place for those who supply a commodity and those who want, or demand, that commodity. The meeting place may be at a specific geographic location, such as an early-morning wholesale produce market in a major city or an organized stock exchange (for instance, the New York Stock Exchange). Or the meeting place may exist through the operation of a communications network by which sellers and buyers negotiate terms (have a "meeting of the minds") while remaining in separate geographic locations. Interbank foreign exchange trading and the over-the-counter securities markets are most often conducted through communications network markets. Developments in modern electronics and computers have tended to allow communications network markets to dominate physical marketplaces when the commodity traded is standard, so that sellers and buyers need not physically view the "merchandise" before agreeing to a trade.

An international capital market is a communications network market having two additional characteristics, obvious from the name. First, the market is *international*, meaning that buyers and sellers are likely to be from different countries. Even when transactions take place between residents of a single country, the nature of the market is such that prices reflect the consensus supply and demand of participants from several countries. Additionally, the commodity traded in an international capital market is *capital*, meaning funds balances denominated in one or another of the world's currencies. Funds balances in any given currency have the requisite characteristic of being standard, so that buyers and sellers need not physically view the money before buying or selling.

INTERNATIONAL FINANCIAL CENTERS

International capital markets exist in international financial centers such as London, New York, and Frankfurt. An international financial center is usually an important domestic financial center that, because of its strength, viability, or geographic location, has attracted international financial business. To draw international financial business, a national financial center needs most of the following: The center should be the locus of a variety of major financial institutions, such as banks, insurance companies, securities firms, and foreign exchange dealers. The center should allow foreign banks or financial institutions to participate on an equal footing with domestic institutions. The center should have a sizable foreign exchange market, which in turn usually means that foreign trade and multinational business are relatively important to the city. Electronic communications should work—meaning, among other things, that the telephone and telegraph system must be efficient and quickly available to those desiring connections. Governmental regulation of financial activity must be dependable, predictable, and generally favorable to business and financial activity. By and large, participants in the financial markets must be free to trade on their own behalf, and the tax burden must not be onerous.

Transactions in an international financial center that is also an important domestic financial center are depicted in Figure 3.1.

A successful international financial center usually depends upon a large body of domestic investors or depositors who supply funds to domestic users. Depicted as (A) in Figure 3.1, this relationship is necessary to obtain a sufficient quantity of financial transactions that financial institutions will find it worthwhile to maintain a presence in the center and that a body of professional expertise is developed in the area.

An international capital market exists when domestic investors or depositors also supply funds to foreign users, or when foreign investors or depositors supply funds to domestic users. These two types of international markets are shown on the diagonals (B) and (C) in Figure 3.1.

FIGURE 3.1: Schematic View of Transactions in an International Financial Center

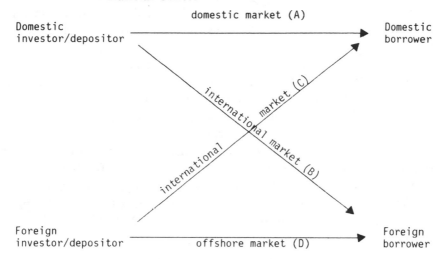

Source: David K. Eiteman and Arthur I. Stonehill, *Multinational Business Finance*, 3rd ed. (Reading, Mass.: Addison-Wesley, 1982), p. 398. Reprinted by permission of the publisher.

Yet a fourth type of international market exists, which is depicted as relationship (D) in Figure 3.1. When foreign investors or depositors supply funds directly to foreign users via a market mechanism that precludes domestic participation in the transaction, the relationship is called an offshore market. Offshore markets usually are created by governments that want to attract specialized financial business without exposing their residents to the freedoms that must be granted to international participants. International participants may always take their business elsewhere, an option that potential domestic participants may not necessarily be granted by their government. The best-known offshore financial centers are the Bahamas, the Cayman Islands, Singapore, Hong Kong, and Panama. (These are discussed in depth in chapter 4.)

Suppliers of funds in an international financial center may be either investors or depositors. Investors supply funds directly to users by purchasing securities such as bonds, commercial paper, or shares of stock. Investors will be attracted to an international financial center by the presence of securities firms, members of international underwriting syndicates, and banks that participate in securities distributions. Depositors supply funds to financial intermediaries, such as banks, insurance companies, and mutual funds, which in turn pool these receipts and make loans or equity investments from the pool.

In a direct investment the supplier of funds looks to the end user for profits (in the form of interest or dividends) or return of principal (for loans). A direct investor must have the means to analyze the quality and financial strength of the end user. In deposit relationships the financial intermediary performs the analysis, and the original supplier of funds has only a claim against the financial intermediary or, alternatively, against the portfolio in which the funds have been commingled. The supplier of funds does not analyze the end user.

The two most important components of the international capital market are the Eurocurrency market and the international bond market.

THE EUROCURRENCY MARKET

The Eurocurrency market is a financial intermediation market. In other words, deposits are accepted by banks, funds are commingled before being reloaned, and the supplier of the funds, the depositor, looks to the bank rather than to a downstream end user for return of capital.

A Eurocurrency is any currency deposited in a bank outside the country where that currency is the unit of account. The most common Eurocurrency, the Eurodollar, is thus a U.S. dollar deposited in a bank outside the United States. Eurosterling deposits are pounds sterling deposited in banks outside the United Kingdom, and Euromarks are deutsche marks deposited in banks outside West Germany. Each Eurocurrency deposit is a large amount of money, usually increments of half a million U.S. dollars, and is in the form of a time deposit, at times including a negotiable certificate of deposit on which interest is paid. Eurocurrency deposits are not demand deposits as that term is understood in the United States.

Eurodollar deposits are held in European banks as well as in banks outside of Europe, since the prefix "Euro-" springs from the function performed rather than from an inherent need for a European location. A market in foreign currency deposits exists in Singapore, where it is commonly referred to as the Asiadollar market, and similar markets exist in other non-European financial centers.

TABLE 3.1. Eurocurrency Liabilities of European Banks, December 31, 1980

Denomination of Liability	December 31, 1980 Millions of U.S. Dollars	Percent of Total
U.S. dollars	$518,730	69.0
Deutsche marks	122,930	16.4
Swiss francs	49,620	6.6
U.K. pounds sterling	12,970	1.7
French francs	11,550	1.5
Dutch guilders	7,430	1.0
Other currencies	28,010	3.8
	$751,240	100.0

Source: Bank for International Settlements, *Annual Report* (Basle, Switzerland: BIS, June 15, 1981), p. 113. Reprinted by permission of Bank for International Settlements.

The size of the Eurocurrency liabilities of European banks is shown in Table 3.1. These data are collected by the Bank for International Settlements in Basle, Switzerland, and therefore include only foreign currency liabilities of European banks. As can be seen, the dominant portion of the market, almost 70 percent, is denominated in U.S. dollars, causing the whole market to be referred to at times as the Eurodollar market. Deutsche marks are next in importance, at 16 percent, followed by Swiss francs and pounds sterling.

Growth in the size of the Eurocurrency market (European banks only) from 1974 through 1980 is shown in Figure 3.2. In those years total deposits rose from approximately $200 billion to $750 billion, an equivalent annual growth of about 20 percent. The bottom half of Figure 3.2 shows the quarterly amount of dollar, deutsche mark, and Swiss franc deposits plotted on a semi-logarithmic scale. As can be seen, the growth rate has been extremely constant.

FIGURE 3.2: Currency Structure of the Euromarket: 1974-80:
External Assets in Foreign Currencies of Reporting
European Banks
(quarterly figures, amounts outstanding)

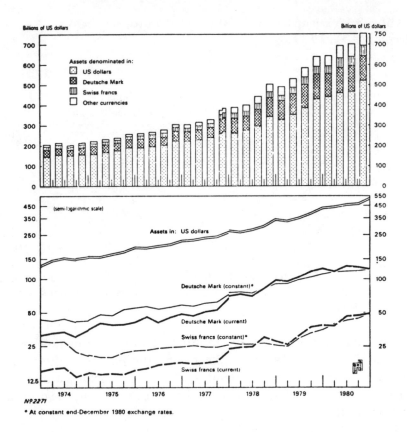

Source: Bank for International Settlements, *Annual Report* (Basle, Switzerland:
BIS, June 15, 1981), p. 112. Reprinted by permission of Bank for
International Settlements.

History of the Eurodollar Market

The modern Eurodollar market arose shortly after World War II,
when the Soviet Union and East European holders of dollars were
afraid to deposit their dollar balances in the United States because

those deposits might be attached by U.S. residents with claims against Communist governments. European banks had accepted limited amounts of dollar deposits before the war, and in the postwar period dollars were again deposited in such banks. As the postwar market grew, additional funds came from banks and central banks seeking higher yields than were available in the United States. Still more deposits came from European insurance companies and from holders of international refugee funds.

In the 1960s the United States responded to the growing weakness of the U.S. dollar by segmenting its capital market from the rest of the world, a step that enhanced the attractiveness of offshore financing and boosted the Eurodollar share of short-term international dollar financing. When the restrictions were removed in the early 1970s, the market continued to thrive, primarily because it had become highly efficient at attracting both depositors and borrowers away from purely domestic financial intermediaries, an ability fostered by the accumulated experience in international money matters available in London.

The key factor attracting both depositors and borrowers to the Eurodollar market has been, and remains, the availability of a narrower interest rate spread between deposit rates and lending rates than is available in the United States. As shown conceptually in Figure 3.3, the effective lending rate in the United States tends to be higher than that in the Eurodollar market, while simultaneously the effective deposit rate in the United States is below that usually available in the Eurodollar market.

The narrower spread in the Eurodollar market arises for a number of reasons. The Eurodollar market is to a large extent an interbank market with a large portion of the depositing and lending between banks, a process referred to as "chaining." An additional reason is that market activity is in fairly large amounts—half a million dollars or more—and is usually conducted on an unsecured basis. Nonbank borrowers are generally large corporations or government entities that qualify for low rates because their risk is perceived to be low. Finally, the Eurodollar operation does not carry much of the overhead of the banks in the market.

Interest rates in the Eurodollar market are normally quoted as premiums above the London Interbank Offered Rate (LIBOR), which is the deposit rate offered by London banks to other banks. The premium over LIBOR reflects adjustments for maturity and for

FIGURE 3.3: Concept of Narrower Spread Between Lending and
Deposit Rates in the Eurodollar Market

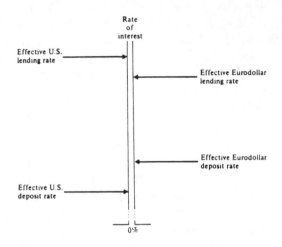

Source: David K. Eiteman and Arthur I. Stonehill, *Multinational Business Finance*, 2nd ed. (Reading, Mass.: Addison-Wesley, 1979), p. 318. Reprinted by permission of the publisher.

additional credit risks. Many Eurodollar credits are extended on a floating rate basis, meaning that the rate for a maturity longer than three or six months is set at the short-term LIBOR rate and then adjusted (or "rolled over") at the new rate every three or six months. This process assures borrowers of funds for longer periods of time while simultaneously protecting the bank from a squeeze if short-term rates rise while the bank is committed to a longer-term loan. When U.S. interest rates rose substantially above European rates in 1980 and 1981, some Eurodollar rates were quoted as a premium over the U.S. prime rate rather than over LIBOR. Compromise rates also have been used.

Asian Currency Market

An Asian version of the Eurocurrency market was created in 1969 when commercial banks in Singapore were allowed to accept

TABLE 3.2. Asian Currency Units: Assets and Liabilities,
March 31, 1980

	Millions of Dollars	Percent
Assets		
Loans to nonbank customers	$ 8,902.7	21.0
Interbank funds		
In Singapore	1,105.2	2.6
Inter-ACU	7,285.0	17.1
Outside Singapore	22,444.6	52.8
	30,834.8	72.5
Other assets	2,770.3	6.5
Total	$42,507.8	100.0
Liabilities		
Deposits of nonbank customers	$ 6,577.3	15.5
Interbank funds		
In Singapore	1,472.8	3.5
Inter-ACU	7,284.9	17.1
Outside Singapore	23,975.0	56.4
	$32,732.7	77.0
Other liabilities	3,197.8	7.5
Total	$42,507.8	100.0

Source: Monetary Authority of Singapore, Annual Report 1979/80, p. 49.

foreign currency deposits. The idea for this Asiadollar market, as it is sometimes called, arose from the observation that many Asian residents, including both multinational firms and overseas Chinese, had dollars or other foreign currencies that were being loaned or deposited in Europe and the United States rather than being put to use closer to home. A regional version of the Eurocurrency market would serve both investors and entities that wanted to borrow American or European funds by providing a mechanism to reinvest in Asian projects.

The Asian currency market has grown rapidly, and by March of 1980 some 108 banks or other financial institutions were licensed by the Monetary Authority of Singapore to operate Asian currency units (ACUs). An ACU is a section within a bank having authority and separate accountability for Asian currency market operations.

The size of the Asian currency market is shown in Table 3.2. The market is primarily an interbank market, with 75 percent of assets being loans to other banks and 77 percent of liabilities being deposits of other banks. Interest rates are expressed in relation to the Singapore Interbank Offered Rate (SIBOR), which moves closely with LIBOR. In some Asian countries SIBOR is the base rate from which other rate quotations are determined.

Creation of Eurodollars

The process of creating a Eurocurrency is best illustrated with a U.S. dollar example. As has already been explained, a Eurodollar is a U.S. dollar-denominated time deposit held in a bank outside the United States. Beginning in December 1981, U.S. banks within the United States were allowed to establish special "international banking facilities" to accept Eurocurrency deposits and make Eurocurrency loans. Although physically within the United States, these new facilities operate separately and keep their books separate from normal domestic banking. For our example we will use a traditional Europe-based bank.

Assume that a Danish corporation has a $1 million time deposit with a New York bank, possibly in the form of a negotiable certificate of deposit, on which it is earning 8 percent. The balance sheet of the New York bank and the Danish corporation would appear as shown below.

NEW YORK BANK

	Time deposit due Danish corporation (costing 8%) $1,000,000

DANISH CORPORATION

Time deposit in New York bank (earning 8%) $1,000,000	

The Danish corporation learns that a bank in London will pay 8.25 percent on a dollar-denominated time deposit. When the New York deposit matures, the Danish corporation redeposits the funds in the London bank. The physical transfer is effected by wire, and the net result leaves the three parties as shown below.

NEW YORK BANK

	Demand deposit due London bank (costing no interest) $1,000,000

DANISH CORPORATION

Time deposit in London bank (earning 8.25%) $1,000,000	

LONDON BANK

Demand deposit in New York bank (earning no interest) $1,000,000	Time deposit due Danish corporation (costing 8.25%) $1,000,000

Redeposit of the dollar funds in the London bank has created a Eurodollar deposit, for now a bank outside of the United States (in London) has a liability denominated in dollars.

In New York, the New York bank created a demand deposit for the Danish corporation when the time deposit matured. If the time deposit had been in the form of a negotiable certificate of deposit, the Danish corporation could have sold it at any time rather than waiting for maturity. In either case the Danish corporation initially acquired a demand deposit, which it then transferred to the London bank. This transfer, one must note, did not result in a reduction in dollar deposit liabilities of U.S. banks or in the quantity of money in the United States. The transfer just meant that on the books of the New York bank, funds were now owed to a London bank rather than to a Danish corporation.

The Danish corporation previously had $1 million on which it was earning 8 percent per annum. After the transfer it has $1 million in a London bank on which it is earning 8.25 percent. Because the deposit remains a bank obligation denominated in U.S. dollars, the Danish corporation has not changed its foreign exchange risk vis-à-vis Danish kroner, nor has it changed the potential purchasing power of the dollar principal of the deposit.

The London bank acquires a demand deposit in a New York bank, on which it presumably earns nothing, and simultaneously incurs a liability denominated in dollars on which it must pay 8.25 percent interest. The London bank has no foreign exchange risks because it has a dollar asset equal in value to its dollar liability, but for the moment the bank is in a disadvantageous earnings position, in that the cost (interest paid) on its deposit liability exceeds the earnings (nothing) on the demand deposit in New York that it acquired.

This profit dilemma is quickly resolved by the London bank's making a dollar loan at a rate greater than 8.25 percent. In fact, if the London bank did not know that it could reloan the funds at a rate greater than 8.25 percent, it would not have agreed to pay the Danish corporation 8.25 percent for the deposit. Assume that the London bank reloans the dollars to an Italian bank at 8.375 percent per annum. Such a very narrow spread would be normal, because the Eurodollar market is very competitive and transaction sizes are very large. The balance sheet of the Danish corporation would not change; in fact, since the Danish corporation looks only to the London bank, a financial intermediary, it would not know that its funds had been reloaned. (In practice, of course, funds are commingled and the London bank would think only of lending its free U.S. dollar balances, not the particular funds acquired from the Danish corporation.)

After the London bank loaned and transferred the funds to the Italian bank, the balance sheets would appear as shown below.

NEW YORK BANK

	Demand deposit due Italian bank (costing no interest)	$1,000,000

LONDON BANK

Loan to Italian bank (earning 8.375%)	$1,000,000	Time deposit due Danish corporation (costing 8.25%)	$1,000,000

ITALIAN BANK

Demand deposit in New York bank (earning no interest)	$1,000,000	Time deposit due London bank (costing 8.375%)	$1,000,000

After clearing the day's cable transfers, the New York bank now finds that it owes $1 million more to an Italian bank and $1 million less to a London bank. The London bank is paying 8.25 percent interest to the Danish corporation on funds that it has loaned to an Italian bank at 8.375 percent, for a gross spread of 0.125 percent. The Italian bank now owns the noninterest-earning demand deposit, and at the same time is obligated to pay the London bank 8.375 percent interest on the funds acquired.

At this moment the Italian bank is in a disadvantageous profit position. It would reloan the funds at another small increment in interest rate to yet another bank, which in turn could lend them to still another bank, creating a chain of interbank deposits at ever slightly higher interest rates. Although such chains of interbank deposits do occur, the ultimate purpose is to make a loan at the end of the chain to a user that needs the funds for productive business purposes.

For simplicity, let us assume that the Italian bank is the last in the chain of interbank deposits. The Italian bank loans the funds at 8.5 percent interest to Alitalia, the Italian state airline, which plans to purchase spare aircraft parts from McDonnell Douglas Corporation in California. After the loan to Alitalia, but before the purchase of the spare parts, the balance sheets that change because of the transaction would be as shown below.

NEW YORK BANK

	Demand deposit due Alitalia (costing no interest) $1,000,000

ITALIAN BANK

Loan to Alitalia (earning 8.5%) $1,000,000	Time deposit due London bank (costing 8.375%) $1,000,000

ALITALIA

Demand deposit in New York bank (earning no interest) $1,000,000	Note payable to Italian bank (costing 8.5%) $1,000,000

When Alitalia actually pays McDonnell Douglas, the following accounts would result:

NEW YORK BANK

	Demand deposit due McDonnell Douglas (costing no interest) $1,000,000

ALITALIA

Inventory of spare parts $1,000,000	Note payable to Italian bank (costing 8.5%) $1,000,000

MCDONNELL DOUGLAS CORPORATION

Demand deposit in New York bank $1,000,000	

At the end of this series of transactions, the New York bank has a demand deposit liability to McDonnell Douglas Corporation. From the point of view of the New York bank, the deposit has simply been transferred from one customer to another. Some customers will be commercial firms, and some will be banks. Some will be U.S. entities, and some will be foreign entities. During the entire series of trans-actions, a demand deposit liability has always existed on the books of the New York bank.

In reality the locus of the underlying dollar demand deposit could have shifted within the United States. The Danish corporation could have kept its dollar funds at Morgan Guaranty Bank, the London bank could have kept its correspondent account at Chase Manhattan Bank, the Italian bank could have kept its correspondent account at Bank of America in San Francisco, and Alitalia could have kept its dollar balance at Citibank in New York. McDonnell Douglas might keep its funds at Wells Fargo Bank in California. However, this possibility for the transfer of funds among U.S. banks does not differ from what would occur in any series of domestic banking trans-actions.

Behind the transfer of the dollar deposit in a U.S. bank are a series of Eurodollar transactions. If European banks were asked to report their total dollar liabilities, as they are in fact asked by the Bank for International Settlements, both the London bank and the Italian bank would report a liability of $1 million, for a total Euro-dollar liability of $2 million. Thus, it can be seen that "chaining" of deposits causes the statistical measure of Eurodollar liabilities to rise to a multiple of the underlying deposit maintained in the United States.

During the course of events in the example above, another type of transaction could have occurred. Any sequential holder of the Eurodollar deposit could reinvest the funds in the U.S. money market rather than loan them to someone else. If, for example, the Italian bank chose to purchase $1 million of U.S. Treasury bills, the New York bank would be instructed to make payment to the Federal Reserve Bank of New York for credit to the account of the U.S. Treasury. This would cause a loss of reserves to the U.S. banking system. (However, if the Treasury bills were purchased in the second-ary market, the New York bank would simply transfer the funds to the seller.)

In the original example above, both the London and the Italian bank eventually possessed a dollar-denominated asset that earned more than the cost of the matching liability. The Danish corporation earned what it perceived to be the highest rate of interest available on its dollar balances. One might ask why the Danish corporation did not deposit its funds directly in the Italian bank at 8.375 percent—or, for that matter, why it did not make a loan directly to Alitalia. The Danish firm might not know of these options and might not find it worthwhile to engage in the systematic search and analysis that would be required. Or it might simply perceive that the risk of dealing with other than a London or New York bank is too great.

Alitalia alone remains "exposed," in that it has a dollar-denominated debt and no dollar-denominated assets. Between the time when the loan is taken down and when it is repaid, Alitalia either will have to earn dollars (presumably by selling tickets to passengers who will pay with dollars) or to purchase dollars (with lire or other currencies earned from selling tickets to passengers who pay with lire or other currencies that Alitalia accepts). By maturity Alitalia must acquire sufficient dollars to repay the loan plus interest. When the chain of loans and deposits matures, each participant in the chain will retain that portion of the interest that is its spread, and repay principal and interest to the next party in line. At the end of the chain, the Danish corporation will receive its principal plus interest at 8.25 percent.

Depending on its business needs, the Danish corporation might redeposit the dollars for another interval of time wherever it finds the best rate, use the dollars to pay dollar-denominated expenses (such as the purchase of raw material acquired outside of Denmark), or exchange them for Danish knoner to pay domestic expenses. If the dollars were exchanged for Danish kroner at a Copenhagen bank, that bank would then acquire a dollar deposit in New York and would have to decide if it wanted to make a Eurodollar loan or sell the dollars for some other currency.

THE INTERNATIONAL BOND MARKET

An international bond issue is sold to investors in countries other than the country of the issuing entity. All international bonds are either foreign *bonds* or *Eurobonds*. A foreign bond is issued by a foreign borrower, underwritten by a syndicate composed of members from within a single country other than the country of the borrower, sold principally and denominated in the currency of that country. Foreign bonds sold in the United States are often called "Yankee bonds," and foreign bonds sold in Japan are sometimes called "samurai bonds."

A tombstone ad for an international bond issue is shown in Figure 3.4. The offering of 10.25 percent deutsche mark bonds of 1981,

FIGURE 3.4: Tombstone Ad for an International Bond Issue

New Issue
November 19, 1981

All of these bonds having been placed, this announcement appears for purposes of record only.

INTER-AMERICAN DEVELOPMENT BANK
Washington, D. C.

DM 100,000,000
10¼% Deutsche Mark Bonds of 1981, due 1991

Offering Price 99%
Interest   10¼% p. a., payable on November 15 of each year
Repayment   on November 15, 1991 at par
Listing   Frankfurt am Main, Berlin, Dusseldorf, Hamburg and Munchen

Deutsche Bank
Aktiengesellschaft

Dresdner Bank
Aktiengesellschaft

Commerzbank
Aktiengesellschaft

**Westdeutsche Landesbank
Girozentrale**

Bayerische Vereinsbank
Aktiengesellschaft

Bankhaus H. Aufhäuser

Bank für Gemeinwirtschaft
Aktiengesellschaft

Bayerische Hypotheken- und
Wechsel-Bank
Aktiengesellschaft

Bayerische Landesbank
Girozentrale

Joh. Berenberg, Gossler & Co.

Berliner Bank
Aktiengesellschaft

Berliner Handels-
und Frankfurter Bank

Bankhaus Gebrüder Bethmann

Delbrück & Co.

Deutsche Girozentrale
– Deutsche Kommunalbank –

Deutsch-Südamerikanische Bank
Aktiengesellschaft

DG Bank
Deutsche Genossenschaftsbank

Georg Hauck & Sohn Bankiers
Kommanditgesellschaft auf Aktien

Hessische Landesbank
– Girozentrale –

Landesbank Rheinland-Pfalz
– Girozentrale –

Merck, Finck & Co.

B. Metzler seel. Sohn & Co.

Norddeutsche Landesbank
Girozentrale

Sal. Oppenheim jr. & Cie.

Schröder, Münchmeyer, Hengst & Co.

Trinkaus & Burkhardt

Vereins- und Westbank
Aktiengesellschaft

M. M. Warburg-Brinckmann,
Wirtz & Co.

Westfalenbank
Aktiengesellschaft

Source: Reprinted from *Euromoney*, December 1981, p. 23, by permission of the publisher.

due in 1991, was made in Germany and was underwritten entirely by German banks. The borrower, however, was the Inter-American Development Bank, an international regional development bank headquartered in Washington, D.C., that makes development loans to Latin American countries.

In comparison, a Eurobond is underwritten by a multinational syndicate of banks and other securities firms, and is sold to investors in a number of countries other than the country of the issuing entity. The Eurobond may be denominated in the currency of the country of the issuing entity—for example, U.S. companies that sell Eurobonds in Europe typically denominate them in U.S. dollars. Or it may be denominated in some other major currency, as would occur if a British firm issued a Eurobond denominated in Swiss francs or Eurodollars. Some Eurobonds have been denominated in Special Drawing Rights (SDRs).

A tombstone ad for a Eurobond offering is shown in Figure 3.5.

FIGURE 3.5: Tombstone Ad for a Eurobond Offering

Source: Reprinted from *Euromoney*, December 1981, p. 41, by permission of the publisher.

In this instance a European entity, the European Investment Bank, borrowed U.S. dollars in Europe. The underwriting was from European countries, the Middle East, and Asia. The group had 97 members from European countries (Bank Brussel Lambert N.V., for example), the Middle East (Alahi Bank of Kuwait K.S.C.), Southeast Asia (The Hongkong Bank Group), and Japan (Nomura International, Ltd.) The non-European underwriters maintain European offices in order to participate in such offerings.

In some respects the Eurobond market is similar to the Eurocurrency market. Both markets are "external," in that obligations in a particular currency are written or carried out in a country other than the country whose currency is used. However, the Eurocurrency market is a financial intermediation market, with major world banks operating as intermediaries between depositors (suppliers) and borrowers (users) of Eurocurrencies. By contrast, the Eurobond market is a direct market in which investors hold the securities issued by final borrowers. Institutions in the Eurobond market carry out an underwriting and direct marketing function. These functions are performed by departments of banks, the same banks that conduct a Eurocurrency business. However, underwriting and marketing groups for Eurobonds include many types of securities firms in addition to banks. Eurobonds are debt obligations of leading multinational firms, of governments, or of government enterprises. Most Eurobonds are issued in bearer form and have call provisions and sinking funds.

Table 3.3. shows that in 1980 new international bond issues were just over $41 million, totals of all currencies being expressed in U.S.

TABLE 3.3. New International Bond Issues, 1980

	Millions of Dollars	Percent
Eurobonds	$23,879	57.1
Foreign bonds sold outside the United States	14,521	34.7
Foreign bonds sold in the United States	3,429	8.2
Total	$41,829	100.0

Source: Morgan Guaranty Trust Company, *World Financial Markets*, January 1981, p. 17.

TABLE 3.4. New Eurobond Issues, 1980

	Millions of Dollars	Percent
Category of borrower		
U.S. companies	$ 4,100	17.2
Non-U.S. companies	9,032	37.8
State enterprises	5,755	24.1
Governments	3,045	12.8
International organizations	1,947	8.1
	$23,879	100.0
Category of depositor		
U.S. dollar	$16,340	68.4
Deutsche mark	3,607	15.1
Dutch guilder	1,050	4.4
Canadian dollar	279	1.2
European Unit of Account	65	0.3
Other	2,538	10.6
	$23,879	100.0

U.S. companies include both parent companies and their financing affiliates, either domestic or foreign.

Non-U.S. companies include private companies domiciled outside the United States and their affiliates.

State enterprises include public agencies.

Governments include central and local governments.

Source: Morgan Guaranty Trust Company, *World Financial Markets*, January 1981, p. 17.

dollars. The Eurobond market was the biggest portion of the market, comprising just over 57 percent of all new issues. Foreign bonds sold outside the United States accounted for almost 35 percent of the total, while foreign bonds sold within the United States were only about 8 percent.

The Eurobond market owes its existence to several unique factors. National governments sometimes impose tight controls on foreign issuers of securities denominated in their local currency and sold within their national boundaries. However, such governments are often much more flexible about securities denominated in foreign currencies and sold to local residents already possessing those foreign currencies.

Other reasons for the popularity of the Eurobond market are its freedom from the stringent and time-consuming registration requirements of domestic agencies such as, in the United States, the Securities and Exchange Commission. This freedom saves both time and money. The fact that Eurobonds appear in bearer form is also an attraction, since the country of residence of the investor is not a matter of public record and interest paid is generally not subject to a withholding tax. (By comparison, foreign residents who hold bonds issued in the United States are subject to a 30 percent withholding tax by U.S. authorities.)

Statistics on the Eurobond market in 1980 are shown in Table 3.4. U.S. companies are relatively modest borrowers, taking down only 17 percent of all issues. Non-U.S. companies borrowed almost 38 percent of all funds, and state enterprises borrowed another 24 percent of all funds. U.S. dollars are the main currency invested, providing 68 percent of total funds. The deutsche mark, at 15 percent, is a distant second in importance.

Currency Cocktail Bonds

Fluctuating exchange rates have increased the sensitivity of financial executives to the potential for unexpected changes in the cost of servicing bonds denominated in foreign currencies. One response has been to issue bonds denominated in one of several multicurrency units or "currency cocktails," composed of a weighted average of several currencies.

TABLE 3.5. Number of New International Bond Issues Offered in 1977-81, by Currency of Issue

	1977	1978	1979	1980	1981
Individual currency issues					
U.S. dollars	193	107	149	187	283
Deutsche marks	78	94	45	58	35
Dutch guilders	9	11	8	17	12
French francs	–	3	12	16	8
Luxembourg francs	4	1	–	–	–
Canadian dollars	20	–	12	6	16
Hong Kong dollars	3	–	–	–	–
Singapore dollars	–	–	–	–	1
Australian dollars	1	2	1	2	–
Austrian schillings	–	1	2	1	–
Kuwaiti dinars	7	16	13	1	3
Bahraini dinars	2	1	–	–	–
U.K. pounds sterling	6	8	4	18	9
Norwegian kroner	–	–	1	4	3
Japanese yen	2	1	2	4	5
Saudi riyals	1	–	–	–	–
Currency cocktail issues					
European Units of Account	1	6	6	3	4
Special Drawing Rights	–	1	2	1	4
European Currency Units	–	–	–	–	5
Total	327	252	257	318	388

Source: Euromoney, February 1982, p. 113.

Table 3.5. shows the number of currency cocktail bond issues offered in 1977-81, relative to new offerings in single currencies. The total number is not large; in 1981, for example, 13 of the 388 new international bond offerings were denominated in a currency cocktail.

Actual subscription to the bonds, and interest and principal payments, are not made in the currency cocktail, since the unit is not a means of payment or an instrument of exchange. Rather, payments are made in any of the component currencies in an amount sufficient to "buy" other components of the unit at current exchange rates and in the proportion defined by the unit. The underlying logic of a currency cocktail bond is that, because of the effects of diversification, the cost of service will be more stable than the cost of servicing a single-currency bond. Portfolio theory has shown that a portfolio of securities will have a lower standard deviation of expected returns than the standard deviation of expected returns from a single security within that portfolio. The same reasoning has been applied to the portfolio of currencies used in a currency cocktail.

As shown in Table 3.5, three currency cocktails are in general use. The Special Drawing Rights (SDRs) are defined by the International Monetary Fund as the value of a basket of five currencies. The quantities of each of the five are shown in Table 3.6, along with the implicit weighting. This definition became effective January 2, 1981, and replaced an earlier definition based on 16 currencies.

TABLE 3.6. Composition and Weighting of Multicurrency Units

	Special Drawing Rights (SDR)		European Currency Unit (ECU) and European Unit of Account (EUA)	
	Composition	Jan. 2, 1981 Weighting	Composition	Mar. 1, 1979 Weighting
U.S. dollar	0.540	42.5%	—	—
Deutsche mark	0.460	18.3	0.828	33.02%
Pound sterling	0.071	13.3	0.0885	13.15
French franc	0.740	12.8	1.15	19.89
Japanese yen	34.000	13.2	—	—
Italian lira	—	—	109.0	9.58
Dutch guilder	—	—	0.286	10.56
Belgian franc	—	—	3.66	9.23
Luxembourg franc	—	—	0.14	0.35
Danish krone	—	—	0.217	3.10
Irish pound	—	—	0.00759	1.11
		100.0%		100.00%

Note: Items do not add to totals due to rounding.

Source: SDR composition described in International Monetary Fund, *IMF Survey*, January 12, 1981, p. 6; EUA and ECU components in European Investment Bank, *Annual Report 1980*, p. 8.

The European Currency Unit (ECU) was created in March 1979 by the countries of the European Economic Community, and consists of the amounts of each of the nine member countries' currencies shown in Table 3.6. The ECU was set equal to another currency cocktail, the European Unit of Account (EUA), which was revised to its present form in 1975. The EUA had been originally intended as a legal standard of value for settlement between members of the European Economic Community. At present both the ECU and the EUA have the same composition.

SUGGESTED REFERENCES

Bank for International Settlements. *Fifth-First Annual Report.* Basle, Switzerland: Bank for International Settlements, June 15, 1981.

Dufey, Gunter, and Ian H. Giddy. "Innovations in the International Financial Markets." *Journal of International Business Studies,* Fall 1981, pp. 33-51.

———. *The International Money Market.* Englewood Cliffs, N.J.: Prentice-Hall, 1978.

Eiteman, David K., and Arthur I. Stonehill. *Multinational Business Finance.* 3rd ed. Reading, Mass.: Addison-Wesley, 1982.

Finnerty, Joseph E., Thomas Schneeweis, and Shantaram P. Hedge. "Interest Rates in the Eurobond Market." *Journal of Financial and Quantitative Analysis,* September 1980, pp. 743-55.

Folks, William R., and Ramesh Avanti. "Raising Funds with Foreign Currency." *Financial Executive,* February 1980, pp. 44-49.

Hodjera, Zoran. "The Asian Currency Market: Singapore as a Regional Financial Center." *IMF Staff Papers,* June 1978, pp. 221-53.

Quinn, Brian Scott. "The International Bond Market for the U.S. Investor." *Columbia Journal of World Business,* Fall 1979, pp. 85-90.

Senbet, Lemma W. "International Capital Market Equilibrium and Multinational Firm Financing and Investment Policies." *Journal of Financial and Quantitative Analysis,* September 1979, pp. 455-80.

Starr, Danforth W. "Opportunities for U.S. Corporate Borrowers in the International Bond Markets." *Financial Executive,* June 1979, pp. 50-59.

4 OFFSHORE BANKING CENTERS

Bowman Brown and
Emmanuel N. Roussakis

OVERVIEW

Until World War II banking was primarily a domestic enterprise. But, at the end of the war, a truly international financial community emerged, originally preoccupied with furnishing the capital to rebuild a war-torn Europe, and later eager to contribute to other aspects of the developing international commerce.

Initially the international financial centers were extensions of existing domestic centers; after all, the support facilities, trained personnel, and communications networks were already present in domestic centers. London was already the most important center for international finance, and New York rose into a position of considerable international importance. In time, however, especially after 1970, other areas not known for their existing banking facilities grew to become important centers for international banking, usually because their governments implemented regulatory and taxation policies favorable to the banking business and because their geographical locations became advantageous in a world where Asian and Middle Eastern economies suddenly rivaled those of Western Europe and of the United States. Recognizing the advantages these new locations offered, U.S. and European banks began establishing offices in these foreign lands in the late 1960s and early 1970s. Thus, these countries became offshore banking centers (OBCs) for the American and European banking industry and have, in recent years, closed in on London and New York as international banking centers of considerable significance within the international financial community.

Conceptually, four kinds of banking transactions may occur: between domestic borrowers and domestic lenders, between domestic borrowers and foreign lenders, between domestic lenders and foreign borrowers, and between foreign borrowers and foreign lenders. The first case is purely a domestic situation, and of no interest to us here. The remaining three cases are examples of international banking transactions. By definition, entrepôt financial centers permit all three kinds of international transactions; "offshore banking," on the other hand, is a term usually applied only to the last category, in which transactions are conducted between two or more foreign parties. Because most host countries discourage the mixing of foreign banking with domestic, entrepôt centers are subject to far greater regulation than offshore centers.

OBCs exist primarily to facilitate international transfer of funds in a business environment supportive of that goal. They tend to enjoy the following advantages over other banking centers: a regulatory climate in which controls are lax enough to permit the unrestrained transfer of capital among nonresidents, and minimal taxation and relatively small reserve requirements. Historically, those OBCs that have been most successful have benefited from the political stability of the host countries and from flexible regulatory policies that permit easy adaptation to new circumstances. In general, OBCs are most frequently and most productively used for funding, syndicating, booking, and administering loans. They are also employed, to a lesser extent, for the management of nonresidents' tax-sheltered trusts. Though some host governments have allowed hybrid cases by permitting unrestricted banking activity, in most instances OBCs are limited to international transactions and are barred from participating in the host country's economy.

Perhaps the most attractive feature of OBCs is their freedom from the strict regulatory provisions present in such established financial centers as London and New York. Usually, to protect the OBC customers, the host countries substitute restricted access to the offshore market for severe regulations. Thus, in most offshore markets only banks with substantial assets and established integrity are granted licenses. Hong Kong, for example, insists that a bank possess assets of more than U.S. $3 billion before it is allowed entry into the market.

Once in the market, foreign banks enjoy reduced regulations, freedom from exchange controls on nonresident transactions, and, usually, tax advantages. Moreover, very often transactions that appear on an OBC's books in fact are handled at the home office. This procedure has a double advantage. First, it allows the home bank to use its highly trained personnel and sophisticated facilities. Second, it reduces the risk of loss of funds due to political intervention by the host country, since the funds exist within the host country on the books only, and not in actual fact.

Another advantage of the OBC is that it eliminates time zone problems that otherwise would exist between parties located on opposite sides of the world. With an OBC in Singapore, a London parent bank, for example, can conduct business in the Far East during normal business hours, something that would be impossible if the transactions had to be conducted through the London office. Crucial to the growth and success of OBCs has been the boom in satellite and computer technology, which has permitted rapid communication between the parent office and the OBC. OBCs cannot thrive in areas that lack dependable communications systems and support services.

One final attribute of OBCs, which some deem advantageous, and others disadvantageous, is the high degree of confidentiality in which most of the data concerning financial transactions are kept. The extent of the confidentiality varies from host country to host country, but usually secrecy prevails; and the fact remains that it is more difficult for U.S. agencies, such as the Internal Revenue Service, to gain access to records officially housed in a foreign country than to records in the United States. The Cayman Islands, in particular, have protected holders of OBC accounts against attempts by the U.S. government to secure their funds.

INTERNATIONAL BANKING FACILITIES

International banking facilities (IBFs) were first proposed in the late 1960s to enable U.S. banks to circumvent the Voluntary Foreign Credit Restraint Program and to continue lending to nonresidents from their head offices rather than through their foreign branches. Concern about the negative impact on the domestic control of money supply led the Federal Reserve to reject the idea in 1974. The

IBF proposal was revived in 1978, this time by the New York Clearing House banks, partly in an effort to propel New York into a position of international financial eminence and partly to stimulate the then ailing economy of the city. After a period of discussion and debate, the Federal Reserve introduced the IBF on December 3, 1981. Located within the United States, instead of offshore, IBFs can accept time deposits in either dollars or foreign currency from foreign customers, free of reserve requirements (Regulation D) and of interest rate limitations (Regulation Q). They can also extend credit to foreigners. IBFs have been further strengthened by legislation in New York and other states that exempts them from state and local income taxes. The incentive for other states to introduce IBF legislation has been to strengthen their competitive position in international banking. Table 4.1 shows the states that had passed IBF legislation, or had such legislation pending, by September 1981.

TABLE 4.1. IBF Legislation

State	Legislation Passed	Legislation Pending	Legislation not Adopted
California	X		
Connecticut	X		
Florida	X		
Georgia	X		
Illinois	X		
Maryland	X		
New York	X		
Hawaii		X	
Massachusetts		X	
Washington			X

Source: Board of Governors, Federal Reserve System.

IBFs possess some advantages and disadvantages that distinguish them from bank operations through foreign locations. On the positive side they make entry into the Eurocurrency market easier for smaller banks, because those banks no longer need to establish a foreign office. Another important advantage for U.S. banks is that in operating through an IBF instead of through an OBC, they can reduce costs for facilities and personnel, have more direct management and control, and use support services and facilities that are already in place. The U.S. jurisdiction offered by IBFs provides greater assurance to foreign investors that their principal is safe and that they will have unimpeded access to their funds. By contrast, OBCs fall under the jurisdiction of the host country; consequently, deposits are exposed to sovereign risk.

On the other hand, though less regulated than their parent companies, IBFs are still more heavily regulated than most OBCs. This fact constitutes their most dramatic limitation. The regulations exist to ensure that IBFs can serve only nonresidents. Specifically, IBFs must receive written acknowledgment from their customers that deposits do not support activities within the United States and that loans granted through the IBF finance only operations outside of the United States. IBFs are prevented from offering demand deposits or transactions accounts that could possibly substitute for such accounts that nonresidents now hold in U.S. banks. IBFs also are prohibited from offering negotiable certificates of deposit. Consequently, they can offer only time deposits. Time deposits offered to nonbank foreign residents require minimum deposits and withdrawals of $100,000, and either a minimum maturity or two business days' notification before withdrawal is permitted. This provision thus precludes the offering of overnight deposits. Finally, for foreign banks it is disadvantageous to transfer business from their non-U.S. offices to the IBFs of their U.S.-based branches and agencies, because in so doing they would subject such transfers to U.S. federal tax liabilities.

IBFs are still new, and it remains to be seen to what extent their advantages will outweigh their disadvantages. As they become better understood, and their position within the Eurocurrency market better known, it is conceivable that existing regulations may loosen. This may become possible, for example, by eliminating the two-day minimum maturity requirement on foreign nonbank deposits. Another requirement, which was removed by Congressional action shortly after the introduction of the IBFs, called for FDIC coverage of deposits where the parent institution's deposits were insured. Exempting IBF deposits from insurance coverage eliminated the cost disadvantage of these deposits (about six basis points annually) vis-à-vis the OBC deposits of U.S. foreign branches. If further relaxation of existing regulation were to occur, IBFs might pose a more substantial threat to OBCs. But in either case it is unlikely that IBFs will obviate the need for OBCs.

OBC LOCATIONS

Because they possess the crucial combination of diminished regulation and taxation, stable and receptive government, a local supply of skilled labor, convenient time zone locations, and the presence of sophisticated telecommunications networks, OBCs have grown significantly since the early 1970s. Specifically, between 1970 and 1981, OBCs' share of the Eurocurrency market increased from 8.7 percent to 28.5 percent. This growth contributed to the decentralization of the Eurocurrency market, which until 1970 existed almost exclusively in London and in a few other West European centers. Some of the sites that have emerged as major OBC locations are the Bahamas and Cayman Islands, Singapore and Hong Kong, Bahrain, Panama, and the Netherlands Antilles. Luxembourg is another important OBC site that offers the industrial European countries the advantage of offshore banking within their own time zone.

TABLE 4.2. Gross Eurocurrency Liabilities* of Major Offshore Banking Centers, 1970-81
(billions of dollars, end of year)

OBC	1970	1975	1980	1981
Bahamas	7	55	126	157
Singapore	—	13	54	86
Luxembourg	3	27	84	82
Bahrain	—	2	38	51
Hong Kong	—	4	32	46[a]
Cayman Islands	—	7	33	42
Panama	—	9	35	42
Netherlands Antilles	—	—	7	8[b]
Total	10	117	409	514

Note: Data include the activities of branches of both U.S. and foreign banks except for Cayman Islands, which reflect only U.S. branch activity.

*These are considered "gross" liabilities because interbank claims are not netted out.

[a]Liabilities to nonresident banks only.

[b]Estimate.

Source: Morgan Guaranty Trust Company, New York.

Table 4.2 shows the gross sizes of the major Eurocurrency offshore centers and their relative importance.

As seen in Table 4.2, the gross Eurocurrency liabilities of the major offshore centers at the end of 1981 were $514 billion. The most important of these centers has been Bahamas, whose share of the market amounted to $157 billion at the end of 1981. If the market share of the Bahamas is combined with that of the Caymans, the two centers jointly account for 38.7 percent of the offshore market. In Asia, Singapore and Hong Kong combine to account for 25.7 percent of the offshore market.

Bahamas and Cayman Islands

The two primary Caribbean banking centers, the Bahamas and the Cayman Islands, represent two of the oldest OBCs and share many characteristics. Relying primarily upon U.S. investment, these centers emerged in the late 1960s as an outlet for medium-size U.S. banks to the growing Eurocurrency market.

At present they constitute the third largest Eurocenter, after London and New York. As indicated in Table 4.2, by far the majority of the Eurocurrency liabilities are found in the Bahamas, though the Cayman Islands' portion has grown significantly in recent years, partly as a result of real and anticipated Bahamian policy changes.

Both centers are characterized by the factors, enumerated above, that are necessary for successful OBCs. They have excellent communications networks and easy accessibility to the United States, in whose time zone they lie. The cost of establishing and operating a facility in the Caribbean is far lower than in London; moreover, government interference is minimal. Both centers permit "shell operations," which allow parent companies to conduct their business elsewhere but enter the transactions in the shell's books. The shell often requires no more than a single employee and a post office box; consequently, it is not uncommon in the Bahamas to find a single attorney "running" ten different banks. It is estimated that over 75 percent of Bahamian OBCs are such operations, but recent pressure from central banks and foreign tax authorities has led to some change in that tendency. Though numerically superior, these shell operations do not account for much of the Eurocurrency business.

Neither the Bahamas nor the Cayman Islands have reserve requirements, and they do not impose exchange controls. They are also characterized by the confidentiality of their banking transactions: records of depositors' accounts are secret, except in the rare instance when the U.S. Supreme Court orders them revealed. Neither center imposes stringent reporting requirements on OBCs. Fees for banking licenses are small, considering the amount of money that is handled on the books. In the Bahamas there is an annual fee of $9,000 for an unrestricted license (which permits the bank to serve the general public, except for the local population). Fees for clearing banks are somewhat higher, and fees for restricted licenses are lower (restricted licenses permit the bank to conduct business only with those parties named on the license). The fees in the Caymans are comparable. The Bahamas, in particular, have stringent licensing standards, and on several occasions the government has refused applications and charter renewals. As of 1981, 215 banks had unrestricted Bahamian licenses and 99 had restricted licenses. There were 348 licensed banks and trust companies in the Cayman Islands.

The Cayman Islands remain a British colony, while the Bahamas are a relatively new, sovereign country (they received independence in 1973). However, both offer a stable political climate in which to conduct business. Initial doubt about the Bahamas' ability to retain stability upon receiving independence, which led some institutions to move to the Caymans, has largely been laid to rest. However, a "bahamianisation program" that denies work permits to foreign personnel if local talent is available to perform the same work, has created some personnel problems there. This policy has induced some institutions to transfer their business to the Caymans.

A more serious threat to both centers comes from the U.S. decision to allow the creation of IBFs. Because they share the same time zone and derive their strength from their accessibility to the United States, the Bahamas and Cayman Islands stand to lose more than any other banking centers from the competition from IBFs, which offer those same advantages. However, it is not expected that the damage will be too severe, since the Bahamas and Caymans retain other competitive edges in terms of a more liberal regulatory environment, greater secrecy, and tax advantages.

Singapore and Hong Kong

Though they differ in many important respects, Singapore and Hong Kong are often discussed jointly because they represent the major Far Eastern financial centers. Combined, they accounted for $132 billion in gross Eurocurrency liabilities in 1981, with Singapore accounting for about two-thirds of that figure. Certainly the one main attraction that the two centers share is their proximity to the Asian markets. Conducting business from within the same or nearly the same time zone is much easier and more efficient than trying to make transactions when it is daytime for the client and nighttime for the banker. Also, travel to Asian centers is considerably more convenient from Hong Kong or Singapore than from London or New York. With the rise of the Asian international market, these two cities together have assumed the status of the world's fourth largest Euromarket center.

Nonetheless, Singapore and Hong Kong create very different operating environments for banks. In Singapore the domestic market is segregated from the international, and only in exceptional cases may Hong Kong residents enter the international market, or international investors participate in the domestic market. Singapore's growth as a foreign money market resulted from a calculated policy decision by the Monetary Authority of Singapore (MAS), which performs most of the duties of a central bank, except for issuing currency (no central bank exists in Singapore). Unlike the regulatory agencies in other offshore centers, the MAS pursues a policy of active regulation of banking activity; however, it compensates for this by offering a relatively attractive tax situation. Net earnings attributable to offshore activity are taxed at only 10 percent.

Other MAS actions conducive to OBCs are exemption of nonresidents from the 40 percent withholding tax on interest earned on Asiadollar deposits; abolition of stamp duties on certificates of deposit and bills of exchange; and abolition of the 20 percent liquidity-ratio requirement for Asian Currency Units. The MAS grants three kinds of licenses—full services, restricted, and offshore—each of which carries its own set of comprehensive regulations. A fully licensed bank can serve the domestic market in addition to the foreign market, while a restricted license bank may not accept time deposits of less than $250,000, offer savings accounts, or operate more than one branch. An offshore license bank may transact all types of business with nonresidents of Singapore, but may not accept fixed deposits of less than S. $250,000 or savings deposits from such customers. They may not accept fixed savings or interest-bearing deposits from local residents, but may conduct other kinds of business with them. In any case, an offshore bank may not lend, without special approval by the MAS, more than S. $30 million to Singapore residents at any one time. At the end of 1981, Singapore had 37 fully licensed banks, 13 restricted license banks, and 58 off-shore banks.

In many respects Hong Kong's treatment of OBCs is the reverse of Singapore's. Unlike Singapore, which is characterized by aggressive regulation and diminished taxation, Hong Kong is characterized by minimal regulation and extensive taxation. It has no central bank nor monetary authority, few capital or foreign exchange controls, and only minimal regulation of foreign banking. In place of regulation, it imposes stringent entry and licensing standards. To enter the market, a foreign bank must hold assets of greater than U.S. $3 billion and must have an established reputation of integrity. Hong Kong is more centrally located within the market than Singapore, and it offers a greater range of financial facilities, including four separate stock markets. It enjoys a stable and supportive government (it is a British Crown Colony), and it allows licensed foreign banks to take advantage of a well-established business community that possesses a high degree of professionalism. English is spoken widely in Hong Kong, which is particularly useful to American and British bankers. Other support facilities and communications networks are well developed.

Whereas the MAS has taken steps to isolate Singapore's domestic banking market from foreign intrusion, Hong Kong's Monetary Affairs Branch does not impose such restrictions. This fact has earned Hong Kong the reputation of by far the most hybrid OBC. Besides licensing foreign banks, Hong Kong licenses deposit-taking companies, locally incorporated or registered for the purpose of accepting deposits. In 1981, Hong Kong had 115 licensed banks, 346 deposit-taking companies, and several bank representative offices. No Hong Kong legislation deals specifically with the status or activities of the Hong Kong representative offices of overseas banks.

Hong Kong's major drawback, from the perspective of foreign banking, is the high level of taxation it imposes of foreign profits. There is a 15 percent withholding tax on gross interest paid on deposits, and a 17 percent tax on net earnings. This level of taxation, more than anything else, accounts for Singapore's attracting greater Eurocurrency liabilities, despite its greater regulatory climate.

Bahrain

Relatively new to the international banking scene, Bahrain, in the Persian Gulf, has emerged as the newest major OBC, and now accounts for more Eurocurrency activity than Switzerland ($35 billion), and almost as much as Singapore. Its stature has been enhanced by a special treaty with Great Britain that designates Bahrain as the center of British administration of its Persian Gulf responsibilities. Among other things, this arrangement has resulted in the development of transport and telecommunications facilities, which in turn have benefited the local service offerings and have made Bahrain more attractive as an international finance center. The creation in 1973 of the Bahrain Monetary Agency (BMA) provided some direction for Bahrain's development. Another important factor has been its success in convincing other Persian Gulf governments to use its market instead of depositing their reserves in London or New York.

BMA issues four types of licenses to foreign banks: full commercial licenses, which permit these banks all types of domestic retail banking activity; offshore banking unit licenses, which allow banks to engage only in offshore business; investment bank licenses, which authorize banks to engage in the securities business; and representative office licenses. As has generally been the case with other OBCs, foreign banks have been especially interested in the offshore banking unit licensing. Recognizing the lending opportunities of the Persian Gulf region, and in some instances of the broader Middle East area, many international banks have established a presence in Bahrain to engage in offshore banking. The financial needs of the area proved so significant that between 1975 and 1981, Bahrain's share of the Eurocurrency market increased from $2 billion to $51 billion. This record reflected essentially the activities of Bahrain's offshore banking sector, which in 1981 numbered 65 banks (the domestic banking sector numbered 19 banks).

Bahrain offers a conducive legal and regulatory environment for offshore banking. However, the fact that the law of Bahrain is that of Islam makes some Western banking authorities uneasy, because it prohibits the charging of interest. Though offshore banks cannot participate in domestic banking activities—they can neither accept local currency deposits nor enter into transactions with Bahrain residents—they are not hampered by government regulations. Tax and foreign exchange obstacles do not exist, and regulatory requirements are minimal. However, Bahrain has been selective in granting permits, issuing them only to prestigious banks.

Bahrain does not permit shell operations—any loan booked there must be administered locally. This has had a positive effect on the local financial community, though it diminishes some of the convenience to foreign banks. The OBCs must be fully staffed and operational. They may offer nonresidents all banking services except checking accounts.

Finally, confidentiality of banking transactions is assured in Bahrain. Unauthorized disclosure of confidential information is covered by the Bahrain Penal Code, and offending bank officers are subject to fines and imprisonment.

Panama

Like Singapore, Panama has consciously decided to become a major foreign banking center and has taken deliberate steps to achieve that end. The most important of those steps was the Banking Law of 1970, which imposed some regulation on banking, without unduly restricting the operations of foreign banks.

Activities in the 1960s that led to the development of Panama as an international commercial center included the designation of a free zone for bonded warehousing and manufacture within the city of Colón, and legislation favorable to the shipping industry. In 1970, with a substantial shipping business intact, the financial community already had the experience of handling large-scale monetary transactions and of dealing with issues of international scope.

Panama's Banking Commission issues both general and international banking licenses; the former permit domestic and international activity, while the latter are restricted to transactions that are completed outside of Panama. Banks with international licenses may receive only deposits that originate outside of Panama, and they may not lend to companies or individuals conducting business in Panama. Licenses also are given for representative offices, which may not actually conduct business. Shell banks are prohibited—licensed banks must maintain actual premises and staff. Only banks possessing recognized international standing within the banking community are licensed. As of 1981, 114 banks were registered to do business in Panama. These are spread out fairly evenly in terms of national affiliation, though U.S. banks outnumber all others with 17.

There had been some consternation concerning Panama's political stability because of the crisis over the Panama Canal. However, since that problem has been resolved, the political uncertainty has largely vanished. Because of its established shipping industry and its affiliation with the United States, Panama possesses the support technology that OBCs require. Another advantage it offers is a bilingual indigenous population familiar with the English language. More important, because the U.S. dollar is the accepted medium of exchange in Panama, funds are free from the risk of devaluation vis-à-vis the dollar. Also, Panama imposes no exchange controls.

Another important advantage that Panama offers OBCs is full tax exemption for offshore business earnings and for interest derived from either domestic or offshore accounts. Accounts may be held in any currency, and no interest rate ceilings exist. No reporting requirements are imposed, and there is minimal government regulation. Nor is there a central bank to monitor transactions. In place of lender of last resort, every foreign bank must maintain, with an overseas bank, a guaranteed line of credit in U.S. dollars equal to 10 percent of its outstanding loans and investments. Panama, like other offshore centers, has strict confidentiality laws.

The Panamanian government is seeking to improve Panama's status as an international finance center. It has worked hard to develop a Latin American export paper market and has established the first Latin American reinsurance market. Communications to North and South America are being expanded and improved, and plans exist to expand the free trade zone and to liberalize the trust laws. Panama today has been compared to Singapore six years ago, a country on the verge of becoming a major worldwide financial center.

Luxembourg

Though landlocked, Luxembourg is one of the oldest and most established OBCs. Catering primarily to European interests (of the 113 foreign licensed banks in 1981, all but 17 were from European countries), Luxembourg began to establish itself as a financial center in 1929, when it exempted holding companies from significant taxation. As a result, by 1981 the number of holding companies had grown to 5,118. Another important measure that encouraged Luxembourg's growth was its approval of strict bank secrecy laws, an action that further enhanced its attractiveness to foreign institutions. It has grown substantially since 1970, and now ranks as the third largest Eurocurrency center in Europe after London and Paris. Apart from their active role in the Eurocurrency market, Luxembourg banks also manage, place, list, and trade Eurobonds. In 1980 they participated in U.S. $4 billion of Eurobond syndications, which accounted for 20 percent of all Eurobond issues.

Luxembourg has no central bank, and all banks there operate under a general license, which covers receipt of deposits and loans, and dealing in currencies and securities. Luxembourg enjoys many advantages within the European market. First, it is in the same time zone as many European capitals and is easily accessible to them. Both transportation and communications networks are of high quality. Moreover, support personnel are frequently multilingual, and they receive smaller salaries than their counterparts in London. That fact, coupled with Luxembourg's lower property values (compared with London's), has in many instances made the establishment and operation of a Luxembourg bank less costly than running a bank in London. Some banks, in fact, have found that they can buy commercial space in Luxembourg for about the equivalent cost of renting the same amount of space in London for a year.

Moreover, Luxembourg's regulatory policies have attracted banking business. In comparison with the strict banking policies in neighboring Germany and Belgium, Luxembourg places no reserve requirements on Eurocurrency deposits and no withholding tax on interest. The stamp tax on certificates of deposit has recently been abolished. There are few restrictions on the flow of currency into Luxembourg, and Luxembourg banks have been especially successful in securing deposits in deutsche marks and Belgian francs.

Netherlands Antilles

Formerly Dutch island colonies off the coast of Venezuela, the Netherlands Antilles is now an autonomous state composed of two groups of islands in the Caribbean. Though their regulatory environment is not as lax as those of other OBCs, their favorable tax climate for foreign banks has led the Netherlands Antilles to become one of the growing centers for offshore banking in the Eurocurrency market.

Financial institutions can be placed in one of three categories: local, international, or general; the last permits both domestic and international activity. Strictly speaking, however, only one type of license is granted (no fee is charged for licensing). In actual practice the Central Bank distinguishes between local and offshore operations; moreover, the tax advantages extend only to offshore transactions. One unique characteristic of the legal environment in the Netherlands Antilles is that banks offering general services can divide their income into offshore income, taxed at the lower rate, and local income, taxed at the standard rate.

The Central Bank supervises offshore activity more closely than do regulatory authorities in other OBCs. Though a general atmosphere of confidentiality prevails—violators are subject to criminal action—the Central Bank is permitted to request a bank to furnish information concerning foreign exchange violations and credit practices. It is also expected to consult with banks to ascertain that they are adhering to sound monetary policies, and it has the authority to issue general directives to ensure that such policies are implemented. However, the Central Bank has historically favored voluntary compliance, and directives have been issued rarely, if ever. Under recent legislation offshore banks must file quarterly reports with the Central Bank; usually they have the form of a condensed balance sheet. The Central Bank prohibits shell operations, insisting that the management be experienced and that at least one of the directors be a resident of the Netherlands Antilles, though no nationality requirements exist.

On the other hand, offshore banks are exempt from several regulatory requirements that apply to domestic institutions. These include exemption from liquidity and solvency requirements. Moreover, offshore banks are not restricted in the services they may offer. The major inducement, however, is the tax situation. The general profit tax for offshore companies is 2.4 percent on the first 100,000 florins net profit and 3 percent on the rest. No withholding tax is placed on dividends. The Netherlands Antilles also enjoy the presence of a well-developed banking infrastructure, and the community is served adequately by local bankers, lawyers, and accountants. Finally, the area benefits from a stable political climate, liberal foreign exchange regulations, and a time zone convenient for U.S. activity.

SUMMARY

Since the early 1970s OBCs have grown considerably and have assumed a role of importance and prominence within the Eurocurrency market. As the world economy grows and international trade expands, the Eurocurrency market will likewise grow. Thus, we can expect the role of OBCs to expand and new centers to emerge. Their favorable taxing and regulatory climate will continue to attract banks, while the prestige they offer and their contribution to the economies of the host countries will continue to induce smaller countries to welcome offshore banks.

Though guessing the future is of course always problematic, there is reason to believe that new OBCs may emerge. The extent of their growth will be affected by the overall international monetary situation and, in some instances, by the success or lack of success that the newly established IBFs experience in attracting business away from OBCs. Despite some existing pressures to regulate the Eurocurrency market, which would carry negative implications for OBCs, it remains unlikely that widespread regulation will occur. Disharmony among aims and policies of sovereign governments, and the appeal of any other freer market, diminish the chances of significant, widespread regulation. This strengthens the prospects for OBCs, which no doubt will play a significant role in international finance at least through the end of the 1980s.

SUGGESTED REFERENCES

Beers, H. C. *An Introduction to the Financial System of the Netherlands Antilles.* Willemsted, Curacao: Bank van de Nederlandse Antillen, 1980.

Brown, Bowman, ed. *International Banking Centers.* London: Euromoney Publications, 1982.

Department of the Treasury. "Report to Congress on Foreign Government Treatment of U.S. Commercial Banking Organizations." (Typed manuscript.) September 17, 1979.

Dufey, Gunter, and Ian Giddy. *The International Money Market.* Englewood Cliffs, N.J.: Prentice-Hall, 1978.

Goodstadt, Leo. "How Hong Kong Came of Age as a Euromarket Centre." *Euromoney*, February 1982, pp. 54-63.

"International Banking Facilities." Morgan Guaranty Trust Company, *World Financial Markets*, November 1981, pp. 6-11.

Ireland, Jenny. "Luxembourg Looks to Its Future." *The Banker*, May 1981, pp. 75-86.

——. "The Growing Respectability of the Bahamas." *The Banker*, December 1979, pp. 55-61.

Mendelsohn, M. S. "Hong Kong's Challenge." *The Banker*, May 1981, pp. 143-47.

Miller, Richard B. "The Caymans—Offshore Banking Paradise." *The Bankers Magazine*, January-February 1981, pp. 39-42.

"Panama After the Treaty." *The Banker*, May 1979, pp. 65-67.

Parker, Carol. "Foreign Banks in London—Annual Review." *The Banker*, November 1981, pp. 101-11.

"Yankee, Come Back!" *Forbes*, October 30, 1978, p. 142.

5 ASSET AND LIABILITY MANAGEMENT

Lazaros P. Mavrides

Asset-liability management (also called sources and uses of funds management) generally refers to the process of setting policy regarding the size and composition of the balance sheet. The main purpose of such policy is to manage liquidity risk and interest rate risk. For a U.S.-based multinational bank, the scope of this process is necessarily global, combining the bank's operations worldwide. Thus, asset-liability management is viewed from both a domestic and an international perspective. Sound management of both domestic and international assets and liabilities is crucial to the operation of a multinational U.S. bank.

Throughout the 1950s low and stable interest rates prevailed in the United States, with long-term rates usually higher than short-term rates. Banks found it profitable to borrow short term and lend long term, and were not terribly concerned with interest rate risk, devoting much more attention to liquidity risk.

The relative importance of liquidity risk has diminished gradually since the early 1960s because the introduction of the negotiable certificate of deposit (CD) and the development of the Eurodollar market made it much easier for banks to obtain funds by bidding competitively in the domestic and international financial markets.

On the other hand, interest rates increased to double digits in recent years, and many banks were suddenly in the position of having to borrow at very high rates in order to support assets that had been booked earlier at much lower rates. Furthermore, following the all-important decision by the Federal Reserve on October 6, 1979, to manage the money supply by targeting bank reserves rather than the federal funds rate, interest rate volatility has increased sharply, even within a single day. The federal funds rate increased in the spring of 1980 to 20 percent, then moved down to the vicinity of 9 percent in the summer, moved back up to the 20 percent area by the end of 1980, back down to the vicinity of 13 percent by March 1981, back up again to the 20 percent level in the summer, and back down again to the vicinity of 12 percent by the late fall of 1981.

These unprecedented interest rate developments had a pronounced effect on bank earnings. From being relatively stable through several economic cycles (as opposed to earnings of other industries), they suddenly became highly volatile. As a result, bank managements started paying increased attention to interest rate risk. Most large commercial banks now have an asset-liability committee (also called sources and uses of funds committee) that includes the chief executive officer and meets on a weekly or biweekly basis. The main purposes of these meetings are to review the development of interest rates in the financial markets, to evaluate the bank's exposure to future interest rates, and possibly to realign the bank's balance sheet in order to reduce or increase this exposure. Considerably less attention is now devoted to the bank's liquidity exposure.

BALANCE SHEET STRUCTURE

The principal components of the balance sheet of a U.S.-based multinational bank are shown below.

Assets	Liabilities
Domestic loans	Demand deposits
Euroloans	CDs
Redeposits	Eurodeposits
Investment account securities	Federal funds
Trading account securities	Repurchase agreements
Other assets	Long-term debt
	Other liabilities
	Capital

Domestic Loans

Domestic loans represent a substantial part of a multinational bank's asset picture. Domestic loans for working capital and other short-term borrowing needs of corporations are usually made under lines of credit. On the other hand, longer-term loans for capital expenditures, acquisitions, or permanent working capital needs are generally made under committed facilities, which are usually structured as revolving credits and/or term loans.

Loans under committed facilities are generally long-term agreements, usually having an original maturity of five to eight years. The bank is committed to honor the agreement throughout, subject to such preagreed conditions as financial covenants on working capital, liquidity, leverage, retention of earnings, and interest coverage. Amortization usually begins after a few years, and the borrower generally has the right to prepay the loan. In extending such loans, banks place a great deal of importance on the value of the long-term relationship with the borrower.

Most loans under committed facilities are based on the prime rate, with the most creditworthy customers paying the prime rate and less creditworthy ones paying higher rates. For the latter the spread over the prime rate depends on market conditions as well as on the borrower's credit. Some alternative pricing formulas have been introduced in recent years, with the interest rate varying at a fixed spread over the comparable effective domestic CD rate or LIBOR (London Interbank Offered Rate). Under such facilities the borrower is usually allowed to pick the interval for which the interest rate will be fixed from a number of possible intervals (usually one, two, three, or six months), and to change to another interval at the end of each interval.

Prime-based loans in general can be prepaid at any time, whereas CD-based and LIBOR-based loans can be prepaid only at the end of each interest interval. Many committed facilities are presently of the "either-or" type, where the borrower has the right to pick among two or three of these pricing formulas.

The traditional pricing of prime-based loans included (in addition to the rate) balance requirements of around 10 percent on the total facility and 10 percent on the usage, with some variation around these numbers. However, this practice started breaking down in the mid-1970s, and the balance requirement on the usage is now substantially lower or nonexistent. At present the balance requirement on the total facility generally varies between 0 and 5 percent, depending on market conditions. Whatever the pricing option, the usual practice under committed facilities is to charge a commitment fee of 0.375 to 0.50 percent on the unused portion of the total facility.

Various other pricing formulas have been introduced in recent years, usually involving credit lines that have a balance requirement of 5–10 percent on the total amount of the line, or a fee in lieu of balances to earn a comparable return to the bank. The pricing options under such lines may include an adjustable rate, varying daily at a stated or implied spread over the federal funds rate, or a fixed rate, at a stated or implied spread over the rate on a money market instrument of similar maturity. These are very much relationship loans, but under a line of credit they do not involve a legal commitment and the bank can either cancel the line or adjust the lending rate as the borrower's credit or market conditions change.

In addition, some banks have been making a limited number of long-term, fixed-rate loans maturing in several years. The pricing of these loans is generally based on a funding instrument of comparable maturity.

Banks also make tax-exempt loans to municipalities and, through local authorities, to corporations for funding projects such as pollution control and industrial development facilities. Most such loans are floating at a percentage of the prime rate (usually 60–75 percent), depending on market conditions and the borrower's credit, although on occasion tax-exempt, fixed-rate loans maturing in several years have been made.

Other types of domestic loans that a multinational bank might wish to make include secured loans to stockbrokers and government dealers (usually overnight), overdrafts (overnight), and acceptances. Acceptances are promissory notes by importers that are endorsed or guaranteed ("accepted") by a bank, and are traded at a discount in the money market. For accepting such drafts, banks generally charge a fee of 0.75 to 1.5 percent, depending on market conditions and the borrower's credit. When a bank discounts and holds acceptances of other banks or buys acceptances in the open market, these notes are in effect marketable fixed-rate loans guaranteed by other banks. The maturity of acceptances is usually 90–180 days, and such financing must be supported by a current trade transaction. In some historic cases, and again more recently, large acceptances of several years' maturity have been provided by syndicated groups of banks.

The pricing of fixed-rate or floating-rate loans that are repriced at fixed time intervals is easy to evaluate, in the sense that there is a "neutral" funding cost provided by the market. That is, if the bank does not want to assume any interest rate risk, it can match these loans with funds of similar maturity and thus lock in a spread. However, if the bank feels strongly that in the future interest rates will move down more than implied by the market yield curve, it may wish to fund such loans with shorter-term instruments.

On the other hand, it is not obvious what constitutes a neutral strategy for funding prime-based loans, since the date at which the prime rate will next be changed is not known. A 1982 study[1] concluded that the prime rate from mid-1979 to mid-1981 was correlated best with the average cost of a portfolio of federal funds and CDs having an average maturity of around 20 days. This was a simulation study that examined 70 different funding strategies with average maturities ranging from 1 to 45 days. Based on this observation, a bank that wishes to apply a neutral funding strategy may seek to fund prime-based loans with federal funds and CDs having a moving average maturity of around 20 days. However, the past is not always a good predictor of the future; the behavior of the prime rate relative to funding rates may change over time.

Euroloans

Euroloans are usually either on a fixed-rate basis to maturity or repriced at fixed time intervals. The maturities of the straight fixed-rate loans are usually less than five years, whereas the maturities of the repricing loans are usually from one to seven years, and can be longer than ten years. The interest rate is usually at a preagreed spread above LIBOR, and this spread may be higher for later years. The borrower has the option of picking the repricing interval, which usually varies from one to six months. At present such loans usually involve a front-end fee of around 0.375 percent on the unused portion of the commitment, and in syndicated loans there is a management fee of around 0.5 percent.

The spreads over LIBOR vary with the borrower's credit, the maturity of the loan, and market conditions. The spreads for the most creditworthy customers are at present around 0.375 percent. In the past, prime-customer spreads over LIBOR have usually been 0.375–0.75 percent. The spreads for lesser credits have been up to 2 percent or more. In periods of high liquidity in the market (as was the case in 1977), the spreads narrow, and the differences in the spreads for prime and lesser credits diminish or even disappear.

By pricing Euroloans at a fixed spread above LIBOR, banks lose the flexibility to increase this spread in the future if the borrower's credit worsens or if market conditions change. This applies to domestic CD-based loans as well. It is less true in the case of prime-based loans, since the prime rate can be adjusted to reflect market conditions.

Eurodeposits and Redeposits

Redeposits are Eurocurrency loans to other banks in the interbank market. The maturity of these loans is from one day to one year or longer. Banks are active participants on both sides of this market. The spread between the quoted bid and asked rates is usually around 0.125 percent. Thus, it is theoretically possible to make around 0.125 percent in this market by taking funds at the bid rate and redepositing them at the asked rate for the same maturity. However, this practice is limited by the fact that the spread is small, and is probably offset by the small credit risk involved and by the fact that it increases the size of the balance sheet.

The main reason for making redeposits is that they enable banks to rapidly adjust their interest rate exposure when their outlook changes. Thus, if it is felt that the outlook for lower interest rates in the near future has become brighter, a bank may swiftly bid or take in short-term deposits at the asked rate, and redeposit them at other banks in longer maturities. A secondary but fundamental reason is the importance of being seen by other banks as participating on both sides of the market.

If redeposits are used to change the bank's interest rate exposure in response to a change in the outlook for future interest rates, and the outlook soon changes back to the original, then the bank's interest rate exposure can be changed back to the original—at the expense of increasing the size of the balance sheet (new deposits must be taken in and redeposited in different maturities).

The establishment of IBFs (international banking facilities) in the United States as of December 3, 1981, has made it possible for banks to accept time deposits from foreign customers, free of reserve requirements and interest rate limitations, and to make loans to foreign customers. IBFs are prohibited from engaging in such activities as accepting deposits from or making loans to U.S. residents or to non-U.S. residents for U.S. purposes, issuing negotiable instruments, offering demand deposit accounts, and accepting overnight deposits from nonbank customers.

Investment Account Securities

The investment account of a multinational money center bank contains mainly U.S. Treasury, agency, and municipal securities. Some banks also maintain a relatively small portfolio of foreign securities.

The government market is huge and highly liquid (around $900 billion marketable U.S. Treasury and agency securities by the end of 1981), which makes it possible to buy or sell substantial quantities in this market without causing unacceptable price swings. There are frequent auctions of U.S. Treasury securities, in which a huge quantity can be obtained almost certainly by placing a bid only a few basis points below the expected average auction rate. Banks concentrate on the two to ten years' maturity range of the government market. Investors that have steady sources of long-term funds, such as pension funds and insurance companies, concentrate on the long end of the market.

The size and the liquidity of the government market provide banks with the flexibility to change the structure of the balance sheet quite rapidly. Moreover, the government market makes it possible to reverse the decisions implemented, should conditions change subsequently. This is the main reason for having a government portfolio.

Agency securities are relatively less liquid than Treasury securities, but they carry yields 50–100 basis points higher and have similar credit risk (they are both backed by the full faith and credit of the U.S. government). Banks generally keep a portion of their government portfolios in agency securities, because of their higher yield, but usually keep relatively more Treasury securities, because of their higher liquidity.

Banks are also important participants in the municipal market, primarily because the after-tax income from such securities generally is substantially higher than the income from taxable assets. Municipal securities are not subject to federal taxes, although they may be subject to state and local taxes. Banks are not permitted to borrow tax-deductible funds to invest in tax-exempt assets. However, by borrowing to finance taxable assets, they can use demand deposits and capital to invest in tax-exempt assets (tax-exempt loans as well as securities). The net effect of this is to reduce federal taxes, because the tax-deductible funds and the state and local taxes on the interest from the tax-exempt assets (if applicable) act to lower the bank's federal tax bill.

A bank's tax position is a limiting factor on the size of its municipal portfolio (along with the tax-exempt loan portfolio). When federal taxes drop to zero, additional tax-exempt assets become less attractive, because the tax benefits generated would have to be postponed, and possibly lost altogether if they could not be utilized in time.

The municipal yield curve has usually been upward-sloping, even when the government yield curve has been downward-sloping, because of heavy demand for short-term tax exemption by individuals and other investors. As a result, to the extent that a bank wishes to invest in fixed-rate assets to reduce long-term exposure to interest rates, it makes sense to invest in long-term municipals and medium-term governments, rather than the other way around.

Some U.S.-based banks maintain a portfolio of foreign securities in the United States as well as overseas. The two main reasons for this are to provide head office personnel with training in such securities, and to pursue a worldwide approach to investing, by comparing economic conditions and other factors in different countries.

Trading Account Securities

In addition to holding government and municipal securities for investment purposes, many banks maintain a trading account for such securities. The original reason for establishing such an account was to provide a service to correspondent banks and other clients by underwriting such securities and retailing them quickly, in order to avoid interest rate risk. Although this generally continues to be the main purpose of the municipal trading account, the government trading account in many banks often is also used to take substantial positions, seeking to profit from anticipated short-term changes in interest rates.

For tax and reporting purposes, trading account securities are usually marked to market, and changes in market values affect operating earnings whether or not such gains or losses have been realized. Some banks use the lower-of-cost-or-market method. On the other hand, investment securities are carried at book value; gains or losses in the market values of such securities arising from changing interest rates do not affect operating earnings, and are taken into net income when they are realized through selling the securities.

Another difference between trading and investment securities is that the former can be sold short (a bank can borrow a security to sell it in the market, and later buy it back for delivery to the original owner), whereas selling short cannot be done with the latter.

Demand Deposits

Demand deposits are kept in a bank by corporations either for transaction purposes, or as balance requirements in connection with credit facilities, or as balance requirements in payment for operations services provided by the bank.

Domestic demand deposits are interest-free. As such they are largely like fixed-rate liabilities at rate zero. However, the portion of demand deposits that pertains to operations services is generally based on short-term interest rates, and it is varied in such a way that the imputed charge to the corporation remains roughly constant. As such, demand deposits for operations services are like floating-rate liabilities.

Until the 1950s banks relied primarily upon demand deposits as a funding source. The ability of banks to accept demand deposits was unique, and separated them from other financial institutions. Demand deposits are subject to reserve requirements, which are to be reduced in steps from 16.25 percent in 1980 to 12 percent in 1984, and to FDIC fees, which amounted to about three basis points in 1981 and were increased to about seven basis points at the beginning of 1982.

Certificates of Deposit

Demand deposits are a passive source of funds. The introduction of large CDs in 1961 provided banks with an active source, because they could bid for such funds competitively. CDs are fixed-rate instruments with original maturities not less than 14 days (the legal limit was 30 days until recently). Typical maturities range from one to six months.

There is a very close relationship between Eurodollar and domestic CD rates. Domestic CDs are subject to a reserve requirement of somewhat over 3 percent, depending on the individual bank (to be reduced in steps to 3 percent by 1984 for all banks), and to FDIC fees, which amounted to about four basis points in 1981 but were increased to about eight basis points at the beginning of 1982. Eurodollar CDs, on the other hand, are free of both. As a result Eurodollar rates are generally higher than domestic CD rates, roughly by the cost of the reserve requirement and the FDIC fees to the banks. In 1966 and 1969, when Regulation Q limited the ability of banks to sell domestic CDs at competitive rates, Eurodollar rates became much higher because banks relied on them heavily in order to meet loan demand.

Since reserve requirements on CDs issued for maturities less than six months were much higher than for longer maturities in the late 1970s (6 percent, 4.5 percent, and 1 percent for maturities of one to six months, six months to four years, and longer than four years, respectively, with a temporary supplement of 2 percent for all maturities), banks came up with a new instrument, variable-rate CDs. The interest rate on these was adjustable every one, two, or three months, whereas the final maturity was six months or longer. In this manner the lower reserve requirement was applicable.

The reserve requirements introduced in 1980 are uniform for all CDs maturing within four years. Nevertheless, banks continue to issue variable-rate CDs for liquidity reasons. The interest rate on these is generally about ten basis points higher than that for fixed-rate CDs of similar maturity. By paying this small additional charge, banks secure the availability of the funds over longer periods. Thus, when a bank expects interest rates to drop and would like to issue short-term CDs, but is concerned about its liquidity position, variable-rate CDs provide a way to satisfy both objectives.

Federal Funds

Federal funds are excess reserves that banks lend to one another. The federal funds market has grown substantially over the years. As many foreign banks established offices in the United States, the number of active participants increased considerably and contributed to the integration of this domestic interbank market into the international interbank markets.

Money center banks are usually buyers of federal funds. Regional correspondents are often regular providers of federal funds to money center banks, which sometimes, for relationship purposes, take the funds even when they do not need them, and unload them in the open market.

Term federal funds are excess reserves loaned at a fixed rate for a period longer than one day. Typical maturities are 30, 60, and 90 days, and occasionally 180 days. The viability of the borrowing institution is a factor in this market, especially for the longer maturities.

Repurchase Agreements

Repurchase agreements (RPs or repos) are essentially borrowings collateralized by securities or loans. The borrower sells securities and simultaneously contracts to buy them back at a specific future time and at a price that will produce the agreed-upon implicit borrowing rate. Term RPs are RPs with a maturity longer than one day. Treasury securities are the most desirable collateral, and command relatively better rates. Many banks make it a practice to repo their entire government portfolio.

The RP rate is usually 25–75 basis points lower than the federal funds rate, but can be lower or higher, depending on market conditions, particularly on the amount of securities in the hands of the traders that can be offered as collateral. The spread practically disappears when there is an abundant supply of securities available as collateral, while it can rise to 200 basis points or more when there is a shortage of collateral.

Long-Term Debt

Banks, as well as other corporations, can raise long-term funds in the United States at fixed interest rates. Whereas a long-term corporate bond market does not exist in most countries, it is highly developed in the United States. Consequently, corporate bonds represent an interesting option for multinational banks. Unlike government securities, corporate securities are generally callable after a number of years, and may or may not have sinking fund provisions. Original maturities extend to 30 years or longer.

Interest rates in the corporate bond market have generally been higher than in the government market, because of the higher credit risk and the call protection. The spread depends on the issuer's credit risk, the maturity of the bonds, the call terms, and market conditions. The spreads for AAA bank securities have generally been similar to the spreads for A industrial securities in the past, and have varied from less than 50 basis points to 200 basis points or more. At times when investors have been reluctant to commit funds to long maturities (as has been the case recently), government bond issues have tended to crowd out corporate bond issues, thus leading to higher spreads.

A large number of original issue, deep discount bonds have been issued recently by banks as well as other corporations. These carry a coupon rate substantially lower than current yields for comparable maturities at the time of issue, and are sold at a discount from par. In effect, the difference in coupons is borrowed at the original rate throughout the life of the bond. Zero coupon bonds have recently been issued for maturities up to around 10 years, whereas bonds with coupon rates of 5 percent or more have been issued for maturities up to around 30 years.

With original issue, deep discount bonds, the discount is amortized straight-line for tax purposes for both issuer and holder, which is favorable to the former and unfavorable to the latter. These bonds are generally callable at par from the outset, but the size of the original issue discount makes it unlikely that they will ever be called. Tax-exempt investors such as public and private pension managers have found these instruments attractive relative to current coupon bonds, primarily because of the increased effective call protection and the lower reinvestment risk. The tax consequences are not important to these investors, since for the most part they are not subject to taxes. Original issue, deep discount bonds have been issued recently at yields of 50–125 basis points below current coupon yields for bonds of similar maturity. However, the high spreads came at a time when the yield curve was sharply downward-sloping (implying that the market was anticipating a sharp drop in rates). The behavior of this spread at more normal times with an upward-sloping yield curve remains to be seen.

Recently the U.S. corporate bond market has absorbed a variety of other instruments, such as convertible bonds (convertible to common stock at a premium over the current market price) and bonds with detachable stock or bond warrants. The yields on these instruments have been lower than the yields on comparable straight coupon bonds, reflecting the conversion and warrant values to the investor. Floating-rate notes with a final maturity around 15 years and a rate adjustable every 3 years or so, according to an index based on 3-year Treasury rates, have been issued in the private placement market. And the Eurodollar market has seen floating-rate convertibles at a fixed spread below comparable Eurodollar rates. In addition, some banks and other corporations have recently exchanged low-coupon bonds for common stock (the largely realized bond discount is not taxable in such recapitalizations). Many other new fixed-rate and floating-rate instruments may come into the U.S. market in the near future, since the number of possible combinations is practically infinite.

Other Borrowings

Some other ways through which banks can raise funds are Treasury tax and loan account, borrowings from the Federal Reserve Bank, and loan participations. Moreover, the holding company can raise funds either in the money markets (commercial paper) or in the capital markets (long-term debt, preferred stock, or common stock), then channel these funds into the bank. If the holding company issues commercial paper and channels it into the bank, the bank is subject to reserve requirements, depending on the maturity of the funds (if 14 days or longer, the reserve requirements on CDs are applicable, otherwise the funds would be reservable at the much higher rates pertaining to demand deposits).

Capital

The three primary sources of a bank's equity capital are retained earnings, its own common stock, and its own preferred stock. Preferred stock can be perpetual or finite (with or without a sinking fund), generally pays a fixed dividend that is not tax-deductible for the issuer, and is senior to common stock and junior to debt. For the corporate investor 85 percent of preferred stock dividends are excluded from federal taxable income, and they are partly excluded from state and local taxable income. Convertible preferred stocks are also issued occasionally, at a dividend rate lower than that for straight preferred stock of similar maturity.

In December 1981 the comptroller of the currency and the Federal Reserve Board issued guidelines for assessing capital adequacy to the financial institutions they supervise. Two categories of capital are to be used, primary and secondary. Primary capital will consist of common stock, perpetual preferred stock, capital surplus, retained earnings, reserves for contingencies and other capital reserves, mandatory convertible instruments, and the allowance for possible credit losses. Secondary capital will consist of limited-life preferred stock, and subordinated notes and debentures having an original maturity of at least seven years. If the remaining maturity is five years or longer, then 100 percent of such instruments will be included in secondary capital; the includable portion will be reduced by 20 percent each year thereafter.

The guidelines provide two principal ratio measurements of capital: primary capital to total assets, and total capital to total assets. Capital guidelines for the 17 multinational banking organizations with assets in excess of $15 billion will continue to be formulated and monitored on an individual basis, taking into account their present and prospective financial condition, and supervisory policies will be modified to insure that appropriate steps are taken to imprive the capital positions of these banks over time. A minimum level of primary capital to total assets was established at 5 percent for regional banking organizations (all other institutions with assets in excess of $1 billion) and 6 percent for community organizations (total assets of less than $1 billion). The agencies also established guidelines for regional and community organizations for the total capital: total assets ratio, ranging from 5.5 to 7 percent. All guidelines are to be applied in a flexible manner on a case-by-case basis, taking into account relevant qualitative factors.

MANAGING LIQUIDITY EXPOSURE

Liquidity risk refers to the possibility of not being able to renew or replace maturing liabilities or to retire an equal amount of assets.

As mentioned earlier, the importance of liquidity management has gradually diminished since 1960, as new and highly liquid domestic and foreign markets for funds have been generated. Nevertheless, liquidity management is still considered very important, because these markets become practically closed to a bank that is regarded to be in danger of being unable to meet its commitments. Furthermore, liquidity is considered to be highly important by bank examiners.

At the Morgan Bank the Sources and Uses of Funds Committee regularly reviews the liquidity position of the bank at its weekly meetings. It uses two measures of liquidity. The first is the difference between liquid assets and short-term liabilities. Liquid assets include government securities of all maturities and all other assets that are to mature within 30 days and are not relationship business. Government securities of all maturities are liquid assets because they can be sold readily. Short-term liabilities refer to all liabilities maturing within 30 days, except a portion of the federal funds that the bank obtains from regular suppliers of such funds. The amount of such funds that is not included among short-term funds is a judgmental figure, based on past flows from such suppliers. For this computation the final maturity, rather than the interest rate adjustment period, determines whether an item is short-term or not. Thus, 6 x 1 variable-rate CDs are not considered short-term, even though their interest rate is adjusted every month, because the final maturity is six months.

If the value of this liquidity measure is zero, the implication is that the bank could retire the liquid assets if it suddenly became impossible to renew or replace any of the short-term liabilities. If at any time the value is much above zero, the question arises of whether the bank should reduce the excess liquidity by meeting new funding requirements through short-term funds. However, if interest rates are expected to rise in the next six months more than implied by the market yield curve, the decision may be taken to stay overly liquid for rate considerations, expecting six-month CDs ultimately to be less costly than one-month CDs.

In addition to this liquidity measure, the Sources and Uses of Funds Committee looks at the portion of the liability book that is expected to be replaced within 4 weeks, within 13 weeks, and within 26 weeks, based on forecasts for loans and demand deposits. The values of these ratios are tracked on a chart going back a year. Whenever the present figure appears to deviate significantly from past figures, this deviation triggers a discussion on whether corrective action is indicated.

MANAGING INTEREST RATE EXPOSURE

Balance sheets for both domestic and multinational banks are largely composed of financial assets and liabilities, with variable or fixed interest rates, as discussed earlier. Holding a fixed-rate asset and funding it with variable-rate liabilities subjects a bank to a risk of lower earnings, since if interest rates rise in the future, the income from the asset will stay constant, whereas the cost of funding will increase. Similarly, holding a variable-rate asset and funding it with fixed-rate liabilities exposes a bank to a risk of lower earnings from falling interest rates. Thus, bank earnings depend heavily on the maturity structure of the balance sheet and on the future course of interest rates. A bank of course has control over its balance sheet, but almost no control over interest rates.

The first step in measuring the interest rate exposure of the bank is to divide the balance sheet into repricing categories (for instance, 0-1 month, 1-3 months, 3-6 months, 6-12 months, 1-2 years) and to compute the "gap" within each such category—that is, the difference between the assets and liabilities that either mature or are subject to a rate adjustment in that maturity interval. A positive gap in a particular time interval means that more existing assets than liabilities would be repriced in that interval. Therefore, a positive gap would benefit from higher interest rates, assuming that the interest rates on both the assets and the liabilities increased by similar amounts. The opposite holds for negative gaps.

One can obtain a rough indication of the sensitivity of the present balance sheet to changes in interest rates from the present to some future time by looking at the cumulative gap up to that time. For example, if the cumulative gap up to one year is positive, this means that there are more assets than liabilities to be repriced within one year. This in turn means that the full balance sheet would benefit from higher interest rates one year out, again assuming that interest rates on different balance sheet items of similar maturity moved by similar amounts.

Although different interest rates of similar maturity do not always move by similar amounts, large moves in one rate are almost always associated with large moves in the other. Thus, by multiplying the cumulative gap up to a particular point in time by a hypothetical change in interest rates, one can obtain a rough measure of the impact of such a change in interest rates on earnings up to that time. For example, if the cumulative gap up to one year is positive $100 million, this means that if interest rates increase immediately by 100 basis points, then pretax earnings within one year will be roughly $1 million higher. However, this is a very rough measure. The precise measure depends not only on the relationship between movements in different interest rates of similar maturity, but also on the detailed repricing pattern of the balance sheet within one year. That is, the impact will be different if the assets and liabilities that are repriced within one year are repriced at the beginning of the year, toward the middle of the year, or toward the end of the year.

Many different bank models have been built to assist top management in estimating interest rate exposure and in making asset-liability decisions. The majority of these are "simulation models," which estimate future income statements on the basis of certain assumptions about the future economic environment and specific asset-liability decisions to be implemented. The economic assumptions would be based on future levels of interest rates, loans, demand deposits, and so on. The decisions would be on future levels of various controllable balance sheet items, such as governments, municipals, federal funds, CDs, and Eurodollars. By entering different sets of assumptions and asset-liability decisions, the user can play a "what if" game, and in this manner gain insight on the bank's exposure to interest rates.

On the other hand, some bank models go one step further, seeking to estimate the optimal size and composition of the balance sheet. These are "optimization models" (also called mathematical programming models), and are much more difficult to formulate and solve. These two types of models are reviewed in current literature.[2]

The Morgan Bank has devoted several years to developing a comprehensive optimization model for asset-liability management (hereafter referred to as "the bank model"). This model uses probabilistic forecasts of interest rates produced by a process (discussed below) to develop a number of interest rate scenarios. It then measures the bank's short-term exposure to interest rates by estimating the three-month and six-month income statements associated with each scenario. Subsequently it measures the long-term exposure to interest rates by estimating the effect of changes in interest rates on the net earnings from every fixed-rate asset and liability until maturity. Finally, the model can derive an optimal strategy, if given additional information on the time and risk preferences of the decision maker.[3]

Forecasting Interest Rates

The sensitivity of earnings to interest rates can be reduced, and possibly eliminated, by matching maturities on opposite sides of the balance sheet. It is not necessary to specifically assign liabilities to assets on an item-for-item basis. This can be done for certain special-purpose activities, but would be time-consuming, costly, and impractical to do for the full balance sheet. The same purpose can be achieved by dividing the consolidated balance sheet into repricing categories and matching the asset and liability totals within each category. However, it would not generally be desirable to eliminate all sensitivity to interest rates, since this might also eliminate considerable opportunities for profit. Where expectations are strong that interest rates will move in a particular direction, a bank may be willing to mismatch maturities on opposite sides of the balance sheet to profit from such a development. Thus, forecasting interest rates is of central importance to asset-liability management.

There are econometric models that forecast interest rates on the basis of factors such as inflation, economic growth, internal generation of funds, total funding requirements, and government deficit. In general such models contain equations that tie together the important factors affecting interest rates and, given forecasted changes in the factors, estimate the effect on interest rates. Such models can be useful in understanding the processes shaping interest rate developments over time. However, interest rates in the short run are affected by a multitude of political as well as economic perceptions that cannot possibly be incorporated into an econometric model.

At the Morgan Bank a special effort has been made to design a subjective interest rate forecasting process on which to base asset-liability decisions. A group of senior officers from various divisions meets once a week to develop probabilistic forecasts of interest rates for various money market and bond market instruments. These forecasts have come to be known as "histograms," because they are displayed graphically by bar charts stating the possible outcomes and the associated probabilities of occurrence.

The process starts with each participant independently preparing his own histogram. Subsequently they all meet to discuss the reasons underlying their individual histograms and to exchange information. As a result some participants may modify their views and revise their histograms, particularly if information previously unknown to them has been brought up by another participant. Finally a consensus histogram is derived for each interest rate under consideration by averaging the individual histograms.

The participants bring to this meeting a number of different perspectives, representing their different kinds of expertise. The process provides a forum for senior officers to communicate their views to one another, and to establish common ground on which to base the bank's asset-liability policy. The process has been in existence at the Morgan Bank since about 1970, and it is held to be of great value in formulating asset-liability policy.[4]

The consensus histograms that are produced by this forecasting process are fed into the bank model. Using these, the model develops five interest rate scenarios, having 10, 20, 40, 20, and 10 percent probabilities of occurrence.

Short-Term Interest Rate Exposure

A bank's short-term exposure to interest rates can be measured by estimating the short-term income statement for each of a number of future interest rate scenarios considered possible. The effect of interest rate changes on short-term earnings can then be seen by analyzing these income statements.

The bank model measures the short-term interest rate exposure of the bank by estimating the income statements for the next three and six months, for each of the five interest rate scenarios, assuming that the existing asset-liability mix is maintained throughout.

The main purpose of asset-liability management is to make decisions that will affect the interest rate exposure of the bank. Thus, the Sources and Uses of Funds Committee pays particular attention to two income statement components: domestic and foreign net interest earnings (interest received from all interest-earning assets, less interest paid on all interest-paying liabilities).

At the Morgan Bank domestic net interest earnings often increase with higher interest rates. This generally happens when the domestic component's demand deposits, fixed-rate borrowings, and capital are larger than its fixed-rate assets. Thus, on a net basis, domestic floating-rate assets are often funded by fixed-rate liabilities. As a result, if interest rates go up, the interest earned on the floating-rate assets increases, whereas the interest paid on the fixed-rate liabilities remains constant—and, therefore, the net earnings go up.

This variability of domestic net interest earnings can be reduced by purchasing Treasury securities or other fixed-rate assets and funding them with short-term liabilities. In fact, if enough of this is done, the variability can be eliminated and even reversed. Conversely, the variability can be increased by selling fixed-rate assets, or by replacing federal funds and other maturing liabilities with longer-term CDs.

On the other hand, foreign net interest earnings at the Morgan Bank often decrease with higher dollar interest rates, resulting from longer maturities on assets than on liabilities overall. Again the variability can be reduced or increased by reducing or increasing the mismatch. This hedge between the domestic and foreign components of the bank is practical for structural reasons: the domestic component has sizable demand deposits, long-term debt, and capital, whereas the foreign component has many regular sources of short-term funds from the Eurodollar market.

The bank's short-term exposure to interest rates cannot be judged by looking at any one component in isolation. It is the total picture that counts. The bank model allows the Sources and Uses of Funds Committee to look at the total short-term earnings exposure over the five interest rate scenarios. If this variability appears to be uncomfortably high, then it may be decided to change the maturity structure of the balance sheet. The decision would be implemented either through the domestic or through the Eurodollar market, whichever happens to be more attractive and feasible at the moment. On the other hand, if there is very little variability when there is a strong conviction that interest rates are likely to change in a particular direction, then it may be decided to increase the combined exposure.

Long-Term Interest Rate Exposure

Banks with identical short-term earnings can have very different earnings subsequently if their balance sheets have very different repricing structures. In general a bank that has more (less) fixed-rate assets than liabilities in long maturities will suffer (benefit) from rising interest rates, because changes in interest rates affect floating-rate assets and liabilities immediately, while fixed-rate items continue at the same rate until maturity.

According to the "expectations hypothesis," the change in the market value of a security is equal to the perceived (by the market) total change in the net earnings from this security, discounted (present-valued) and adjusted for time and risk preferences. This holds, subject to all other things (other than interest rate expectations) remaining the same. Although interest rates can change for reasons other than interest rate expectations, such reasons rarely carry significant weight relative to interest rate expectations, except possibly in the less-than-six-months Treasury bill market. This market is often used by foreign institutions to invest dollars acquired in currency stabilization operations, as well as by other investors to temporarily place dollars ultimately intended for long-term investments; when the demand from these investors is unusually strong, it places a downward pressure on Treasury bill rates (pressure that is not related to interest rate expectations).

Following the expectations hypothesis, the bank model uses the change in the market value of any marketable security (largely Treasury, agency, and municipal securities) over the next three months as a measure of the change in the anticipated net earnings from this security from three months to maturity.

Government securities can be assumed, for all practical purposes, to be free of any risk of default. This is not true of other marketable securities, such as corporate and municipal bonds. Changes in the market values of such securities incorporate perceived changes in credit risk, as well as anticipated changes in financing cost.

Nonmarketable fixed-rate assets, such as fixed-rate loans, do not have a changing market value. Nonetheless, their earnings outlook is affected in the same way: interest received remains constant until maturity, whereas the financing cost may change with short-term interest rates. Changes in credit risk are accounted for by the provision for possible credit losses, which is included as an expense in the income statement. On the other hand, assuming no default, the change in net earnings will be about the same for a fixed-rate loan as for a Treasury security of similar maturity. Therefore, the bank model uses the change in the market value of a Treasury security as a measure of the change in the anticipated net earnings of any non-marketable fixed-rate asset of similar maturity.

Fixed-rate liabilities can be analyzed similarly. Changes in short-term interest rates do affect the value of a fixed-rate liability. Without that liability the bank would have to borrow the funds in the short-term markets. Therefore, fixed-rate liabilities can be treated as negative fixed-rate assets, and the change in the value of any fixed-rate liability can be taken to be the same as the negative of the change in the market value of a Treasury security of similar maturity.

The bank model follows the approach outlined above to estimate the implicit market value change over three months for every fixed-rate asset and liability, and for each of the five interest rate scenarios. Again, these represent anticipated changes in future net interest earnings discounted (present-valued) and adjusted for time and risk preferences.

Actually the bank model breaks down these discounted long-term earnings effects in three ways. The first component measures the effect of changes in interest rates during the next three months on earnings from the end of the three months to the end of the calendar year; the second estimates the effect on earnings in the following year; and the third estimates the effect on earnings in all subsequent years. The information that enables the bank model to obtain these separate effects is contained in the yield curves at the beginning and end of the three months. Actually, by comparing these two yield curves, it is possible to break down the total effect on long-term earnings into as many components as is desired.

The bank's earnings exposure in each of the above three time intervals can be assessed by looking at the variability of the earnings effect over the five interest rate scenarios. If it appears that earnings in some time interval decrease excessively with lower interest rates, this exposure can be reduced by buying government securities or other fixed-rate assets maturing toward the end of this time interval, and funding them with shorter-term liabilities. On the other hand, if it appears that earnings in some time interval decrease excessively with higher interest rates, this exposure can be reduced by selling government securities or other marketable fixed-rate assets maturing toward the end of this time interval, and reducing federal funds. Alternatively, the same purpose can be achieved by raising new funds maturing toward the end of the time interval to replace federal funds or to invest in short-term assets.

Optimal Strategy

As discussed, the bank model can be used to measure both short-term and long-term exposure to interest rates with the present balance sheet. If the short-term exposure appears to be either uncomfortably high or too low, then it can be changed by varying the levels of short-term assets and liabilities, particularly money market instruments in either the domestic or the Eurodollar market, whichever appears to be more attractive and feasible at the moment. On the other hand, if the long-term exposure appears to be unsatisfactory, it can be changed by varying the levels of long-term, fixed-rate assets and liabilities, particularly government securities.

Once the decision is taken to change the short-term or long-term interest rate exposure, the bank model can help decide the best way to bring about the change. The model considers decisions in the government and municipal bond portfolios on the assets side of the balance sheet and in domestic and Eurodollar money market instruments on the liabilities side. All other balance sheet components are forecasted judgmentally. Given hypothetical values for the decision variables, the model will estimate the implied short-term and long-term earnings exposure for each of the five interest rate scenarios. After comparing the implications of a number of strategies, the decision maker can choose the one having the most desirable outlook.

Depending on the maturity structure of the present balance sheet and on the interest rate outlook, different decisions will have different implications regarding the timing of future earnings and their sensitivity to interest rates (interest rate risk). Decision makers differ in preferences regarding timing and risk. Therefore, the optimal strategy depends on the preferences of the particular decision maker. The optimal strategy also depends on any regulatory or self-imposed constraints, such as limits on liquidity ratios and debt: equity ratios.

Among the possible asset-liability strategies, the bank model derives the optimal strategies for two extreme decision makers: the optimal strategy for a decision maker who is completely indifferent to risk (his objective being to maximize expected earnings without regard to variability over different interest rate scenarios), and the optimal strategy for a decision maker who is completely averse to risk (his objective being to maximize earnings under the condition that all sensitivity to interest rates is eliminated).

Given a set of time and risk preferences for a particular decision maker, the bank model will derive the implied optimal strategy for that decision maker. Such preferences can be quantified through questionnaries. However, one must not rely completely on such questionnaires, because it is very difficult to quantify preferences that are based largely on intuition. Furthermore, no mathematical model can incorporate all the factors affecting real asset-liability decisions. Noneconomic factors may exist that are not quantifiable.

The optimal strategy derived by the bank model is intended to be used as a guide to focusing the attention of senior management on a specific strategy that appears to be the best on the basis of economic factors and a crude quantification of time and risk preferences. It may be useful to compare the implications of this strategy with those of the optimal strategies for the two extreme decision makers. In the final analysis, however, senior management must use judgment to account for the factors that are not quantifiable, and to provide the extra intuition to supplement the crude quantification of the time and risk preferences.

Hedging with Financial Futures and Options

If, on a net basis, a bank has long-term assets funded by short-term liabilities, its earnings are exposed to higher interest rates. The bank may wish to reduce this exposure. As discussed earlier, this can be done by selling fixed-rate assets, by replacing federal funds or other maturing liabilities with long-term liabilities, or by selling short long-term governments. Alternatively, this can be done by hedging with financial futures or options.[5] A futures contract for a security is a commitment to buy or sell that security at a specified future time at a specified price. A bank can hedge a portfolio security by selling a future in that security, if a market for such a future exists. Then, if interest rates go up, the price of the portfolio security will go down, but the loss will be offset by delivering the security at the price specified in the futures contract sold earlier, or by buying back the futures contract (the latter can be done prior to the specified delivery date). Similarly, if interest rates go down, the price of the portfolio security will go up, but the gain will be eliminated by a loss on the futures contract.

However, there is only a limited number of financial instruments for which there is a viable futures market. If such a market for a particular security does not exist, a future for another security can be used for hedging, assuming that the price volatilities of the two securities are similar. Prices of long-term securities are generally more volatile than those of short-term securities. The historical relationship between the price movements of the two securities must be derived mathematically in order to determine what amount of the existing future is needed to hedge the security for which there is no futures market. However, such indirect hedging does not guarantee complete insensitivity to changing interest rates, because interest rates for different financial instruments do not always move in the same manner relative to one another.

As of December 1981 a viable futures market existed for the following financial instruments: 90-day Treasury bills, 90-day CDs, GNMAs, and long-term Treasury bonds. Futures for 1-year Treasury bills, 30-day and 90-day commercial paper, and 2-year and 4-year Treasury notes had been started, but these markets have not become viable. Ninety-day Eurodollar CD futures had been just introduced, and futures for other interest rate instruments were in the planning stage.

A fixed-rate asset could be hedged against rising interest rates by buying a "put" option for it, or for a security of similar maturity. If the put is for a security other than the hedged asset, then the relative price volatilities of the two assets must be estimated, and the quantity of the hedging asset must be such that its total price volatility is equal to that of the hedged asset, if complete hedging is desired. The put would give the bank the option to sell the underlying security at a specified price by a specified date. Thus, if interest rates increased, the market price of the asset would go down, but the loss would be offset by a gain in the price of the put. On the other hand, if interest rates decreased, the market price of the asset would go up, while the loss in the put would be limited to the price paid for it.

If a bank finds itself with long-term liabilities funding short-term assets on a net basis, and wishes to reduce the exposure to lower interest rates, this can be done by acquiring fixed-rate assets, by buying back its fixed-rate liabilities to the extent this is feasible, by buying a future in a security of similar maturity, or by buying a "call" option in a security of similar maturity. The future would offset the changes in the market value of the fixed-rate liabilities in both directions. On the other hand, the call, which would give the bank the option to buy the underlying security at a specified price by a specified date, would offset the downside risk from lower interest rates, but would not reduce the benefit from higher interest rates, except by the price paid for the call.

Hedging with puts and calls is essentially buying insurance to protect the bank against movement of interest rates in a particular direction, but leaving unrestrained the potential benefit from the other direction. Options could also be used to hedge both directions, in which case the cost of hedging the risk from one direction would be reduced by "writing" (selling) an option that would offset the benefit from the other direction. A fixed-rate asset could be hedged in this manner by simultaneously buying a put and writing a call, while a fixed-rate liability could be hedged both ways by simultaneously buying a call and writing a put.

There were no options on interest rate instruments as of January 1982, but both put and call options on GNMAs were scheduled for introduction as early as February, subject to court approval, and options on Treasury securities and other financial instruments were planned for introduction at the same time or shortly thereafter. Options can be used to hedge the downside risk of fixed-rate assets while leaving the upside potential unrestrained.

Banks have not yet actively used the futures market for hedging purposes. The main reasons for this have probably been lack of viable futures markets in the intermediate maturity range of two to ten years, where government securities of bank portfolios are concentrated, and cumbersome and uncertain accounting rules (the Financial Accounting Standards Board was expected to rule on this subject sometime in 1982).

In general, the gross amount of securities underlying futures and options contracts, as well as short sales, is not reported in the balance sheet, while both unrealized and realized gains or losses are included in operating earnings. For Federal Reserve reporting purposes, the latter holds even for hedging contracts. For tax and public reporting purposes, exceptions to this mark-to-market approach are acceptable when the short sales and futures or options contracts are identified as hedging specific assets, liabilities, or commitments, and the hedging instrument has a high price correlation with the hedged item. In this manner hedging contracts can be used to hedge publicly reported as well as real earnings, but it is necessary to keep two sets of books. Moreover, the accounting treatment of certain complicated hedging operations is uncertain.

The accounting treatment of interest rate futures is discussed in a 1978 report by Arthur Andersen and Company.[6] The American Institute of Certified Public Accountants issued a revised accounting guide for savings and loan associations in 1979[7] that is consistent with the accounting treatment in the Arthur Andersen and Company report.

As a result of the astronomical rise in interest rates in 1980 and 1981, many banks are understandably reluctant to invest in fixed-rate loans of very long maturities. This could lead to a much steeper upward-sloping yield curve in the future than has normally been the case in the past. However, if viable futures and options markets are generated over a broad maturity range, and if the accounting treatment of hedging contracts is simplified, banks may find it profitable to invest in fixed-rate loans as well as in marketable securities, and to hedge the interest rate risk. In this manner banks could earn a normal banking spread while passing the interest rate risk to speculators.[8]

FOREIGN EXCHANGE RISK

Though foreign exchange risk is discussed in chapter 10, it is worth noting here some of the practical implications of currency translations. Under Financial Accounting Statement 8, which was adopted in 1975, translation gains or losses arising from exchange rate fluctuations had to be included in operating earnings. Such gains or losses resulted from translating into dollar equivalents the net non-dollar-denominated financial assets and earnings of foreign entities, the foreign tax credits that are based on the exchange rates in effect at the time of payment, and any nondollar-denominated securities held in the United States. Certain balance sheet items (largely fixed assets, in the case of banks) had to be translated into dollars at historical exchange rates (pertaining to the time of acquisition).

A new rule, Financial Accounting Statement 52, was issued in December 1981. It is to be effective for fiscal years beginning on or after December 15, 1982, with earlier adoption permitted. Under the new rule translation gains or losses from conversion from the functional currency into the reporting currency are to be reported as a separate component of the stockholders' equity, leaving operating earnings unaffected. However, translation of gains or losses arising from nondollar-denominated securities held in the United States will continue to be included in operating earnings. Furthermore, the translation gains or losses accumulated over time are to be removed from the translation adjustment component of stockholders' equity upon sale of an item, at which time they must be netted out with the gain or loss from the sale, and must be included in operating earnings.

A bank may hedge its net nondollar-denominated assets and foreign tax credits by engaging in foreign exchange futures contracts, in such a way that a translation gain (loss) is offset by a loss (gain) in the futures holdings. Moreover, the bank may forecast the income from each foreign branch and try to hedge this income as well. However, it is not always possible to hedge perfectly, because there is no futures market in some currencies.[9]

Some banks have been at least partly hedging their foreign exchange exposure in order to reduce the impact of currency fluctuations on operating earnings under Financial Accounting Statement 8. Under the new rule this reason for hedging has not been completely eliminated, since future operating earnings will be affected by the accumulated translation gains or losses upon the sale of an item. In any case, banks may wish to hedge in order to reduce the impact of currency fluctuations on the balance sheet, particularly on stockholders' equity. Moreover, the need for hedging translation gains or losses arising from nondollar-denominated assets held in the United States remains the same, because the treatment of such gains or losses has not changed.

CONCLUSION

The sources and uses of funds committee is the central body controlling the worldwide liquidity and interest rate exposures of the bank. The various offices and subsidiaries of the bank are generally allowed to manage their own liquidity and interest rate exposures independently, subject to certain size and exposure limits. These independent decisions may at times offset one another in determining the overall interest rate exposure, while at other times they may all contribute to increasing this exposure. In order to evaluate the overall exposure of the bank, it is necessary to combine the individual exposures.

When the sources and uses of funds committee looks at the overall exposure and decides to change it because it appears to be either excessive or too small in the face of interest rate expectations at the time, it effectively offsets some decisions taken in the individual offices or subsidiaries. It is essential to have such a central control mechanism, since the individual offices and subsidiaries cannot possibly know how their decisions will affect the combined exposure. The alternative would be to set narrow exposure limits in each maturity category, so that the overall exposure can never be too large. Such an approach would preclude substantially mismatching the balance sheet, which the bank's management may be willing to do at times when interest rates are strongly expected to move in a particular direction. Moreover, this approach would be likely to inhibit somewhat the development of individual initiative and financial acumen. Thus, the establishment of a central decision-making body at the head office actually makes it possible to give greater freedom to the branches; if the independent decisions of the branches lead to excessive or insufficient combined exposure, the central body can always take corrective action.

The ability to forecast interest rates is the determining factor in asset-liability management. If a bank does not feel that it can forecast interest rates better than the implicit forecast imbedded in the market yield curve, then the optimal strategy for that bank will be to eliminate all sensitivity to interest rates. This does not necessarily mean that every asset should be matched with a liability of similar maturity. It may be that hedging with financial futures or options is more profitable than matching at a particular point in time.

On the other hand, a bank does not need to forecast much better than the market yield curve in order to be able to derive substantial profit from mismatching the balance sheet. A prudent strategy may be to avoid mismatching substantially in longer maturities, and to take more risk in the short end. In this manner it will be possible to generate substantial profits over time through proper mismatching, and if interest rates go the other way, the bank's earnings will not suffer for long.

NOTES

1. R. A. Robertson, "Rate Behavioral Maturity of Prime," presented at the European Congress on Operational Research, Institute of Management Sciences meeting at Lausanne, Switzerland, July 1982.

2. K. J. Cohen, S. F. Maier, and J. H. Vander Weide, "Recent Developments in Management Science in Banking," *Management Science* 27, no. 10 (October 1981): 1097–1119.

3. The use of the bank model by the Sources and Uses of Funds Committee of the Morgan Bank is discussed in L. P. Mavrides, "Funds Management, Morgan Style," *ABA Banking Journal*, August 1981, pp. 96, 99–100. Also see D. B. Riefler and L. P. Mavrides, "Sources and Uses of Funds Management," *American Banker*, February 26, 1982, pp. 4–7. Solution methods for a class of mathematical problems that includes the bank model are in L. P. Mavrides, "Nonlinear Programming Under Triangular Constraint Substructure, with Applications to Sequential Decision Processes," Ph.D. diss., Yale University, 1973. Also see L. P. Mavrides, "A Finite Step-Size Procedure for the F-W Method," *Journal of Computer and System Sciences* 21, no. 1 (1980): 24–29.

4. The procedure is discussed in detail in I. Kabus, "You Can Bank on Uncertainty," *Harvard Business Review*, May-June 1976, 95–105.

5. For a detailed treatment of financial futures, see M. J. Powers and D. J. Vogel, *Inside the Financial Futures Markets* (New York: John Wiley and Sons, 1981). For a thorough discussion of options, see L. G. McMillan, *Options as a Strategic Investment* (New York: New York Institute of Finance, 1980).

6. Arthur Andersen and Company, *Interest Rate Futures Contracts—Accounting and Control Techniques for Banks* (Chicago: Arthur Andersen and Co., 1978).

7. American Institute of Certified Public Accountants, *Audit and Accounting Guide for Savings and Loan Associations* (New York: AICPA, 1979).

8. S. Rose, "Restoring Bank Profitability," *American Banker*, December 1, 1981, pp. 1, 4, 8.

9. For further details on this subject, see Powers and Vogel, op. cit.

6 PROFITABILITY OF INTERNATIONAL BANKING

Arturo C. Porzecanski

The involvement of the major U.S. commercial banks in international activities, which took root during the 1960s, deepened noticeably in the early 1970s, and widened to encompass medium-size, regional banks in the latter half of the 1970s, was driven by the expectation of greater profitability and by the potential for accelerated asset growth. The attainment of these objectives was made possible by a combination of favorable circumstances: the absence of legal restraints on the kinds of services banks could render (for instance, out-of-state and investment banking activities); the need of multinational corporations for large-scale, multicurrency funding and cash management advice; the rapid growth and increased complexity of international trade; and the opportunity to intermediate between surplus OPEC countries and deficit, oil-importing industrial and developing nations.

This chapter reviews the banks' international experience since the mid-1970s and, in particular, attempts to quantify recent performance in three related areas: asset growth, profitability, and risk minimization.

INTERNATIONAL LENDING

The earnings of commercial banks, especially the large ones that are the major participants in the Eurocurrency market, are derived from net interest income, bond and foreign exchange trading activities, trust and agency services, and other fees and commissions. Despite the apparent variety of sources, however, the overwhelming portion of earnings attributable to overseas operations is a direct or indirect function of the banks' lending activities.

Since the mid-1970s the volume and geographical distribution of international loans by U.S.-chartered banks have been monitored by the Federal Reserve System. Data for American banks and for banks operating in Canada, Japan, 12 West European countries, and various offshore banking centers are supplied by their respective regulatory agencies to the Bank for International Settlements, in Basle, Switzerland. These statistics, which are presented in Table 6.1, make possible an analysis of recent trends in what is the backbone of international banking.[1]

The heyday of overseas lending for U.S. financial institutions (at least in relation to banks in other countries) was the early 1970s, during which time they held about 40 percent of all international claims. From 1975 on, banks in the other industrial countries increased their international portfolios at an average annual rate of 28 percent, compared with loan growth averaging 17 percent per year for American banks. Thus, the U.S. share of international outstandings gradually fell to below 30 percent of total. Nevertheless, American banks' foreign loan portfolio increased from almost $105 billion as of the end of 1975 to an estimated $400 billion by the end of 1981, well in excess of their domestic loan growth.

The composition of U.S. banks' international holdings has changed surprisingly little over the years. At the end of 1975, 37 percent of all foreign loans were to public and private entities in the major industrial countries (principally the United Kingdom, Japan, France, and Germany); 23 percent were booked in offshore banking centers (mainly the Bahamas and the Cayman Islands); 23 percent in non-OPEC developing countries (such as Brazil and Mexico); 7 percent in smaller developed countries (such as Spain and Norway); 5 percent in OPEC countries (mainly Venezuela); and a mere 2 percent in East European nations (principally Yugoslavia). At the end of 1980, the only significant changes were a decline to 33 percent of total for the major industrial countries and an increase to 26 percent of total for offshore banking centers. When these centers are excluded from the geographical breakdown, the two main groupings become the G-10 countries plus Switzerland (accounting for 48 percent of total in 1975 and 44 percent of total in 1980) and the non-

TABLE 6.1. Outstanding International Claims of Commercial Banks Reporting to the Bank for International Settlements, 1975–80
(billions of dollars)

Claims on	Dec. 1975	Dec. 1976	Dec. 1977	Dec. 1978	Dec. 1979	Dec. 1980
G–10 countries and Switzerland[a]	204	236	291	387	472	578
Non-U.S. banks	150	171	217	302	380	470
U.S. banks	55	65	73	84	92	108
U.S. share	27%	28%	25%	22%	20%	19%
Offshore banking centers	58	79	93	117	149	180
Non-U.S. banks	24	28	35	51	73	94
U.S. banks	34	51	59	66	76	86
U.S. share	59%	65%	63%	57%	51%	48%
Smaller developed countries[b]	38	51	71	84	98	112
Non-U.S. banks	28	37	55	67	79	90
U.S. banks	10	14	16	18	19	21
U.S. share	27%	27%	22%	21%	20%	19%
OPEC countries[c]	14	24	39	56	64	70
Non-U.S. banks	7	11	19	35	44	49
U.S. banks	7	13	20	22	20	21
U.S. share	52%	53%	51%	39%	32%	31%
Non-OPEC developing countries	63	81	99	122	159	195
Non-U.S. banks	29	39	52	72	100	122
U.S. banks	34	42	47	50	59	73
U.S. share	54%	52%	48%	41%	37%	37%
East European countries[d]	23	32	42	53	63	69
Non-U.S. banks	20	27	36	47	56	62
U.S. banks	3	5	6	6	7	7
U.S. share	14%	15%	14%	11%	11%	11%
Miscellaneous and unallocated[e]	9	11	15	19	24	29
Non-U.S. banks	4	6	10	11	12	16
U.S. banks	5	5	5	8	12	13
U.S. share	54%	50%	35%	43%	49%	45%
World total[a]	411	514	650	839	1,029	1,233
Non-U.S. banks	263	319	424	584	744	903
U.S. banks	148	195	226	225	285	330
U.S. share	36%	38%	35%	30%	28%	27%

Note: Figures may not add to totals because of rounding. Shares were computed from unrounded numbers. Data for 1977–80 are not strictly comparable with data for 1975–76.
[a]Excludes claims on the United States.
[b]Other West European countries plus Australia, South Africa, and Turkey.
[c]Includes Bahrain and Oman.
[d]Includes Yugoslavia.
[e]Includes Liberia and New Zealand.
Source: Board of Governors, Federal Reserve System.

OPEC developing countries (30 percent of total in both 1975 and 1980).

American banks have lost their share of the market throughout the geographical groupings in the wake of accelerated foreign lending by West European, Japanese, and Canadian banks. The decline was most pronounced in the OPEC countries, where between the end of 1975 and the end of 1980, U.S. loans outstanding tripled but loans by non-American banks rose sevenfold. In these countries a U.S. market share of 52 percent dwindled to 31 percent in five years' time. The other notable market share loss took place among the non-OPEC developing nations, where loans by American financial institutions more than doubled during 1975–80, while outstandings by West European and other banks virtually quadrupled. In this part of the world, the drop in market share was from 54 percent to 37 percent. In Eastern Europe, where U.S. banks traditionally have had a very small presence, the market share loss was minimal (from 14 percent to 11 percent).

The often-discussed involvement of commercial banks in developing countries merits some additional quantification, which is provided in Table 6.2. The available data reveal, first, that the presence of U.S. banks was, and remains, heavily concentrated in six countries that account for almost three-quarters of total American claims on non-OPEC developing nations: Brazil, Mexico, South Korea, Argentina, Taiwan, and the Philippines. Politically and economically this is a subgrouping of diverse countries among which are, for instance, a major oil exporter (Mexico) and a country that is virtually self-sufficient in energy (Argentina). In the case of non-U.S. banks, lending to developing countries has become increasingly centered on this same subgroup, although as of December 1980 the six countries still represented less than two-thirds of the total non-OPEC developing nation exposure of non-American institutions.

The data show, second, that the U.S. market share loss has been greatest in Chile, Mexico, Malaysia, the Philippines, South Korea, and, starting from a much lower base, in Morocco. In these countries the loss was or exceeded 20 percentage points. On the other hand, non-American banks lost least in Taiwan and Thailand, where U.S. market share actually increased slightly, and displacement of American banks was low in Egypt and Israel.

TABLE 6.2. Outstanding International Claims of Commercial Banks Reporting to the Bank for International Settlements on Non-OPEC Developing Countries, 1976 and 1980 (billions of dollars)

Claims on	December 1976			December 1980		
	Total	U.S. Banks	U.S. Share (percent)	Total	U.S. Banks	U.S. Share (percent)
Non-OPEC developing countries	80.9	41.9	52	195.1	72.7	37
Argentina	3.4	1.9	57	18.9	7.1	38
Brazil	21.2	10.9	52	43.3	15.7	36
Chile	1.1	0.8	72	6.7	3.5	52
Colombia	1.6	1.3	77	4.3	2.7	63
Mexico	17.9	11.7	66	41.0	15.9	39
Peru	2.8	1.8	62	3.9	1.8	46
Malaysia	1.0	0.5	50	2.3	0.7	30
Philippines	2.6	2.0	76	7.0	3.8	54
South Korea	3.9	3.0	77	14.0	6.7	48
Taiwan	2.6	2.0	77	5.1	4.0	78
Thailand	1.4	0.6	41	3.2	1.4	44
Egypt	1.2	0.4	30	3.1	0.8	26
India	0.5	0.2	52	0.9	0.3	33
Israel	2.5	1.0	39	4.7	1.5	32
Morocco	0.5	0.2	34	3.0	0.4	13
Zaire	0.8	0.3	31	1.1	0.2	18
Others	15.8	3.7	23	32.6	6.1	19

Note: Figures may not add to totals because of rounding. Shares were computed from unrounded numbers. Data for 1980 are not strictly comparable with data for 1976.

Source: Board of Governors, Federal Reserve System.

INTERNATIONAL PROFITABILITY

In the early and mid-1970s profits from overseas lending and from other cross-border banking services were much higher than today. There are several reasons for this decline in profitability: the aggressive entry of many relatively less-exposed, less-experienced West European and medium-size American banks into the international lending arena; the increased financial sophistication of multinational corporate and foreign government borrowers; and the growing familiarity of the parties involved, which contributed to a more realistic appraisal of the (previously exaggerated) risks entailed. The continuous drop in average and lowest loan spreads observed in publicly announced, medium-term Eurocurrency loans is a reflection of these factors. In 1976 average loan spreads exceeded 1.5 percent over the London Interbank Offered Rate (LIBOR), and the lowest such spreads were 1 percent over LIBOR; by 1979 loan spreads averaged 0.75 percent and the minimum spread became 0.25 percent above LIBOR.

The fall in profitability is evident from an examination of the financial statements of the ten largest American banks. Several years ago these institutions accounted for about three-quarters of all U.S. cross-border lending; at present, and given the previously noted overseas expansion of the so-called regional banks, the top ten firms hold no more than two-thirds of the total international loans made by American banks. They are the ones, however, that have provided the best data on their overseas operations and for the longest time span.[2]

The profit margin on international assets at these banks declined from a weighted average peak of 0.67 percent in 1975 to a low of 0.44 percent in 1979. Table 6.3 shows a detailed breakdown for 1976, when the composite return of international assets was 0.52 percent, and for 1980, when, for reasons detailed later, profitability improved (relative to 1979) to 0.48 percent. The long-term decline is also striking in relation to margins on domestic assets, which averaged a low of 0.39 percent in 1975 and recuperated steadily to a composite peak of 0.57 percent in 1979. Table 6.3 documents the increase from 0.4 percent in 1976 to 0.52 percent in 1980, a year in which the banks' return on domestic assets fell somewhat relative to 1979. The decline in international margins was sharpest and steadiest at Citicorp, Manufacturers Hanover, and First Chicago Corporation, and was minimized at J. P. Morgan, Chemical New York, and Bankers Trust New York.

TABLE 6.3. Return on Domestic and International Assets
at Ten Largest U.S. Commercial Banks, 1976 and 1980
(percent)

	1976 Return on Assets		1980 Return on Assets	
	Domestic	International	Domestic	International
Citicorp	0.4	0.8	0.5	0.4
BankAmerica	0.1	0.4	0.55	0.6
Chase Manhattan	0.4	0.5	0.5	0.45
Manufacturers Hanover	0.3	0.6	0.4	0.4
J. P. Morgan	0.7	0.7	0.6	0.8
Chemical New York	0.3	0.4	0.45	0.4
Bankers Trust New York	0.2	0.4	0.4	0.6
Continental Illinois	0.6	0.2	0.6	0.5
First Chicago	0.7	0.45	0.4	0.0
Security Pacific	0.6	0.1	0.7	0.4
Weighted average	0.4	0.52	0.52	0.48

Source: Salomon Brothers, U.S. Multinational Banking: Semiannual Statistics (New York: Salomon Brothers, various issues).

In spite of the inferior performance of international assets in both absolute and relative terms, most of the top banks apparently have continued to accumulate them at a faster pace than domestic assets. It is estimated that during 1976-80, international assets growth occurred at an annual average rate of 15.6 percent, while domestic assets rose at a yearly rate of 10.6 percent. Only in 1980, following several years of declining profitability, did international assets expand more slowly than domestic (10 percent versus 11.5 percent). The statistics suggest, therefore, that asset growth has been regarded as a legitimate objective of international banking.

The rapid accumulation of international assets during 1975-79, at a time of eroding profitability, inevitably led to a fall in the contribution of overseas earnings to total bank earnings. For the ten bank holding companies listed in Table 6.4, the weighted average earnings contribution declined from 52 percent in 1975 to a low of 43 percent in 1979. It then recuperated partially to 47 percent of total in 1980. The international earnings share drop was most precipitous at Chase Manhattan, BankAmerica, Citicorp, and First Chicago. During 1976–80, the overseas earnings of the ten largest banks increased by about 13 percent per annum (versus an estimated 20 percent yearly during 1973–76), which contrasts with domestic earnings growth of approximately 18 percent per year.

The available earnings data of the ten top bank holding companies cannot be disaggregated to reveal the quantitative importance of the various sources of international earnings. Nevertheless, commercial banks have begun to publish some comparable statistics on the main contributing factors to income attributable to international business. One relevant distinction is between interest and noninterest income. The former is derived from the spread between interest earned on loans and interest paid on funds. The latter follows from foreign exchange and other trading account profits and commissions, corporate and other trust and agency income, and various fees, commissions, and translation gains.

**TABLE 6.4. International Earnings of Ten
Largest U.S. Commercial Banks, 1975–80
(as percent of total earnings)**

	1975	1976	1977	1978	1979	1980
Citicorp	71	72	82	72	65	62
BankAmerica	55	47	42	35	38	45
Chase Manhattan	64	78	65	53	47	49
Manufacturers Hanover	47	59	60	51	49	49
J. P. Morgan	60	46	48	51	52	58
Chemical New York	41	41	39	42	35	38
Bankers Trust New York	59	61	83	68	51	58
Continental Illinois	14	23	17	18	18	33
First Chicago	33	15	20	16	4	0
Security Pacific	12	7	12	15	10	13
Weighted average	52	51	51	46	43	47

Source: Salomon Brothers, *U.S. Multinational Banking: Semiannual Statistics* (New York: Salomon Brothers, various issues).

TABLE 6.5. Interest and Noninterest Income Attributable to Overseas Operations of Five Largest U.S. Commercial Banks, 1978–81
(in millions of dollars and as percent of international earning assets)

	1978	1979	1980	1981*
Citibank				
Interest income	1,134	1,256	1,083	660
As percent of earning assets	2.48	2.29	1.98	1.24
Noninterest income	390	388	636	876
As percent of earning assets	0.85	0.71	1.17	1.65
BankAmerica				
Interest income	643	721	862	872
As percent of earning assets	1.91	1.91	2.20	2.26
Noninterest income	244	249	357	384
As percent of earning assets	0.73	0.66	0.91	0.99
Chase Manhattan				
Interest income	482	634	653	779
As percent of earning assets	1.74	2.32	1.90	2.19
Noninterest income	221	227	296	356
As percent of earning assets	0.80	0.83	0.86	1.00
Manufacturers Hanover				
Interest income	216	355	361	419
As percent of earning assets	1.50	2.19	1.65	1.88
Noninterest income	8	75	92	111
As percent of earning assets	0.06	0.46	0.42	0.50
Morgan Guaranty				
Interest income	297	416	493	531
As percent of earning assets	1.70	2.27	2.19	2.27
Noninterest income	140	107	161	170
As percent of earning assets	0.80	0.58	0.71	0.73

*First-half results annualized.

Source: Salomon Brothers, U.S. Multinational Banking: Semiannual Statistics (New York: Salomon Brothers, various issues).

The data on interest and noninterest income at the five largest American banks, shown in Table 6.5, point to a significant change in these sources of international profitability. Traditionally, noninterest income has always made a smaller contribution to earnings from overseas operations than has spread income. During 1978–79, for example, noninterest income at the five banks represented at most one-third, and usually less than one-fourth, of total pretax income attributable to international business. But this changed in 1980 and in the first half of 1981. The ratio of noninterest income to earning assets increased from a range of 0.06–0.85 percent in 1978 to a range of 0.50–1.65 percent as of mid-1981. Meanwhile, the ratio of interest income to earning assets decreased from a range of 1.50–2.48 percent in 1978 to one of 1.24–2.27 percent by the middle of 1981. In 1980, for instance, three of the four banks that suffered a decline in profitability due to reduced interest income as a percent of earning assets were able to counter it—fully, in two cases—through higher earnings from fees, commissions, trading income, and the like.

The point is that these latter sources of income may assist in the reversal of the trend of eroding international profitability. This would require, however, greater management emphasis on rendering financial and other services that do not burden the banks' balance sheets because they do not entail the commitment of funds inherent in lending.

INTERNATIONAL RISK

No analysis of trends in international lending and profitability is complete unless reference is made to the risks entailed in overseas operations. However, the measurement of risk is no easy matter. Some risks lead to actual losses, while others deteriorate the quality of a bank's assets less perceptibly; some originate in a bank's loan portfolio, while others come from funding activities or foreign currency translation. In short, some risks can be quantified and linked to international business, while others cannot.

The key measure of risk from international banking is provided by the record of net loan losses after recoveries. For the ten largest bank holding companies in the sample, domestic net loan write-offs declined from a peak of $1.1 billion in 1975 to a low of $550 million in 1979, then rose somewhat to $840 million in 1980. On the international front, losses peaked at about $300 million in both 1976 and 1977, and subsequently fell steadily to half that amount by 1980. As a percent of total, therefore, international net loan write-offs rose from 13 percent in 1975 to 29 percent in 1977, then diminished to 15 percent of total in 1980, an average of 21 percent for period 1975–80 as a whole (see Table 6.6).

TABLE 6.6. Net International Loan Losses of Ten Largest U.S. Commercial Banks, 1975–80 (as percent of total net loan losses)

	1975	1976	1977	1978	1979	1980
Citicorp	33	46	41	46	13	20
BankAmerica	5	18	51	25	44	19
Chase Manhattan	11	35	51	39	42	15
Manufacturers Hanover	1	*	1	14	23	6
J. P. Morgan	7	15	17	25	*	8
Chemical New York	2	3	12	7	*	10
Bankers Trust New York	4	9	7	*	9	5
Continental Illinois	10	6	10	20	29	*
First Chicago	5	8	13	17	*	21
Security Pacific	13	26	11	9	*	19
Weighted average	13	23	29	26	22	15

*Not meaningful because of net international or total loan recoveries.
Source: Salomon Brothers, *U.S. Multinational Banking: Semiannual Statistics* (New York: Salomon Brothers, various issues).

These percentages are certainly very low when compared with either the share of international assets in the banks' total assets (an average of 47 percent during 1975–80) or the proportion accounted for by international earnings (a mean of 48 percent of total earnings during the same period). Moreover, their level and evolution may help explain the decline of profitability as a proper reflection of the fact that international lending appears to involve relatively little, and falling, loan loss risk.

TABLE 6.7. Principal International Loan Charge-offs of U.S.
Commercial Banks, 1975–80
(millions of dollars)

	Cumulative Totals for 1975–80
G-10 countries and Switzerland[a]	
United Kingdom	130.3[b]
West Germany	35.9[b]
Belgium	18.4
Switzerland	16.5
France	15.1
Italy	12.9[b]
Japan	4.6
Netherlands	3.9
Smaller developed countries	
Greece	48.8
Australia	42.2
Spain	19.9[b]
Norway	12.9
Austria	5.7
Turkey	5.6[b]
OPEC countries	
Iran	22.6[b]
Venezuela	17.4
Indonesia	3.0
Nigeria	1.0
Non-OPEC developing countries	
Mexico	57.9[b]
Brazil	31.0
Nicaragua	34.6[b]
Argentina	17.2
Honduras	8.1
Guatemala	7.5
Costa Rica	7.2
Taiwan	7.1
Zaire	5.6[b]
Thailand	3.4
India	3.2
Jamaica	2.2[b]
El Salvador	2.2
Egypt	1.4

[a]Excludes the United States.
[b]Includes charge-offs to governments, government agencies, and government-owned banks.
Source: Robert Morris Associates, Report on Domestic and International Loan Charge-Offs (Philadelphia: RMA, various years).

Given the somewhat controversial nature of bank lending to developing countries, perhaps it would be appropriate to make some observations on how the loan loss data by groups of foreign countries compare with the statistics presented in Tables 6.1 and 6.2 on the banks' international loan portfolios. The information released by individual banks does not permit any meaningful geographic disaggregation, but there is an alternative data base generated by an annual survey of over 100 American banks. The survey asks respondents to identify five countries in which the largest international loan charge-offs were incurred.[3]

The results of the 1975–80 surveys are highlighted in Table 6.7. A comparison of the international loan exposure of U.S. banks with their loan loss record during the period reveals that, on the whole, those losses are lowest in the main industrial countries and highest in the smaller developed countries. OPEC and non-OPEC countries alike do not stand out as particularly risky or nonrisky. For example, the ratio of loan charge-offs during 1975–80 to end-1980 outstanding is 0.25 percent for the eight major industrial countries, 1.07 percent for the six smaller developed countries, 0.36 percent for the four OPEC nations, and 0.40 percent for the fourteen non-OPEC developing countries. When comparing individual countries across the global spectrum, the loan loss experience appears most adverse in Australia, Greece, the five Central American republics, Jamaica, Zaire, and Iran, and least adverse in Japan, the Netherlands, France, Belgium, Taiwan, and Nigeria. The charge-off record in Brazil is similar to that in Italy, and the one in Mexico resembles that in West Germany. Interestingly, write-offs to government agencies and state-owned banks appear in all four main groupings.

To be sure, these loan-loss statistics cannot adequately capture and quantify the risks involved in overseas lending but, like all the other data presented throughout this chapter, they provide a necessary perspective on the complex, yet rewarding nature of international banking.

NOTES

1. The statistics on American banks include both their domestic offices and foreign branches, and appear in Table 3.20 of each monthly issue of the *Federal Reserve Bulletin*. The Bank for International Settlements data, which are made

public through a quarterly press release, cover banks in Belgium, France, Germany, Italy, Luxembourg, the Netherlands, Sweden, Switzerland, the United Kingdom, and, since December 1977, Austria, Denmark, and Ireland, as well as the offshore banking centers of the Bahamas, Cayman Islands, Panama, Hong Kong, and Singapore. To allow full comparability between the Federal Reserve and B.I.S. data, the following adjustments were made by the Division of International Finance of the Board of Governors of the Federal Reserve System: Yugoslavia, New Zealand, and Liberia were shifted to new categories; intrabank claims were restored for U.S. banks; claims held by the foreign branches of U.S. banks on local customers were removed, since such local currency claims are not covered by the B.I.S.; and claims held by U.S. bank branches outside the B.I.S.-reporting area were omitted. I am grateful to Rodney H. Mills, Jr., senior economist, Board of Governors, Federal Reserve System, for supplying me with these data.

2. The statistics on the ten largest bank holding companies are taken, derived, or estimated from those in Salomon Brothers, *U.S. Multinational Banking: Semiannual Statistics* (New York: Salomon Brothers, various years), and compiled by Thomas H. Hanley, senior analyst, Bank Securities Department, Salomon Brothers.

3. The surveys are conducted by Robert Morris Associates, and the results appear annually in *Report on Domestic and International Loan Charge-offs* (Philadelphia: RMA, various years).

Part III

LEGAL ISSUES, LENDING POLICIES AND PRACTICES

7 LEGAL ISSUES IN
INTERNATIONAL LENDING:
GENERAL CONSIDERATIONS

Laurel A. Nichols

International lending transactions are relatively more complicated than purely domestic ones (where the lender and the borrower
are located in the same jurisdiction) because of the involvement of
more than one country (and, therefore, more than one legal system)
and, consequently, the need to deal with the differences between
those systems. At the very least two systems of law will be applicable
to any international lending transaction: the law of the country in
which the lender is located and that of the country in which the borrower is located. If other parties to the transaction, such as guarantors
or additional lenders, are located in still other countries, or if the
lender is making the loan from an office outside its home country,
the number of applicable laws increases correspondingly. Principles
of international law may also come into play from time to time,
particularly with respect to the enforcement of judgments. (The
situation in international lending is not unlike that in lending between
two states in the United States, where state laws differ with respect
to various matters and federal law also affects some aspects; interstate lending, however, is generally somewhat less complex than international lending because state laws have a common heritage in
English common law, are generally similar and sometimes identical—

The author wishes to express her appreciation to her colleagues at Sage Gray
Todd & Sims for their assistance in the preparation of this chapter.

for instance, the Uniform Commercial Code, and operate within the framework of "full faith and credit.")

It is important, particularly for the lender, that the legal aspects of the financing be made as predictable as possible by structuring and documenting the transaction within a known legal framework. The most important choices in establishing that framework are the choice of one system of law to govern the substantive aspects of the transaction and the choice of a particular forum in which the parties may resolve any disputes that arise.

There will always, however, be some legal aspects of any international financing that cannot be changed by agreement of the parties (for instance, exchange control regulations applicable to the borrower or guarantor, and government authorizations required for the particular transaction). Although the parties may choose one system of law to govern their transaction substantively, the transaction and its documentation must nevertheless function under more than one legal system. It is important for the lender and its counsel to work closely with local counsel in the borrower's country who is knowledgeable and experienced in international credit transactions, in order to achieve the optimal structure and documentation under the relevant legal systems (see the section "Use of Local Counsel," below).

The balance of this chapter covers the choice of law and the choice of forum, the closely related topic of sovereign immunity, and a number of other matters related to international lending transactions that should be considered by the lender and its counsel. These subjects are treated in the context of a U.S. lender financing a borrower located outside the United States; the discussion is equally applicable with respect to the legal relationships between the U.S. lender and any guarantor of the credit that is located outside of the United States. The same general concerns arise in international transactions not involving U.S. entities, but the particular considerations and solutions may differ.

While the following discussion is intended to highlight certain areas in which legal advice is essential in order to structure and document an international lending transaction in the way that is most effective for the lender, lenders should nevertheless keep in mind that the legal documentation only gives the rules of the game agreed at its commencement and a bargaining position for the lender if the credit goes bad. Foreign laws and policies change rapidly, as may a borrower's attitude toward a credit or its financial condition, and neither counsel nor the documents can furnish a guaranty that the credit will be repaid; the best assurance of that remains the sound judgment of the lender with respect to the creditworthiness of the borrower and to any need for collateral security or third-party guaranties.

CHOICE OF GOVERNING LAW FOR THE TRANSACTION

The lender to a foreign borrower wants the financing governed by a developed and predictable system of substantive law that is not subject to change by or for the benefit of the borrower (particularly if the borrower is a government or government entity) and that is, preferably, familiar to the lender. For a U.S. lender that system is in most cases the law of the state in which the lender is located, which includes any applicable federal laws. (In a syndicated credit the law chosen is usually the law of the jurisdiction in which the agent or the majority of the lenders is located.) A typical choice-of-law clause reads "This Agreement shall be governed by, and construed and interpreted in accordance with, the laws of the State of X."

The local law of the forum in which any action is brought will determine whether the parties' choice of governing law can be accepted in the forum. In most American jurisdictions the courts will respect the parties' choice of law if that choice bears a reasonable relationship to the transaction. Indicia of such a relationship include the following: where the lender's and the borrower's offices are located, where the credit is negotiated, where the documents are signed, where funds are disbursed to the borrower, and where payments are to be made by the borrower.

In a number of countries, particularly in Latin America, the local constitution or statutes may require the use of local law. In Latin America this reflects what is known as the Calvo Doctrine (after a nineteenth-century Argentine jurist), which developed out of the experience of those countries during the nineteenth century with diplomatic and military intervention in their affairs on behalf of foreign investors and lenders. The Calvo Doctrine states basically that a foreigner doing business in a country is entitled only to nondiscriminatory treatment under local law, and that by choosing to do business in the country, the foreigner implicitly agrees to be treated as a local resident. In other cases, borrowers, usually governmental, may refuse, out of a sense of national pride, to accept any law other than their own as the governing law.

The validity of the choice of governing law under both that law (and, if different, the law of the chosen forum) and the law of the borrower's country should always be confirmed by the lender's U.S. counsel and by counsel in the jurisdiction in question ("local counsel"). If the choice is held invalid, the court or other tribunal so holding will make its own selection of the governing law, an introduction of a considerable element of uncertainty that might have been avoided had the validity of the parties' choice been verified.

A lender whose normal choice of governing law is rejected by the borrower or is not permitted under any local law that is likely to be relevant has available several options:

1. The choice of the law of a neutral jurisdiction, that of neither the lender nor the borrower, may be acceptable to the borrower (but not, of course, if the borrower's local law forbids use of any other law in international transactions). If that law is acceptable, the lender's counsel and local counsel should investigate whether the chosen forum would apply that law, and whether a judgment rendered under that law would be enforced in the borrower's country. If the chosen forum jurisdiction is not the jurisdiction whose law is selected to govern the transaction, then the ease or difficulty of proving the content of the selected governing law in the forum courts should be taken into account.

2. The documentation may remain silent as to the choice of governing law, in which case the forum court or tribunal will determine the proper law to be applied in case of a dispute. The disadvantage of this option is that the governing law of the financing becomes unpredictable because it is dependent upon the particular facts of the financing and the forum in which enforcement of rights is sought. The forum court is likely to apply its own law if it can find any basis upon which to do so, because that enables it to decide the case under the law with which it is most familiar.

3. The law of the borrower's country may be expressly designated as the governing law, and that may well be an acceptable alternative if all or most of the assets that may be available to the lender in case of default by the borrower are located in the borrower's country, so that the lender would have to enforce any judgment there and pos-

sibly bring suit there in the first instance. This choice (or, for that matter, the express selection of any particular governing law) has the advantage over alternative (2) of identifying the governing law, and thus making it possible to mitigate drawbacks in that law, so far as possible, by appropriately structuring and documenting the transaction.

In some cases there may be reasons to specify that one law is to be followed if proceedings occur outside of the borrower's country and that the borrower's local law is to be applied if proceedings are brought in its country. This could be the case, for example, if the local courts in the borrower's country would not apply foreign law in suits tried before them but would enforce foreign judgments rendered under foreign law. This is not an altogether satisfactory solution to the choice-of-governing-law problem because of the practical difficulties created if the two laws attach different consequences to a lender's particular action (or inaction) and the lender acts (or fails to act) at a time when it does not know in which forum any related claim will be tried.

The choice of the governing substantive law for a transaction does not affect the rules of procedure and remedies available in the forum court or tribunal where any dispute is brought for resolution (which rules of procedure and available remedies should be reviewed by counsel in those jurisdictions where a suit is likely to be brought, usually the jurisdiction of the chosen forum and the jurisdiction in which the borrower is located). Neither does the choice eliminate the applicability to the parties and to the transaction of "regulatory" laws, such as applicable lending limits, local bankruptcy law, and requirements for government approval for the borrowing or for the obtaining and use of foreign exchange.

CHOICE OF FORUM FOR THE RESOLUTION OF DISPUTES

The forum chosen as the one in which the parties may resolve disputes usually follows, although it need not, the choice of law—that is, the courts of the jurisdiction whose substantive law governs the transaction are specified as a place in which any litigation may be maintained. This choice of forum avoids the need for the parties to prove the substance of a foreign law to the court (which proof may involve translation from one language to another, resulting in increased possibilities for error) and allows the court to apply a law with which it is familiar rather than its perception of the substance of the foreign law. The international lender also prefers a forum having impartial judges experienced in commercial matters and an adequate number of courts and competent attorneys, so that any litigation may proceed expeditiously. The choice of a forum should be a nonexclusive choice—that is, it should be available if the complaining party chooses, but its use should not be mandatory. The lender should retain the flexibility of using a different forum if it appears more advantageous when the need arises (for instance, if the borrower has assets in a different jurisdiction that may disappear before the lender is able to obtain a judgment in the contractually specified forum).

The choice of forum may be specified directly by a provision such as "The parties agree that all disputes relating to this Agreement may be tried before the courts of the State of X or the courts of the United States sitting in X," or indirectly through the borrower's submission to the personal jurisdiction of the chosen forum (discussed below). Forum selection clauses are generally upheld if they are not unreasonable, contrary to public policy, or the result of fraud or an abuse of bargaining power (but see the next paragraph). In choosing a forum, the lender should consult with its counsel and local counsel to confirm that the chosen forum will have subject matter jurisdiction over any dispute brought before it, that a judgment rendered by the chosen forum will be enforced in jurisdictions where the borrower's assets are located, and under what circumstances a forum non conveniens argument might be made successfully.

Forum non conveniens is a legal doctrine in the United States that enables courts to refuse jurisdiction over a case if another forum is available, offers effective redress, and would be more just and convenient for the parties. In some state courts only the parties may move for dismissal of a suit on the basis of forum non conveniens, but in other state courts and in federal courts, the courts themselves may be able to raise the issue in order to prevent an unnecessary expenditure of court resources when a more appropriate forum is available. In federal courts a successful forum non conveniens motion leads to the transfer of the suit to a more appropriate federal court, if there is one with jurisdiction over the parties, or to dismissal of the suit (transfer to a state or foreign court not being possible; a federal court may condition its dismissal of the federal case on the plaintiff's ability to institute its suit in another court). Similarly, in state courts a successful motion generally leads to the suit's transfer to a more appropriate state court or, if there is none, to its dismissal.

The documentation for an international loan usually includes a waiver by the borrower of its right to raise a forum non conveniens objection to the court in which any case is being tried. Although the waiver will not preclude a federal court judge or judges in some state courts from considering the forum non conveniens issue on the court's own motion, the waiver would be a factor to be considered in ruling on the motion; the waiver should also prevent the parties from raising the issue themselves.

SUBJECT MATTER AND PERSONAL JURISDICTION

Before the parties to an international lending transaction make their final choice of the forum in which to resolve disputes arising out of the transaction, the lender's counsel should confirm that the forum courts will have both subject matter jurisdiction with respect to disputes and personal jurisdiction over the borrower and any other potential defendant. Subject matter jurisdiction is a question of the court's intrinsic power to adjudicate the claims raised in a case before it. In the United States subject matter jurisdiction, unlike personal jurisdiction, cannot be created by consent of the parties[1] (neither may the parties deprive a court of subject matter jurisdiction by agreement—when it exists, it exists).

Personal jurisdiction is a question of the court's power to bring before it and to deal with the litigants; today this power depends principally upon adequate notice to any defendant of the claim(s) asserted against it and upon the existence of a sufficient relationship between the court trying the case and the defendant to justify the court's rendering of a judgment against the defendant. The bases for personal jurisdiction over a foreign state or foreign state agency are now statutorily specified (see the section "Sovereign Immunity," below). Personal jurisdiction over a nongovernment defendant may generally be founded on one or more of the following bases: the defendant's presence or conduct of business in the forum jurisdiction, the defendant's consent to the personal jurisdiction of the forum court, or the application of a "long-arm" statute (a statute that provides that certain contacts between a transaction or event and the forum jurisdiction will give the forum courts personal jurisdiction over the parties to the transaction or event[2]).

Jurisdiction over a nongovernment defendant to the extent of its assets located in the forum jurisdiction (known as *quasi in rem* jurisdiction) may be obtained by attachment of the defendant's assets located in that jurisdiction. In the case of a foreign borrower, the lender cannot be certain that the borrower will be present or conducting business in the forum jurisdiction or that a long-arm statute will apply to the borrower when a dispute arises. Obtaining jurisdiction by attaching the defendant's assets is effective only if the defendant has assets in the forum jurisdiction; it has the disadvantage that any judgment is enforceable only against those assets, and not against the borrower personally. (Jurisdiction over a sovereign or sovereign entity may not be obtained by attaching its assets—see the section "Sovereign Immunity," below.) Consequently, a consent by the nongovernment borrower to the personal jurisdiction of the courts of the chosen forum should be included in the documentation for the transaction. An example of such a provision is as follows:

> The Borrower hereby irrevocably submits to the nonexclusive jurisdiction *in personam* of any court of the State of X [the forum state] or any Federal court sitting in the State of X in any action or proceeding arising out of or relating to this Agreement.

Occasionally a borrower argues that as a matter of parallel treatment of the parties, the lender should also expressly submit itself to the personal jurisdiction of courts in the borrower's country. The lender should resist this request, because such a submission may have untoward tax or other consequences if the submission results in the lender's being held to be present or doing business in the borrower's country when it would not otherwise be so held.

The consent-to-jurisdiction provision usually also provides for one or more methods for service of legal process on the borrower in the forum jurisdiction, including the appointment of an agent in that jurisdiction to receive process on behalf of the borrower. The submission-to-jurisdiction provision given above might, for instance, continue as follows:

> The Borrower hereby irrevocably appoints A, with offices on the date hereof at (address in State X), and its successors ("Process Agent") as

its agent to receive on its behalf and on behalf of its property service of all legal process that may be served in any such action or proceeding. Such service may be made by mailing or delivering a copy of such process to the Borrower in care of the Process Agent at the Process Agent's address provided herein or such other address as the Process Agent shall designate in writing to the Lender, and the Borrower hereby irrevocably authorizes and directs the Process Agent to accept such service on its behalf. As an alternative method of service, the Borrower also irrevocably consents to the service of any and all legal process in any such action or proceeding by the mailing via certified mail of copies of such process to the Borrower at its address set forth on the signature page hereof or at such other address as shall be designated by the Borrower in writing to the Lender. Nothing herein shall affect the right to service of process in any jurisdiction in any other manner permitted by law.

The agent may be any person or entity, but care should be taken to choose an agent who can properly exercise the responsibility of receiving process and forwarding it to the borrower. Borrowers, particularly governments and government agencies, sometimes request that their consul or a diplomatic officer in the forum jurisdiction be designated as the agent to receive process. This request is often honored, but it should be avoided unless alternative methods of service are also available, because the consul or other officer and the consular premises may be entitled to diplomatic immunity, which would make it possible to avoid proper service of process. If the consul is named as the agent for service of process, the documents should specifically provide for service on the consul by mail, because service by that means may be sufficient (as it is in New York) and the consul cannot effectively avoid service without stopping the delivery of all mail to the consulate. Corporate service organizations accustomed to acting as such agents are located in most major cities in the United States, and provide this service for a relatively small fee (which normally must be paid in full in advance).

In some cases (particularly countries where the Calvo Doctrine exists) the borrower's local law may prohibit it from submitting to the jurisdiction of foreign courts. In such cases the lender may wish to provide for disputes to be settled by arbitration. However, this alternative should be carefully considered with counsel before it is decided that arbitration is preferable to silence on the question of jurisdiction. Arbitrators have a bias toward "splitting the difference" between disputants, which is not a satisfactory outcome for the lender when the problem is an unpaid debt. Also, the arbitrator will not necessarily be bound by rules of evidence that apply to courts, there may be limited rights of appeal from the arbitrator's decision, and enforcement of the arbitral award may not be certain. These problems can be alleviated by the choice of the jurisdiction in which the arbitration will take place (for instance, in England questions of law may be taken to the courts for decision during an arbitration) and by a careful setting out of the rules that the arbitrator is to follow in the arbitration, but it is a complex area and the lender may prefer to be silent as to jurisdiction and take its chances on where and how jurisdiction over the borrower may be obtained when the occasion arises.

SOVEREIGN IMMUNITY

Sovereign immunity is the doctrine under which the courts of one sovereign state forgo the exercise of jurisdiction over another sovereign "as a consequence of the absolute independence of every sovereign authority, and of the international comity which induces every sovereign State to respect the independence and dignity of every other State."[3] The absolute theory of sovereign immunity holds that a sovereign cannot be made to answer in the courts of another sovereign without its consent. This theory was followed by the U.S. Supreme Court as early as 1812[4] and was not expressly disavowed until 1952, when the U.S. Department of State, to whose determinations the courts were accustomed to defer in matters of sovereign immunity, stated in a letter (commonly known as the "Tate Letter") from the acting legal adviser to the attorney general[5] that the department would thereafter follow the restrictive theory of sovereign immunity when presented with requests for the granting of such immunity. The restrictive theory distinguishes between a sovereign's public and sovereign acts and its private and commercial acts, and restricts sovereign immunity to the former.

There is no uniform practice worldwide as to which theory is followed, although the trend is away from the absolute theory and toward the restrictive theory. Governments have become increasingly involved in economic matters that are not within their traditional spheres of administration and management, and the unfairness of denying to private parties conducting business with governments and government entities the use of courts to settle disputes with the government parties has been increasingly recognized. The restrictive theory has relatively recently been adopted by statute in both the United States and the United Kingdom.[6]

The U.S. Foreign Sovereign Immunities Act of 1976[7] (FSIA), which took effect on January 19, 1977, gives to state and federal courts in the United States exclusive jurisdiction to decide whether sovereign immunity is available in any given case brought before them. The FSIA basically codified the existing law on the application of sovereign immunity, and it eliminated the uncertainties that had previously existed when requests for sovereign immunity were made to the State Department (which was subject to political and diplomatic considerations in deciding whether to grant the requests, and unsuited to making any necessary findings of fact) and the courts deferred to the State Department's decisions (or made their own decisions if no request for immunity had been made to the State Department). The FSIA does not change the substantive law of liability that applies in any case,[8] questions of diplomatic or consular immunity, or the division of responsibility among the various entities of a foreign state; it only provides the standards upon which the availability of sovereign immunity is to be decided by state and federal courts in the United States and the means by which process may be served on a nonimmune sovereign to bring it before the courts. It should also be noted that the provisions of any applicable international treaty to which the United States is a party take precedence over the FSIA in case of any conflict between them.

The FSIA distinguishes between immunity from jurisdiction and immunity from attachment, arrest, and execution, providing somewhat different rules in the two cases (and even more restrictive rules in the case of attachment before judgment than in the case of postjudgment attachment). This is a distinction that has long existed in jurisdictions following the restrictive theory of sovereign immunity, because it is generally recognized that taking a foreign sovereign's property in the forum state in execution of a judgment is even more likely to be met with diplomatic protests and outrage than is the rendering of the judgment in the first place.

While state courts continue to have whatever subject matter jurisdiction their particular state laws give them over cases involving sovereigns, the FSIA now expressly gives U.S. district courts subject matter jurisdiction over any nonjury civil action against a foreign state (in the FSIA and in this section the term "foreign state" embraces a political subdivision, agency, or instrumentality of a foreign state, including a corporation owned by the government, unless otherwise noted) when that foreign state is not entitled to immunity from jurisdiction under the FSIA or any applicable international agreement. The federal district courts are also given jurisdiction over all civil actions involving $10,000 or more between citizens of U.S. state and citizens or subjects of a foreign state or between a foreign state as plaintiff and citizens of one or more U.S. states.[9] Suits begun by plaintiffs in state courts may be removed by the foreign state defendant to a federal district court.[10]

If the action against a foreign state is brought in federal court, the proper judicial district in which to bring the action is any such district agreed upon by the parties or that has one or more of the enumerated contacts with the dispute (essentially, a substantial part of the events giving rise to the asserted claim occurred there, property that is the subject of the action is located there, or the agency or instrumentality of a foreign state being sued is licensed to do or is doing business there). If the action is brought against a foreign state or political subdivision thereof (but not an agency or instrumentality), the U.S. district court for the District of Columbia is a proper forum, regardless of contacts with the cause of action.[11]

The FSIA begins with the presumption that a foreign state is immune from the personal jurisdiction of federal and state courts unless one of the statutory exceptions to immunity provided in the FSIA exists.[12] The exceptions of most importance to lenders are the following:

1. The foreign state waived its immunity expressly or implicitly (and a waiver may not be withdrawn except in accordance with its own terms).
2. The suit is based upon a commercial activity of the foreign state carried on in the United States, an act performed in the United States in connection with the foreign state's commercial activity elsewhere, or an act outside of the United States in connection with commercial activity of the foreign state outside of the United States, which act has a direct effect in the United States.
3. The action is a suit in admiralty to enforce a maritime lien against the foreign state's vessel or cargo, the lien is based upon the foreign state's commercial activity, and notice of the suit is given as provided in the statute.[13]

Other exceptions relate to expropriations, U.S. property acquired by inheritance or gift, U.S. real property, certain torts, and counter-claims with respect to which the foreign state would not be immune were the claim brought in a separate action and certain other counter-claims.[14]

In prescribing how service of process may be made, the statute distinguishes between foreign states and their political subdivisions, and agencies and instrumentalities of foreign states. An "agency or instrumentality of a foreign state" is defined as any entity that is a separate legal person; an organ of a foreign state or a political sub-division of a foreign state, or an organ of which the majority is owned by the foreign state or political subdivision; or a corporation not incorporated in or having its principal place of business in any state of the United States, any of its territories, the District of Columbia or Puerto Rico, nor created under the laws of any third country. Service of process upon a foreign state or a political sub-division of a foreign state may be made by any of four methods:

1. By any means agreed upon between the plaintiff and the foreign state or political subdivision
2. If no such agreement exists, in accordance with an applicable international convention[15]

3. If service cannot be made by method 1 or 2, by having the court clerk send the process and a notice of suit (in a form prescribed by the U.S. secretary of state), together with translations of those documents into the foreign state's official language, to the head of the ministry of foreign affairs of the foreign state by mail requiring a signed receipt
4. If service cannot be made by any of the foregoing means, by sending the process, notice of suit, and translations to the U.S. secretary of state for transmittal to the foreign state through diplomatic chan-nels.[16]

Service of process upon an agency or instrumentality of a foreign state may be made by any of three means:

1. In accordance with any arrangements agreed upon between the plaintiff and the agency or instrumentality
2. If no such arrangements exist, by delivery of the process to an officer, a managing or general agent, or any other authorized agent, or in accordance with an applicable international convention

3. By a means reasonably calculated to give actual notice of the suit and as directed by an authority of the foreign state, or by mail requiring a signed receipt, or as directed by the court.[17]

Attachment of sovereign property as a means of obtaining *quasi in rem* jurisdiction is not permitted by the FSIA.

In the area of the immunity from attachment, arrest, and execution that is to be accorded property of a foreign state, the statute also begins with the presumption that a foreign state's property is immune from any attachment, arrest, or execution,[18] and then provides exceptions to the presumption. The exceptions most pertinent to a lender are that U.S. property of a foreign state used for a commercial activity in the United States is not immune from attachment in aid of execution or from execution upon a judgment if:

1. The foreign state waived its immunity expressly or implicitly (again, no withdrawal of a waiver is permitted except in accordance with the waiver's own terms)
2. The property is or was used for the commercial activity on which the claim is based.

Other exceptions with respect to property used for a commercial activity in the United States involve expropriation, inherited property or property received by gift, real property located in the United States, and insurance covering tort liability.[19] In addition, U.S. property of an agency or instrumentality of a foreign state engaged in commercial activity in the United States is not immune from attachment in aid of execution or from execution on a judgment if the agency or instrumentality has waived such immunity, or if the judgment relates to certain of the types of claims from which the agency or instrumentality is not immune (that is, arising out of commercial activities having a connection with the United States, expropriation, torts, or maritime liens), regardless of whether the property is or is not used in the activity upon which the claim is based.[20] The court must in all cases allow a reasonable time for the defendant to satisfy any judgment before a permitted attachment or execution is carried out, except that an attachment may be made prior to the lapse of that time in order to assure the availability of assets upon which to execute the judgment if the defendant foreign state has expressly waived its immunity from attachment prior to judgment.[21]

Express and specific waivers of immunity are necessary to create two other exceptions to the general rule of immunity from attachment, arrest, and execution. First, the property of a foreign state used for a commercial activity in the United States may be attached prior to judgment if the foreign state has expressly waived its immunity from attachment prior to judgment, and if the purpose of the attachment is to assure the availability of assets to satisfy the judgment that may be entered against the foreign state—and not to obtain jurisdiction over it.[22] Second, the property of a foreign central bank or monetary authority held for its own account is immune from attachment in aid of execution and from execution in the absence of an express waiver of such immunity by the bank or authority of its parent government.[23] Military property of a foreign state is always immune from attachment and execution.[24]

Under the International Organization Immunities Act,[25] international organizations in which the United States participates and which are designated by presidential executive order are entitled to the same immunity from suit and judicial process that is granted to foreign governments unless they expressly waive such immunity. The status under the FSIA of international organizations that do not come within the coverage of the International Organization Immunities Act and of foreign regimes that are not officially recognized by the United States (Taiwan, for example) is unclear.

"Commercial activity" is defined by the FSIA as either a regular course of commercial conduct or a particular commercial transaction or act. The courts are directed to determine whether an activity or transaction is commercial by looking at its nature rather than at its purpose. The existing case law has not developed a clear line of distinction between commercial and noncommercial activities.[26] Given this lack of clarity, it is advisable to include in the documentation a representation by the borrower that the particular transaction is a commercial transaction; this may at least prevent the borrower from claiming otherwise in court.

Lenders' concern with limiting borrowers' possible claims to sovereign immunity has given rise to sophisticated waivers of immunity in the documentation of international transactions with sovereigns or sovereign entities. Such a waiver might read as follows:

To the extent that the Borrower or any of its property has or hereafter becomes entitled to any immunity, whether on the grounds of sovereignty or otherwise, from the jurisdiction of any court, from any legal process (whether through service or notice), from attachment prior to the entry of judgment, from attachment in aid of execution, from arrest or from execution upon a judgment in any jurisdiction, the Borrower hereby irrevocably waives such immunity for itself and its property (including property held for its own account) in respect of its obligations under this Agreement to the fullest extent permitted by applicable laws in any jurisdiction where any action or proceeding arising out of or relating to this Agreement may be brought.

The waiver should expressly cover both immunity from jurisdiction and immunity from attachment in aid of execution, and execution, because an express waiver of one may not be an implicit waiver of the other and, in the case of central bank assets, only an express waiver is effective; it also should expressly waive immunity from attachment prior to judgment, because implicit waivers of that immunity are ineffective. A lender should be certain that the person or entity signing the waiver has the necessary authority to bind all government entities and/or the government that the lender wishes to have bound by the waiver. It should be remembered, in any case, that if a borrower does not have assets in the forum jurisdiction or a third country in which the lender's judgment can be enforced, the borrower may be able to avoid paying the lender, irrespective of any sovereign immunity, if the lender cannot obtain and enforce a judgment against the borrower in the latter's own country.

ENFORCEMENT OF JUDGMENTS

A consideration related to the lender's choice of the law to govern a particular transaction and the forum in which disputes are to be settled is the question of the enforceability in the jurisdiction(s) where the borrower and its assets are located of a judgment rendered in the chosen forum under the chosen law. If a jurisdiction in which the lender wants to enforce its judgment will not recognize a judgment rendered by a foreign court or under a foreign law, the lender will gain nothing by providing that suits should be tried in the foreign court and/or under the foreign law.

The question of the enforceability of foreign judgments in the local courts should always be taken up with the lender's local counsel. Some countries are simply not receptive to foreign judgments; others will enforce a foreign judgment unless it violates principles applied by the local courts to foreign judgments. Factors often considered by courts in jurisdictions where "proper" foreign judgments will be enforced include the finality of the foreign judgment (whether all possible appeals have been taken or the time to appeal has expired); whether notice of the suit to the defendant borrower was given in a manner considered sufficient under local law, so that the foreign court had proper personal jurisdiction over the borrower;[27] whether the underlying obligation was valid under local law; whether the choice of law applied to the transaction in question by the foreign court was appropriate; whether the judgment in any way violates local or international law (including the local concepts of due process and fairness) or is contrary to local public policy; and reciprocity of enforcement in the courts that granted the judgment of judgments rendered by the local courts. The enforcement of foreign judgments may also be the subject of international treaties, and counsel should consider whether any treaty is applicable to a particular case (the United States is not a party to any such treaty except with respect to the enforcement of arbitral awards). Local courts will rarely enforce a foreign judgment against local real property (such as a foreclosure), because real property is considered to be by its very nature subject to the dominion of local authority exclusively.

In the United States the recognition and enforcement of foreign judgments are largely a matter of common law rather than of statutes; only ten states have adopted the Uniform Foreign Money-Judgments Recognition Act (which was intended by its authors only to codify the existing common law), and no statutes dealing with the subject have been adopted on the federal level. The common law decisions look to factors such as those given in the preceding paragraph in determining whether a specific foreign judgment should be enforced.

In civil law countries a foreign judgment is enforced by *exequatur*, which is a writ making the foreign judgment executory in the local jurisdiction. The exequatur proceeding is an adversary proceeding in which the plaintiff-judgment holder must present proof of the foreign judgment and the court may consider matters such as those listed in the second paragraph of this section. If the court refuses to issue the writ, the plaintiff may then bring an action de novo in the local courts.

An ancillary issue in the enforcement of judgments is the currency in which the judgment will be given, because any variation from the currency in which the credit transaction is denominated creates an exchange risk for the lender. In federal courts, judgments must be expressed in U.S. dollars,[28] and that is also the general rule in state courts. The rate of exchange used to calculate the dollar equivalent of damages ascertained in a foreign currency may be the rate of exchange in effect on the date of default or on the date of judgment, depending on the court and the facts of the particular case. In some countries a judgment may be given in a foreign currency; enforcement of the judgment within the country, however, may be legally required or permitted in the local currency. This raises the question of the exchange rate to be used in determining how much local currency is required to satisfy the foreign currency judgment.

To reduce these exchange risks, the documentation for an international lending transaction should include a provision to the effect that recoveries by the lender, whether pursuant to a judgment or otherwise, will discharge the debt only to the extent that the lender receives payment in the currency in which the debt is denominated. The following is a typical provision:

> If for the purpose of obtaining or enforcing judgment in any court it is necessary to convert a sum due hereunder in United States dollars into another currency (the "Second Currency"), the rate of exchange that shall be applied shall be that at which, in accordance with its normal banking procedures, the Lender could purchase United States dollars with the Secondary Currency on the business day preceding that on which final judgment is given. If payment of any sum due hereunder is made to or received by the Lender, whether by judgment (and notwithstanding the rate of exchange actually applied in giving such judgment) or otherwise, in a Second Currency, the obligations of the Borrower hereunder shall be discharged only in the net amount of United States dollars that the Lender in accordance with its normal bank procedures is able lawfully to purchase with such amount of Second Currency. If the Lender is not able to purchase sufficient United States dollars with such amount of Second Currency to discharge the United States dollar obligations to the Lender, the Borrower's obligations to the Lender shall not be discharged to the extent of such difference, and any such undischarged amount will be due as a separate debt and shall not be affected by payment of or judgment being obtained for any other sums due under or in respect of this Agreement. If the Lender is able to purchase an amount in United States dollars in excess of the amount

necessary to discharge such United States dollar obligations, the Lender shall promptly remit such excess to the Borrower.

Such provisions are generally untested in courts at this time, and one cannot be certain that they will be entirely effective to protect the lender from exchange risks, especially if a court thinks the lender is taking unfair advantage of the borrower in applying the provision to a particular situation.

TAXES

The lender in an international financing should investigate with its counsel and local counsel, as early as possible, whether taxing authorities in the borrower's country will withhold taxes from payments to lender of interest, fees, commissions, and other amounts. Any withholding that cannot be recouped promptly or otherwise compensated for by the lender will reduce the lender's return, and the lender must decide whether it will bear all or part of that cost, or pass it on to the borrower.

If withholding taxes exist, tax treaties between the borrower's country and the lender's country may reduce the rates of withholding. Such rate reductions may, however, require the submission by the lender of a withholding exemption certificate to the taxing authorities in the borrower's country. In such event lender's counsel should consider the representations required of the lender in such a certificate.

If the lender does not intend to bear the cost of withholding taxes and there is no tax treaty in effect that eliminates the withholding, then the preferred solution is to require the borrower to "gross up" for the withheld taxes—that is, the borrower is required to pay an additional amount to the lender such that after the taxes on the total amount are withheld from that amount, the lender will receive the net amount it would have received had there been no withholding. The additional amount may be identified as just that, or it may be described as an increase in the interest rate. Local counsel should consider whether the additional payment will count as additional interest for the purposes of local usury laws, exchange control rules, and so on.

If the borrower pays withholding taxes without deducting the amount of such taxes from interest owed to the lender, the tax payments made on the lender's behalf may be considered additional income to the lender. That additional income may be subject to further withholding in the borrower's country, resulting in a pyramiding of taxes payable by the borrower on behalf of the lender and substantially increasing the cost of the borrowing. The "gross up" payments may also constitute additional income to the lender in its own country. In order to offset that additional taxable income, a U.S. lender will want to claim a credit against its U.S. income taxes for the foreign tax paid. To do so, the withheld tax must be a kind that is creditable against U.S. income taxes and the lender must be able to provide proof satisfactory to the Internal Revenue Service of payment of the foreign taxes. Local counsel can advise the lender on what kinds of documentary evidence of payment are obtainable from the tax authorities.

An experienced borrower that agrees to a gross-up provision, thus increasing the cost of the financing to it, will often seek in return the lender's agreement to share any tax benefits derived by the lender from payment of the foreign taxes. These benefits are subject to limitations based on the amount of the lender's income, the percentage of its income that comes from foreign sources, and the effects of other credits, loss carry-forwards, and loss carry-backs; consequently the amount of benefit attributable to any single foreign tax credit is often difficult, if not impossible, to calculate. Also, if a lender has more foreign tax credits than it can utilize, it faces the potential problem of having agreed to share more benefits than it actually receives. Accordingly, many lenders resist any such sharing of benefits; agree to sharing, if they must, only on a fixed percentage or other formula basis; and require the borrower to return any shared benefits if the claimed benefits do not materialize.

Some countries do not permit lenders to impose payment of local taxes on the borrower by grossing up for the withholding. In such cases the lender may be able to reprice the credit and absorb the taxes (so long as the increased price does not then violate usury laws or other laws or regulations affecting the credit). If the lender does agree to absorb the local taxes, that decision is based on the current rate of taxation, and any increase in the rate will affect the lender adversely; the lender should consider whether it wants to provide for prepayment of or renegotiation of the terms of the credit if the local taxes are increased. In some cases it may also be possible to avoid incurring local taxes by proper structuring of the credit—for instance, if the borrower's country offers, as an incentive to development, an exemption from taxation for loans used for particular purposes, it may be possible to restrict use of the loan proceeds to those purposes.

Many jurisdictions also impose stamp, registration, or other taxes on documents related to credit transactions; it is generally accepted that borrowers pay these taxes. It is best to require payment of these taxes at the beginning of a transaction even though the tax may not be incurred until a later date (as in the case of a stamp tax that is payable only if and when the document is brought into the jurisdiction imposing the tax). If the tax has not been paid by the time the borrower defaults, the lender may expect to pay the tax itself for obvious reasons, particularly if payment of the tax is the first step in commencing a lawsuit against the borrower.

LENDING LIMITS

Banks in the United States and in some other countries are subject to lending limits (usually statutory or regulatory) intended to prevent overexposure to the credit risk of any one borrower. These limits are generally written in terms of a fixed percentage of a bank's capital funds. The specifications of the limits (the applicable percentage[s], what "capital funds" includes, what constitutes a single borrower, what constitutes a loan or extension of credit subject to the limits, and the exceptions to the general rules) vary from jurisdiction to jurisdiction. In the United States the most widely used general rule limits loans to any one borrower to an amount not exceeding 10 percent of the bank's capital funds; exceptions to the general rule usually relate to the collateral securing the loan or the governmental nature of the borrower.

In international lending banks must frequently determine whether loans to a government entity are required to be aggregated with loans to the government itself for lending limit purposes. The question often arises when dealing with socialist and mixed economies, where the government owns otherwise apparently separate entities. The U.S. comptroller of the currency promulgated a regulation[29] applicable to national banks setting forth two tests to be used in determining whether loans to a government agency or instrumentality should be aggregated with loans to its parent government: the "means" test—

whether the borrower has resources or revenues of its own sufficient over time to service its debt obligations—and the "purpose" test— whether the loan is obtained for a purpose consistent with the borrower's general business. If the borrower fails to meet either test at the time a loan is made to it, then the loan is counted against the lending limit applicable to the parent government. Edge Act corporations are required to aggregate with loans to a foreign government all loans to its departments or agencies that derive their current funds principally from general tax revenues.[30] The rules governing state banks vary from state to state, and appropriate counsel should be consulted by a state bank lender to ascertain the aggregation rules applicable under its state law.

A second question of aggregation arises with respect to loans to corporations and their subsidiaries; here again the rules vary among the regulatory authorities, and appropriate counsel should be consulted. By way of example, the comptroller of the currency requires national banks to aggregate loans to a corporation with loans to all subsidiaries in which it owns or controls a majority interest; but if the parent corporation is not borrowing, loans to the several subsidiaries need not be combined except in certain specified situations.[31] New York State, on the other hand, does not require New York state banks to combine loans to a subsidiary corporation with loans to its parent corporation unless the loan to the subsidiary is made for the benefit of the parent.[32]

Counsel should also be consulted to learn whether a particular credit transaction will count against lending limits, because the treatment of such transactions as leases of personal property, letters of credit, and contingent obligations (including standby letters of credit) varies from jurisdiction to jurisdiction.

USE OF LOCAL COUNSEL

The use of local counsel for the lender in the borrower's country is extremely important in international transactions. The advice of local counsel regarding the local legal system applicable to the borrower and the transaction is vital in structuring and documenting the transaction so that it is enforceable in the borrower's jurisdiction as well as in other jurisdictions chosen by the lender. Local counsel can be of invaluable assistance in structuring the transaction and documentation to take advantage of, or reduce the disadvantages of, the borrower's legal system as it affects the transaction; for instance, it may be possible to use promissory notes that meet the local requirements for being enforced in executory proceedings, which may be speedier than the normal court procedures necessary if the notes do not meet those requirements. Local counsel also help by being present to handle in person matters such as discussions with any government authorities whose approval of the transaction is required.

In addition to advising the lender and its counsel with respect to topics previously discussed in this chapter, local counsel's advice may cover such matters as whether there are any preferences or priorities for one class of creditors over another (such as local lenders over foreign lenders, lenders whose documents have been notarized or otherwise formalized over lenders with unformalized documents), the existence of requirements as to approval by or registration of the transaction with regulatory authorities, whether further approvals are needed if the transaction is altered after it is entered into, and whether the lender itself must register or be licensed in the borrower's country in order to make or enforce the loan to the borrower. Local counsel are also essential in the jurisdictions where any assets being taken as collateral security are located. Since the lender's rights in such collateral would almost invariably have to be enforced in the local courts and under local law, the liens in favor of the lender should be created, documented, and perfected in such a way that they will be readily enforced in the local courts. Local counsel are the best persons to achieve the desired result expeditiously and effectively.

Local counsel should also be requested to render an opinion to the lender covering the transaction, which can be more or less extensive, depending on the nature of the transaction and the extent to which the lender and its counsel are prepared to rely on the borrower's counsel.[33] It should cover at least the existence of the borrower; its ability to enter into and carry out the transaction; the legality, validity, and enforceability of the documentation; the existence of all government authorizations and approvals necessary for the borrower to enter into and carry out the transaction; the fact that the transaction will not violate local laws and regulations; the binding effect of the choice of governing law specified in the documents; the borrower's submission to the jurisdiction of the chosen forum for litigation and any waiver of immunity; and whether the documentation is in proper form for enforcement in the borrower's country. The opinion will, of course, be rendered under local law, and local counsel should not be expected to opine with respect to the law of any jurisdiction where they are not qualified to practice law.

NOTES

1. For example, in U.S. federal courts the citizen of one state may sue an alien, but if another alien is joined as a plaintiff with the state citizen, then the complete diversity of citizenship required for the diversity jurisdiction of the federal courts is destroyed and, if there is no other basis for subject matter jurisdiction (for instance, a question of federal law or a specific statutory grant of jurisdiction), those courts may not adjudicate the suit even though all parties have submitted themselves to the personal jurisdiction of the court. This aspect of federal court diversity jurisdiction should be kept in mind in syndicated loans where one or more of the lenders, as well as the borrower, are foreign. (If one of the plaintiffs is a national bank or the defendant is a foreign state or foreign state entity, that fact may provide a basis for federal court jurisdiction even when there are aliens on both sides of the case. But see note 9.)

2. The types of contacts required vary from statute to statute, but generally include such matters relevant in the context of lending transactions as the making of an in-forum visit by the defendant (or its agent) during which business is carried on, or the breach of an agreement in the forum by failing to perform acts required by the agreement to be performed in the forum.

3. *Parlement belge*, 5 P.D. 197 at 214 (1880).

4. *The Schooner Exchange* v. *McFaddon*, 11 U.S. (7 Cranch) 116 (1812).

5. *Department of State Bulletin* 26 (1952): 984.

6. The United Kingdom statute is the State Immunity Act of 1978.

7. Public Law 94-583, 90 Stat. 2891, *codified* at 28 U.S.C. 1330, 1332(a) (2), (4), 1391(f), 1441(d), and 1602-11 (1976).

8. It appears that the Act of State Doctrine continues to be alive and well even after the codification of the restrictive theory of sovereign immunity, although four Supreme Court justices thought in a 1976 case that it should not be extended to acts committed in purely commercial operations (*Alfred Dunhill of London, Inc.* v. *Republic of Cuba*, 425 U.S. 682). That doctrine holds that courts in the United States may not inquire into the validity of the public acts of a recognized sovereign done within its own territory. While sovereign immunity can be raised as an issue only by a sovereign or sovereign entity, the Act of State Doctrine may be used by any litigant.

9. 28 U.S.C. 1330(a), (b), 1332(a)(2), (4) (1976). A Second Circuit Court of Appeals case, *Verlinden B.V.* v. *Central Bank of Nigeria*, 647 F.2d 320 (1981), held that the federal courts do not have subject matter jurisdiction under section

1330 over cases involving only aliens on both sides. The U.S. Supreme Court granted certiorari, agreeing to review the Second Circuit's decision.

10. 28 U.S.C. 1441(d) (1976).

11. 28 U.S.C. 1391(f) (1976).

12. 28 U.S.C. 1604 (1976).

13. 28 U.S.C. 1605(a) (1), (2), (b) (1976).

14. 28 U.S.C. 1605(a) (3), (4), and (5); 1607 (1976).

15. The only such convention to which the United States is currently a party is the Hague Convention on Service Abroad of Judicial and Extrajudicial Documents, 20 U.S.T. 361.

16. 28 U.S.C. 1608(a) (1976).

17. 28 U.S.C. 1608(b) (1976).

18. 28 U.S.C. 1609 (1976).

19. 28 U.S.C. 1610(a) (1976).

20. 28 U.S.C. 1610(b) (1976).

21. 28 U.S.C. 1610(c), (d) (1976).

22. 28 U.S.C. 1610(d) (1976).

23. 28 U.S.C. 1611(b) (1) (1976).

24. 28 U.S.C. 1611(b) (2) (1976).

25. 22 U.S.C.A. 288–288f-1 (West 1979); 22 U.S.C.A. 288f-2 (West Supp. 1981).

26. In contrast with the FSIA, which provides no definition of commercial transaction (other than to refer to its "nature") and requires a connection with the United States, the United Kingdom's State Immunity Act (1978) takes the opposite course, requiring no connection with the United Kingdom but defining "commercial transaction" as a contract for the supply of goods or services, a loan or other transaction for financing and any guarantee or indemnity with respect to the same, and any other transaction or activity other than in the exercise of sovereign authority.

27. For instance, the parties may agree contractually that service may be made personally on an agent in the U.S. jurisdiction where any suit is to be tried, and by mail to the defendant-borrower. That service would usually be sufficient in the U.S. jurisdiction, but might not be sufficient in the borrower's local courts if their rules require actual service personally on the defendant.

28. 31 U.S.C. 371 (1976).

29. 12 C.F.R. 7.1330 (1981).

30. 12 C.F.R. 211.6(b) (2) (1981).

31. 12 C.F.R. 7.1310 (1981).

32. N.Y. Banking Law 103(e) (McKinney 1971).

33. The lender, having had the option of selecting its local counsel, will (one hopes) have chosen counsel who understand the problems involved in an international credit transaction and who can assist in pointing out problems under the local law and possible solutions; the borrower's counsel, who will probably not have been retained with the particular transaction in mind, may not be similarly experienced in the area.

SUGGESTED REFERENCES

Corse, C. Thorne. "International Term Loan Agreements and Loan Syndications." 60 *The Journal of Commercial Bank Lending* 12 (March 1978).

Delaume, G. R. "Jurisdiction of Courts and International Loans." 6 *American Journal of Comparative Law* 189 (1957).

Dellapenna, Joseph W. "Suing Foreign Governments and Their Corporations: Sovereign Immunity." 85 *Commercial Law Journal* 167, 228, 298, 364, 497 (May, June/July, August/September, October, November 1980).

Donaldson, T. H. *International Lending by Commercial Banks*. New York: John Wiley and Sons, 1979.

Mathis, F. John, ed. *Offshore Lending by U.S. Commercial Banks*. 2nd ed. Washington, D.C. and Philadelphia: Bankers' Association for Foreign Trade and Robert Morris Associates, 1981.

Reodell, Robert S., ed. *International Financial Law*. London: Euromoney Publications, 1980.

Steiner, Henry J., and Detlev F. Vagts. *Transnational Legal Problems*. 2nd ed. Mineola, N.Y.: The Foundation Press, 1976.

von Mehren, Robert B. "The Foreign Sovereign Immunities Act of 1976." 17 *Columbia Journal of Transnational Law* 33 (1978).

8 INTERNATIONAL LENDING POLICIES AND PRACTICES

Douglas A. Hayes and
Philip G. Moon

Most objectives of lending policies and practices in the international area are identical to those associated with commercial lending in the domestic market. They include the following:

- Provide loan commitments to regular customers in amounts legitimately required to finance their short-term and intermediate-term needs
- Establish an information system to obtain adequate data for appraising credit and other possible risks on prospective and active borrowers
- Provide credit on terms that control risk exposures at reasonable levels but do not unreasonably constrain operations and financial capabilities of customers
- Offer loan pricing options that are reasonably competitive but also result in adequate levels of profitability
- Establish a set of policy constraints to obtain adequate risk control and diversification of the loan portfolio; these constraints may be set both on maximum amounts of individual credit exposure and on certain definable types of credit exposure (industry or country limits).

However, international lending activities frequently include a dimension that more closely resembles impersonal investments in financial markets rather than personalized customer loans. These may include discretionary interest arbitrage (defined as the purchase of funds in one market or maturity sector and their concurrent sale in another market or maturity sector). The Eurocurrency markets, which are structured to accommodate large unit transactions on a continuous basis, represent a major source for the implementation of these operations on the asset or liability side, or both.

In addition, the large size of many international credits has led to the syndicated loan format. Except for the syndicate managers, the criteria for a decision to purchase a participation in a syndicated loan are essentially similar to those used to purchase a government or municipal bond: the yield, credit quality, maturities, and other terms are evaluated relative to alternatives available in the financial markets. Then the purchase is made or rejected strictly on whether the yield is adequate, given the evaluated risk. For reasons considered below, the decision to participate in a syndicated loan may sometimes include other considerations, but these cases represent exceptions rather than the general rule.

Finally, most banks actually engaged in extensive international lending activities find it convenient to become dealers in the interbank markets for the several leading Eurocurrencies. This means they maintain continuous offers to buy or sell time deposits in these currencies at prevailing market rates. As a consequence these banks are able to obtain considerable amounts of funds in the Eurocurrency markets to meet funding requirements on their loan commitments, usually at slightly more favorable rates than nondealer banks. Strictly viewed, placements with other banks to implement the dealer operation can be considered a part of the loan portfolio, and they are so reported in the macro statistics on foreign loans of U.S. banks. However, it is essentially a trading activity subject to specific constraints, and not lending in the usual sense of the word.

Policies and practices with respect to investment-type loans logically should be differentiated from those applicable to credits extended to customers, because the criteria for the one may be quite different from those applied to the other. The primary focus of this chapter will be on the customer sector of the international portfolio, but brief consideration of the "investment" sector will be included.

PROFILE OF INTERNATIONAL PORTFOLIOS

The data in Table 8.1 provide a rough profile of the international loan portfolios of major U.S. banks. The following comments on

TABLE 8.1. Cross-Border and Nonlocal Currency Claims of 153 U.S. Banking Organizations as of December 31, 1980 (millions of dollars)

		Claims on			Maturity Distribution		
	Total Claims	Banks	Government Units	Other Private	1 Yr. or Less	1 to 5 Yrs.	Over 5 Yrs.
Developed countries	$141,111.4	$ 91,321.3	$12,594.5	$37,193.4	$111,122.8	$21,039.6	$ 8,948.8
Eastern Europe	7,938.9	4,047.8	2,960.9	932.1	3,538.6	3,394.5	1,005.8
Oil Exporting Countries	21,381.3	5,426.5	8,308.3	7,646.4	14,188.4	5,693.0	1,501.9
Latin America and Caribbean	50,068.7	16,065.3	14,915.7	19,088.6	28,467.7	15,163.2	6,437.7
Asia	21,472.0	9,437.2	5,265.1	6,769.6	15,517.4	4,239.9	1,713.6
Africa	3,875.6	894.4	2,357.5	623.6	2,375.0	1,153.8	346.6
Offshore Banking Centers	40,476.0	31,319.4	938.3	8,218.2	35,425.4	3,258.8	1,792.7
Total	$286,324.3	$158,512.2	$47,340.7	$80,472.3	$210,635.6	$53,943.1	$21,747.5
Percent of Total		55.4	16.5	28.1	73.6	18.8	7.6

Note: Individual items do not necessarily add up to totals.
Source: Federal Financial Institutions Examinations Council, *Statistical Release*, Federal Reserve System, no. E 16 (126) (May 28, 1981).

these data might be appropriate to suggest the nature of the port-folio mix. First, about 55 percent of the total represents claims against foreign banks; as indicated above, a large proportion of this amount represents dealer operations in Eurocurrencies and not loans in the usual sense. But at the same time it is undoubtedly true that interbank lending is more important in international lending activities than in the domestic area.

Second, commitments to government units are of considerable importance in the international sector; indeed, such commitments tend to dominate in the so-called less-developed countries. For exam-ple, in Africa loans to governments represent 61 percent of the total. In many of these countries, loans to the private sector are of nominal proportions, either because private business is on a small scale or be-cause the economies operate under a socialist structure. As a conse-quence, credit policies must include a format to appriase political trends and external debt capacities of countries as a whole. These appraisals may result in the selective elimination of all commitments in some areas because of the difficulties associated with country risk evaluations.

Third, loans to the private sector are of dominant importance in the developed countries (located principally in Europe, but also in-cluding most of the British Commonwealth countries and Japan). It should be noted, however, that commitments made to foreign sub-sidiaries of U.S. companies are included here, and parent company guarantees are sometimes obtained to support these commitments. In many of these cases, therefore, the loans can essentially be construed as domestic credits in which the proceeds are allocated for use abroad. On the other hand, the data do not include loans made in the United States to subsidiaries of foreign countries, which in spirit can be construed as international loans whose proceeds are designated for use in the United States.

Finally, the data in Table 8.1 suggest that short-term credits heavily dominate international portfolios. However, because the data include short-term interbank placements, the proportion of conven-tional loans that extend beyond a year really is considerably larger. Therefore, maturity and amortization policies on term loans are of considerable significance in the international sector.

INTERNATIONAL LENDING POLICIES: SUMMARY OF ISSUES

The above summary review of the scope of international lending activities and the profile of international portfolios suggests that the following policy considerations are of major significance in the structuring and monitoring of an international loan portfolio:

1. The determination of the major categories of loans that will be considered or emphasized among the following alternatives:
   a. Foreign subsidiaries of U.S. companies
   b. Foreign customers overseas, and possibly their U.S. subsidiaries
   c. Direct loans to foreign governments or agencies thereof
   d. Participation in syndicated loans
2. The establishment of an approved list of foreign banks eligible for loans and deposit placements, and determining individual credit exposure limits
3. The establishment of policies to obtain adequate risk control of the portfolio in terms of criteria considered to be significant
4. The determination of maturity and amortization policies on term loans made to various categories of borrowers
5. The setting of policy guidelines for requiring guarantees of parent companies on subsidiary loans and for government or bank guarantees on loans to companies domiciled in foreign countries
6. The determination of policy guidelines for the conditions under which specific asset collateral should be required
7. The determination of pricing and funding policies on various categories of loans, which would include alternative pricing options to be offered borrowers; yield spread targets for both non-syndicated and syndicated loans; and policies with respect to the degree of interest rate risk that can be tolerated consequent to a mismatch of rate maturities on assets related to liabilities
8. The degree of loan authority to be granted to officers overseas and in the home office; policies here must compromise the desire to centralize major lending decisions, in order to achieve maximum control over the portfolio structure, with the competitive need to permit decentralized decisions, in order to achieve maximum flexibility and customer satisfaction.

PORTFOLIO PROFILE: LOAN CATEGORIES

There is a wide variation between banks in the degree to which they participate in the international credit markets.[1] At one extreme the participation may be limited almost entirely to the financing of foreign trade under the letter of credit and acceptance mechanism, supplemented on occasion by a line of credit or loan to a correspondent bank or the purchase of a small piece of a syndicated loan. At the other extreme a few money center banks have extensive networks of branches, subsidiaries, and affiliates, and as a consequence are able to provide banking services of all types on a worldwide basis. In the first case there is no need for a unique set of policies applied to international loans as such, and in the second case it becomes very difficult to differentiate international from domestic policies.[2] In between these extremes are a number of large regional banks that have one or more branches overseas and actively engage in international banking, including lending to a variety of customers.

In order to obtain some indication of the possible range of lending policies covering this heterogeneous universe, we sent a detailed questionnaire covering the major policy issues outlined above to a selected set of banks. A few money center banks and a few that had very limited operations were included, but most were large regional banks that had a significant international portfolio that could be readily differentiated from the domestic portfolio.

Table 8.2 shows the relative importance of various categories of loans in the respondent banks that were able to provide the requested data. In the nonsyndicated category it is clear that loans to foreign banks and governments (or their agencies) are of major importance, whereas such loans are usually of nominal significance in domestic commercial lending. Indeed, all respondents had extended various forms of credit accommodation to foreign banks; a majority had fairly substantial direct commitments to government units, and for a few these were more than 25 percent of the total portfolio.

Direct loans to subsidiaries of U.S. companies or to foreign corporations were of high or moderate importance in slightly over half of the respondents' portfolios. It may well be that funds advanced to banks or government units are then advanced to foreign corporations, and of course the data excluded acceptance financing in connection with foreign trade transactions. It is also notable that loans to foreign company subsidiaries operating in the United States are of

TABLE 8.2. Relative Importance of Participation in International
Loan Categories, by Type of Borrower
(number of respondent banks)

	Relative Importance			
	High	Moderate	Low	None
Nonsyndicated (direct) loans				
Domestic customers, foreign subsidiaries	5	4	6	2
Foreign banks (excluding deposit placements)	10	7	–	–
Foreign corporations				
In country of domicile	6	6	3	2
In U.S.	–	7	4	6
Foreign governments and agencies	4	7	4	2
Syndicated loans				
Foreign banks	2	3	5	6
Foreign corporations	–	2	7	5
Foreign governments and agencies	5	5	3	3

Note: Several respondents indicated that internal breakdowns of their portfolios did not make possible the estimates requested.
Source: Authors' data.

only modest proportions despite the reported large expansion of
such activities in recent years.

By and large the data in Table 8.2 suggest that syndicated loan
participations have not been attractive to most banks in recent years.
In general, interest in these loans was concentrated in the money center banks, which often receive underwriting fees in addition to the
interest spread return. Some may feel obliged to participate in government offerings of countries in which they have significant indigenous business through branches or representative offices.

PORTFOLIO PROFILE: MATURITY DISTRIBUTION

Table 8.3 shows the estimated distribution between short-term and term loans in the portfolios of respondent banks with at least moderate commitments in the particular sector indicated.

TABLE 8.3. Maturity Distribution Profile (number of banks)

	Percent of Total Short Term				Percent of Total Term Loans			
	0-20	21-40	41-60	60+	0-20	21-40	41-60	60+
Nonsyndicated								
Domestic customers, foreign subsidiaries		1	1	7	1	6	2	
Foreign banks	1	2	1	10	7	2	3	1
Foreign corporations								
In country of domicile	4	5	1	4	2	3	3	6
In U.S.	1	4	1	4	3	2	1	4
Foreign governments and agencies	5	5	1				5	6
Syndicated								

All reported that more than 80 percent of loans in this sector were term loans.

Note: Distribution shown for respondents having significant loans in sector and willing to estimate distribution.
Source: Authors' data.

The following comments on prevailing practices would seem relevant. First, a very large proportion of syndicated loans are for extended maturities; thus maturity limit policies, quality constraints (including credit and country risk evaluations), and rate spread targets would be involved in decisions to accept or reject participations in these loans.

Second, at the other extreme, in the case of direct commitments to foreign banks, the short-term sector dominates; most of these are usually lines of credit subject to annual review. Third, in the case of other private-sector direct loans, the portfolios are generally balanced between term and short-term commitments; indeed, in many instances both types of credit are extended at the same time. Finally, governments and their agencies apparently focus on term credits even when they are made on a direct basis.

CREDIT POLICIES: FOREIGN BANK
PLACEMENTS AND LOANS

As indicated in Table 8.2, direct loans to foreign banks are of major significance in most international portfolios. Interbank credit exposures also include deposit placements in the Eurocurrency markets, short-term liabilities arising from foreign exchange transactions, and contingent exposures arising from credit guarantees. The short-term commitments are usually extended under lines of credit or "authorizations." The "authorization" commitment is used only in international finance, and differs from a line of credit in that it is considered somewhat less binding than a line, and advances under it can be denied—for example, because total country limits have been reached. Under either lines or "authorizations" a bank may extend clean advances (an unsecured loan), offer confirmation of letters of credit on behalf of the foreign bank or its customers, and accept time drafts drawn by the foreign bank (bankers acceptance). Thus contingent liabilities as well as advances of funds arise under these commitments.

As a consequence, prevailing practice is to establish and monitor an approved list of foreign banks eligible for deposit placements and, if required, loan and credit accommodations. Total credit exposure limits are then set for each bank on the list. The policy issues under this format are the appropriate number of banks to be included on the list; the credit criteria to be used in establishing exposure limits; whether contingent liabilities should be included in the limits; and whether "off-beat" banks should be included on the approved list.

TABLE 8.4. Interbank Loan and Placement Policies, Selected Sample of U.S. Banks

Number of banks on approved list	Respondent Banks
0–50	1
50–100	3
100–200	1
over 200	17

Credit analysis factors determining exposure limits	Very Significant	Significant	Minor Significance	Not Used
Size of bank	6	13	1	
Location of bank (country)*	13	7	1	
Relationship with government	5	12	4	1
Capital adequacy analysis	10	11	1	
Asset quality evaluation	5	14	2	1
Earnings record	3	17	1	
Reputation of management	15	5	1	1
Liquidity evaluation	9	10	3	1

Amounts included in limits	Yes	No
Standby credit commitments	21	1
Potential acceptance liabilities	21	1
Amounts of loan guarantees	20	2
"Day" risk on foreign exchange settlements	15	7
Total country risk exposure limits	19	3

Placements allowed with	Yes	No
Consortium banks	4	18
Merchant banks (England)	9	13
Specialty banks	2	20

*Related question: Because of country risk appraisal, does the bank avoid all placements to banks in certain countries?

Yes	No
22	—

Source: Authors' data.

Table 8.4 shows the policies and practices of the respondent banks with respect to these issues. Several comments on these data might be made. First, it apparently is common practice to maintain a large number of banks on the approved list; the great majority of respondents indicated more than 200. However, on the negative side, exclusion solely because of adverse country risk appraisal was universal practice; thus, a "good" bank in a "bad" country would be avoided. Second, there are total country limits. In other words, a total country "quota" is established, and then other criteria are used to divide the quota among a set of banks.

Third, to establish individual exposure limits, the most important determinants were capital adequacy, liquidity evaluation, size, and general managerial reputation. Some banks also considered asset quality and past earnings record to be of major significance. However, several respondents mentioned that adequate data for evaluation along these lines frequently are not available from published reports. As a result these banks indicated these factors to be of minor importance in establishing exposure limits. Fourth, because private-sector banks in many countries have close working relationships with the government, it was hypothesized that an assessment of this relationship might be significant. In general, however, it appeared that this factor was considered of only moderate importance.

Fifth, general practice was to establish a total exposure limit and then to reduce it, for deposit placement and loan purposes, by the amount of contingent liabilities arising from nonlending relationships. Acceptances and guarantees of loans were particularly noted as of major significance. "Day" risk on foreign exchange settlements has been reduced by recent electronic transfer clearing systems, so this factor now seems to be of less importance than formerly.[3]

Finally, Table 8.4 shows that the majority of respondents limited the approved list to well-established commercial banks, and would not consider specialty banks (such as those involved primarily in real estate or consumer finance), consortium banks, or merchant banks. The facts that in these areas credit problems have been more numerous and general correspondent relationships are usually not involved are probably the major reasons for the exclusions. However, a significant minority of respondents included some of the major English merchant banks on their approved lists. These banks have had a long history of successful operations and, in addition, have the expertise and contacts useful in structuring financing packages in the overseas markets.

CREDIT POLICIES: MATURITY LIMITS AND AMORTIZATION

Table 8.3 showed that, except for commitments to foreign banks, term loans represent a major portion of the total portfolio. Therefore, most respondents had established general policy guidelines for acceptable maturity limits.[4] Such limits logically should be related to amortization policies, because if bullet loans or balloon maturities are acceptable, then effective maturities are likely to be well beyond nominal maturities. This inference is based on the logical presumption that under these circumstances many borrowers will request an extension of the original commitment.[5]

Because risk necessarily increases as maturities are extended or amortization is delayed, it might be presumed that banks would prefer relatively short maturity schedules with full, straight-line amortization. On the other hand, many borrowers logically prefer relatively long maturities and perhaps minimal contractual amortization re-

TABLE 8.5. Term Loan Maturity Policies, Respondent Banks

	Maximum Maturity (years)[a]					
	5–7		7–10		Over 10	
	Syndi-cated	Other	Syndi-cated	Other	Syndi-cated	Other
Type of loan						
Government project	4	8	13	10	1	1
Government balance of payments[b]	6	6	9	7		
Foreign subsidiary of U.S. company	4	5	11	11		2
Foreign company	8	12	9	7		4

Reported exceptions

Over 10 years made on an exception basis

[a]Response omitted if loans not made in indicated category.
[b]Some banks reported that all balance-of-payments loans are against policy.
Source: Authors' data.

quirements, in order to avoid potential cash-flow problems and/or obtain maximum flexibility in the use of cash flows. As a result, maturity and amortization policies must necessarily represent a competitive compromise and also be reasonably flexible to accommodate valued customers.

Given these caveats, Table 8.5 shows the normative maturity limits for the major categories of international loans in which term loans represent a major proportion of the total outstanding amounts. The data indicate that in most categories seven- to ten-year limits represent prevailing practice. However, in two sectors many banks indicated shorter maturity limits: loans to foreign companies and government balance-of-payments loans. In the first case the primary reason cited was the lack of adequate financial data (compared with U.S. requirements) to support long-term credits; in the second case a general uneasiness with country risk on balance-of-payments loans appeared to be the causative factor. Indeed, several banks indicated these loans generally were avoided entirely.

As might be expected, there was a modest tilt toward allowing somewhat longer maturities on loans to foreign subsidiaries of U.S. companies, probably because of greater familiarity with the credits and the availability of parent company guaranties. Also, it appears that maturity limits are moderately more generous on government project loans; in this case the realities are that many projects (especially larger ones that require syndication) require extended terms to make them viable.

Prevailing policies with respect to amortization options are shown in Table 8.6, and while policy preference is generally for full amortization over the life of the loan, the delayed amortization option

TABLE 8.6. Term Loan Amortization Policies, Respondent Banks

	Frequently	Sometimes	Rarely	Never
Straight line over life	11	6	4	
Delayed amortization	15	6		
Straight line with balloon		7	13	1
Bullet loan (no amortization)		3	15	2

Note: Several banks indicated that complete amortization over life is preferred, but that competitive conditions limit the availability of such loans.
Source: Authors' data.

appears to be the most frequently used in practice.[6] Because considerable time may elapse between loan takedown and cash flow generation from a completed project, delayed amortization often becomes a necessary corollary of the financing arrangement.

Respondents indicated a general antipathy for both bullet loans and modest amortization with a large balloon at maturity. One bank indicated that the most common type of bullet loan was a long-term deposit placement, perhaps up to eight years, in a few foreign banks. Since banks are constantly engaged in rolling over funds in the financial markets with no reduction in total liabilities expected, the bullet loan may be appropriate in this case. But in the nonfinancial sectors the uncertainty regarding the ability to meet a large single maturity some years hence increases risk.

CREDIT POLICIES: GUARANTEES AND COLLATERAL

For several reasons third-party guarantees are often associated with certain types of international credit commitments. First, the U.S. government has established specific guarantee programs to encourage export finance and other loans to certain areas of the world. Therefore, the risk on qualified commitments can practically be eliminated through guarantees by U.S. government agencies; but, except for export transactions, criteria for qualification considerably limit the universe.[7] Second, U.S. parent companies may consider it expedient to capitalize foreign subsidiaries on a minimum basis, in which case loans to the subsidiaries logically require guarantees of the parent.

Third, since contacts with foreign banks have historically been the points of entry into many countries, and bank guarantees on behalf of commercial customers are the essence of the traditional acceptance mechanism, the extension of this practice to various types of loans became a logical step. Difficulty in obtaining adequate financial data on some foreign applicants to justify loan requests should also be cited as a contributing factor. For example, the international loan policy of one bank states:

> The requirement for financial statements may be waived only . . . in cases where we hold an unquestioned guarantee by an acceptable government, bank, or first class domestic or foreign parent company.[8]

Finally, in socialist or quasi-socialist countries, government-owned or -sponsored companies often constitute those of significant size that require financing in amounts beyond the capacities of the local financial markets. These firms are the logical loan customers of foreign banks, and because their continued viability requires government support, guarantee by the related government becomes a natural requirement.

TABLE 8.7. Frequency of Use of Loan Guarantees, by Type (respondent banks)

Type of Guarantee	Use			
	Frequently	Sometimes	Rarely	Never
U.S. government agencies	5	11	4	
Parent company guarantee	1	15	4	
Parent company "comfort" letter	3	13	3	1
Foreign bank guarantee	8	11	1	
Foreign bank "comfort" letter	1	4	11	4
Foreign government guarantee	5	11	4	

Source: Authors' data.

Table 8.7 shows the estimates of the respondent banks as to their use of various sources of guarantees. As expected, more loans are made under foreign bank guarantees than under any other source. Government support, by both U.S. and foreign agencies, is next in importance, although a significant minority of banks indicated only rare use of these sources. The policy with respect to parent company support of loans to subsidiaries seems more ambiguous and controversial. The data in Table 8.7 indicate that unqualified parent company guarantees are not frequently obtained; indeed, several banks stated they are rarely obtained. So-called "comfort" letters, which purport to establish a "moral" obligation of the parent, are somewhat more frequently used, although a few banks consider them generally unacceptable.[9] According to one source, the problem here is that many large corporations refuse to offer unqualified guarantees for subsidiary loans, but nevertheless can obtain the required financing from many banks.[10] In essence, an evaluation of a "comfort" letter's value in support of a loan is really a "character" assessment of parent company management: whether a parent company conceivably would disclaim the obligations of its subsidiaries even though it had the legal right to do so.

Because procedures for taking security interests against specific assets of borrowers usually require special on-site legal assistance, and perhaps other costs, it is logical to expect that loans domiciled abroad would less frequently involve collateral than those domiciled in the United States.[11]

TABLE 8.8. Frequency of Collateral Usage by Domicile of Loan and Type of Collateral
(respondent banks)

	Frequently		Sometimes		Rarely		Never	
	U.S.	Non-U.S.	U.S.	Non-U.S.	U.S.	Non-U.S.	U.S.	Non-U.S.
Working capital loans								
Receivables	3	—	11	6	5	12	2	3
Inventory	2	—	10	5	5	10	4	6
Fixed assets (equip.)	1	—	11	6	6	9	3	6
Land and buildings	2	—	10	5	6	12	3	4
Term loans								
Fixed assets (equip.)	4	—	7	8	6	6	2	5
Land and buildings	3	—	10	8	5	7	2	5

Note: U.S. refers to loans domiciled under the laws of the United States; non-U.S. refers to loans domiciled in foreign countries where their laws control lien rights.

Source: Authors' data.

The data in Table 8.8 confirm this hypothesis. In the case of loans subject to liens structured under U.S. law, mainly to U.S. subsidiaries of foreign companies, most respondents stated that the terms either frequently or sometimes included asset liens of some sort. Receivables assignments and real estate mortgages were the most common types of collateral; the first were applicable to working capital loans, and the second to term loans.

In contrast, a dominant majority indicated that security interests were rarely if ever taken on loans domiciled outside the U.S.; indeed, not one bank considered that collateral was a frequent feature of any type of loan in such a case. Moreover, a significant minority of respondents were willing to take the extreme position that collateral was never taken on such loans.

TABLE 8.9. Reasons for Requesting Guarantees or Collateral

	Very Significant	Significant	Not Significant
Credit quality of borrower	18	3	0
Sponsorship of loan	7	11	2
Eligibility for government guarantee	6	9	5
Country risk of borrower	11	7	2

Source: Authors' data.

The major purpose for requesting guarantees or collateral is of course risk avoidance, and Table 8.9 indicates that avoidance of both credit and country risks are indeed the primary reasons cited in this connection.[12] But Table 8.9 suggests that there may be two additional reasons. First, if U.S. or foreign government guarantees are normally associated with a specific type of commitment, then the support may be routinely requested, assuming the associated costs are reasonable. Second, if a third party (say a foreign bank) introduces and recommends a borrower to a bank, then the guarantee of the third party may be requested as tangible evidence of the positive recommendation.

PRICING-FUNDING POLICIES

The pricing process in the international sector is usually a pure spread management operation, whereas in the domestic area other considerations often enter into the pricing, such as compensating balances or the profitability of other service packages extended to customers (pension fund management, for example).[13] Spread management in this context means that specifically defined funding costs, plus a negotiated spread, determine interest rates on loans. This pricing policy is particularly identified with loans funded in the Eurocurrency markets; in this case loan rates are routinely tied to the London Interbank Offered Rate (LIBOR) for the particular currency in which the loan is denominated.

As shown in Table 8.10, all respondents indicated that LIBOR

TABLE 8.10. Pricing-Funding Policy Options: Frequency of Use

	Frequently	Sometimes	Rarely	Never
Pricing option				
Tied to U.S. prime rate	9	13	—	—
Tied to LIBOR	22	—	—	—
Option of borrower to use LIBOR or prime	4	12	6	—
Tied to Fed funds or CD rates	—	1	17	4
Rate gap policy option*				
Matched book required	9	4	6	—
Moderate gap based on slope of yield curve	6	8	2	3
Moderate gap based on interest rate forecast	4	9	3	2

*Several banks stated that they were unable to answer this question. This may be construed to mean that gap policy is not implemented in the international department or that it is considered a very sensitive area and they do not wish to disclose the controlling policy.

Source: Authors' data.

rates for Eurocurrencies are the primary basis for pricing international loans; typical practice here is to quote a loan rate equal to the prevailing rate on a particular Eurocurrency maturity (one, three, or six months), plus a negotiated spread. The loan rate is then adjusted to current market levels at intervals equal to the specified Eurocurrency maturity.

As a result, it is possible for a bank to maintain a "matched book" on the entire portfolio in which all interest rate risk is eliminated: liability maturities can be closely matched with the rate adjustment intervals on the loans.[14] If the maturities of the purchased funds do not match the intervals for adjusting loan rates, then a "rate gap" exists. This can improve average spreads if the maturities actually used to fund the loans have an average cost less than the maturities used to establish the rates on the loans. But a policy to allow "rate gaps" on the portfolio also increases risk, particularly if short-term funds are used to fund (say) six-month rate adjustment intervals. Then if interest rates increase, funding costs will rise, and may well exceed the yields on the loans for several months.

A deliberate "rate gap" may be introduced into the portfolio for two reasons. First, under the presumed normative conditions of up-sloping yield curves (rates in a given market increase as maturities lengthen), funding with very short maturities against loan rates based on longer maturities will increase spread margins as compared with the "matched book" alternative. Second, if a bank attempts to forecast interest rates and desires to obtain benefits from "bets" on the forecast, then a controlled "rate gap" is a convenient means of implementation. If rates are expected to decline, funding maturities (liabilities) will be shorter than asset (loan) maturities, and vice versa if rates are expected to increase.

Because interest rates have been highly volatile in the past several years, both the risks and the potential rewards of a policy permitting a significant "rate gap" to exist on the loan portfolio have increased. As a consequence appropriate policy on the issue has become highly controversial. Prevailing "rate gap" policies reflected this fact. While the general preference seemed to be for a "matched book" policy, a significant number of respondents indicated that their policies allowed moderate "rate gap" management on a frequent basis. In contrast, the opposite view received considerable support in the form of policies that either completely prohibited "gapping" or would consider it only rarely.

Policies regarding acceptable spread margins have become controversial. It is common knowledge that spreads have generally declined in recent years, as a result of a significant growth in the number of banks aggressively seeking active participation in the international markets. As a result these are considerable differences in views on the appropriate approach to spread policies. At one extreme is the view that low spreads are acceptable because, on a marginal-cost approach, any returns on increments to the portfolio contribute to earnings (on the assumption that marginal direct costs are close to zero on some categories of loans).

A second view is that marginal costs should include a return-on-capital requirement, on the assumption that an increase in purchased funds and loans should have capital support. In other words, the ratio of capital to assets (deposits) cannot expand indefinitely. For example, if policy requires capital of 5 percent of total assets and 20 percent is the pretax objective for the return on capital, then a minimum spread target can be established as follows for a $1,000 incremental increase in the loan portfolio:

$$\$1,000 \times \text{spread} = 5\%(1,000) \times 20\% = 1\%.$$

The solution to set minimum spreads at 1 percent, given these assumptions, is justified on the ground that acceptance of lower spreads would represent a dilution of the return on capital.[15]

A third view is that the marginal-cost approach should be applied only to those participations in syndicated loans where credit risks and servicing costs are negligible. Otherwise, net yields should include additional returns for risk premiums and departmental costs that would suggest spread targets on direct loans of between 100 and 200 basis points.[16] In this case, however, it is usually conceded that in practice some exceptions are required for valued customers in a strong bargaining position (access to several alternative banks).

Table 8.11 shows the estimated frequency of various ranges of yield spreads obtained by the respondent banks. The dispersion of the results inferentially suggests considerable differences in pricing policies on both nonsyndicated and syndicated loans. In the nonsyndicated sector the policy of accepting spreads of less than 100 basis points suggests a marginal-cost approach; some banks indicated that this level dominated both lines of credit and term loans. In contrast, others indicated that 100 to 200 basis points was the dominant

TABLE 8.11. Yield Spreads of Respondent Banks: Basis Points

	Frequently		Sometimes		Rarely		Never	
	Term	Lines	Term	Lines	Term	Lines	Term	Lines
Spread of basis points (non-syndicated)								
Less than 100	5	17	9	6	7			
100–200	10	3	10	14	1	5		1
200–300			5	1	13	10	2	10
Over 300*			3	1	4	3	14	18
Spread of basis points (syndicated)								
25 to 375			1		11		10	
375 to 50		1	7		10		4	
50 to 75		8	10		3		1	
75 to 100		10	10		2		—	
Over 100		5	11		6		—	

*On loans funded in local currencies, spreads of 300 basis points or more obtained frequently, according to some respondents.
Source: Authors' data.

level, and was required to obtain adequate returns on capital or assets. However, it is clear that yield spreads over 200 basis points are difficult to obtain except, perhaps, on some term loans.

As expected, spreads in the syndicated sector were considerably lower than on direct customer loans. But again some policy differences seemed apparent. Several banks would only rarely consider purchasing a participation where the spread was less than 75 basis points, whereas others would accept such a spread on a frequent basis. Indeed, several banks would accept spreads of less than 50 basis points; purchases at these levels suggest a policy based on the first approach to spread policies discussed above.[17] In general, the most frequent spread levels obtained on syndicated loans was 75 to 100 basis points. At leverage levels of 20 to 25 (loans to capital), such spreads would provide a reasonable return on capital, and since such capital ratios are not uncommon among very large banks, a case can be made that purchases on this basis are entirely justified.

LOAN AUTHORITY POLICIES

There are two conflicting views as to appropriate delegation of lending authority. The first holds that because under U.S. banking law senior management (including directors) can be held legally responsible for lack of participation in major loan decisions, only nominal authority should be given field officers, and final decisions should largely be made in the home office. The second emphasizes that in order for field officers to command respect from and offer prompt service to customers, they should be granted considerable discretionary authority to make loan commitments within broad policy parameters established in the home office. In a competitive context the first view is generally considered a "conservative," and the second an "aggressive," policy.

It should be noted that this inherent conflict in objectives applies to a lesser proportion of international loans than to domestic loans. Decisions regarding purchases of syndicated loans, exposure limits for foreign banks, and government loans requiring extensive country risk evaluations would logically be made in the home office, because field officers usually would not possess all of the information needed to reach decisions in these areas. And, as indicated in Table 8.12, these types of loans often represent an important segment of the international portfolio. In addition, commitments to very large multinational companies may include a package of domestic and international loans to foreign subsidiaries with parent company support that can best be appraised and structured in the home office.

However, vigorous penetration of the indigenous private-sector loan markets abroad, in which yield spreads may be most attractive, may necessitate reasonable delegation of loan authority to field officers on the scene. Therefore, it might be presumed that a policy to seek such penetration would result in at least moderate decentralization of lending authority. However, the contrary argument can be made that modern communications technology makes prompt service possible even if most decisions are made in the home office.

Table 8.12 shows the views of respondent banks with one or

TABLE 8.12. Loan Authority Policies of Respondent Banks

| | Amount of Authority | | | |
	Large	Moderate	Small	None
Overseas offices				
General manager alone*	2	5	9	1
General manager with other branch officers	2	7	7	1
Other branch officers		3	8	6
Head office				
Senior international officer alone	6	5	5	1
Combination of officers	11	2	3	1
Foreign general manager with senior international officer	6	7	3	1
Head office loan committee	15			2

Note: "Loan authority policy" is defined as discretionary lending limits of indicated persons or committee.
   *Some banks indicated that authority varied between branches.
   Source: Authors' data.

more active overseas offices (as contrasted to a "shell" branch for tax purposes) on the question of loan authority. The data clearly indicate the dichotomy of policies in this connection. Although less than a majority, a significant proportion grant overseas field officers only nominal loan authority. In contrast, a few give the senior overseas officer authority to make legal limit commitments, and several others grant moderate loan authority to these officers. There was, however, a general policy to limit strictly the authority of subordinate branch officers.

In the home office the preponderance of respondents granted the senior officer alone, or in combination with others, considerable discretionary loan authority. In addition, in most banks the senior officer abroad had only to contact the senior officer in the head office in order to extend large or moderate commitments. This arrangement seemed to represent the prevailing compromise between the conflicting objectives outlined above. Because the head office loan committee, probably including senior executive officers, represents the control body for the entire international portfolio, it was generally empowered to render decisions on any type of major commitment. Several banks apparently following the "conservative" philosophy reserved all decisions above the moderate range to this group. In contrast, two banks indicated that a formal committee was not used for this purpose. Although by no means certain, it may be conjectured that these banks were oriented to the "aggressive" decentralized approach to decision making.

NOTES

1. A number of banks, of course, concentrate entirely on the domestic market. Reference here is to banks that have established an international department within the organization.

2. The following statement is illustrative of the money center bank situation: "Because of the close integration of the Corporation's foreign and domestic activities, it is difficult to estimate the assets, liabilities, income and expenses attributable to international activities. Such amounts are based on internal allocations and allowances, which are necessarily subjective." Chase Manhattan Corporation, *Annual Report for 1980*, p. 63.

3. This refers to CHIPS (Clearing House International Payments System) operating in New York City. Payments made through CHIPS provide for "same day" settlements, but may be recalled at any time up to 5:30 P.M. New York time.

4. However, the majority of international term loans are not made under loan agreements that include the specific financial covenants typical of domestic term loans. The reason is that many substitute guarantees of third parties or are extended to banks or government agencies. Only a modest number are made on an unqualified basis to moderate-size companies in which special financial constraints are considered necessary.

5. Large companies (or governments) with access to the public markets usually have the alternative option of refunding large maturities through public sale of securities or through a banking syndicate.

6. Delayed amortization means that payments on the principal of the loan are deferred for one or more years. For term loans of seven to ten years, a two-year delay is most typical, but a three- or four-year delay in amortization may be associated with term loans of ten years or more.

7. For example, the criteria for guaranties by the Overseas Private Investment Corporation (OPIC) are as follows: "Assisted projects must be financially sound, new investments (or expansion of existing projects) in friendly developing countries. Such projects must contribute to the social and economic progress of the host country and be consistent with the economic interests of the U.S." F. John Mathis, ed., *Offshore Lending by U.S. Commercial Banks*, 2nd ed.

(Washington, D.C., and Philadelphia: Bankers' Association for Foreign Trade and Robert Morris Associates, 1981), app. II, p. 321.

8. Defaults and consequent losses in 1981 on two large loans made to Japanese companies by a group of external banks (including U.S. banks), in which guarantees were waived for competitive reasons, despite the apparent lack of adequate evaluation data, suggest the desirability of this policy. *Wall Street Journal*, December 16, 1981, p. 24.

9. The loan policy of one respondent includes the following: "Generally 'comfort' letters are not an acceptable substitute [for unqualified guaranty] although rare exceptions may be made with the concurrence of the Commercial Loan Committee or other appropriate authority."

10. Mathis, op. cit., p. 152. For a more complete discussion of the moral and legal nuances of "comfort" letters, see pp. 152-55 of Mathis.

11. For example, one policy statement in this connection: "Because of great distances between us and the borrowers and the possible legal and technical difficulties involved in the foreclosure and liquidation of collateral, our policy is to be very cautious toward granting loans which cannot stand up on an unsecured basis."

12. A number of respondents indicated that in the case of loans to nonbank financial institutions (leasing and finance companies) where the assets are easily hypothecated with nominal servicing costs, pledges of such assets are frequently requested. However, such loans are unlikely to be of major significance in the portfolio.

13. In the case of large multinational U.S. companies, worldwide credit packages can be structured in the home office, where the entire relationship is considered in the pricing arrangements. However, these cases are really outside the scope of this chapter, because the domestic relationships with respect to balances and other services rendered the customers tend to dominate the negotiations on credit terms.

14. This statement assumes that risk "tiering" is not a problem—in other words, that the bank will be able to acquire funds at the best LIBOR rates, regardless of conditions in the financial markets. Because of risk perceptions related to the condition of certain banks, the availability to them of funds purchased in the Eurocurrency markets may be limited or obtainable only at premium rates. In this case, even if a "matched book" is maintained, the result can be negative spreads in the portfolio.

15. In an article advocating this approach, the senior officer in charge of an international department prepared a table to show the return on capital at various money costs and spreads, given an assumed leverage ratio of loans to capital. It was the conclusion of this article that policies of regional banks should achieve minimum spreads of 1.25 percent. D. M. Mandich, "International Loans: Profit Center or Loss Lender," *Journal of Commercial Bank Lending*, September 1972, pp. 41-42.

16. The desirability of this approach is implicit in the following critical comment on international banking returns: "But on a return on assets basis—a more significant measure—profits from overseas banking have proved to be surprisingly thin at many banks, what's more, in all likelihood these returns will dwindle

further unless bankers act decisively to save themselves." *International Banking, Institutional Investor*, June 1981, p. 239. Return on assets is of course calculated by deducting both money costs and all other expenses from the gross yield and then dividing by the amount of the portfolio.

17. It is possible that underwriting fees as syndicate managers will increase the returns to money center banks, which often act in that capacity, and that reciprocal participation in syndicated loans is required to achieve recognition as a potential manager of a syndicate.

Part IV
RISK AND CREDIT ANALYSIS

9 COUNTRY RISK
Ingo Walter

By their very nature, international banks ply their trade across the political frontiers of sovereign nation-states—countries that have their own histories and their own futures. A bank that makes a cross-border loan to a national government or government-guaranteed entity is exposed to *sovereign risk*. A bank that makes a cross-border loan to a private borrower in a particular country naturally incurs credit risk as well as—given the chance that even a creditworthy borrower may not be able to convert local currency into foreign exchange—*transfer risk*.

Both of these concepts are part of what is generally called *country risk*, focusing on the possibility that private borrowers in particular countries may be unable to service debt to foreign banks because of internal or external economic or political conditions in their countries; government borrowers are unable or unwilling to honor their external debt commitments; or private- or public-sector entities under government guarantee default because the government is unwilling or unable to honor that guarantee. Country risk is therefore closely related to other dimensions of risk in international banking—indeed, it is sometimes inseparable from them.

COUNTRY EXPOSURE AND LIMITS

The first thing an international bank needs to know is its exposure to country risk around the world. To do this, it needs to develop an information system that captures all cross-border loans, investments, and other forms of exposure, and to classify them by type, maturity, borrower, and other characteristics that will keep management constantly informed of its exposure in each country where it does business. This means that no matter where in the world a loan to a borrower in a particular country originates, the information must be promptly and accurately transmitted to a central exposure tracking facility at the head office. It must then be made available to bank officers developing business and making decisions on the bank's activities in that country.

In addition, given the outlook for business and its assessment of the risks involved, bank management must decide on a *country limit* beyond which its exposure will not ordinarily be allowed to go. This limit, in turn, may be divided into several sublimits, usually by maturity and sometimes by borrower type. For, given expectations regarding future returns, exposure limits will normally be lower, the higher the assessed degree of country risk. For very high-risk countries, moreover, the term sublimit (over one year) ordinarily will be a relatively small proportion of the total, and bank exposures will be concentrated largely in shorter maturities, particular trade credit, and special-purpose financing where recovery of interest and principal from noncountry-related sources is virtually assured. Changes in country futures that may give rise to changes in risks and expected returns from a bank's activities in a particular country thus will ordinarily lead to a reassessment of that country's limit.

Country exposure is not quite so easy to measure as first appears. For example, a loan to a Nigerian borrower guaranteed by its Swiss parent has to be recorded as Swiss exposure, not Nigerian. A loan to a Mexican affiliate of an American multinational accompanied by a comfort letter or keepwell from the parent, however, is Mexican risk, and not American. Shipping loans and similar kinds of exposure likewise pose problems of proper allocation. The point is that the country of lending and the country of exposure are not necessarily the same.

Finally, it might be of interest for management to know the extent to which it has deposits from each of the countries in which it is exposed. These should not be netted out against that exposure, but they might provide a certain degree of comfort in the event of serious debt service difficulties under the "right of set-off," as experienced most dramatically in the Iranian crisis of 1979-80.

COUNTRY RISK ASSESSMENT

The purpose of country risk assessment or, more accurately, *country analysis*, is to forecast the political and economic futures of countries in order to ascertain the prospective risks and returns associated with a bank's lending and other types of exposure in a particular country. In particular, will a country be willing and able to service its outstanding debt, both public and private, in future periods?

A simple view of the problem focuses on risk that arises out of structural (supply-side) elements, demand-side and monetary elements, external economic and political developments, and the quality of the national economic management team and the domestic political constraints bearing upon decision makers. One might begin with a relationship such as

$$Y + M = A + X$$

representing real flows of goods and services in an economy, where Y is output, M is imports, A is domestic absorption (consumption, investment, and public-sector spending), and X is exports, all in real terms. Clearly, supply-side changes in Y with unchanged demand will require shifts in imports or exports—reduced production capabilities, for example, mean either increased imports or a more limited capacity to export. Similarly, demand-side shifts affecting A with unchanged supply can be examined—increased government spending will, for example, have to be met from expanded imports or will deflect export production to meet domestic needs. Monetary variables can affect the picture as well—growth in the domestic money supply will, unless reflected in exchange rates, tend to raise A relative to Y and, therefore, increase M, decrease X, or both.

In order to bring the money side into the picture explicitly, we can develop an equally simple equation describing international financial flows:

$$VX - VM - DS + FDI + U - K_o = DR - NBR.$$

Here, VX and VM represent the money value of imports and exports, respectively; DS represents debt service payments to foreigners (usually part of VM in conventional balance-of-payments accounting); FDI is net flows of nonresident foreign direct investments; U represents net flows of private and public-sector grants such as foreign aid; K_o is net capital flows undertaken by residents; DR is the change in international reserves of the country in question; and NBR is its net borrowing requirement. An overall negative balance on the left-hand side of the equation clearly means that the country will have to increase its foreign borrowing or use up some of its international reserves. At the same time, increases in foreign borrowing will mean increases in DS in future time periods.

Effective country analysis requires evaluation of a country's economic structure, with respect to the evolution of domestic supply and demand; its monetary policies; trade and other external factors (some of which are beyond control of the country itself); its international liquidity and ability to borrow further in international financial markets; and internal and external political developments, most of which are linked to the various economic elements.

Structural Aspects

The question here is whether developments in the internal workings of a national economy, on both the supply and the demand sides, will seriously threaten markets, profitability, or the ability to service external obligations. We are interested first in the linkages between the supply side's ability to produce export, import-competing, and nontraded goods, and in the qualitative and quantitative dimensions of the labor force, the capital stock, the natural resource base, technology, and entrepreneurship that combine to determine this capability. At the same time we are interested in the contributions of real capital inflows to these supply capabilities made possible by foreign borrowing, foreign direct investment, and other types of financial transfers.

Historical measures of supply-side economic performance abound: labor force growth and participation rates, unemployment rates, migration and labor force distribution trends, savings and investment trends, productivity trends, natural resource availability, and the like. The quality, timeliness, and comparability of the relevant data vary widely, but the real problem obviously lies in ascertaining whether the past is likely to be a good guide to the future. Here a great deal of judgment is required in order to identify and project, for example, various types of quantitative or qualitative labor supply ceilings and possible market disruptions, social and economic infrastructure bottlenecks, capital adequacy problems, natural resource constraints, and so on.

Of prime importance is the evaluation of government policies that will influence domestic savings and investment, capital flight and foreign direct investment, risk-taking and entrepreneurial activity, supply conditions in labor markets, the adequacy of economic and social infrastructure, exploitation and forward processing of natural resources—the entire underlying complex of incentives and disincentives built into the nation's fiscal and regulatory system. In many cases such policies are anchored in government planning documents, in which case an assessment of the degree of realism embodied in these plans may be quite important—government attempts to force the supply side of an economy into a mold that does not fit, but to which a political commitment has been made, can lead to severe domestic and international distortions in the real sector, ballooning of external borrowing, and, ultimately, debt service problems. These are summarized in Figure 9.1.

On the demand side we are interested in factors affecting taxes, government expenditures, transfer payments, and the overall fiscal soundness of the public sector, as we are in prospective patterns of demand for goods and services from the private and export sectors. Once again, historical data series covering consumption spending, government taxation and expenditures, gross national product or gross domestic product, and other conventional economic indicators are usually available on a reasonably timely basis to permit an evaluation of the demand picture over a number of years. But forecasts depend in large part on the ability to predict government demand management and income distribution policies, as well as exogenous demand-side shocks that may emanate from the foreign sector, changing expectations, or other sources.

In attempting to develop a defensible prognosis of the structural aspects of country futures, therefore, the analyst must start from as complete an information base as possible about the historical track record of the domestic economy and its current situation, and then try to project both the demand-side and the supply-side dimensions. This may not be a serious problem in the short term, where the exogenous and policy elements are relatively fixed, but the sources of error multiply as the forecasting period is extended, and few or none of the important determinants of economic performance can be

FIGURE 9.1: Sample Country Analysis Checklist: Domestic Economy Supply Side

Describe numerically the prospects during the next seven to ten years for the country's balance of payments.

	Favorable			Unfavorable	
	1	2	3	4	5
TRADE:					
Export growth					
Export diversification[1]					
Import growth					
Import diversification[2]					
Import compressibility[3]					
FINANCIAL FLOWS:					
Investment flows (net)					
Foreign aid receipts					
Capital flight					
Foreign borrowing ability					
RESERVES AND DEBT:					
Size of foreign debt					
Debt service "burden"[4]					
External reserves					
IMF position[5]					
EXCHANGE RATE:					
Deviation from market rate[6]					
EXTERNAL BALANCE SUMMARY:					
Balance of trade					
Terms of trade[7]					
Balance of payments					
External reserves					
Foreign debt					

---

[1] Adequacy of existing or prospective financial institutions to channel savings into investment.

[2] For example, rail lines, highways, port facilities, telecommunications.

[3] For example, schools, hospitals.

Source: Prepared by author.

considered constant. What will happen to taxes, transfers, government regulation, the pattern of subsidies and other market distortions, consumption and savings patterns, investment incentives, treatment of foreign-owned firms, and similar factors five or ten years into the future? Everything is up for grabs, and forecasting has to rely in large measure on the basic competence of the policy makers, their receptivity to outside advice, and the pattern of social and political constraints under which they operate. Assuming the cast of characters remains the same, past experience in macroeconomic management and reactions to outside shocks may not be a bad guide to the future. But this assumption itself is often open to question.

Monetary Aspects

A part of the task of projecting future country scenarios—and some would contend the most important part—lies in the monetary sector. Whereas most country analyses contain extensive descriptions of the national financial system, the critical factors obviously relate to prices and exchange rates. Useful indicators are the domestic monetary base, the money supply, net domestic credit, and available price indices, together with net foreign official assets and net foreign debt. Monetary disturbances may originate domestically or from the foreign sector (for instance, major increases in external reserves that become monetized). Apart from their inflationary and exchange-rate aspects, of course, such disturbances may also have real-sector influences on consumption and savings, capital formation, income distribution, expectations, and the like.

Once again, whereas the mechanisms relating monetary developments to country risk problems are well understood, and the requisite data usually are more readily available than most others, near-term assessments are far easier than formulating a defensible long-range outlook. It is, after all, possible to evaluate the relationship of the existing exchange rate to some hypothetical market-determined rate based on a calculated purchasing power parity index, and to project this deviation for the near term on the basis of relative inflation trends. The larger the degree of currency overvaluation, for example, the greater will the need for increased external borrowing tend to be, as well as the likelihood of reserve losses and/or the prospects for a tightening of controls on international trade and payments. Much more difficult is the task of forecasting government responses to problems in the monetary sphere: devaluation, liberalization of controls, domestic monetary stringency, and the like—and particularly the timing of such measures. And in the longer term the problem once again boils down to the competence of the monetary policy makers and the political pressures upon them.

FIGURE 9.2: Sample Country Analysis Checklist:
               Domestic Economy Demand and Monetary Factors

Describe numerically the prospects during the next 7 to 10 years for the following elements of the aggregate demand and monetary characteristics of the national economy.

AGGREGATE DEMAND FACTORS:	Favorable			Unfavorable	
	1	2	3	4	5
Consumer spending					
Investment spending					
Government spending					
Net foreign demand[1]					
Income redistribution pressure					
Government deficit					
MONETARY FACTORS:					
Money supply growth					
DEMAND-SIDE SUMMARY:					
Unemployment					
Inflation rate					
Realized GNP growth[2]					
ECONOMIC POLICYMAKERS:					
Assessment of competence					

[1] Exports minus imports.
[2] Outlook for actual (as opposed to potential) GNP growth.
Source: Prepared by author.

The demand-side and monetary elements are summarized in Figure 9.2.

External Economic Aspects

Because of the importance of foreign exchange availability in projecting debt service, country assessments usually must pay a great deal of attention to outside factors affecting a country's balance of payments and external finance. On the export side this requires evaluation of both long-term trends and short-term instabilities. Increasing product and market diversification might be a sign of greater export stability and reduced vulnerability to shifting economic and political conditions, or protectionist trends in a country's major markets. Shifts in the ratio of exports to gross national product may signal changing future balance-of-payments conditions, and an analysis of demand and supply characteristics for major export products may indicate possible sources of future instability in export receipts. Domestic export-supply constraints and export-competing demand elements link back into the analysis of structural problems, outlined above. Export policies set by the national government and by governments of competing exporters may also be important, along with exchange rate policies. In general, we are interested here in alignment of a country's exports with its international competitive advantage, in diversification of export risk, and in home-country and third-country policies that might pose a threat to future export earnings.

On the import side as well, concern must focus on both long-term trends and short-term instabilities. The ratio of imports to gross national product, for example, says little about country risk, but abrupt and sizable shifts in this ratio may be important. The ability to compress imports in times of balance-of-payments trouble may be considered in terms of measures such as the ratio of food and fuel to total imports, or the ratio of food, fuel, intermediate goods, and capital equipment to total imports. Import price volatility, supplier concentration among trading partners, and trends in import-replacement production are among the other measures that can help identify risk elements originating on the import side. Here, as in the case of exports, we are also interested in the policy context—the structure of effective tariff and nontariff protection, and its impact on domestic resource allocation and efficiency in production.

We have already noted the importance of foreign direct investment for the supply side of a national economy, in terms of its contribution to aggregate and sectoral capital formation; technology transfer; development of human resources, management, and entrepreneurial activity; access to markets; and access to supplies—the traditional multinational corporate "bundle" of services. Besides the balance-of-payments gains associated with capital inflows, induced exports, and import-replacement production, outflows may occur via induced imports of goods and services, and profit remittances. Each foreign investment project evidences a more or less special balance-of-payments profile, in magnitude as well as in timing.

Policies affecting foreign direct investment (such as taxation, restrictions on earnings remittances, indigenization pressures, nationalization, and expropriation) may seriously alter this profile, and thereby influence country prospects as viewed by international lenders. Multinational companies often are extraordinarily sensitive to changes in national policy environments, and because they can portend change in the overall creditworthiness of countries, shifts in foreign direct investment patterns deserve careful attention. So do capital outflows on the part of domestic residents, which frequently are highly sensitive to the domestic outlook, especially in times of possible discontinuous policy changes.

Finally, it may be important to analyze the magnitude and types of grants and concessional loans that a country receives from abroad, and prospective developments in these flows. Here domestic developments in the donor countries, donor-recipient relations, and the economic and political attractiveness of the recipient for such transfers may be important. Moreover, is there a "lender of last resort"? Countries of strategic or economic importance are obviously prime candidates for future intergovernmental "rescues" that may to some extent backstop private bank lending exposure in severe problem situations, and increase the interest of major financial powers in resolving country problems.

Liquidity Aspects

The aforementioned issues usually involve medium- and long-range forecasts of such aggregates as the balance of trade, the current account, and various other "flow" measures. These naturally will be reflected in a country's future international reserve position and in its access to international financial markets for future financing needs. Near-term "liquidity" assessments generally focus on such measures as changes in a country's owned reserves and IMF position, and on ratios, such as reserves to monthly imports, intended to indicate in some sense the degree of "cushioning" provided by reserve holdings. Ability to borrow additional sums abroad, or to refinance existing debt, naturally depends on the projected state of financial markets and assessment of country creditworthiness by international banks and official institutions at the time of need. Favorable financial market and country conditions sometimes lead to "preemptive" borrowing to restructure outstanding debt at market terms and to build up reserves for future use or to improve future creditworthiness.

Analysis of the size and structure of country indebtedness and debt service payments is equally important in this regard. Ratios such as total debt to exports or to gross national product, and long-term public debt to exports or to gross national product are used in virtually all country analyses, as are the amount of and trends in overall external indebtedness, current versus term debt, and total and short-term bank claims. The "debt service ratio"—debt service payments to exports or "normal" exports—is perhaps the most common, and can be criticized on various grounds. For example, by using only exports in the denominator, it ignores the potentially equivalent contributions of import substitution to debt service capabilities. And a particular debt-service ratio (say 0.3) may mean entirely different things for different countries as far as creditworthiness is concerned. Additionally, the ratios of foreign capital inflows to debt service payments, exports plus capital inflows and aid receipts to current debt, vital imports plus debt service payments to exports plus capital inflows and aid receipts ("compressibility ratio"), and the reciprocal of the average maturity of external debt ("rollover ratio") are commonly used.

All such ratios must be interpreted cautiously, and have different meanings for different countries and for the same country at different times and stages of development. There are no valid rules of thumb. The skill lies in the interpretation of any ratios used, particularly changes in them, and in the specific context of particular country situations. Yet even if a good analyst recognizes the limitations of some of the more pedestrian indicators, they may nevertheless figure heavily, and perhaps mechanically, how the market views the situation in a debt rollover context—and, therefore, may have to be monitored carefully.

The external stock and flow factors are summarized in Figure 9.3.

FIGURE 9.3: Sample Country Analysis Checklist: Trade, Capital Flows, Reserves, and Debt

Describe numerically the prospects during the next 7 to 10 years the following elements of the supply side of the national economy.

	Favorable			Unfavorable	
	1	2	3	4	5
Labor force quantity					
Labor force quality					
Labor supply bottlenecks					
Labor supply disruptions					
Savings rate					
Financial intermediation[1]					
Investment levels (domestic)					
Economic infrastructure[2]					
Social infrastructure[3]					
Agricultural development					
Natural resources					
Energy					
Foreign direct investment					
Productivity					
Entrepreneurship					
Character of the people					

SUPPLY-SIDE SUMMARY:	1	2	3	4	5
Real growth potential					
Emergence of bottlenecks					
Ability to withstand adverse shocks					

---

[1] Diversification across export markets and products.
[2] Diversification across import sources of supply (trading partners).
[3] Imports of "necessities" like food and fuel (which cannot be reduced under adversity) as a percentage of total imports.
[4] For example, debt service payments as a percent of exports.
[5] Net borrowings from the International Monetary Fund.
[6] Is the currency "overvalued" or "undervalued," as projected?
[7] Movement of export prices relative to import prices.
Source: Prepared by author.

Political Aspects

Besides domestic structural and monetary factors and external stock and flow variables, country analysis related to term exposure always requires astute political forecasting. Most closely related to the economic variables just reviewed, of course, is the "competence" or "wisdom" of the economic managers—which, insofar as it relates to the cast of characters on the stage, is basically a political matter. Small changes in the actors can cause enormous changes in the quality of the play. There is also the question of whether the technocrats have a full political mandate to "do what is necessary" from a debt service point of view, and ultimately whether the government itself is firmly enough in the saddle and has the political "guts" to carry it out. Recent "horror stories," ranging from Turkey and Zaire to Jamaica, Peru, and Poland, illustrate the critical importance of evaluating and forecasting the political "overlay" of national economic policy making—the degree of resolve, the power base, and the tools available for implementing sound policy decisions. Banks and corporations that are leaders in country analysis generally place a great deal of stress on this particular dimension, which requires an entirely different sort of prognostication and information base than some of the more fundamental political developments that need to be sorted out, monitored, and forecast as well.

Internal political change may range from gradual to abrupt, systemic to nonsystemic, and cataclysmic to trivial in terms of its importance to international firms. For example, political drift to the right or left may mean a great deal in terms of the internal and external workings of the national economy and the quality of economic management, as the recent history of countries like Brazil, Mexico, Chile, and Sri Lanka demonstrates. The symptoms make themselves felt in domestic fiscal and monetary policies, relations with foreign countries, pressures for nationalization or indigenization of foreign direct investments, imposition of exchange controls, and the like. Adverse shifts in this respect may result in soaring imports, reduced capacity to export, drying-up of foreign direct investment, capital flight, aid cutoffs, and problems in gaining access to international capital markets. The point is that it is necessary to fix on the direction, magnitude, and timing of political drift, if any, before very much that is sensible can be said about future macroeconomic scenarios.

A more dramatic version of the same thing relates to violent internal political conflict, which may ultimately produce the type of political "drift" discussed above, but in the meantime may have serious direct economic consequences as well. Strikes, terrorism, sabotage, and popular insurrection may seriously disrupt the workings of the national economy, with potentially dramatic consequences for the balance of payments. Export industries like tourism are particularly sensitive to such problems. The direct and indirect import requirements of government anti-insurgency efforts can be significant as well. It is obviously necessary to assess the strength of both the insurgency movement and the government in order to forecast the duration and outcome of the conflict, which (if it results in systemic change) may even lead to repudiation of external debt. As the Iranian case shows, such forecasts are as treacherous as they are critical to the whole process of country analysis. The assassination of South Korean President Park Chung Hee illustrates the insignificant-reaction end of the range of possible outcomes of a discrete event of political violence, while the Iranian revolution of course represents political and economic overthrow of the existing order.

External political conflict can likewise take a variety of forms, ranging from invasion (Afghanistan) and foreign-inspired or -supported insurgency (Zaire, Morocco, Tunisia) to border tension and perceived external threats (Peru, Israel, Thailand). Threats from abroad often require far-reaching domestic resource reallocation in the form of an inflated defense establishment—causing probably adverse trade shifts—and for most countries involve large direct foreign exchange costs as well. Military hardware, human resources, and infrastructure in an economic sense generally have low or negative productivity in terms of the domestic economy or the balance of payments. Such distortions alone may have a serious bearing on the risk profile of a country as viewed from abroad.

These problems reside in both potential and actual external conflict. The latter simply makes the various distortions worse—to the extent that the costs are not absorbed by foreign political allies—to which must be added the supply-side possibilities of physical and human-resource destruction and dislocation, obsolescence, and reconstruction costs (to the extent that these are not partly offset by reparations or aid receipts). Even if external political conflict is won, there may be derivative internal political upheavals and possibly sizable costs of occupation. If the conflict is lost, continued internal resistance and reparations obligations may have a debilitating effect on the home economy, quite apart from the possibility of debt repudiation by the successor regime. All such assessments have to be undertaken in probabilistic terms, but they are of far more than casual interest in lending to countries like South Korea, Taiwan, Thailand, Yugoslavia, Pakistan, and even Malaysia and Singapore.

Shifting political alliances, regional political developments, and bilateral relations over such peripheral issues as human rights and nuclear proliferation can provide additional sources of political events. Heavy lending exposure in Eastern Europe and China (insofar as the banks are not backstopped by their home governments) carry risks related both to future political developments and to the ability of the borrowers to sever links to Western trade and financial markets at acceptable economic cost to themselves.

Both the internal and the external political factors relevant for country risk assessment are presented in Figure 9.4. From this it should be evident that political forecasting is an art that, despite its central role in plotting the future creditworthiness of countries, remains in its infancy. Indices of political stability developed by political scientists say little that is very reliable about the future or about the ultimate implications for traders, investors, or lenders. The more sophisticated projections and even on-line information systems detailing possible sources of internal and external political conflict, while useful and necessary, usually leave the critical judgments largely up to the user of the information. There are also problems in the completeness and currency of political information, as well as the inevitable biases embedded in external and in-house information that consensual approaches such as the "delphi" technique have only begun to attack. It is not surprising, therefore, that political forecasts by banks and others "missed" on dramatic cases like Iran and South Korea, or less dramatic ones like Zaire and Turkey. It hardly means, however, that significant advances cannot still be made.

DESIGNING A COUNTRY RISK INSTRUMENT

From a managerial perspective a key question is how the results of country assessment can be boiled down to "ratings" that can be effectively used in decision making. Clearly, to describe a country's prospects fully would require an extensive and detailed narrative

FIGURE 9.4. Sample Country Analysis Checklist: Political Factors

Leadership Change

Mark the combination which seems to describe best the country's leadership:

	Democratically elected majority party	Democratically elected majority coalition	Non democratically elected ruling party/coalition/faction	No real ruling party/coalition/faction
Leadership in power for past 4-5 years				
Leadership in power for less than 4-5 years				
Leadership facing fragmented opposition				
Leadership facing strong, organized opposition				

Describe numerically the level of violence displayed during demonstrations, riots or strikes by both demonstrators and polic (army?) during the past 2-3 years.

low 1	2	3	4	high 5

Describe numerically the level of terrorism (both internally and abroad, by organisations belonging to the country).

Goal change

YES	NO	DON'T KNOW

Fundamental issues are being debated and the leadership is deeply divided over them

If the answer is YES, answer the following:

Does the content of these debates touch on matters of economic policy?

Yes	No

Although they do not touch on matters of economic policy, the debates themselves strongly influence the leadership's economic policies

If the answer is NO, answer the following:

Although fundamental issues are not being debated, they do exist and are potentially divisive

Yes	No

Strong pressure groups within the country are likely to bring up requests or demands whose implementation requires a drastic change in officially stated systemic goals

Policy change

The way laws, regulations, rules and orders are implemented has changed over the last 4-5 years

No 1	2	3	4	Yes 5

Administrative procedures are currently being revised and changed

The need for a thorough administrative reform having deep implications on how rules are implemented is felt

Capability

	Favorably				Unfavorably
	1	2	3	4	5

How do you rate the country's...

efforts to set up and manage an efficient educational system (elementary and high schools, vocational schools, institutes of higher learning)?

efforts to use its natural resources (land reclamation, extraction of minerals, etc.)?

efforts to utilize its human capital (providing employment and incentives to specialists, financing research, etc.)?

enforce its own laws (prevention and punishment of crime)?

avoid and prevent deviance or morally condemnable behavior?

cope with environmental problems (pollution, health, etc.)?

welfare programs?

other programs for the underprivileged?

wage and price policy?

ability to project a good image of the government among its own citizens?

ability to project a good image abroad?

ability to convince the public opinion of the worthiness of its own government?

ability to cope with internal natural emergencies (earthquakes, drought, etc.)?

ability to cope with social and political emergencies (strikes, terrorism, etc.)?

ability to effectively respond to explicit military threat from abroad?

Structural differentiation

Does the political system have specialized structures able to perform the following activities:

-- rule making
-- rule implementation
-- rule adjudication (tribunals)

	High Spec.				Low Spec.
	1	2	3	4	5

Does the political system have specialized structure able to convert popular demands and widely felt needs into a suitable output (a new law, an administrative reform, etc.) through the following activities:

-- rule making
-- rule implementation
-- rule adjudication

	High Spec.				Low Spec.
	1	2	3	4	5

Ideological polarization

Check the existence of the following:

Opposing groups characterized by widely differing systems of thought

Historically rooted cleavages among groups

Intolerance among groups and unwillingness to compromise

Use of violence justified and encouraged by the opposing groups

	low				high
	1	2	3	4	5

Subsystem autonomy

Amount of political participation allowed through elections and party/trade union activism (or whatever group has an official status)

Amount of political participation allowed or tolerated through demonstrations, propaganda, lobbies, professional associations etc. (informal interest groups)

Level of the activity actually occurring

	high				low
	1	2	3	4	5

215

Internal political summary | Favorable | | | Unfavorable |
| 1 | 2 | 3 | 4 | 5 |

Prospects for avoidance of domestic
political violence

Prospects for avoidance of "systemic"
political change

Prospects for avoidance of adverse economic
effects of emerging political change

Mandate given to economic policymakers

External political factors

| 1 | 2 | 3 | 4 | 5 |

Prospects for avoidance of border warfare
or tensions

Avoidance of geopolitical tension spillovers

Stabilizing effects of regional political
alliances

Avoidance of economic warfare

Source: Prepared by author.

216

backed up by large quantities of economic data and forecasts. Such extensive and relatively unstructured "country studies" would clearly be cumbersome and of limited value in business decision making. Moreover, they would be relatively noncomparable among countries, and highly sensitive to differences in competence among country analysts. Some technique, therefore, may have to be found to organize as much country information as possible and boil it down into usable form. This is the task of "country risk rating" systems.

FIGURE 9.5: Sample Country Review Checklist: Summary and Compilation of Country Rating

Assign weights to factors A through F in the second-to-last column, according to your assessment of the relative importance of each summary factor. Weights must add up to 100. Then multiply the value you have assigned to each factor by its weight, and add all of the products for items A through F. Your total ("weighted country rating") will lie somewhere between 100 (most favorable) and 500 (least favorable).

Favorable Unfavorable

	1	2	3	4	5	Weights	Products
A. Economy: supply side							
B. Economy: demand and monetary factors							
C. Balance of payments, reserves, debt							
D. Competence of economic policymakers							
E. Internal political							
F. External political							
				TOTALS		100	TOTAL

WEIGHTED COUNTRY RATING ◄- - - - - - - - - - - - - - - - - - - ┘

Source: Prepared by author.

Figure 9.5 summarizes the checklists used so far, which can be converted into an instrument that might be used to construct a country rating. It involves assigning judgmental values to a series of factors, aggregating them, and then compiling the aggregates into an overall summary "score." This involves the assignment of weights, either explicit or implicit, to the various factors and, clearly, a great deal of subjectivity. Moreover, it is not at all certain that the same weights should be assigned to each country—since the importances of individual factors differ as potential sources of risk from one country to the next.

What a country risk rating approach like this contributes in terms of usefulness, it often loses in capturing highly country-specific sources of risk. For example, few country risk rating systems succeeded in forecasting the 1977 Iranian revolution or its consequences for international banking. For this reason dependence on such "weighted checklist" or "scoring" systems can be quite hazardous. It is recommended that this kind of approach be used only as a preliminary "screen" to identify countries that should be further reviewed in depth with specific reference to a bank's contemplated exposure levels.

Somewhat better are two-dimensional checklist arrangements, where several aspects of country risk are displayed at the same time, such as debt servicing capacity, a product of internal and external fundamental factors like GNP growth, the balance of trade, and domestic monetary expansion; and liquidity indicators, such as available input cover and a country's IMF position. These can be displayed in matrix format, and can locate countries in different risk categories based on specific sources of risk. Multidimensional displays can be used with similar effect to indicate not only the overall level of risk to which the bank is exposed in a particular country, but also the principal sources of that risk—and both can be composed across countries.

In addition, however, banks generally will want to undertake periodic in-depth analyses of countries' economic and political systems and forecasts of the future. Only in this way can some of the critical qualitative factors—particularly with respect to the competence of economic policy makers and internal and external political developments—be fully integrated into the bank's country profile regarding prospective risks and returns associated with specific country exposures.

Given the nature of the country evaluation problem within the context of decisions in international bank lending, and the available techniques, it is useful to discuss briefly the institutional setting within which this process occurs. Figure 9.6 represents a simplified schematic of a decision system, one that will vary to some extent among internationally active banks—the solid lines represent reporting relationships and the broken lines represent information flows.

FIGURE 9.6: Setting, Monitoring, and Evaluating International Risk Exposure

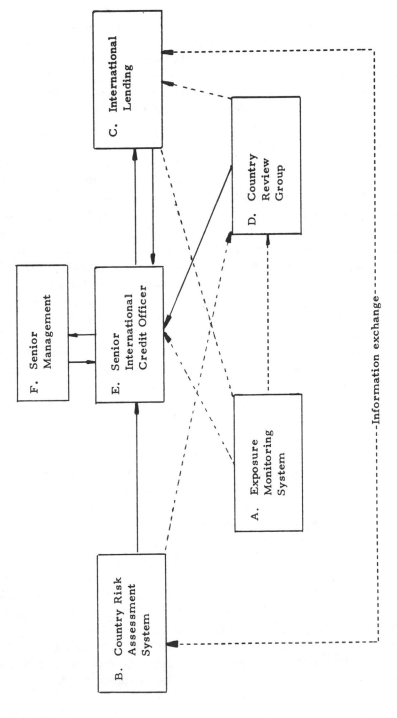

Source: Prepared by author.

Information on cross-border exposure can be maintained by a monitoring system at the head office (A).

There will normally be a substantial two-way exchange of information between those responsible for monitoring the country risk assessment system (B) and line managers (C), insofar as they are not one and the same. If a major loan is contemplated, if a change in exposure limits seems justified by profitability trends, or if an alteration in the perceived riskiness of exposure develops, an ad hoc country review group (D) may be formed, consisting of responsible officers, senior executives with regional responsibility, country economists and other country specialists, and possibly other interested individuals under the chairmanship of the bank's senior international credit officer (E) or that officer's designee. Such a review group may recommend appropriate action in the case involved. The purpose is to bring together as many different viewpoints as possible, often with conflicting opinions—for example, between the country economist emphasizing the risks and loan officers emphasizing business opportunities, competitive positioning, and the associated returns. Ultimate responsibility lies with the senior international credit officer, who reports directly to top management (F) and is charged with monitoring and planning the bank's international loan or investment portfolio within broad policy guidelines.

In the design of a country analysis function, the emphasis clearly must be on the fact that it is the beginning, not the end, of the task. Approaches that try to be overly precise risk triggering arguments among users over irrelevant points. Those that are too general may fail to concentrate on the true sources of risk in country exposure and on the specific concerns facing a particular bank or corporation. Risk to medium- and long-term loan or investment exposure requires a far more complex analysis than risk to short-term lending or trade credit.

The twin temptations of "quick and dirty" and "overloaded" country assessments often seem to confront international bankers. The first approach promises mechanical shortcuts and the use of low-priced talent to grind out results at reasonable cost, but often appears to succeed only in producing nonsense—there is no substitute for high-quality analysis, flexibility, judgment, and familiarity. The second approach may rely on well-qualified internal personnel at high cost, yet encounter a dangerous narrowing of country expertise, possibly cause dissension, and create bottlenecks in the decision-making process.

The conflicting demands of country assessment—ranging from high levels of usability, auditability, and comparability and the need to capture exceedingly complex and country-specific qualitative judgments over extended periods of time, to the need to avoid abuse of the results in decision making—probably mean that there is no such thing as an "ideal" system. "Appropriate" systems will certainly differ for different banks or corporations.

The key may reside as much on the "human resources" side as on the "technology" side. To train line executives in using reasonably unsophisticated yet sensible country assessments properly, and in being sensitive to changing country risk profiles as they go about their business, may in the end contribute more to sound decisions than comparable resources devoted to the design and implementation of more elegant systems. This would appear to follow from the view of multinational banks' general competitive advantage as "information factories" to which their global operations and headquarters-affiliate links are ideally suited.

Country assessment should be an integrated managerial process that focuses the network of information and actively involves individuals with different functions and perspectives. It will thus have intangible benefits all its own, quite apart from its more visible output in the form of defensible country-by-country evaluations. Mechanization and decentralization of the country review process will tend to cut down, and perhaps eliminate, this benefit, and may thereby help to stifle an environment conducive to sound international lending decisions.

SUGGESTED REFERENCES

Association of Reserve City Bankers. *Country Exposure and Reporting Practices of Member Banks.* NY: ARCB, March 1977.

Avramovic, Dragoslav, et al. *Economic Growth and External Debt.* Baltimore: Johns Hopkins University Press, 1968.

Brainard, Lawrence J. "Recession Will Hit the Weakest Hardest." *Euromoney*, April 1979, pp. 125, 127-28, 131.

Caldwell, J. Alexander, and J. Antonio Villamil. "U.S. Lenders Are Learning to Discriminate." *Euromoney*, April 1979, pp. 135-59.

Dhonte, Pierre. "Describing External Debt Situations: A Rollover Approach." *IMF Staff Papers* 22, no. 1 (1975): 159-86.

Donaldson, T. H. *Lending in International Commercial Banking.* New York: Halsted-Wiley, 1979.

Duff, Declan, and Ian Peacock. "A Cash Flow Approach to Sovereign Risk Analysis." *The Banker*, January 1979, pp. 41-46.

Ensor, Richard. *Assessing Country Risk.* London: Euromoney Publications, 1981.

Feder, G., and R. Just. "A Study of Debt Servicing Capacity Applying Logit Analysis." *Journal of Development Economics* 4, no. 1 (1977): 25-38.

Frank, Charles R., and William R. Cline. "Measurement of Debt Servicing Capacity: An Application of Discriminant Analysis." *Journal of International Economics* 1, no. 3 (1971): 327-44.

Gladwin, Thomas N., and Ingo Walter. *Multinationals Under Fire: Lessons in the Management of Conflict.* New York: Wiley-Interscience, 1980.

Goodman, Stephen. "How the Big Banks Really Evaluate Sovereign Risks." *Euromoney*, February 1977, pp. 185-89.

Kobrin, Steven J. "Political Risk: A Review and Reconsideration." *Journal of International Business Studies*, Spring-Summer 1979, pp. 67-80.

Mayo, Alice L., and Anthony G. Barrett. "An Early Warning Model of Developing Country Risk." In Stephen H. Goodman, ed., *Financing and Risk in Developing Countries.* New York: Praeger, 1978.

Nagy, Panchras. *Country Risk.* London: Euromoney Publications, 1979.

———. "Quantifying Country Risk: A System Developed by Economists at the Bank of Montreal." *Columbia Journal of World Business*, Spring 1979, pp. 26-40.

Porzecanski, Arturo. "The Assessment of Country Risk: Lessons from the Latin American Experience." In J. C. Garcia-Zamor and S. Sutin, eds., *Financing Development in Latin America.* New York: Praeger, 1980.

Puz, Richard. "How to Tell When a Country Shifts from A-1 to E-5." *Euromoney*, August 1978, pp. 67-70.

Sargen, Nicholas. "Use of Economic Indicators and Country Risk Appraisal." Federal Reserve Bank of San Francisco, *Economic Review*, Fall 1977, pp. 19-35.

van Agtmael, Antoine. "Evaluating the Risks of Lending to Developing Countries." *Euromoney*, April 1976, pp. 16-30.

10 FOREIGN EXCHANGE RISK
Clas Wihlborg

The international exchange rate regime since the breakdown of the fixed rates at the beginning of the 1970s cannot be described in simple terms. Some countries allow a "clean" float—the exchange rate is allowed to fluctuate without central bank intervention. Other countries peg their rates for long periods to a particular currency or to a basket of currencies. Many countries subscribe to some system between these extremes. In other words, they intervene at times while allowing the market to determine the exchange rate at other times. Such a system is often called a "dirty" or "managed" float. (Note, however, that theoretically all countries except one can independently determine their exchange rates relative to all other countries.) Thus, the price of the dollar in terms of other currencies is under the influence of other governments' interventions even if the Federal Reserve does not intervene at all.

Germany, France, the Netherlands, Belgium, Luxembourg, Italy, Ireland, and Denmark participate in the European Monetary System (EMS). Exchange rates are fixed within the EMS, but these countries' rates float relative to the dollar. Other European countries allow their currencies to float more or less cleanly (the United Kingdom), while others peg to a basket of currencies (Sweden, Spain, Norway).

The author wishes to thank Kaj Areskoug for valuable comments on a draft of this chapter.

Most developing countries peg to the currency of their most important trading partner or to a basket of currencies.

The shared reality for residents of all countries is that they face a number of exchange rates, most of which are flexible to some degree.

The above is a short description of the environment within which commercial banks and firms with international business must operate.

Banks with international operations participate directly or indirectly in foreign exchange markets in several ways. First, commercial banks buy and sell foreign currencies from and to individuals and firms. Second, banks act as "market makers" in foreign exchange markets under the present regime, as opposed to a pegged regime, under which central banks play that role. Third, banks are involved in arbitrage operations between different currencies and different money market centers. Fourth, banks sometimes take deposits and make loans in foreign currencies. Fifth, banks provide forecasting services and advise corporate clients on how to manage foreign currency positions.

The first section of this chapter contains a short description of the foreign exchange markets and banks' role in them. Different kinds of arbitrage operations by international banks are described in the second section. The third section considers various types of "currency risks," of which exchange risk is one. Forecasting of exchange rates is discussed in the last section. In particular I address the conditions under which it would be worthwhile to apply resources to forecasting.

FOREIGN EXCHANGE MARKETS AND COMMERCIAL BANKS

Definitions of Foreign Exchange Markets and Foreign Exchange Rates

Any purchase (sale) of one currency with (for) another is a foreign exchange transaction. All such transactions together constitute the *foreign exchange market*.[1] The actual purchase and sale can take more or less organized forms. Two persons meeting in the street can negotiate a transaction, or people can buy (sell) foreign currencies from (to) commercial banks at preannounced prices. The main reason for the existence of foreign exchange markets is the use of different means-of-transaction monies in different geographical areas. Anybody buying goods, services, or assets from individuals and firms in a different currency area generally must purchase the accepted means of payment in this area or be willing to pay a higher price. We can assert that the demand and supply for one currency in exchange for another is derived from the demands by individuals in one currency area for goods, services, and assets produced by individuals in another currency area and therefore ultimately payable in a foreign currency.

A *foreign exchange rate* is simply the price of one currency (money) in terms of another. There is no direct link between the exchange rate and relative prices in one area compared with relative prices in another. Exchange rates are relative prices of monies in terms of other monies—purely nominal variables—translating prices denominated in one currency into equivalents in other currencies.

The Intermediary Role of Banks

The advantage of a monetary economy relative to a barter economy is that the person who wishes to sell, for example, chickens for carpets need not spend time finding another person wishing to sell carpets for chickens. The monetary economy is more efficient because transaction and search costs are lower.

Banks in foreign exchange markets perform a role similar to that of money in the markets for goods and services. The person who wishes to buy 1,000 pounds sterling for dollars needs to find a person with these pounds in supply—who may not exist—if there are no intermediaries. Every individual who wants to buy or sell any amount of foreign currency benefits from being able to buy from and sell to a common intermediary that attracts a large number of sellers and buyers of different currencies. Banks perform this intermediary role in foreign exchange markets as they do between lenders (depositors) and borrowers in financial markets.

It is obvious that a bank performs its intermediary role better the more buyers and sellers it can attract, because the likelihood increases that it can satisfy a particular currency demand. Accordingly, there are substantial economies of scale in the intermediary function in foreign exchange markets.

Banks as Market Makers

Theoretically, one can imagine that banks act merely as brokers in foreign exchange markets, simplifying contact between the demander and the supplier of, for example, 1,000 pounds sterling, or between one person who wishes to buy 1,000 pounds and 10 persons, each of whom wishes to sell 100 pounds. This kind of system works well as long as trade in goods, services, and assets between two currency areas is balanced at all times. A bank can improve its foreign exchange services, however, if it is willing to buy a certain currency from a person without having another person selling the same currency to it at the same time. Trade, then, is not balanced between two currencies hour by hour, day by day, or even over a year. It follows that the intermediary role of a bank is improved if, as a kind of dealer, it is willing to take a position in a currency for some time—that is, to buy an amount of a currency with the expectation of selling it at the same or a higher price in the future. *Market making* involves exactly this.

Central banks act as market makers under a fixed-exchange-rate regime. They promise to buy and sell any amount of foreign currency at a specific price (or at certain price floors and ceilings). In such a case commercial banks do not take any risk by holding positions in foreign currencies. Under a flexible regime, however, central banks do not guarantee to buy and sell currencies at particular prices. Thus, open positions that are taken by banks are risky. Nevertheless, for the system to function smoothly, somebody must be willing to take positions. In other words, private market makers are needed to bridge the time gap between demand and supply for a currency by individuals and firms.

Every bank that handles foreign exchange transactions with individuals and firms cannot avoid performing a market-making role to some extent, because it is impossible for a bank to keep positions balanced at all times.

The above definition of a market maker differs somewhat from the common use of the term. It is often reserved for the bigger banks that trade with each other without underlying demand and supply from customers. Such interbank trade is based entirely on differential expectations among the parties to the transactions, and helps smooth out rate fluctuations when the underlying demand from customers is temporarily out of balance. Other, "nonmarket-making" banks sell the foreign exchange positions that arise in their dealings with individuals and firms to the larger market-making banks. Nevertheless, any bank dealing in foreign exchange must take positions for at least the time it takes to sell it to another bank. In this sense all banks participate in market making to some extent.

Foreign Exchange Contracts and Foreign Exchange Quotations

The most commonly quoted exchange rate is the spot rate. This rate is properly a two-day rate, since the interbank spot market is a two-day market. In other words, the parties to a spot transaction determine a price for currency to be delivered in two business days (the value date). Banks can trade for "next day" or "cash" as well, but this is rarer because of time zone differences. The number of transactions completed in less than two days has expanded recently with electronic fund transfers. In particular, transactions between Europe and New York can now be completed during one day.

Firms and individuals can buy currencies from banks for immediate delivery. The relevant exchange rate for such transactions is the spot rate plus/minus the bank's fee. This is reflected in the *bid/ask spread*—the difference between the prices at which a bank is willing to buy (bid price) and sell (ask price) a currency.

Foreign currency also is traded in *forward markets.* Individuals and firms can buy a currency for delivery and payment at a future date at a price determined when the forward contract is entered. Similarly, banks trade forward with each other by entering contracts for delivery and payment beyond two days. Forward contracts for a few currencies may mature as far in the future as five years, but the most common contracts are for one, three, or six months.

The demand for and supply of foreign exchange in the forward markets reflect the payment terms for the underlying transactions in goods, services, and asset markets. An importer of goods might obtain a trade credit for, say, 90 days. This importer can enter a forward contract with a 90-day maturity, and thereby make sure how much domestic currency will be needed at the payment date.

Futures contracts are similar to forward contracts in the sense that contracts are fulfilled at a future date. The futures markets in which these contracts are traded differ from forward markets, however. Futures markets are organized markets like stock exchanges. This means that contracts are standardized in terms of maturity and amount. A limited set of maturities and amounts is available. The International Money Market in Chicago is the most prominent market for futures contracts. Forward contracts, on the other hand, can be entered for any maturity and amount, though active trading in the interbank forward market is limited to "even" maturities such as one week, one month, or two months.

Foreign exchange contracts among banks can take on more complicated forms than simple spot and forward contracts. One buy and one sell contract with different maturities can be combined into a swap. For example, a "spot against forward" swap involves the spot purchase (sale) and forward sale (purchase) of one currency for another. Swaps are used mainly in interbank trade, but an exporter/importer with one receivable and one payable of equal size but different maturities could utilize a swap to cover against the exchange risk between the two maturity dates.

Exchange rates can be quoted in "*European terms*" as the number of foreign currency units per dollar, or in "*U.S. terms*," as the number of dollars per unit of foreign currency. Forward rates can also be expressed as swap rates, as opposed to the above outright rates. A *swap rate* shows the number of points ($.0001 per unit of foreign currency) at which a currency is at a premium or discount in the forward market relative to the spot rate.

An example can clarify these terms. Assume that we have a spot rate equal to $2.00 per pound sterling. The three-month forward rate is $2.005 per pound sterling. This means that the pound is at a premium in the forward market relative to the dollar. (The dollar is at a discount relative to the pound.) The swap rate for the pound is a 50-point premium relative to the dollar.

Another way to express a forward rate is as premium and discount in terms of percent per annum. The pound is at a 1 percent premium in the above illustration. Mathematically, the premium is

$$\frac{2.005-2.000}{2.000} \cdot \frac{12}{3} \cdot 100 = 1.$$

The dollar is, naturally, at a 1 percent discount. The general formula for premiums/discounts is

$$\frac{\text{Forward rate-spot rate}}{\text{spot rate}} \cdot \frac{12 \text{ months}}{\text{months to maturity}} \cdot 100$$

where all rates are expressed as dollars/unit of foreign currency.

The above quotations were "midpoints" between the bid and ask prices. The actual quotation a customer can receive by calling a bank must necessarily distinguish between bid and ask prices. An example of a quotation is the following:

Price of pounds: 1.9998/2.0002   28/32   47/53   7/13   13/7.

These figures show outright bid and ask prices, as illustrated below.

Dollars/Pound, Outright Prices

	Bid	Ask
Spot	1.9998	2.0002
1 month	2.0026	2.0034
3 months	2.0045	2.0055
6 months	2.0005	2.0015
12 months	1.9985	1.9995

The first two figures in the quotation show the spot prices (bid/ ask). The figures thereafter show forward rates (bid/ask) for one month, three months, six months and one year, respectively, in the form of points premium or discount. The foreign currency is at a premium when the bid figure is lower than the ask figure (for instance, 28/32). We add the points to the spot rate to arrive at outright forward rates. The foreign currency is at a discount when the bid figure is higher than the ask figure (13/7). In this case we deduct the number of points from the spot rate to arrive at the outright rate.

Some Institutional Characteristics of Foreign Exchange Markets

Banks performing their intermediary role may not be willing to hold open positions, and therefore sell these positions to other banks. These other banks are the more dominant ones in market making. They trade with each other on the basis of different expectations about exchange rate developments, and are willing to hold open positions for shorter or longer periods. The expectations of different banks depend on general information and on signals from their customers in the international business community.

The *interbank foreign exchange market* is one in which the exchange rate is determined under a flexible exchange rate regime. This market is not an exchange like the New York Stock Exchange; instead, most transactions are carried out by telephone or telex, and trading departments in each bank deal with trading departments in other banks continuously.

The foreign exchange market is truly global. There is a 24-hour market in the sense that foreign exchange trading is going on somewhere in the world at any time during any 24-hour period. Moreover, at almost any time there is some overlap between continents. Morning trading in New York corresponds to afternoon trading in Frankfurt and Zurich. Late afternoon trading in San Francisco corresponds to morning trading in, for example, Singapore. As a result of this continuous global trading, exchange rates can move continuously, and news and new information spread nearly instantaneously among traders in different parts of the world.

Though the markets are global, each country's monetary authority imposes its specific regulations on foreign exchange activities. Some central banks set severe restrictions on the size of the open positions of the banks under their jurisdiction, and have to authorize the banks before they are allowed to trade in foreign exchange. Other countries, like the United States, do not regulate market practices and do not require authorization.

Banks in the United States deal with each other and foreign banks through *direct dealings* or through *foreign exchange brokers*. Direct dealings occur mainly among established market makers, and rely on a large amount of trust and reciprocity. Contracts are made verbally by phone. Naturally, it becomes known to every trader in the world if one bank has broken a verbal contract. This bank would not be able to participate further. Reciprocity is important, because different banks specialize in market making in different currencies. One bank specializing in, for example, pounds sterling offers market-making services to another bank specializing in, say, deutsche marks, knowing that the latter bank will offer the same services in deutsche marks. Market-making banks offer *two-way bids* in direct dealings. In other words, one bank quotes a bid and an ask price to another bank upon request, and stands ready to buy or sell, knowing that the latter will do the same in another currency.

Foreign exchange brokers help to arrange transactions among banks. Thus, they serve as intermediaries for banks. They do not take open positions, but arrange communication between the two sides of the market. A bank that contacts a broker for a desired sale cannot be sure that a transaction will take place, because the broker may not have another customer willing to buy at the same time. However, the broker will use its market knowledge to search for a buyer. The advantage of handling transactions through brokers is that foreign exchange contracts become more formalized than in direct dealings, and need not rely on trust and reciprocity. Smaller, nonmarket-making banks can therefore participate in the markets via brokers.

Foreign Exchange Exposure in Foreign Exchange Trading

Any bank dealing in foreign exchange must accept the risk that the exchange rate may change before an offsetting transaction can be made. Any open position is exposed to this foreign exchange risk. Some banks trying to stay out of market making may be exposed only for minutes. However, under a flexible regime this time may be sufficient for exchange rates to move substantially during periods of rapid change and turmoil. Once news hits the market, it spreads extremely rapidly and rates adjust quickly.

The more involved a bank is in market making, the larger the open positions it must take and the longer it must hold such positions. The scope for gains and losses due to exchange rate changes are enormous for these banks. Foreign exchange traders tend individually to specialize in one currency and in a specific time horizon, since the same piece of information—for example, from a central bank—may have different impacts on currencies and time horizons. Detailed fingertip knowledge of the market is necessary for a trader.

The swaps mentioned above are subject to interest rate risk or forward exchange rate risk. A one-month forward purchase of pounds sterling and a simultaneous three-month forward sale of pounds sterling do not leave an open position on the books. However, the "mismatch" of maturities implies that the bank will receive an open pound position in one month and that it will not be offset for another two months. The open position can be viewed as exposed to interest rate changes because the pounds can be held on deposit for the two months at an uncertain interest rate as of the day of the contract. Alternatively, we can look at this risk as forward rate risk because the pounds that the bank receives in one month for two months' holding can be sold forward at the time of receipt at an uncertain two-month rate. Forward rate risk and interest rate risk are normally equivalent because changes in the relative interest rate between two currencies typically correspond to changes in the forward premium/discount between the currencies. (Compare "Covered Interest Arbitrage" in subsection "Covered Arbitrage.")

We need not go into the actual management of currency positions here. Some positions occur by design, and these naturally are not a problem, although banks impose limitations on their individual traders' positions. Other positions occur as a result of services provided to customers, and need not be the desired ones. Then the bank tries to obtain the desired position and maturity composition in trades with other banks. An undesired mismatched maturity composition in a currency can be offset by an opposite swap.[2] Rates may change, however, before the bank is able to make such a deal.

ARBITRAGE OPERATIONS AND SPECULATION IN FOREIGN EXCHANGE MARKETS

An important part of the foreign exchange market operations of commercial banks is arbitrage operations of different kinds.[3] The definition of arbitrage is "the simultaneous purchase and sale of the same or equivalent security in order to profit from price discrepancies."[4] This definition implies that the security-specific risk is irrelevant in a pure arbitrage transaction (equivalent security). It is based entirely on more or less lasting disequilibriums in markets. Arbitrage has an important role in its contribution to smoothly functioning markets, in the sense that the price of a particular security should be independent of the location and identity of the seller.[5]

Arbitrage activities are similar to "speculative" activities, but the latter are risky, since the securities purchased and sold in such a transaction are not equivalent. Speculative transactions are based on differential expectations about future prices or different degrees of risk acceptance among the partners to a transaction. The swaps discussed above are speculative activities. A one-month forward contract and a two-month contract cannot be considered equivalent securities because the risks differ. A swap cannot take place without different expectations or risk attitudes, with respect to the two maturities, by the two partners to the transactions. Nevertheless, swaps are often called *time arbitrage.*

Common *pure* arbitrage transactions performed by banks in foreign exchange markets and other international financial markets are the following:

- Triangular arbitrage
- Covered arbitrage
- Arbitrage between the U.S. and the foreign money markets in dollar-denominated securities.

Triangular Arbitrage

Assume that 1 pound sterling costs U.S. $2.00 in the spot market while 1 deutsche mark costs 50 cents. The implicit mark/pound rate (*a cross rate*) can be calculated to be 4 deutsche marks/pound sterling. If any of these rates alone would differ from the above figures, there would be scope for triangular arbitrage—so called because a transaction would typically involve banks in three locations.

Take a case when the dollar/pound rate in London is $2.02/£, the deutsche mark (DM) rate in New York is $.50/DM, and the mark/pound rate in Frankfurt is DM4/£. Obviously the pound is too cheap in Frankfurt or too expensive in London. Therefore, use $50 to buy DM 100 in New York, and sell these DM for £25 in Frankfurt. Then, use the £25 in London to purchase $50.50. The arbitrageur makes a profit of 50 cents on these transactions. They can be carried out by telephone.

Triangular arbitrage was more common when traders did not have rapid communications via screens on which currency prices in different locations can be shown simultaneously. Electronic developments have made the international market very efficient, and rates in one market are often based on rates in the others because the potential for immediate triangular arbitrage exists. This kind of arbitrage is therefore important implicitly, though there are seldom actual opportunities to pursue it.

Covered Interest Arbitrage

Covered interest arbitrage is a transaction composed of borrowing one currency for, say, three months, purchasing another currency spot, depositing the funds for three months, and selling the future proceeds three months forward against the currency in which the loan was taken. There is no exchange risk on this transaction. Alternatively the arbitrageur may sell a security denominated in one currency while purchasing an identical security denominated in another currency. A forward sale of the latter currency covers against exchange risk.

Covered arbitrage is easily illustrated with the following figures:

- 3 months' interest rate in dollars: 8%
- 3 months' interest rate in pounds: 12%
- Spot exchange rate: $2/£
- 3-month forward rate: $1.95/£
- Borrowing and lending rates are equal in each currency.

Consider the following transaction:

- Borrow $100
- Buy £50 at spot rate ($100/($2/£))
- Deposit £50 and in three months receive $£[(\$100/2)(1 + .12/4)] = 50(1.03) = 51.5$
- Sell $£[(100/2)(1 + .12/4)]$ at the initial time in the three-months' forward market and in three months receive
$$\$(1.95/2) \times 100 \times (1 + .12/4) = \$100.4$$
- Pay back loan with interest $= \$100(1 + .08/4) = \$102.$

In this case the arbitrageur would suffer a loss. Accordingly it is necessary to make the opposite arbitrage transaction with the above figures in order to make a gain:

- Borrow £50
- Buy $100
- Invest in deposit at 8% interest in dollars
- Sell $/buy £ forward $[(\$100(1 + .08/4)]$
- In three months receive pounds and pay back loan.

Covered arbitrage can occur in the markets for Treasury bills, certificates of deposit, and other money market instruments in different currencies. Many of these are necessarily issued in different countries as well as different currency denominations. For example, a pound Treasury bill and a dollar Treasury bill are issued by the British and the American treasuries, respectively. The two securities are therefore different in terms of country risk, and the investors' demand for a risk premium enters the calculation in such a way that arbitrage may not occur at small incentives.[6] Only in the Eurodollar market can one find securities that differ only in terms of currency denomination. Accordingly, covered arbitrage incentives exist until the difference between the interest rates in two currencies is equal to the forward premium. When this is the case, interest rate parity holds. The formula describing this equilibrium relationship is

$$(1 + r_1/n) = (1 + r_2/n)\frac{F}{S} \text{ or } (1 + r_1) = (1 + r_2)(1 + f)$$

where r_1 and r_2 are nominal interest rates
$n = 12/\text{number of months to maturity}$
F = forward rate (country 1 currency units/unit of currency 2)
S = spot rate
f = forward premium on currency 2 (discount on currency 1)

The above formula is often approximated as $r_1 = r_2 + f$. The latter holds well when r_1, r_2, and f are small.

Interest rate parity holds within very narrow margins (due to transactions costs) among the major currencies.[7] In fact, banks may often use the interest rate differential to set their forward rates. As a result, covered arbitrage transactions need not take place very often. Traders in banks would rapidly observe deviations from parity, and this knowledge prevents banks from trying to set forward rates inconsistent with interest rate parity. Exceptions may occur in periods of turmoil in the markets and for exchange rates of currencies in which, as a result of exchange controls, the arbitrage opportunities are limited.

Arbitrage Between the U.S. Money Market and the Eurodollar Market

Similar money market instruments denominated in dollars are issued in the United States and in Europe or other Eurodollar centers. Arbitrage between these markets is naturally free from exchange risk, but country risks may differ as a result of exchange controls or uncertainty about future tax rules. Banks can arbitrage between, for example, certificates of deposit issued in New York and London but, if one country is considered relatively risky, interest rates need not become completely equal in the two markets. Small interest rate differentials are actually observed between money markets located in different countries.[8] Different reserve requirements in the two markets may also explain differences between quoted nominal interest rates for one currency. "Effective" interest rates for banks may nevertheless be equal.[9]

Speculation

Speculative transactions, as well as pure arbitrage transactions, do not technically require any particular amount of wealth at the time the transaction is initiated. Speculation is risky, however, and may result in a loss. It is therefore essential for the speculator to have a "cushion" to absorb such a loss. One kind of speculation is a swap or mismatched maturities in otherwise offsetting forward market positions.

"Pure" speculation in foreign exchange markets involves only the purchase of a forward contract. At the maturity date the speculator purchases or sells in the spot market the foreign exchange necessary to fulfill the contract. As with swaps, this kind of transaction is based on different expectations or risk perceptions of the parties to the contract. Assume, for example, that the forward pound sterling for three-month forward delivery costs $2.10. The speculator who expects the spot rate to be above $2.10—say $2.15—buys pounds forward for dollars. At the maturity date the speculator expects to be able to sell each pound for $2.15, thereby making $.05 profit per pound. Naturally the speculator suffers a loss if the pound falls below $2.10.

The speculator must find a party to the above contract. In other words, somebody must be willing to sell pounds forward at $2.10. This could be a speculator having the expectation that the pound will fall below $2.10, or it could be a risk-avoiding U.S. exporter to the United Kingdom with receivables in pounds. In the former case expectations differ among the parties, and risk perceptions differ in the latter case.

Another speculative transaction is often called "uncovered interest arbitrage." This is a mixture of covered interest arbitrage and

pure speculation. The only difference between covered and uncovered interest arbitrage is that the arbitrageur/speculator in the
latter case does not cover the future receivable in the foreign currency. Both transactions consist of borrowing in one currency and
investing in another. Incentives for uncovered arbitrage exist when
the expected rate of change of the exchange rate differs from the
interest rate differential between the two currencies.

Note, finally, that the forward rate will be equal to the expected
future spot rate and, therefore, the forward premium will be equal to
the expected rate of change of the exchange rate, which in turn will
be reflected in the interest rate differential when both covered
arbitrage and speculation occur rapidly in response to profit incentives. Formally, under this condition

$$(1 + r_1)/(1 + r_2) = (1 + f) = 1 + \text{expected annual rate of appreciation}$$
$$\text{of currency 2 relative to 1}$$

Interest rate parity due   Premium-expected exchange rate change
to covered arbitrage   due to "perfect" price speculation

Interest rate differential reflects expected
exchange rate change due to "perfect" uncovered
arbitrage (international Fisher parity)

Empirical evidence shows that interest rate parity holds nearly
perfectly. The other relationships cannot be easily tested, because
expectations cannot be observed. (I return to this issue in the last
section of this chapter, since it is important for the forecasting of
exchange rates.)

CURRENCY RISKS AND MANAGEMENT

Foreign Exchange Risk and Other Currency Risks

In "Foreign Exchange Markets and Commercial Banks" exchange
rate risk related to banks' trading operations was assumed to depend
on uncertainty about the future value of foreign currencies in terms
of the domestic currency of the trading bank. This is a fair description of the risk related to the holding of open positions in currencies

for short time horizons, from a day up to a quarter of a year.[10] Over longer time horizons it is necessary to take into account that changes in the value of each money are reflected in changing money prices of goods and services. Most investors are concerned about the future purchasing power of their wealth, and therefore must consider inflation in the domestic currency. (We shall see below that the more exchange rate changes reflect differential inflation rates in different countries, the less relevant is exchange risk as it has been described above.)

A more general view of currency risks is of interest to banks, because they hold foreign currency positions for varying periods as a result of borrowing and lending in foreign currencies. Also, banks with foreign subsidiaries may receive dividends from the subsidiaries' host country activities. Thus, banks may hold foreign currency positions over many different maturities and in monetary as well as real assets. A bank may also be involved in currency management of a corporation in its role as foreign exchange adviser.

In earlier writings I have presented a theoretical view of currency risks and have applied their concepts to firms in an international environment.[11] A brief summary follows.

Underlying the taxonomy of currency risks is the concept of *purchasing power parity*. Absolute purchasing power parity holds when $e = p_1/p_2$ —the exchange rate (for instance, of dollars to pounds) is equal to the ratio of price levels in two countries. (Here p_1 is the American price level; p_2, the U.K. price level.) Since price levels are usually described by indexes that express one period's price level relative to another period's, the absolute version of purchasing power parity is seldom useful. It is more common and meaningful to express purchasing power parity in relative terms: $(1 + \hat{e}) = (1 + \hat{p}_1)/(1 + \hat{p}_2)$ or approximately $\hat{e} = \hat{p}_1 - \hat{p}_2$ where denotes a percent rate of change, $\hat{e}$ is the rate of change of the exchange rate, and $\hat{p}_1$ and $\hat{p}_2$ are the inflation rates in countries 1 and 2, respectively.

Deviations from purchasing power parity can occur over any time horizon, but there is widespread agreement among economists that it holds well over the long run.[12] The important question is: How short is the long run? This depends on the currencies considered. Purchasing power parity between the United States and Canada may hold over two-year periods, while purchasing power parity between the United States and Thailand may never occur.

A general exchange rate formula can be written as

$$\hat{e} \equiv \hat{p}_1 - \hat{p}_2 + \hat{u}$$

where $\hat{u}$ is the rate of change of deviations from purchasing power parity.

Figures 10.1 and 10.2 show that most exchange rate changes over periods up to a quarter reflect deviations from purchasing power parity. For longer periods exchange rate changes may reflect inflation differentials to a large extent.

Assume now that an investor in country 1 wishes to evaluate the real rates of return (r^R) on securities in two denominations. Then $r_1^R = r_1 - \hat{p}_1$, where r_1 is the nominal interest rate, and $r_2^R = r_2 + \hat{e} - \hat{p}_1 = r_2 - \hat{p}_2 + \hat{u}$. These expressions can be used to illustrate two kinds of currency risk in more detail.

Inflation Risk

An investor or borrower faces the risk that inflation in the currency of denomination of the asset or liability will differ from the expected, unless the nominal interest rate is precisely linked to inflation. An unanticipated rise of the rate of domestic inflation lowers the real rate of return on assets denominated in the domestic currency. It does not affect the real rate of return on foreign-currency-denominated assets when the foreign currency appreciates commensurate with higher domestic inflation relative to the foreign. A foreign investment is in fact a hedge against domestic inflation risk.

Exchange Risk

This is a risk on foreign currencies in particular, and is often set equal to the variance of the exchange rate. However, when purchasing power parity holds ($\hat{u} = 0$), there is only inflation risk. Exchange risk can therefore be defined as uncertainty about deviations from purchasing power parity.[13] (Note that exchange risk is a risk on currencies that are foreign relative to the future transaction currency— currency 1 in this example.)

Deviations from purchasing power parity may occur as a result of relative price changes, whereas the above formulations imply that the deviations occur for all commodities. The relative price between, for example, exportables and importables could be correlated with the

FIGURE 10.1: Annual Percentage Rates of Change in the Deviation
from Wholesale-Price Purchasing Power Parity for the
United States, the United Kingdom, and Germany
over Quarters and Years, 1967-76

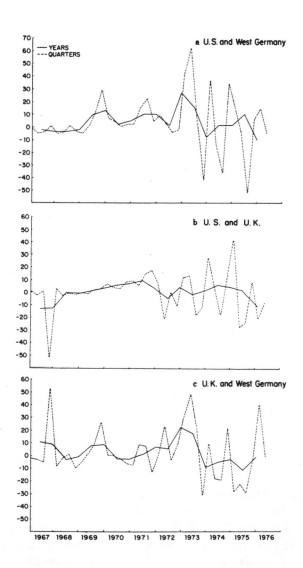

Source: C. G. Wihlborg, "Currency Risks in International Financial Markets,"
Princeton Study in International Finance no. 44 (1979).

FIGURE 10.2: Relative Unit Labor Costs in Dollars, Relative Consumer Prices in Dollars, and Exchange Rates, 1973-77

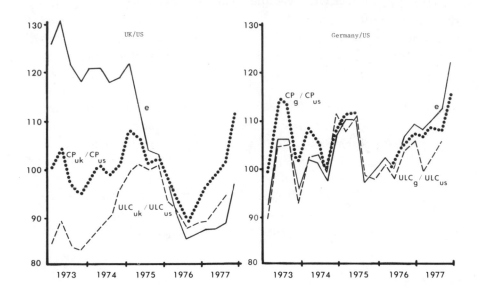

Note: ULC = Unit labor costs
     CP   = Consumer prices
     e   = Exchange rates.
ULC_{uk}/ULC_{us} and ULC_g/ULC_{us} show the development of relative unit labor costs in dollars for U.K.–U.S.A. and for Germany–U.S.A., respectively.
CP_{uk}/CP_{us} and CP_g/CP_{us} show the development of relative consumer prices in dollars. Index 100 represents purchasing power parity, and is calculated as an average for 1974–75.
Source: OECD, *Main Economic Indicators*, various issues.

exchange rate when the price of one of these commodity groups is determined primarily in world markets while the price of the other group is determined mainly by domestic cost considerations. The evaluation of risk, in terms of purchasing power, of holding an asset or liability in a particular currency must then depend on the shares of exportables and importables.[14] In the following, this kind of risk is neglected.

Corporations are often concerned about their net worth as represented by their balance sheets. This leads us to consider accounting risk. Many countries have instituted rules for translating accounts denominated in foreign currencies at consolidation dates. For example, the United Kingdom has the rule that all assets and liabilities should be translated at the current exchange rate. The recently agreed-upon rule in the United States (FAS 52) is similar, but through 1980, American corporations followed FAS 8. According to the latter rule, monetary assets and liabilities are translated at the current rates while inventories, and plant and equipment, are translated at historical rates. These rules have very different exposure implications. However, all rules have in common that the accounting exposure differs substantially from the economic exposure as defined by the exposure of shareholders to changes in the purchasing powers of their wealth as a result of unanticipated exchange rate changes.[15]

One reason for this difference is that accounting is in general conducted in nominal prices. Also, firms usually do not know their actual exposure, but still have to design some method for translation. Whatever translation method is applied, the book value of a firm will fluctuate positively or negatively with fluctuations in the exchange rate. Most firms regard this as a source of worry because the stock market's valuation of a firm may depend on reported net worth or variations thereof.

Portfolio Management Principles

We can now proceed to discuss the exposure and management of different kinds of foreign currency assets and liabilities. I distinguish between the management of short-term assets and liabilities and the management of long-term assets and liabilities.

Short-Term Assets and Liabilities

Short-term positions are exposed mainly to exchange risk. Inflation risk may also be relevant, but in the short run the inflation rate can be viewed as much more stable and predictable than the exchange rate.

Exchange risk exists on assets (liabilities) that cause future cash inflows (outflows) in currencies different from those in which future cash outflows (inflows) are denominated. The implication of this view of exposure for short-term management can most easily be seen under the assumption that the firm wishes to minimize exchange risk. The firm would distribute its gross short-term assets among currencies in such a way that future receivables exactly correspond to the distribution of payables in each currency.

This can be illustrated by an example. Assume that a bank or another kind of firm has the following positions in currencies A, B, and C with regard to a certain future date.

Inflows	A	B	C
Cash	100	50	0
Accounts receivable	200	150	50
Outflows			
Accounts payable	50	50	150
Wages due	150	100	
Dividends to be paid	50		
Net flow	+50	+50	-100

The firm has a subsidiary in B where wages have to be paid. After balancing the inflows with expected payments in different currencies, a net positive position remains in currencies A and B, balanced by a 100 liability position in C. Accordingly, the firm can become risk-free by transforming, in one way or another, its positive A and B positions into an additional 100 of currency C.

Note that the above analysis includes the expected cash flows for the corporation as a whole. In this illustration both parent and subsidiaries balance their cash flows in different currencies for each future date. Such a policy differs substantially from the balancing of positions on a balance sheet.

No firm can operate with the target of minimizing risk, however, without consideration of costs. Accordingly, relative expected returns must influence the short-term position. For example, if the effective rate of return/cost of borrowing is relatively high in A and relatively low in B, the firm's opportunity cost of balancing its currency position is high. A profit-maximizing firm would want to hold a positive position in currency A and a negative position in B.

The choice of an optimal portfolio of currencies becomes a trade-off between risk and return considerations. The more risk-averse the firm, the more closely its portfolio will approximate the risk-free balanced portfolio. The risk-neutral firm will maximize its liability position in the low-expected-return currency and invest in the high-expected-return currency. These expected returns must include interest rates and expected exchange rate changes. Without being "speculative" the firm would tend to hold a positive asset position in the currency that is expected to appreciate.

Naturally, the firm's portfolio choice is not limited to the three currencies in which it has transactions. If there was a fourth currency, D, that gave a very high return, the firm would want to hold a positive asset position in this currency. It would possibly be a risky position in terms of expected cash flows, but on the other hand, the more currencies the firm holds, the more diversified the portfolio is. The marginal risk on an asset depends on its covariance with other assets, and not on an individual variance. A negative correlation between currency D and the other currencies could therefore decrease the total risk on the portfolio.

Management of Long-Term Financial Positions

The principles of diversifying long-term positions are simpler, since the exchange rate usually follows relative price levels closely. A firm or a bank is exposed to changes in the price level in the currency of denomination of a loan, domestic or foreign, unless there is an offsetting long-term asset in the same currency. Domestic assets or liabilities may accordingly be as risky as, or more risky than, foreign.

An optimal loan portfolio is typically diversified among currencies. The less risk-averse the firm, the more it will concentrate its net long-term position in high-return currencies. The more risk-averse it is, the more it will try to diversify into many currencies in which inflation rates are not perfectly correlated.

It is often argued that a manufacturing firm should raise capital in the country in which it invests and operates. However, the diversification argument above is completely independent of the country in which the real assets are located, because the returns on these assets are likely to rise with inflation. Real long-term investments are therefore hardly exposed to any currency risks. The argument for local financing in the country of operation rests upon accounting measures of exposure.

FORECASTING EXCHANGE RATES

An important part of banks' foreign exchange advisory services is the forecasting of foreign exchange rates. This section contains a brief description of the empirical evidence on the success or failure of forecasting services.[16]

Explicit forecasting of the future exchange rate is profitable only if there is no easily available market price incorporating the best possible forecast. Many economists argue that relative interest rates and the forward rate reflect all available information about the future. Firms or investors need only study the interest rate differential on identical assets in two currencies in order to obtain the optimal forecast. The forward exchange rate provides the same information, because the forward premium or discount reflects the interest rate differential as a result of covered interest rate arbitrage.

The conditions under which no gains can be made by forecasting the exchange rate in order to obtain a favorable currency position are strict. The best available information must be incorporated in interest rates and forward rates. Only a small part of all market participants have access to the best information. Therefore, these must have unlimited access to funds for arbitrage and speculation, and they must not be risk-averse in order for the forward rate and interest rates to incorporate all available information. There are profit opportunities for individuals, banks, or firms with good information and with little risk aversion, if any of the above conditions does not hold. These opportunities reveal themselves in the formulas for equilibrium presented earlier in this chapter.

We turn now to empirical evidence on arbitrage conditions in international financial markets. The first important observation is that interest rate parity holds in forward markets among the major currencies represented in Euromarkets.[17] The forward markets in other currencies are not sufficiently developed to conduct tests on them, but it is safe to assume that temporary deviations occur. Thus, forward rates and/or interest rates are biased estimates of the future spot rates. Most likely both estimates are biased.

It is naturally difficult to test whether the forward rate is the best available forecast of the exchange rate. Measures of expectations for the best-informed market participants are necessary. A number of indirect tests have been performed, however. Giddy and Dufey, Levich,[18] and others have studied whether the forward rate's error in predicting the future spot rate is a random variable. If not, the systematic elements of the error over time are a sign of speculative profit opportunities. These studies have not led to conclusive results.

Levich[19] conducted another kind of indirect study of profit opportunities over different periods by tracing the performance of the forecasts of foreign exchange advisory services relative to the forward rate. There is evidence that some services are able to outperform the forward rate consistently, indicating profit opportunities by having access to superior information (or judgment). However, it still remains to be shown that one foreign exchange advisory service can outperform the forward rates among the major currencies, consistently and over long periods. If not, the firm or individual must know when to change adviser. Naturally, this presumes access to superior information by the firm itself.

Under some conditions it is possible to make predictions that are superior to the forward rate even without access to superior information. Specifically, it was mentioned above that arbitrageurs/speculators will not necessarily push the forward rate to the expected future spot rate when they are risk-averse and/or when the supply of arbitrage funds is limited.

Empirical evidence points to the following conclusions:

1. The forward rate and the interest rate differential for major currencies normally can be outperformed only by the forecaster who has superior information or judgment about future determinants of the exchange rate.

2. The investors or borrowers with less risk aversion than the last previous entrant of the market (the marginal market participant) may gain by forecasting even when their available information is also held by the marginal market participant.

3. Exchange rate expectations for currencies without well-developed financial markets are less well reflected in relative interest rates and forward rates. This increases the value of separate forecasts.

NOTES

1. An excellent description of the role of banks in foreign exchange markets is provided by R. M. Kubarych, *Foreign Exchange Markets in the United States* (New York: Federal Reserve Bank of New York, 1978). The subsections "Foreign

Exchange Contracts . . ." and "Some Institutional Characteristics . . ." are based on this source.

2. A balanced net position in pounds with an asset position for one month and a liability position for two months can be offset by a swap involving a one-month forward sale of pounds and a two-month forward purchase of pounds.

3. A description of arbitrage and speculative transactions can be found in most international finance textbooks. See, for example, G. Feiger and B. Jacquillat, *International Finance* (Boston: Allyn and Bacon, 1980).

4. *Webster's New Collegiate Dictionary* (Springfield, Mass.: G. C. Merriam Company, 1977). Compare with Areskoug's discussion in ch. 2 of this volume.

5. Price differentials depending on transactions and transportation costs are not signs of inefficiencies, however, since these costs represent resource utilization.

6. See, for example, R. Z. Aliber, "The Interest Rate Parity Theorem: A Reinterpretation," *Journal of Political Economy*, December 1973, pp. 145–59.

7. J. A. Frenkel and R. M. Levich, "Covered Interest Arbitrage: Unexploited Profits?" *Journal of Political Economy*, April 1975, pp. 325–38.

8. Aliber, op. cit.

9. The effective interest rate on a deposit against which a bank must hold 10 percent in noninterest-bearing reserves is the deposit interest rate/(1-reserve requirement).

10. Uncertainty can be described by the variance of the probability distribution for the future value of, for example, an exchange rate. The risk on a portfolio of currencies is normally less than the sum of the variances of the values of individual positions when different exchange rates are not perfectly correlated. There is a diversification effect of holding many currencies. The total portfolio risk depends on the covariances among exchange rates. See, for instance, J. Makin, "Portfolio Theory and the Problem of Foreign Exchange Risk," *Journal of Finance*, May 1978, pp. 517–34.

11. See C. G. Wihlborg, "Currency Risks in International Financial Markets," *Princeton Study in International Finance* no. 44 (December 1978); "Currency Risks—Taxonomy and Theory," in R. M. Levich and C. G. Wihlborg, eds., *Exchange Risk and Exposure* (Lexington, Mass.: Lexington Books/D. C. Heath, 1980); and "Economics of Exposure Management of Foreign Subsidiaries of MNCs," *Journal of International Business Studies*, Winter 1981, pp. 3–18.

12. See, for example, L. H. Officer, "The Purchasing Power Parity Theory of Exchange Rates: A Review Article," *IMF Staff Papers*, March 1976, pp. 1–60. A consumer price index or a wholesale price index is a very imperfect measure of a price level. The imperfections grow with the length of time considered. Therefore, observed long-term deviations from purchasing power parity are likely to be exaggerated.

13. I assume here that deviations from purchasing power parity are independent of inflation rates.

14. For a more elaborate presentation of these points, see Wihlborg, "Currency Risks in International Financial Markets."

15. Compare with Wihlborg, "Currency Risks—Taxonomy and Theory."

16. A fuller discussion of this issue can be found in C. G. Wihlborg, "Forecasting Exchange Rates," in T. Murray and I. Walter, eds., *Handbook in International Business* (New York: John Wiley, 1982).

17. On this observation see, for example, the work of Frenkel and Levich in note 7; and S. W. Kohlhagen, *The Behavior of Foreign Exchange Markets—A Critical Survey of the Empirical Literature*, Monograph Series in Finance and Economics, New York University, no. 3 (New York: New York University, 1978).

18. I. Giddy and G. Dufey, "The Random Behavior of Flexible Exchange Rates: Implications for Forecasting," *Journal of International Business Studies*, Spring 1975, pp. 1–32; R. M. Levich, "Further Results on the Efficiency of Markets for Foreign Exchange," in Federal Reserve Bank of Boston, *Managed Exchange Rate Flexibility: The Recent Experience*, Conference Series no. 20 (Boston: Federal Reserve Bank of Boston, 1978).

19. See R. M. Levich, "Analyzing the Accuracy of Foreign Exchange Advisory Services: Theory and Evidence," in R. M. Levich and C. G. Wihlborg, eds., *Exchange Risk and Exposure* (Lexington, Mass.: Lexington Books/D. C. Heath, 1980). Also see R. M. Levich, "How to Compare Chance with Forecasting Expertise," *Euromoney*, August 1981, pp. 61–78.

11 CREDIT ANALYSIS OF FOREIGN LOANS

Roger A. Coe and
Emmanuel N. Roussakis

Credit analysis is the process through which a lender determines a borrower's ability and willingness to repay a loan in accordance with the terms of a loan contract. As in all lending, determining the creditworthiness of the borrower is important, but with foreign borrowers there is an additional dimension: evaluating the country and foreign exchange risks associated with the credit.

The method of analyzing a credit proposal is basically standard in most commercial banks. What is less standard, however, is the person who performs the credit analysis. At one extreme it is the international banker who must gather and analyze all relevant information about the loan applicant. This approach is highly effective where loan officers are specialists in specific industries. At the other extreme the credit analysis may be performed by credit departments, which usually are staffed by junior officers or trainees.

Just as in domestic lending, the functions of the credit department are to assemble, record, and analyze credit information, with the objective of ascertaining the degree of risk associated with each loan request and determining the amount of credit that the bank can prudently extend in each case. Once the analysis has been completed, it is addressed to the banker in charge of the specific account. In some banks the credit department may be authorized to make recommendations regarding the loan application; in others it may not.

With the analysis completed, a decision must be reached on the loan request. This stage, too, is subject to important variation among banks engaged in international lending. In some banks the banker handling the specific account is responsible for presenting the credit request to a loan committee. In other banks decision makers are the loan officers, who have authority to lend up to a certain amount. This authority is called a discretionary lending limit. In such instances, banks frequently require the signatures of at least two officers to approve the credit. Where this approach is used, the signatures of two senior officers may be sufficient to commit the bank. In still other banks a combination of these extremes may prevail—that is, low lending limits by loan officers with a credit committee functioning as the senior authority.

Where a bank has foreign branches, these branches are usually given a local lending limit, with authority delegated to the branch manager to implement this limit. There are exceptions, notably European, Canadian, and Japanese banks, which usually require all lending decisions to be made at the head office.

Most banks have "country limits"—the amount of funds the bank is willing to lend in any specific country, to the government of that country, private corporations, individuals, or banks. These "country limits" are usually reviewed on an annual basis, or more often if world events so necessitate. Prudence dictates that the loan portfolio be diversified among different creditworthy borrowers and among countries considered to be of equal creditworthiness or risk.

FACTORS TO BE CONSIDERED
IN CREDIT ANALYSIS

The objective of credit analysis is to evaluate the degree of risk involved in a requested loan and the amount of credit that can be prudently extended to a borrower. To answer these questions, the officer engaged in foreign credit analysis will analyze and evaluate the factors commonly referred to as the three Cs of credit: character, capacity, and capital. In some instances two more Cs are considered: collateral and conditions. Since the loan request originates from a foreign borrower, the analyst must also review the country and foreign exchange risks associated with the loan request. Both of these considerations have been discussed in the two preceding chapters, so this section will focus on the basic factors of credit analysis: character, capacity, capital, collateral, and conditions.

Character

The term "character," as used in lending, implies not just willingness to pay debts but also a strong desire to settle contractual obligations in accordance with the terms of the contract. When the borrower is an individual, character is largely a function of that person's moral qualities, personal habits, style of living, business and personal associates, and general standing in the business and social communities. When the borrower is a country, character is a function of such factors as stability of the government, its philosophy and policies, its relations with other countries and major trading partners, and other considerations. When the borrower is a company, character is a function of management integrity, reputation, and standing in the business and financial communities. In the final analysis, of course, the reputation, integrity, and standing of a company's management are primarily a reflection of the character of the individuals responsible for the formulation and execution of company policies. Whether the borrower is an individual, a country, or a business, the previous record for meeting financial obligations plays a determining role in evaluating the borrower for credit purposes. This points to the importance of having an experienced loan officer on the scene.

Capacity

Capacity has both a legal and an economic connotation. From a legal perspective, lenders are interested to know whether the party requesting the loan can legally obligate itself to borrow contractually. The lender should retain legal counsel in the country of the borrower to make this determination. Specifically, where the borrower is an official entity, the lending bank should determine whether this entity has authority to borrow or must obtain prior approval from a supervisory authority. Furthermore, the bank should determine whether this entity is eligible to borrow abroad for the purpose intended and under the terms proposed. Pragmatic consideration of these issues requires recognition of the different categories of official borrowers. Official borrowers may be broadly classified in four categories:

• Government at the national (federal), provincial (state), and local levels

- Ministries of the national government and central banks
- Statutory authorities and agencies at all government levels
- Public-sector industries, development banks, or utilities, wholly, majority, or minority owned by the government.

Determining the borrowing authority of an official entity raises a number of practical issues for the lending bank, most important of which involves assessing the specific unit in the government hierarchy responsible under law or policy in the event of nonpayment, and the extent of its responsibility. These considerations should not be disregarded, as is often the case, by assuming that the government nature of the would-be borrower necessarily assures the quality of the loan.

In lending to a partnership, the loan officer should ascertain that the signing partner has legal authority (that is, a power of attorney from the other partners) to obligate the partnership. Similarly, in lending to a private corporation, it is advisable to examine the corporate charter and bylaws to determine who has the authority to borrow for the corporation. In the absence of any explicit statement, a bank may accept a corporate resolution that, signed by the board of directors, identifies the person who has authority to negotiate for the company and sign the loan contract.

In considering a corporation's loan request, it is also important to analyze the outstanding loans already made to the corporation, in order to assure that any new loan is not restricted or prohibited by covenants in a previously made loan. A similar analysis is made of loans to private banks, with the additional investigation that the proposed loan is within the banking regulations of the country.

From an economic perspective, capacity implies ability to meet loan payments as they come due. A bank loan may be repaid from a variety of sources—earnings generated from operations, sale of assets, and borrowing from another lender. Of these sources, the least acceptable to a bank is clearly the last one, not only because it encourages the borrower to switch loans from one bank to another but also because of the degree of risk involved: the borrower's position may subsequently deteriorate, rendering it virtually impossible to locate another lender. Nonetheless, banks look closely at a borrower's overall availability of credit lines and line rotation ability. Many banks request 30–60-day line cleanups to test performance. Most banks as borrowers cannot pay back all their obligations from

cash flow, and must refinance from other lines of credit. Neither do
U.S. banks generally favor being repaid from the proceeds of the sale
of assets pledged. Such method of repayment is costly and time-
consuming, and adversely affects a bank's public image. This leaves
one source of debt repayment: income. Income, being an effective
measure of financial performance, has generally been accepted as a
good indication of a borrower's current and potential ability to meet
loan payments as they come due.

If the borrower is an individual, ability to generate income depends in part on business experience, education, good judgment,
ambition, maturity or age, and shrewdness. For a corporation its
power to generate income depends upon such factors as the quality
of goods or services sold, cost and availability of raw materials and
labor, competition, profit sensitivity to cycles, effectiveness of
advertising, and company location. In recent years, however, it has
been increasingly recognized by banks that the single most important
income-generating factor for a company is the quality of its management. Good management is based primarily on the talent and ability
of the individuals responsible for running the company. The success
or failure of a company depends to a large extent on the abilities of
those who manage it. Time and again studies have concluded that in-
experience and incompetence, neglect, and fraud are among the chief
causes of business failures. Thus, management should inspire sufficient confidence as to its ability to adapt to changing conditions,
replace inefficient practices with more efficient ones, take advantage
of opportunities as they arise, and ensure that company products
enjoy a strong customer base because of their price and/or quality.

Evaluation of a company's capacity will rely to a great extent
upon its financial statements, and particularly on the balance sheet
and income statement. International bankers place different emphasis upon each of these statements. Most foreign bankers rely heavily
on balance sheet items because they are basically oriented toward
short-term lending. This orientation is primarily a product of tradition and the absence of developed capital markets in their countries.
In many European countries, for example, the normal form of lending has been through short-term notes or overdrafts, many of which
are of an evergreen nature, thereby functioning as term loans.[1] In
Latin American countries, particularly in those with a high rate of
inflation, the discounting of promissory notes constitutes a regular
method of bank financing. In Japan a dominant form of lending is

the time loan, which is made on a three-month basis with automatic rollover. Secured by a mortgage or other collateral, a time loan is normally granted for financing capital expenditures.

Unlike their foreign counterparts, U.S. banks emphasize both statements, depending upon the maturity of the loan. Thus, when negotiating short-term loans, U.S. bankers place more emphasis on balance sheet items, while in negotiating longer maturity loans greater emphasis is placed upon income statements. Indeed, for medium-term loans U.S. banks look into a company's income statement to determine its ability to generate sufficient income from operations to meet potential loan repayments. The analytical tool used in this respect is the cash flow, which in its simplest definition is the sum of net income plus noncash charges (principally depreciation) minus noncash income. The essence of cash-flow lending is that it enables a bank to analyze a company's financial projections and, if they are acceptable, develop a repayment schedule that reflects its ability to generate cash. Cash-flow lending constitutes an innovative credit technique that U.S. banks introduced in the domestic credit markets immediately after World War II[2] and have since gradually applied to foreign lending as well. An example of a cash flow analysis is provided in the appendix to this chapter.

When the party requesting the loan is a foreign government, the lending officer's task again will be to determine the borrower's ability to create income. However, in this case the sovereign nature of the borrower limits the effectiveness of cash flow as predictor of ability to service potential debt. Specifically, a corporation may go bankrupt and cease to exist, but technically a country, its government, or its central bank does not. Another limitation on using the corporate cash-flow analogy on loans to governments is that a government borrower can always generate the necessary local funds to service a local-currency-denominated debt (that is, through issuance of government securities or the printing of monies). Though such funding may add to the inflationary pressures on the domestic economy, it nevertheless enables a sovereign borrower to meet its debt-servicing requirement.

Even if the loan is denominated in foreign currency, a government would be in a position to generate the necessary foreign exchange to meet debt servicing, should it choose to do so. Clearly, political expedience plays an important role in this respect. Debt servicing can be effected through policies that would be conducive to maintenance of a sustainable balance between payments to and from other countries, on current and capital accounts combined. In this respect it may be observed that in addition to monetary and fiscal policy, a government has at its disposal a variety of measures to influence its balance of payments, and hence enhance its foreign-debt servicing ability. Some of these measures include the following:

- Controlling the availability and/or cost of foreign exchange
- Promoting exports of goods and services and, hence, foreign exchange revenues
- Introducing or stiffening restrictions on imports, thereby preserving foreign currencies
- Encouraging a net inflow of capital by promoting a favorable investment climate (through tax incentives, favorable repatriation provisions for profits and capital, and so forth)
- Drawing on its official reserves (gold, foreign exchange, and special drawing rights)
- Borrowing from other sources
- Obtaining foreign aid.

As a result, in evaluating the debt servicing ability of a government, the lending officer should take into consideration such items as talent and quality of government officials, the efficiency of the government machinery, natural resources, industrial and scientific achievements, rate of economic growth, and generally all those related dynamic indicators customarily reviewed in country risk analysis. If the party requesting the loan is a government agency or other type of official entity, its debt servicing ability would depend, among other things, upon such considerations as sources through which this entity funds its activities—that is, the extent to which its operations are funded through annual allocations from a federal budget, its authority to borrow from the central bank or other government banks, and the right to issue its own obligations in the domestic credit markets; any tax benefits or duty-free import privileges that this entity enjoys and that may affect its operations favorably; its independent access to foreign exchange and its authority to effect payments abroad; and the pricing of its services in the domestic market (whether its services are underpriced for political reasons, in which case the users of the services are actually being subsidized).

Capital

A strongly capitalized company is a more acceptable credit risk than one that is highly leveraged. The utilization of this capital to purchase quality assets is an important factor in determining the financial strength of the company. A borrower's ability to obtain credit would thus be greatly affected by the amount and quality of the assets it owns. For example, a foreign manufacturer that owns modern machinery and equipment will be more certain of obtaining credit than will its counterpart with obsolete machinery and worn-out equipment. Similarly, a foreign retailer with attractive buildings and fixtures, and adequate stock will be favored over his counterpart with rundown buildings and fixtures, and inadequate stock. The amount and quality of the assets owned thus serve as an indication of the prudence and resourcefulness of a company's management.

If the would-be borrower is an official entity, capital is important only to the extent that this entity is a joint-stock corporation, with private interests participating in the capital of the company. Corporations of this type are found in many countries of the non-Communist world—that is, in countries where the means of production, sales, and finance are not owned by the state or workers' cooperatives. Such is the case, for example, of the German corporation Volkswagenwerk A. G., which is owned by the Federal Republic of Germany, the state of Lower Saxony, and private interests. Similarly, in Italy, Olivetti, Montedison, and Fiat are corporations jointly owned by government and private interests. In other countries such joint-stock corporations frequently include public utilities, transportation enterprises, telephone and telecommunication networks, and specialized banks. If the government is a minority shareholder in such a corporation, the amount and quality of the assets owned by this corporation would be a decisive factor in determining the applicant's credit prospects. On the other hand, if the government is a majority shareholder, the borrowings of this corporation may enjoy the support of the government or a government entity (the ministry of finance or the central bank). Should that be the case, any analysis of this company in essence would be an analysis of the government itself.

Collateral

Though banks generally prefer to make short-term, self-liquidating or cash flow loans (that is, loans that would be collectible from the anticipated income or profits of the borrower), on various occasions they may request a would-be borrower to provide security. In some cases security is pledged because the loan is longer term, which increases the risk factor for the bank; in other cases security is requested in order to increase the borrower's sense of responsibility. In most cases assets are pledged because they improve a lender's claim against a borrower. Broadly speaking, the proper function of collateral is to minimize the risk of loss to a bank if, for unforeseen reasons, the borrower's income or profits fail to materialize sufficiently for repayment of the loan. In other words, the purpose of the collateral is to provide a bank a second way out of a loan, and not to be the primary source of repayment. This view is exemplified by the axiom that collateral does not make a bad loan good but makes a good loan better.

The security pledged for collateral should be readily convertible into cash, and its market value should be greater than the value of the loan it secures. The assets pledged may consist of real property (land and improvements attached to land) or personal property (investment securities, accounts receivable, inventory, machinery and equipment). When accepting such assets as collateral, a bank seeks to establish a legally valid security interest in the country where the collateral is located. In many countries this is feasible because of legislation governing the rights of secured lenders. Such is the case, for example, in Mexico, which provides for the registration with the government of liens on fixed assets. The variety in the laws and regulations of different countries stresses the importance for banks to retain foreign counsel. A local law firm will have a thorough knowledge of local laws and procedures, and will be useful in preparing the necessary documentation related to the transaction.

Frequently a borrower may substitute the guarantee of payment by another party for collateral. For example, when the loan request comes from the foreign subsidiary (the production or marketing unit) of a domestic corporation (such as an automobile manufacturer), the latter may offer its guarantee in support of the loan. Parent support would ordinarily be justified on the ground that the operations of the subsidiary so supported are financially an integral part of the parent's. Assuming the explicit guarantee of the parent, the bank's risk is no different from that assumed in a direct loan to the parent itself.

Other instances where guarantees are sought and received by lenders are for support of loans to official borrowers. Bank emphasis on guarantees for such borrowers has increased so much in recent years that they have come to constitute a regular feature of loan agreements. Repayment guarantees may range from a pledge of full faith and credit by a national government to a guarantee by a government-owned enterprise (a commercial bank or a finance institution). This may lead to the question of how much more protection a lender receives from the repayment guarantee of a national government than from that of a government-owned enterprise. The record in recent years suggests that regardless of the level of the government guarantor, rarely have banks found it necessary to invoke a guarantee. Yet there has been an excessive reliance by banks on this concept. To some banks this concept is a substitute for independent analysis and judgment. To other banks it is simply a matter of emulating the lending practices of international organizations and foreign government banks, which have traditionally required such guarantees. For still other banks the merit of this concept is psychological—commitment by an additional official entity is a further evidence of the appropriateness of the transaction, not to mention the influence that the guarantor would have upon the borrower in ensuring repayment of the debt.

Conditions

Another factor to be considered by the lending officer in deciding on a loan request is the economic environment within which the borrower operates. Economic conditions are generally beyond the borrower's control. From a broader perspective, economic conditions reflect the political stability and the effectiveness of the government's fiscal and monetary policies for alleviating or counteracting business cycles. Therefore, evaluating the borrower's economic environment calls for appraising the effectiveness of the government's economic policy—assuming, of course, that the economy operates within a climate of political stability.

From a narrower perspective, evaluating the borrower's economic environment entails identifying the importance of the industry in the country's overall economy. To properly evaluate this factor, the loan officer must become familiar with the characteristics of the industry with which the firm is associated. This aspect of credit analysis has become increasingly difficult in recent years as more companies have grown into multiproduct and multinational concerns. Consequently, many banks have encouraged lending officers to acquire expertise in such industries as energy, shipping, airlines, and mining.

The kind of information that the lending officer should look for is the effect of economic conditions upon the industry, the industry's output relative to gross national product, the market structure of the industry, the applicant's position in the industry, the impact of technology (and technological changes) on the demand for the industry's product or its capital requirements, the industry's distribution methods, trends in industry profits, and the extent to which industry is regulated by the government. Answers to these and related questions will enable the lending officer to obtain a comprehensive understanding of the dynamics of the industry—a basic input for a more pragmatic appraisal of the firm's relative strengths and weaknesses. Clearly, the greater the importance of the industry to the smooth functioning of the economy, the more likely that the loan officer will act favorably on the company's credit application.

SOURCES OF CREDIT INFORMATION

Any evaluation of the applicant's creditworthiness must rely on available information. The bank will certainly need to accumulate information that will be used to evaluate the borrower's character, capacity, capital, collateral, and industry characteristics. Collecting information is the objective of credit investigation, the scope of which varies from case to case, depending upon the specifics of the loan request—proposed size and maturity of loan, collateral offered, applicant's business record—and the existence of any prior relationship with the would-be borrower. Though a bank may draw upon several sources of credit information, some of the more important ones include an interview with the party requesting the loan, the bank's credit files, external sources, in-person visit to applicant's premises, and applicant's financial statements. These sources are applicable primarily to foreign private loan applicants rather than to public applicants. Each of these sources is briefly discussed below.

Loan Interview

It is customary for a loan officer to interview a would-be borrower for the purpose of developing credit information. During the interview the loan officer has the opportunity to inquire—or obtain additional information—about the history of the company, experience and background of the principal officers, the nature of the business, profitability of operations, extent of competition in the marketplace, availability of resources (labor, raw materials, and other essential services) for the smooth functioning of the business, and the objectives of the management as expressed in long-range plans. Other information that the loan officer can obtain from the interview pertains to the purpose for which the proceeds of the loan are to be used. Knowledge of the purpose of the loan is important not only because of risk considerations but also because it enables the loan officer to relate repayment to the nature of the transaction being considered for financing. For example, project loans (such as those to finance the development of raw materials, oil, mineral, and other resources) call for repayment provisions tailored to the cash flow of the project being financed.

The interview, moreover, provides the loan officer with an initial impression of the sincerity, integrity, and capability of the party requesting the loan.

Finally, the interview is an appropriate time for requesting the loan applicant to submit financial statements and any other additional information, and to arrange for a visit to the company.

Bank's Credit Files

A bank's credit files can be an important source of information for a loan officer. Banks establish for each borrower a credit file that contains detailed information on their credit relationship with that specific client. By studying these files, the loan officer can identify how well the customer complied with the terms and conditions of previous loans, and can thereby assess the bank's overall credit experience. The credit information contained in these files, though considered confidential, is customarily shared by banks when they consider extending credit to the same client.

Even if the borrower approaches the bank for the first time, a credit file may exist if the borrower is a sizable concern within the bank's location (a "prospect file").

External Sources

Besides the loan interview and the bank's own records, a loan officer may use external sources of credit information. One such source is other banks. Although banks compete vigorously among themselves, they usually share credit information regarding a mutual customer. This information is presented in a standardized format, as a result of certain well-established customs, and is confidential. The loan officer can find out, for example, the applicant's borrowing and payment record, balances carried in deposit accounts, and other pieces of information about the financial strengths or weaknesses of the applicant.

Other external sources of credit information are credit reporting agencies. One such agency, and one of the best-known, is Dun and Bradstreet. In addition to its coverage of companies in this country, this agency collects information on business activity in a great many countries around the world, mostly in European and other industrialized countries. The data collected enable the company to publish reference books containing concise information about and credit ratings of foreign businesses, on a firm-by-firm basis. Besides the rating services, Dun and Bradstreet issues written credit reports that provide more detailed information on individual firms. These reports contain a brief history of the company, and information on its principal officers, the nature of the business, the ownership, operating data, and other financial data.

Still another external source of credit information is the suppliers and customers of the prospective borrower. Suppliers can share with the lending bank information on the applicant's payment practices. Customers, on the other hand, can give information on the quality of the company's products or services, management's honesty and integrity in its dealings, and other factors.

Other external sources that may be tapped by the bank are public records, where reference is made, for example, to pending lawsuits, bankruptcy proceedings, and transfers of property; trade journals, which report developments and trends in the particular industries in which bank customers are engaged; public accounting firms; and newspapers, magazines, circulars, bulletins, and directories.

If the would-be borrower is an official entity, information about its activities customarily appears in official publications—that is, in government documents or reports of national development banks and/or of the central bank. Often, write-ups on this type of borrower appear in international finance journals and periodicals (such as *Euromoney* and *The Economist*). Country statistics and other economic indicators are ordinarily available in the publications of international organizations and internationally oriented agencies of the U.S. government. For example, data on growth rates and on per capita gross national product (GNP) in constant dollar equivalents for a large number of countries are published by the U.S. Agency for International Development (AID) in its annual publication *Gross National Product*; balance-of-payments figures and foreign exchange reserves for member countries are reported in the monthly publication of the International Monetary Fund (IMF), *International Financial Statistics*; detailed data on the foreign trade activities of different countries are reported in the United Nations' *Yearbook of International Trade Statistics* and periodically in the *Monthly Bulletin of Statistics*; information on the various countries' external public-debt service (including interest and amortization on all public and government-guaranteed debt) with original maturity in excess of one year is published by the International Bank for Reconstruction and Development (IBRD)—also called the World Bank—in its *Annual Report*, *World Debt Tables*, and *World Debt Tables—Supplements*; and data on the capital flows to developing countries are published in the *Development Co-operation Review* of the Development Assistance Committee of the Organization for Economic Cooperation and Development (OECD). Relevant information may also be found in the publications of the Bank for International Settlements (BIS), the Federal Reserve Board, and private banks (for instance, Morgan Guaranty Trust Company's *World Financial Markets* and *Morgan International Data*, the latter including individual and comparative data tables for 80 industrial and developing countries). An interested loan officer can also contact the commercial and economic section of the U.S. embassy in the relevant country.

On-site Visit

The financial status of a loan applicant and the quality of its management usually can be best determined by the loan officer through an on-the-scene visit to the applicant's business. Specifically, a visit to the borrower's business will offer the lending officer firsthand information on the condition and efficiency of its physical facilities; the extent of management sophistication in terms of nature and method of operation, and financial planning; and the local reputation and standing of the firm as perceived by local officials, indigenous bankers, other businessmen, and perhaps its competitors, though in the latter instance such information must be used with great discretion.

The information and impressions gained by the officer from the visit to the borrower's business are helpful not only in properly evaluating the business risk involved but also in offering the applicant sound financial advice. Capitalizing on the confidence and respect that may develop from such a visit, the loan officer can share with the would-be borrower financial expertise on such related issues as ideal capital structure, forecasting the amount and timing of future cash needs and ability to repay the loan, appropriateness of the type of credit requested, and other financial matters. The need for this type of financial counseling is especially apparent in the small and medium-size businesses of developing countries, which suffer from a lack of sophisticated financial planning and management, and the absence of a meaningful capital market.

If the would-be borrower is an official entity, an on-the-scene visit can be equally important. Depending upon the status of the official borrower, the loan officer can arrange for meetings with government officials at various levels, including officials in the ministries of finance, economy, and planning, and the central bank. These meetings may be expanded to the private sector and include discussions with local businessmen, bankers, and other individuals who customarily view the role and importance of official entities from a different perspective. Additional inputs may also be obtained from U.S. embassy officials in that country and specialists in such organizations as the IMF, the IBRD, and the Export-Import Bank.

The large number and diverse nature of the individuals contacted may eventually create the problem of the loan officer's having to cope with opposing views on certain issues. This, of course, is to be expected, and is basically a matter of judgment—that is, a matter of weighing the value of the sources of contradictory information. Clearly, good judgment is a product of experience and intuitive grasp of what makes sense and what does not. It is judgments such as this that make lending an art rather than a mechanical process.

A country visit, beyond its importance in evaluating the creditworthiness of the borrower, enables the loan officer to obtain a realistic picture of the political, economic, and social conditions in the borrower's country. Comprehensive understanding of these conditions will be vital in assessing the country risk associated with the loan. In this respect a country visit offers vital on-the-spot knowledge for which there is no substitute.

Financial Statements

One of the most important sources of credit information is the applicant's financial statements. Because financial statements identify the expected ability of a would-be borrower to repay an indebtedness, their submission is generally required. A firm usually must provide balance sheets and income statements, covering the last three to five years, so that the lending officer can obtain a feeling of company direction. Clearly, when the loan applicant is a national government or a ministry thereof, the lending officer instead considers data reflecting the country's economic performance, its political stability, and its social background (as discussed in chapter 9).

Though loan applicants are required to submit financial statements, the lending officer of a bank operating overseas is often confronted with the inadequacy of the financial information contained in them. Nowhere is this more true than in developing countries, where the inadequacy of financial information may extend to the industry level. Thus, the lending officer who has been trained to analyze historical financial statements, pro forma statements, and cash projections in evaluating a borrower's creditworthiness, is faced with the problem of having to draw conclusions on the basis of insufficient data. This is in striking contrast with his counterpart in an indigenous bank who has a thorough understanding of the local scene and may, therefore, be more favorably inclined to extend a loan on incomplete information or against a name rather than on an amortized cash flow basis. This situation is often encountered in Latin America, where businesses may be owned by families with historical reputation or by individuals having strong political connections.

Similar are the experiences of the lending officer analyzing the financial statements of government-owned businesses and other official entities. The statements of these entities may be out of date, most elementary, quite brief, or simply minimal, either because of a lack of data or because of a desire for secrecy.

Even if the financial statements of a prospective borrower—private or public—are available, the lending officer is confronted with the question of reliability. The validity of any conclusions drawn from such statements are no better than the information contained in them. Assuming, however, the availability and reliability of the financial statements of foreign borrowers, the loan officer is confronted with a set of issues that overlie the typical analytical approach associated with domestic loans. The next section is devoted to the identification of these issues before any discussion of financial statement analysis.

ISSUES UNIQUE TO FOREIGN CREDIT ANALYSIS

Before any analysis of the financial statements of a foreign prospective borrower, the lending officer has to address certain issues that are unique to foreign credit analysis. Specifically, the applicant's financial statements are expressed in his national currency; prepared in accordance with accounting principles and reporting practices followed in his country; audited by an (often) unknown local firm governed by alien auditing standards; and reflective of a different legal tradition. The lending officer must have a good understanding of these issues in order to make a reasoned judgment on the credit transaction.

In addressing the first issue, the lending officer must always bear in mind that any translation into U.S. dollars of figures expressed in a foreign currency will misrepresent the applicant's operating results. For one thing, any dollar translation will be affected by the foreign exchange rate used. Specifically, given the foreign currency depreciation that countries around the world have experienced over the last few years as a result of higher inflation rates, any translation of historical financial data (the income statement) at today's exchange rate would understate the borrower's prior record. This understatement would make today's figures look better, thereby creating the illusion of a trend of growth and improvement in the borrower's performance. If, on the other hand, the translation of historical financial data is done on the basis of the going exchange rate for each corresponding year, the resulting data would be biased by the extent of currency depreciation or exchange rate fluctuations sustained in each individual year. Because of the distorting effect of exchange rates in currency translations, the lending officer is better off analyzing financial statements in the currency in which they are denominated.

The second issue calls for the lending officer to have an understanding of the important differences between U.S. accounting principles and practices and those of the country in which the financial statements originate. This is especially important in view of the prevailing variation in the principles and practices followed by different countries. In fact, in many Latin American, Asian, and African countries, accounting is still in an early stage of development. Awareness, therefore, of prevailing differences in accounting practices enables the lending officer to better understand the basis on which the applicant's financial statements were prepared. Some of the better-known examples of intercountry differences in accounting practices are price-level accounting that is, the practice of certain countries to allow for adjustments in the value of fixed assets for inflation (revaluation); widespread use of unconsolidated statements (statements that do not include the aggregate values of subsidiaries, affiliates, and investees of an entity); greater latitude in the establishment and use of contingency and other reserves; and income tax matters.

Information on the above and related items is ordinarily omitted from financial statements. Disclosure of such information may be requested from the would-be borrower, and is helpful in clarifying and/or adjusting the financial statements.

A related issue is the validity of the foreign auditors' report. The lending officer should use such a report with great discretion. Not only may the professional integrity of the auditing firm be unknown, but so may be the standards followed in the examination of the company's financial statements. In some countries auditors need not have any specific qualifications to examine financial statements, nor need they comply with any governing rules in the performance of such examinations. Even if the auditing firm is known and its integrity is respected, the statement that the would-be borrower has followed generally accepted accounting principles raises questions as to the degree of conservatism that this judgment may reflect. Thus, in the final analysis there is no substitute for knowing the borrower and trusting his honesty and integrity in the preparation of financial statements.

Another issue that the lending officer will have to bear in mind is the fact that the borrower's country of origin has a set of laws different from those of the lender's country. Indeed, differences in legal tradition have influenced the development of law in various countries differently. Specifically, Roman law and the Napoleonic Code have greatly influenced the development of law on the Continent and elsewhere (for instance, Latin America), as against Anglo-Saxon law, which is the basis of the legal systems of England, the United States, and most of the British Commonwealth. Even so, there is important variation in the laws of countries with the same legal tradition. Lack of awareness of such a variation by the lending officer could have an important bearing on financial analysis. For example, liabilities generally represent legal claims on assets. However, an intuitive assumption that the legal claims of various liabilities against assets enjoy the same status or priority as they do in the lending officer's country may lead to decisions that could prove expensive or even disastrous for the bank.

ANALYSIS OF FINANCIAL STATEMENTS

Any analysis of a would-be borrower's financial condition calls for evaluating as accurately as possible current financial statements, examining historical financial statements, and studying pro forma financial statements and cash projections that show the borrower's future profitability and cash requirements. The lending officer should not rely too heavily on historical financial statements, because a prospective borrower's financial condition can change drastically if losses develop. Such caution about historical information is, moreover, justified on the ground that past profits often do not reflect future performance. On the other hand, borrower assumptions about future developments will affect the accuracy of cash forecasts and pro forma financial statements. Hence the importance to the lending officer of the soundness of such assumptions.

The current financial condition is a decisive indicator of the viability of the firm. Consequently, a good understanding of the borrower's financial condition calls for an in-depth evaluation of the significant items in his financial statements. Specifically, the lending officer will need to inquire about each important account and to determine whether the figure cited represents a fair and accurate statement of the value involved. Clearly, such evaluation may result in the trimming or adjustment of items from the figures originally reported by the foreign concern. This approach, however, provides a pragmatic picture of the prospective borrower's financial position. This section thus deals with the evaluation of items in the balance sheet and income statement, and some of the techniques widely used in analyzing financial statements. These techniques, borrowed from domestic practices, can be used in analyzing a foreign borrower's historical and current financial statements as well as his cash projections and pro forma statements.

Evaluation of Asset Items

In evaluating individual asset items, which are usually expressed in local currency, the lending officer will seek to determine their true worth and extent of liquidity. Cash holdings, though a small proportion of total assets, are essential to meeting a company's liquidity needs. The importance of this item in servicing the debt depends on the denomination of the loan and the existence of any foreign exchange restrictions in the borrower's country. For example, a prospective borrower's local cash holdings will be of limited value in servicing a foreign currency loan if the purchase of foreign exchange is prohibited by exchange controls. By contrast, cash holdings will be of significant value if exchange restrictions are nonexistent or if the loan is to be denominated in local currency.

Accounts receivable must be analyzed carefully because they constitute the principal source of repayment of a short-term loan. One of the first considerations is the currency of the receivables, because this may considerably affect the ability of this asset to repay debt. It is also important to determine the age of the receivables and the local repayment practices (that is, how many accounts are current or overdue by local standards, and, if overdue, for what period); the extent to which receivables are concentrated in a few large accounts, which would increase the inherent risk of nonpayment; the existence and/or adequacy of reserves for bad debts; and the bad debts record of the prospective borrower. The loan officer should also inquire whether the prospective borrower has sold any of its accounts receivable—and, if so, whether they were sold with or without recourse. If the accounts receivable are to be pledged to the lender, a system of control should be established.

Understanding the age, liquidity, and market value of inventory is vital to determining the prospective borrower's cash position. It is also important to know the extent to which inventory is exposed to obsolescence or deterioration, and the existence or adequacy of insurance coverage. The lending officer should arrange for a physical confirmation of the inventory as reported by the would-be borrower, and determine the method of inventory accounting: LIFO (last in, first out), FIFO (first in, first out), or NIFO (next in, first out).[3] If the inventory is to be pledged to the lender by the borrower, this pledge should be legally documented and, if possible, recorded at a public registry. In addition, a method of control over the movement of the inventory should be set up between the lender and the borrower.

Fixed assets, too, involve a number of considerations. As was stated earlier, an important accounting question is whether fixed asset values are adjusted for inflation. Indeed, one of the prime differences between U.S. standards and those used in countries of high inflation, such as Chile, Argentina, Brazil, France, and the United Kingdom, is their revaluation of fixed assets. If the would-be borrower comes from one of these countries, it is important to know the basis for revaluation. Another basic question, especially if the request is for intermediate or long-term credit, is the ability of fixed assets to produce income to service the debt. Other important questions relate to the adequacy of insurance coverage, marketability of these assets, and their liquidation value. In addition, the lending officer will be interested to determine if the borrower has made any commitment to acquire new fixed assets and what financial liability will arise from this acquisition. Since lenders are generally interested in tangible assets, limited consideration will be given to intangible assets such as goodwill, franchises, and leaseholds.

When the borrower has made substantial investments, the method of recording these investments should be determined (that is whether at cost or at market value). From the lending officer's perspective, the most conservative method should be used for financial analysis purposes. The lending officer should also determine if there is any intercompany relationship between the would-be borrower and other firms. In some countries prevailing accounting practices do not call for preparation of consolidated financial statements, and hence no disclosure is made of the parent/subsidiary relationship except for the investment, which is carried at cost. Such a practice results in the understatement or overstatement of the value of the parent company, depending upon the market value of the investment.

When the balance sheet shows loans to directors, officers, and their affiliated companies, the lending officer should carefully scrutinize those items. Loans of this type are commonly used by foreign banks, principally in South America. As recent history indicates, this has resulted in the demise of several major financial institutions in Latin America.

Evaluation of Liabilities and Net Worth

Since liabilities represent legal claims on assets, thorough analysis of these items is of primary importance for a lending officer considering extension of credit. The first item of inquiry is notes and accounts payable. The lending officer will need to know the terms and to whom these obligations are owed. Also, if the past-due amount of these debts is large relative to the prospective borrower's scale of operations, the borrower may need additional equity capital or borrowed funds. Slowness in payment of trade obligations is often encountered among the important family-group companies of developing countries, and stems either from inability to raise new capital or from unwillingness to accept the dilution of control that the infusion of new capital would entail.

If the notes payable are not trade-related, but are instead a result of amounts owed by the company to its shareholders or officers, the lending officer will investigate these notes and may ask their subordination to the bank loan, in which case they would serve, in effect, as additional capital. In many cases the lending officer will want to review the amounts accrued for salaries and wages. In several countries these social liabilities constitute claims senior to those of other creditors, and in the event of company liquidation they have preference over all other claims on assets by operation of law. Also, taxes owed to government bodies enjoy preferred creditor status.

Long-term liabilities represent debt due in more than one year. The lending officer will be interested in the type of these liabilities (mortgages, debentures, notes, term loans, and other), their proper reporting in financial statements, the maturity date of each of these liabilities, and the contractual provisions of each debt agreement. These provisions are of particular significance because in each case they reveal such information as the currency of the debt, terms of repayment, the existence of collateral, and the specific conditions under which the particular debt is immediately due and payable (default provisions). Clearly, the lending officer will be especially concerned with what constitutes an act or event of default in each loan agreement. The loan applicant's record of compliance with the provisions of the various loan agreements also will be of interest to the lending officer. Where long-term liabilities include debt due to affiliated companies, determination must be made as to whether this item is actual debt or quasi equity.

The size of the net worth, or equity, is of great significance for the lending officer. As indicated earlier in connection with the "five Cs," capital indicates ownership of assets, and therefore serves as security for a loan. Where a company is closely held by a few individuals (partners or shareholders), it is vital to know and evaluate the net worth of these individuals. It may be prudent in appropriate cases to request, as a condition of making the loan, that the partners or shareholders individually guarantee the loan.

Equity accounts include the original capital paid by the shareholders into the company. It is important for the lending officer to determine that this amount has been actually paid, and does not appear as accounts receivable from the shareholders. Other equity accounts to be reviewed are company earnings, surplus, and reserves. Of these accounts the lending officer will be especially concerned with reserves because of their varied characteristics. Specifically, existing differences in the accounting practices of various countries have contributed to the varied use of reserves, from being treated as a contingent liability to employment as a convenient account used for the smoothing out of annual fluctuations in income. For example, use of reserves as a contingent liability may result from the discounting of accounts or notes receivable with recourse, the endorsing or guaranteeing of the indebtedness of third parties, and the likelihood of additional tax payments. On the other hand, several countries permit companies to transfer income into reserves that later may be used to offset operating losses in any given accounting period. This practice thus enables companies to project to the public a record of continued profitability over the years. Since this practice is not ordinarily disclosed in financial statements, the lending officer will need to ascertain the size of real earnings in any given year. Because of the existing variation in the use of reserves—a potential liability, a means of controlling the earnings trend, or something in between—this account will always be a matter of concern for the lending officer.

Evaluation of the Income Statement

The income statement identifies the sources of revenue of a prospective borrower, the expenses sustained to earn that revenue, and the net income realized in the accounting period involved. The revenue component of the income statement is of vital importance to the lending officer because it constitutes the principal source of cash generation for the repayment of loans. He therefore will be interested in such data as sales volume, composition of sales, selling prices, credit terms, sale returns, markets to which products are sold, size of foreign sales, and exposure to foreign exchange fluctuations.

In some instances the would-be borrower may be a subsidiary or an affiliate company with a scope of activities defined by the parent corporation. In such instances its scope and style of operation reflect its role in the organization. For example, the would-be borrower may operate as a manufacturing subsidiary producing a sizable portion of a global product line sold to sister subsidiaries and affiliates in other countries. This kind of relationship gives rise to different considerations than would otherwise be the case. Specifically, this company will have a higher proportion of its sales on credit than will other companies producing the same line of goods. This practice will have a bearing on the size of the company's accounts receivable and their aging. If these receivables are in different currencies, they add to the subsidiary's foreign exchange exposure, rendering credit analysis more complex. Clearly, the lending officer will have to review these and related questions in the context of the company's relationship to the corporate parent and its importance in the overall corporate picture. The same approach will be used if the would-be borrower functions as a marketing subsidiary selling a product manufactured by a foreign parent.

Another objective of the income statement analysis is to evaluate the costs of goods sold. Clearly, the method of inventory valuation will have an important effect upon costs, as will the consistency of the method used. For example, a change in the method of valuing inventory may be effected for the purpose of increasing profits, thus giving the impression that the would-be borrower has the ability to service the proposed loan. If the inventory is imported, the lending officer will consider, in addition, such information as the size of the overseas supplier, contract prices, the length of the shipment period, the cost effect of foreign exchange fluctuations, and the effect of local import tariffs upon costs. If the source of the imported goods or materials is a foreign subsidiary or affiliate, the lending officer will want to know the corresponding cost of these items, if they are acquired from independent sources. Another issue to be considered is whether local labor is unionized, and thereby increases pressure on costs. This is especially the case in high-inflation countries where union-imposed wage adjustments, combined with controlled prices, can thin out profit margins.

Close scrutiny also will be given to administrative and other expenses. An item of importance in this respect is the amount of officers' salaries and the extent to which they may drain profits. Such concern exists mainly with family-owned or closely held companies, which frequently pay excessive salaries. Other items that may warrant investigation, or call for additional disclosures, include rent payments, the method used in the depreciation of facilities, and the actual size of uncollectible receivables.

A final item to be considered in arriving at net profit or loss is taxes. The lending officer should properly understand the country's tax practices. He will normally be interested not just in the amount of taxes but also in the timing of their payment, since their deferral can be an important source of cash. Reported profits may or may not reflect actual profitability. Closely held companies frequently use a number of devices to divert their earnings out of the country and into tax havens, thereby reducing their overall tax exposure. Awareness of this practice by the lending officer provides for a more realistic evaluation of the prospective borrower's level of income, and hence the ability to repay the proposed loan.

Techniques of Analysis

Though inquiring about the nature and determining the true worth of accounts in financial statements are essential to intelligent analysis of the prospective borrower's business, item-by-item evaluation does not identify any key relationships between accounts or groups of accounts, nor does it enable any judgment on the stability of the company's operations or the efficiency with which it is being managed. To address these and related questions, the lending officer must turn to such basic tools of financial analysis as cash flow; ratios; sources and uses of funds; and common-size analysis. Use of these tools helps the officer recognize exceptional situations quickly and distinctly, and encourages him to seek additional information, or clarification, from the would-be borrower on the reasons behind them. No single tool is by itself a complete method of analysis; instead, each sheds light on a different aspect of the prospective borrower's financial condition. Therefore, each of these tools should not be viewed as an end in itself, but as a means to reaching a reasoned decision.

Clearly, it is important to keep in mind that use of analytical tools in foreign financial statements assumes that the amount and quality of figures reported are satisfactory, and that any differences between domestic and foreign statement-account terminologies are completely understood. Another important assumption is that for any interpretation of the findings to be meaningful, it must take into account the underlying differences in legal, tax, accounting, and financing practices. Unless these assumptions are met, any effort to subject foreign financial statements to the standardized pattern of analysis used for domestic loans will produce only misleading results. For example, when reviewing financial leverage ratios of a Japanese corporation, it will be altogether misleading to evaluate them on standards other than those prevailing in that country. As is generally known, the close cooperation between government and business in Japan has encouraged the extensive reliance of industry on debt financing. As a result the indebtedness of major industrial groups to local banks has risen to unprecedented levels by the standards of the Western financial world. A U.S. corporation with similar reliance on debt financing would be viewed as an unacceptable credit risk. A brief description of some of the basic techniques used in the analysis of foreign financial statements is provided below.

One of the simpler methods that the lending officer may use in analyzing foreign financial statements is the common-size analysis, which expresses all related items as a percentage of a basic magnitude. For the purpose of this analysis, the basic magnitude is given the rating of 100 percent. Thus, all items in the income statement are expressed as a percentage of net sales, and all balance sheet items are expressed as a percentage of total assets or liabilities and equity. Once this is done and is extended to the financial statements of preceding years, the lending officer will be able to compare the relative importance of similar figures for previous periods and to identify any situations that appear to be out of line.

A related technique is the trend percentage method of comparison. This approach calls for establishing as base year the earliest year for which financial statements were submitted by the would-be borrower, and giving each item appearing in that statement a rating of 100 percent. If the corresponding accounts in statements of subsequent years are related to the base year, the lending officer will be able to detect the extent of the increase of each statement account, or group of accounts, over the base year, and the revealed trend over the period under consideration. In some accounts the trend may be upward, and in others downward, while in still others no definite trend may be evidenced. In addition to the direction of the trend, the lending officer will be able to compare the trends of individual accounts, or of groups of accounts, over the period under consideration.

Another useful method of investigating foreign financial statements is the sources-and-uses-of-funds statement. Preparation of a sources-and-uses-of-funds statement is based on the computation of the net changes in the asset, liability, and net worth accounts from one balance sheet date to another. Specifically, the net change in each individual balance sheet item is listed under separate "source" and "use" columns, depending upon what such a change represents. Changes that reflect increases in assets and decreases in liabilities and in net worth are recorded under the "uses of funds" column; decreases in assets and increases in liabilities and in net worth, under the "sources of funds" column. The purpose of this method is ready identification of the sources tapped by the would-be borrower to meet his need for funds during the period under consideration.

Cash flow is still another technique of value to the lending officer in his credit analysis. Since borrowers are expected to repay loans out of income rather than from the sale of assets or refinancing from another lender, the lending officer must look to their future income for debt retirement. Cash flows, thus, are generally prepared from information contained in projected income statements and balance sheets. Hence the importance of always checking the reasonableness of the borrower's projected data against the economic and industry forecasts for the period that the loan will be outstanding. Since the accuracy of a cash flow depends heavily on the assumptions underlying pro forma financial statements, the lending officer may wish to develop cash flows under best, worst, and most likely assumptions in deciding on the borrower's ability to service the debt.

Cash flows are normally requested from would-be borrowers for each year that the loan will be outstanding. These cash flows, in addition to predicting loan repayment, provide important insights into management competence. In other words, a company's sources of cash and its cash needs, and the relative amounts involved, project a clearer picture of the degree of efficiency with which the company is being managed. If, for example, the company's net cash generation is poor because of a rapid growth pattern, this raises questions with respect to the soundness of credit practices, requirements for additional working capital, inventory policies, and payables policies.

A final technique in foreign financial statement analysis is ratios. The objective of ratios is to highlight the internal relationship between figures reported in financial statements. If discriminating calculated and wisely interpreted, ratios can be of considerable assistance in the analysis of these statements. In other words, ratio calculations are meaningful when the figures selected are reliable and come from accounts that bear a fundamental and important relevance to one another. Thus, though a large number of ratios can be computed, only a few are considered basic in analysis work. The lending officer customarily relies on these ratios to make interyear comparisons of borrower performance and to determine the general direction in which a company's financial condition is moving. To the extent that industry data are available, the lending officer may also use ratios to identify a company's relative strengths and weaknesses vis-à-vis other firms in the same industry.

Because of the difficulty often encountered in the proper use and interpretation of ratios for analyzing foreign financial statements, every effort must be made to use relatively simple and basic analysis. Thus, of the various ratios, five are generally considered basic in foreign credit analysis: current ratio, receivables-to-sales ratio, sales-to-inventory ratio, debt-to-net worth ratio, and profits-to-net worth ratio.

Although analytical tools are important in evaluating the financial condition of a would-be borrower, it is necessary to supplement them with specific pertinent facts and direct contact with the borrower. After all, foreign credit analysis is not cut and dried. It is as unique as each individual borrower and each country. Every case involves a different number of variables, the most important of which is always the character of the specific borrower. If a borrower's character is poor, the probability of his respecting the terms of a loan agreement is low.

In summary, this chapter has sought to elucidate the various facets of foreign credit analysis. It has described the various considerations involved in deciding on a foreign loan request, reviewed the factors considered in credit analysis, discussed the sources of credit information, identified some of the issues unique to international lending, and offered some basic guidelines in analyzing financial statements. Arriving at a reasoned decision through use of analytical tools combined with intuitive judgment is common for bank lending officers who conduct domestic credit analysis. However, foreign credit analysis poses additional considerations. Though this chapter has not explored all of the possible refinements, it does review the primary issues involved in appraising foreign credit risk.

APPENDIX: CASH FLOW ANALYSIS

Table 11.1 illustrates the cash flow format used by Morgan Guaranty Trust Company in analyzing foreign loan requests. It is made up of the following components: total cash generated from operations, which includes net income plus depreciation and other sources of cash (that is, decrease in noncurrent assets or increase in senior liabilities); total uses of cash, which include capital and other expenditures as well as changes in net working investment, as determined by separate analysis of current accounts; changes in short-term debt, which may—or may not—constitute an additional source of cash, depending upon the direction of the change; servicing of already contracted long-term debt; and the resulting excess or deficit that identifies the prospective borrower's ability to service the loan under request.

Table 11.1 presents three versions of the cash flow for the same foreign concern: one submitted by the foreign applicant, one developed by the bank's foreign credit analyst, and a third also developed by the bank's analyst but adjusted to exclude monetary correction

TABLE 11.1. Cash Flow Analyses (millions of dollars)

	Company's Estimate of Most Likely Cash Flow					Bank's Estimate of Most Likely Cash Flow				
	1981	1982	1983	1984	1985	1981	1982	1983	1984	1985
Net income	-1	22	37	48	69	-5	-1	6	18	26
+ Depreciation	51	56	60	63	57	48	51	52	55	58
Operating cash flow	50	78	97	111	126	43	50	58	73	84
+ Other sources	11	8	12	13	1	11	8	11	10	1
Total operating cash flow	61	86	109	124	127	54	58	69	83	85
Change in net working investment	-69	48	-1	3	5	24	-6	-17	8	12
Capital expenditures	56	34	36	34	52	56	34	36	34	52
Other uses	7	6	0	1	11	1	12	0	0	1
Total uses	-6	88	35	38	68	81	40	19	42	65
Excess/(deficit)	67	-2	74	86	59	(27)	18	50	41	20
Change in short-term debt*	-29	-8	-7	5	-7	-29	-8	-7	5	-7
Available to service long-term (LT) debt	38	(10)	67	91	52	(56)	10	43	46	13
LT debt repayments	84	64	73	130	71	85	65	73	130	71
Excess/(deficit)	(46)	(74)	(6)	(39)	(19)	(141)	(55)	(30)	(84)	(58)

(continued)

TABLE 11.1 (continued)

Bank's Most Likely Cash Flow, Excluding Monetary Correction

	1981	1982	1983	1984	1985	1986	1987		Cumulative
Net income	-6	-2	6	18	26	34	43		
+ Depreciation	48	51	52	55	58	60	63		
Operating cash flow	42	49	58	73	84	94	106		
+ Other sources	11	8	11	10	1	0	0		
Total operating cash flow	53	57	69	83	85	94	106		
Net working investment	24	-6	-17	8	12	11	12		
Capital expenditures	56	34	36	34	52	17	36		
Other uses	1	12	0	0	0**	0**	0**		
Total uses	81	40	19	42	64	28	48		
Excess/(deficit)	(28)	17	50	41	21	66	58	=	225
Change in short-term debt*	-29	-8	-7	5	-7	-4	3	=	(47)
Available to service LT debt	(57)	9	43	46	14	62	61	=	178
Scheduled repayments	84	0	6	56	64	64	68	=	342
Excess/(deficit)	(141)	9	37	(10)	(50)	(2)	(7)	=	(164)

*Reduction in short-term borrowings as anticipated by loan applicant.
**Borrower projects sizable debt-financed investments in 1985–87, which were omitted for the purpose of this calculation.
Source: Morgan Guaranty Trust Company.

280

TABLE 11.2. Additional Tests of a Company's Financial Condition

	Summary of Statistics					
	1980	1981	1982	1983	1984	1985
Current ratio	1.43	1.49	1.68	1.28	1.72	1.76
Quick ratio	0.45	0.45	0.40	0.32	0.44	0.47
Senior liability/tangible net worth and/or subordinated debt	1.27	1.12	1.13	0.92	0.70	0.54
Total long-term debt/net worth	1.02	0.93	0.93	0.73	0.52	0.38
Total borrowed funds/net worth	1.17	1.01	0.99	0.78	0.57	0.42
Total liabilities and reserves/net worth	1.27	1.12	1.13	0.92	0.70	0.54
Cash flow/total long-term debt	0.12	0.11	0.17	0.25	0.37	0.50
Cash flow/total borrowed funds	0.10	0.10	0.16	0.23	0.33	0.46
Cash flow/total liabilities	0.09	0.09	0.14	0.20	0.27	0.36
EBIT/average total assets	3.58	2.54	4.58	5.75	6.91	8.48
EBIT/average total investment capital	3.76	2.67	4.87	6.16	7.46	9.18
Net after-tax earnings + ½ interest/average total investment capital	2.84	1.29	3.55	4.98	6.29	8.32
Return on average net worth (0/0)	4.18	-0.21	4.46	7.16	8.55	11.10
Times interest earned-EBIT/interest	2.05	0.96	1.85	2.61	3.18	5.31
After-tax fixed charge coverage	3.11	0.93	2.69	4.22	5.36	9.63

(continued)

TABLE 11.2 (continued)

Sources and Uses of Cash Funds: Most Likely Case (Company)
(millions of dollars, constant June 1980)

	1980	1981	1982	1983	1984	1985
Net income after tax	20	-1	22	37	48	69
Depreciation, depletion, and/or amortization	0	51	56	60	63	57
Operating cash flow	57	50	78	97	111	126
Other sources	0	11	8	12	13	1
Total	0	61	86	109	124	127
Change in net working investment	0	-69	48	-1	3	5
Capital expenditures	0	56	34	36	34	52
Other uses	0	1	12	0	0	11
Total uses	0	-12	94	35	37	68
Excess (deficit)	0	73	-8	74	87	59
Change, short-term debt	0	-29	-8	-7	5	-7
Additions to LTD	0	50	70	6	39	20
Repayments of LTD	0	84	64	73	130	71
Net change in LTD	0	-34	6	-67	-91	-52
Change, total debt	0	-63	-2	-74	-86	-59
Decrease in cash and/or short-term investments	0	-6	6	0	-1	0
Total	0	-69	4	-74	-87	-59

Net Working Investment Analysis
(amounts in millions of dollars and percents of sales)

	1980		1981		1982		1983		1984		1985	
	Amt.	%	Amt.	%	Amt.	%	Amt.	%	Amt.	%	Amt.	%
Receivables	89	20.2	60	12.0	65	10.9	68	11.1	71	11.3	75	11.6
Inventory	195	44.4	140	28.1	191	32.1	194	31.7	197	31.3	199	30.8
Adjusted working assets	284	64.6	200	40.1	256	43.0	262	42.8	268	42.6	274	42.4
Other current assets	1	0.2	20	4.0	21	3.5	18	2.9	15	2.3	16	2.4
Total current working assets	285	64.9	220	44.1	277	46.6	280	45.8	283	45.0	290	44.8
Accounts receivable and/or accruals	27	6.1	30	6.0	37	6.2	38	6.2	39	6.2	40	6.1
Other current liabilities	20	4.5	21	4.2	23	3.8	26	4.2	25	3.9	26	4.0
Total current working liabilities	47	10.7	51	10.2	60	10.1	64	10.4	64	10.1	66	10.2

(continued)

TABLE 11.2 (continued)

	1980 Amt.	%	1981 Amt.	%	1982 Amt.	%	1983 Amt.	%	1984 Amt.	%	1985 Amt.	%
Adjusted net working investment (1)	237	53.9	149	29.9	196	32.9	198	32.4	204	32.4	208	32.1
Reported net working investment (2)	238	54.2	169	33.9	217	36.5	216	35.3	219	34.8	224	34.6
Change in reported net working investment	0	0.0	-69	-13.8	48	8.0	-1	-0.1	3	0.4	5	0.7
Ratios												
Accounts receivable and/or accruals/inventory	13.85		21.43		19.37		19.59		19.80		20.10	
Inventory/cost of goods sold (CGS)	57.69		37.84		43.51		44.19		44.57		44.32	
Accounts receivable and/or accruals/CGS	7.99		8.11		8.43		8.66		8.82		8.91	

Note: Percents do not necessarily add to totals.
Source: Morgan Guaranty Trust.

284

(that is, the effect of asset revaluation). The second and third versions of cash flow have their own merits. The second identifies the flow of cash in the context of the company's local economic environment (that is, effects of local inflation). The third is a more conservative estimate, excluding the inflationary effects of asset revaluation.

Table 11.2 highlights some of the additional tests that Morgan uses to analyze foreign companies. These tests include ratios, sources and uses of cash funds, and net working investment analysis.

NOTES

1. Typically an overdraft is a facility used by banks to finance the self-liquidating needs of companies, and is therefore payable on demand. Where this facility is used as a means of medium-term financing, it is customarily referred to as an evergreen overdraft. Banks allowing such a practice usually find it very difficult to call for payment.

2. The "anticipated income" theory of liquidity, developed in 1949, emphasizes that banks, in making intermediate and long-term loans, should rely on the anticipated income of the borrower and its coverage of debt service requirements. See Herbert V. Prochnow, *Term Loans and Theories of Bank Liquidity* (New York: Prentice-Hall, 1949).

3. NIFO is the method of valuing inventory on the basis of the prices of goods on order.

SUGGESTED REFERENCES

Angelini, Anthony, Maximo Eng, and Francis A. Lees. *International Lending, Risk and the Euromarkets.* New York: John Wiley and Sons, 1979.

Donaldson, T. H. *Lending in International Commercial Banking.* New York: John Wiley and Sons, 1979.

Fitzgerald, R. D., A. D. Stickler, and T. R. Watts, eds. *International Survey of Accounting Principles and Reporting Practices.* Scarborough, Ontario: Price Waterhouse International, 1979.

Lees, Francis A. *Reporting Transnational Business Operations.* New York: The Conference Board, 1980.

Mathis, F. John, ed. *Offshore Lending by U.S. Commercial Banks.* 2nd ed. Washington, D.C., and Philadelphia: Bankers' Association for Foreign Trade and Robert Morris Associates, 1981.

Price Waterhouse and Company. *Guide for the Reader of Foreign Financial Statements.* New York: Price Waterhouse and Company, 1971.

Seawahl, Nancy. "Getting Started in International Lending—A Guide to Sources of Printed Information." *The Journal of Commercial Bank Lending*, May 1978, pp. 3-22.

Part V

FOREIGN LOANS
AND FINANCING

12 IMPORT FINANCING
Bob Kurau and
Emmanuel N. Roussakis

Over the centuries international trade transactions have been characterized by limited or no knowledge of the financial strength and reputation of each party, as well as by uncertain delivery and payment. As a result, sellers usually have sought to retain legal control over their goods until receipt of payment, whereas buyers have been reluctant to pay before possessing the goods. Experience and necessity thus have contributed to the creation of instruments intended to reduce risk in international transactions by assuring the seller of payment and the buyer of receipt of the goods. During the last three centuries these instruments have evolved along with institutional financial specialization. Some of the larger European merchant houses eventually found it increasingly profitable to lend their good name to less well-known merchants by accepting these merchants' drafts. Out of this practice grew merchant banking, commercial letters of credit, and bankers' acceptances.

As specialization of functions progressed, banks began to assume an important role in international finance. By the twentieth century commercial banks dominated the financing of foreign trade. The major instruments developed to facilitate the financing of foreign trade transactions are the letter of credit, the draft, and the banker's acceptance. To discuss import financing, it is useful to review these instruments as they arise in the normal sequence of an import transaction. This approach will clarify the role of banks in this process, and place import financing arrangements in their proper perspective. The following sections review the major international financial instruments, identify the documents involved, and analyze the various types of import financing.

INTERNATIONAL FINANCIAL INSTRUMENTS

Letter of Credit

One of the safest and most common ways to finance a transaction between international trading parties is the commercial letter of credit, or simply letter of credit (L/C). This instrument, depending upon the party to which reference is being made, is also referred to as an import letter of credit or an export letter of credit.

A letter of credit is a financial instrument issued by a bank at the request of a customer, whereby the bank undertakes to accept and/or pay drafts drawn upon it by a designated party, provided certain conditions are met by this party. In essence, the letter of credit provides for the substitution of a bank's strength for that of its customer, and assures the exporter payment against delivery of documents rather than of the actual merchandise. The exporter is also protected against government restrictions preventing payment by the importing firm. Experience shows that cases in which governments have prevented banks from honoring already issued letters of credit are limited (if there have been any). The importer is assured that the exporter will not be paid until the documents that transfer title to the merchandise are carefully examined by the bank and are found to be in order.

Issuance of a letter of credit by the importer's bank (*issuing* or *opening bank*) is the product of a process that usually begins with the exchange of correspondence between two parties located in different countries and interested in entering into a transaction. Once agreement is reached, a merchandise contract is concluded between the seller (exporter) and the buyer (importer). Two important features of this contract are the currency of payment and the means through which it is to be effected. If the invoice is to be expressed, and hence be paid, in the exporter's currency, the importer will have to bear the foreign exchange risk of this transaction. On the other hand, if the invoice is to be stated in the importer's currency, the exporter will have to bear the foreign exchange risk. In either case this risk can be reduced by hedging in the foreign exchange market (see chapter 10). The means of payment is another important aspect of this contract. If it is agreed that the transaction is to be paid by means of a letter of credit, the importer will contact his local bank and file a formal application for a letter of credit, which comes in a standardized printed form (see Figure 12.1). The importer's bank will want to know the amount of money involved, the terms of payment, the documents that the bank should receive to effect payment, the time period for which the credit will be valid, and other conditions.

Processing a letter of credit request is similar to processing a loan. The bank will seek to determine the ability and willingness of the importer to provide the funds necessary to honor the letter of credit and to pay the required fees. A well-established importer already has access to a substantial line of credit at the bank, in which case issuing a letter of credit entails no difficulty. The amount to be drawn under the letter of credit is charged against the total available under the credit line. Small and less-known importers, on the other hand, have to provide some type of security, such as a cash deposit (for part or all of the credit) or other collateral.

Once the bank is satisfied with the creditworthiness of the importer, it will proceed to open a letter of credit in favor of the exporter, guaranteeing its payment subject to the terms and conditions contained in the credit (see Figure 12.2). The letter of credit is then forwarded to a bank in the exporter's country (that is, to a correspondent bank or to the exporter's bank), which is instructed to advise the beneficiary of the establishment of a letter of credit in its name. This bank (*advising bank*) has no financial responsibility, nor does it receive fees. After receipt of the letter of credit, the exporter arranges for the shipment of the goods to the importer, to fulfill the conditions of the credit.

Once the goods are shipped, the exporter draws a draft against the issuing bank and attaches it to the required documents, which are submitted to the exporter's bank along with the letter of credit. Assuming that the documents are found to be in order, the exporter's bank forwards them to the issuing bank for payment. If the draft and accompanying documents comply with the terms and conditions of the letter of credit, the issuing bank pays the exporter's bank, which then makes the funds available to its client, the exporter. The issuing bank, in turn, collects from the importer against release of documents that are essential for the latter's physical possession of the merchandise.

The great majority of the letters of credit issued are *irrevocable*— that is, once the beneficiary is notified, the letter of credit cannot be

FIGURE 12.1: Application for Letter of Credit

Commercial Letter of Credit Application and Security Agreement

MANUFACTURERS HANOVER INTERNATIONAL BANKING CORPORATION
MIAMI, FLORIDA 33132

Date March 21, 1982 LC No. AB-100140

Bank use only

Please issue an irrevocable Letter of Credit as set forth below and forward same to your correspondent for delivery to the beneficiary by:
☐ Airmail ☐ Airmail, with short preliminary cable advice ☐ Full Cable

ADVISING BANK (If Blank, Correspondent Bank)	FOR ACCOUNT OF (APPLICANT)
MANUFACTURERS HANOVER TRUST COMPANY Gran Vía Carlos III, 140-142 Barcelona 34, Spain	VENCO IMPORT COMPANY Post Office Box XXXX South Miami, Florida 33133

IN FAVOR OF (BENEFICIARY)	AMOUNT
A & M MANUFACTURERS Apartado de Correos 44 CXI Barcelona, Spain	U.S. $46,000.00 (FORTY SIX THOUSAND AND 00/1.00 DOLLARS) *** Drafts must be negotiated or presented to Drawee on or before (Expiration Date) November 16, 1982

Available by drafts at __Sight, drawn on us__
for __100__ % of the Invoice value.
When accompanied by the following documents, as checked:

CHECK DOCUMENTS REQUIRED

☒ Commercial Invoice, *signed in Original and Three (3) Copies.* **SPECIMEN**
☐ Customs Invoice
☐ Marine ⎫
☐ War ⎬ Insurance Policy or Certificate __for Invoice Value plus 15%__
☐ Air ⎭
(If other insurance is required, please state risks)
☒ Other documents __Certificate of Origin issued by Chamber of Commerce, in three (3) Copies. Packing List, in three (3) Copies.__
☐ Airway Bill consigned to _____
☒ ON BOARD Ocean Bills of Lading (full set required if more than one original has been issued)
    issued to order of: __Manufacturers Hanover International Banking Corporation, Miami__
    marked: NOTIFY __Venco Import Company, Post Office Box XXXX, South Miami, Florida 33133__ Freight: Collect/Paid

COVERING: Merchandise described in the invoice as: (Mention commodity only in generic terms omitting details as to grade, quality, etc.)
__LADIES DRESSES__

Check one: ☐ FAS ☐ FOB ☐ C&F ☒ CIF ☐ C&I

Shipment from: __Barcelona, Spain__
To: __Miami, Florida__

Partial Shipments: ☒ Permitted ☐ Prohibited
Trans-shipments: ☐ Permitted ☒ Prohibited

☒ Documents must be presented to negotiating or paying bank within __15__ days after the date of issuance of documents evidencing shipment or dispatch or taken in charge (shipping documents) but within validity of letter of credit.
☐ Insurance effected by ourselves. We agree to keep insurance coverage in force until this transaction is completed.

UNLESS OTHERWISE INSTRUCTED, DOCUMENTS SHALL BE FORWARDED TO YOU IN ONE AIRMAIL.
Special Instructions: _____

In consideration of your issuing at the request of the undersigned your Commercial Letter of Credit, hereinafter called the "Credit," substantially in accordance with the foregoing application, the undersigned hereby agrees as follows:

Note: This is an incomplete form, with security agreement details and other contractual terms omitted.
Source: Manufacturers Hanover International Banking Corporation.

FIGURE 12.2: Letter of Credit

```
┌─────┐      MANUFACTURERS HANOVER INTERNATIONAL BANKING CORPORATION
│  H  │              100 NORTH BISCAYNE BOULEVARD, MIAMI, FLORIDA 33132
└─────┘
```

DATE **March 21, 1982**

OUR CREDIT NO.	ADVISING BANK NO.
AB-100140	

IRREVOCABLE COMMERCIAL LETTER OF CREDIT
ADVISING BANK

MANUFACTURERS HANOVER TRUST COMPANY
Gran Via Carlos III, 140-142
Barcelona 34, Spain

APPLICANT

VENCO IMPORT COMPANY
Post Office Box XXXX
South Miami, Florida 33133

BENEFICIARY

A & M MANUFACTURERS
Apartado de Correos 44 CXI
Barcelona, Spain

AMOUNT

U.S. $46,000.00 ***

EXPIRY DATE
November 16, 1982

GENTLEMEN:
YOU ARE AUTHORIZED TO VALUE ON us
BY DRAWING DRAFTS AT   Sight   FOR FULL INVOICE VALUE WHEN ACCOMPANIED
BY THE FOLLOWING DOCUMENTS:

- Commercial Invoice, signed in Original and Four (4) Copies.
- Customs Invoice, in Original and Two (2) Copies.
- Insurance Policy or Certificate for Invoice value plus 15% covering Marine, War, and All Risks.
- Certificate of Origin issued by Chamber of Commerce, in Original and Three (3) Copies.
- On Board Ocean Bills of Lading (full set required if more than one original has been issued) issued to order of: Manufacturers Hanover International Banking Corporation, Miami, marked: NOTIFY Venco Import Company, Post Office Box XXXX, South Miami, Florida 33133, Freight Prepaid.

COVERING   LADIES DRESSES, C.I.F.   **SPECIMEN**

SHIPMENT FROM Barcelona, Spain	PARTIAL SHIPMENTS	TRANSHIPMENTS
TO Miami, Florida LATEST	Permitted	Prohibited

DOCUMENTS MUST BE PRESENTED WITHIN 15 DAYS AFTER THE DATE OF ISSUANCE OF THE BUT WITHIN THE VALIDITY OF THE CREDIT.

SPECIAL CONDITIONS:

THE AMOUNT OF ANY DRAFT DRAWN UNDER THIS CREDIT MUST BE ENDORSED ON THE REVERSE OF THE ORIGINAL CREDIT.
ALL DRAFTS MUST BE MARKED, "DRAWN UNDER MANUFACTURERS HANOVER INTERNATIONAL BANKING CORPORATION.
LETTER OF CREDIT NUMBER   AB-100140   DATED March 21, 1982

WE HEREBY ENGAGE WITH THE DRAWERS, ENDORSERS AND BONA FIDE HOLDERS OF DRAFTS DRAWN UNDER AND IN COMPLIANCE WITH THE TERMS OF THIS CREDIT THAT SUCH DRAFTS WILL BE DULY HONORED ON DUE PRESENTATION. IF NEGOTIATED ON OR BEFORE THE EXPIRATION DATE OR PRESENTED TO US TOGETHER WITH THIS LETTER OF CREDIT ON OR BEFORE THAT DATE.	ADVISING BANK'S NOTIFICATION
Yours very truly,	
AUTHORIZED SIGNATURE	

[left margin, vertical text] EXCEPT SO FAR AS OTHERWISE EXPRESSLY STATED THIS CREDIT IS SUBJECT TO THE UNIFORM CUSTOMS AND PRACTICE FOR DOCUMENTARY CREDITS (1974 REVISION) INTERNATIONAL CHAMBER OF COMMERCE (PUBLICATION NO 290)

Source: Manufacturers Hanover International Banking Corporation.

cancelled prior to the expiration date or altered in any way without the prior consent of all parties to the transaction, including the beneficiary. If the letter of credit is *revocable* the credit is subject to cancellation or modification at any time before payment and without notice to the beneficiary. Not infrequently the exporter may request the advising or notifying bank to add its own liability to that of the opening bank. In such a case the letter of credit becomes *confirmed*, meaning that both the issuing and the confirming bank are obligated to honor drafts drawn in compliance with the credit. If both the irrevocable and the confirmed features are combined in the same letter of credit, such a letter is virtual guaranty of payment once the conditions of the credit are fulfilled, and is referred to as an *irrevocable and confirmed letter of credit*.

Over the years, because of particular needs of importers and/or exporters, there have been other important variations of the basic document to accommodate different conditions. Thus, a letter of credit may provide for advances to the exporter prior to shipment (*red clause letter of credit*); call for payments not at the time of shipment but later, in accordance with scheduled dates over the life of the credit (*deferred-payment letter of credit*); make possible the transfer of proceeds by the beneficiary (a trading intermediary) to another party (a supplier) in the transaction (*transferable letter of credit*); permit the exporter to seek the most favorable foreign exchange rate among those quoted by different banks or exercise its judgment as to the bank that would be most desirable to effect collection (*negotiable letter of credit*); or cover more than one transaction through successive reinstatements of the letter of credit, renewing the amount involved and extending the expiration date (*revolving letter of credit*).

Whatever the specific features of the letter of credit, the terms and conditions should be clear and simply stated. Reference to the quality or condition of the merchandise and other details are not customarily included in the letter of credit. No one would expect bank employees to open and examine the contents of boxes or crates—and even if they did, they would hardly be qualified to express an opinion on the state of these goods. If the exporter is dishonest, a letter of credit will not prevent shipment of inferior goods, or even rocks. Since banks deal only in documents, they cannot be held liable in such instances. However, the bank can withhold payment from the exporter if there is some irregularity in the necessary documents (those covering shipment and insurance of goods) or if some of the terms and conditions stated in the letter of credit have not been met.

Drafts and Acceptances

The final phase in the letter of credit financing process is the actual payment, which is effected by means of a *draft* or bill of exchange. A draft is a written order to pay, signed by the drawer, requiring the party to which it is addressed to pay on demand, or at some future date, a stated sum of money to the order of a named party or to the bearer. As follows from this definition there are three parties to a draft: the *drawer*, the *drawee*, and the *payee*. The drawer or maker is the exporter, who, after the goods are shipped, originates the draft and presents it—along with the required documents—to its bank for payment of what is due. The drawee is the party to which the draft is addressed—the importer or its bank—and which is asked to pay the stipulated amount in accordance with the terms of the document. The payee is the beneficiary in favor of whom the draft is payable—that is, the exporter or the exporter's bank.

Another feature of the draft is the time of payment, often called a draft's tenor. Depending upon the prior agreement between importer and exporter, a letter of credit may call for a sight or a time draft. If the letter of credit provides for a sight draft, the issuing bank will make immediate payment once the draft and certifying documents are received and are found to be in accordance with the terms of the letter of credit. If provision is made for a time draft, payment by the importer is due 30, 60, 90, or some other specified number of days after the date of the draft. As this implies, the main purpose of a time draft is to provide the importer with sufficient time to claim and dispose of the goods, and meet the maturity of the underlying draft.

Issuance of a time draft calls for an additional step in the financial transaction, its acceptance by the importer's bank and, hence, the creation of a *banker's acceptance*. The draft is changed into an acceptance by a stamp across the face of the draft that includes the word "accepted," the date, the signature of an authorized officer, the name of the bank, and other information. Clearly the accepting bank will charge its client a commission for creating this acceptance.

The banker's acceptance may be returned to the exporter, to be held until maturity and then collected.

Alternatively, the exporter may discount (sell) the draft to its bank or to an investor, receiving payment immediately. When the accepting bank is a U.S. bank, foreign exporters usually favor authorizing the U.S. bank to sell its dollar-denominated acceptance in the domestic money markets. This is because the U.S. money markets are generally more liquid and have lower transaction costs than is true for markets in most other currencies. Such a request presents no problem, especially if the accepting bank has a strong reputation in international trading circles. The stature of the accepting bank makes it a prime asset—that is, a high-quality investment for banks and other institutional investors interested in holding liquid assets of this type. The selling of the acceptance will be at a discount from the face amount based on the going discount rate for bankers' acceptances. Since the importer may have agreed in advance to pay for this discount, the accepting bank will remit the exporter's bank the full amount of the draft for payment to the exporter. The investor, in turn, will hold the accepted draft until its maturity, then present it to the bank for payment. The accepting bank will then look to its customer for reimbursement.

In many cases, businesses well known to each other may find use of a letter of credit unnecessary, and instead agree on payment through drafts to be collected through banking channels. In other words, the banks involved act only as agents in performing a collection function, thereby earning a collection fee. Specifically, after shipment of the merchandise, the exporter draws a draft on the importer (rather than on its bank), in accordance with the terms agreed upon by the two parties, and submits it, along with the other documents necessary for the transaction, to its bank for collection. The exporter's bank then forwards them to its correspondent in the importer's country, which arranges for collection of the funds due the exporter. If the draft is a sight draft, the documents are turned over to the importer upon payment of the draft. If the draft is a time draft, the documents are released to the importer when the latter accepts the draft liability, which is then known as a *trade acceptance*.

In either case the collecting bank may choose to time the presentation of the drafts to the importer—for payment or acceptance—when the merchandise arrives in the importer's designated port. On the basis of an exporter's letter of instruction to the collecting bank, the latter collects from the importer the stipulated amount (plus any fees) and remits it to the exporter's bank for payment. Clearly, should the importer fail to make any payment or go into bankruptcy after accepting the draft, the collecting bank has no obligation or commitment to pay. The risk of nonpayment is carried by the exporter.

DOCUMENTS

Whether drafts are part of a letter of credit transaction or merely items for collection, documents are an integral part of the transaction. These documents generally certify title to the goods and condition of shipment. With banks functioning as intermediaries between exporters and importers, it is only natural that they be concerned about these documents and make every effort to assure that they are in good order. Following is a list of the documents required in most international transactions.

Commercial Invoice

Once a merchandise contract is concluded, the exporter issues an invoice in the name of the buyer, describing the merchandise and its attributes, unit prices, the terms of sale, and the total value of the transaction. The invoice includes information pertaining to shipping terms and charges, such as CF (cost and freight), CIF (cost, insurance, and freight), FOB (free on board), and FAS (free alongside). The data contained in the invoice should be consistent with the corresponding data on the letter of credit.

Bill of Lading

A key document in the financing of a foreign trade transaction is the bill of lading. This document, issued by steamship companies, airlines, railroads, and other common carriers, provides a description of the terms and conditions under which a shipment is accepted. It is a receipt from the carrier that it has accepted goods for transportation; a contract with the shipper for the transport and delivery of goods to a designated party or its order; and a transferable title to the goods, provided it is negotiable (made out "to order"). These attributes of the bill of lading render it the principal document supporting the exporter's draft and, hence, its claim for payment.

Insurance Certificate

Another important document stipulated in the letter of credit is insurance to protect the shipment from different types of risk. The question of insurance is a major one in a foreign transaction. The variety and magnitude of risks threatening the profitable conclusion of transactions have always been greater in foreign trade than in domestic. Distances are usually longer, and the number of handlings to which goods are subjected is generally greater. As a result, the chance of financial loss is bigger. Hence the need for proper insurance coverage to protect not only the individual parties to the transaction but also the bank that is financing it.

Depending upon the terms of the merchandise contract, insurance may be placed by the exporter for his account or for the account of the importer; or it may be placed by the importer with his own underwriting firm. Active importers and exporters usually maintain open or floating policies on the basis of which they issue insurance certificates for individual shipments; these certificates accompany the required title documents. Marine insurance policies cover the normal hazards of voyage, usually referred to as *shipping risks.* These risks range from total loss of goods through sinking of the vessel to losses resulting from fire, collision, or fuel oil or freshwater damages.

In addition to sea perils, there are a number of other real risks that can interrupt the commencement and/or the completion of the voyage: strikes, riots, civil commotion, and war. Of these risks, strikes are the most common peril faced by traders today. Strikes can prevent the transfer of the shipment from the dock to the vessel or vice versa. This can be especially disastrous for the importer when the shipment consists of perishables. The same is true for seasonal items—for example, Christmas ornaments are landed in time for the season but are delayed by a longshoremen's strike. If insurance is desired to cover against strikes or any of the other risks, it can be included in the marine insurance policy by endorsement. The exception is war risk, which requires a separate contract.

Upon arrival of the vessel at the port of import, and after the shipment is unloaded at the docks, it is exposed to the added risks that include theft and pilferage, which are usually referred to as *dockside risks.* These are also subject to marine insurance coverage.

The vast variety of risks against which insurance coverage can be obtained makes it all the more important for the importer's bank to review thoroughly the insurance arrangements associated with the import transaction and to make sure that the policy is adequate, transferable, and written by a reliable firm.

Other Documents

Other documents that may be required by a letter of credit are a *certificate of origin*, which certifies the country where the goods are grown or manufactured; a *weight list*, which itemizes the weight of each package or bale; a *packing list*, which identifies the contents of individual packages, especially when these are numerous; an *inspection certificate*, which is usually issued by a third or independent party to verify the contents or quality of the shipment. Since banks deal only in documents, this certificate assures the importer that it is receiving what it ordered.

Occasionally the shipment arrives in the importer's designated port in advance of the title documents, or the latter may be received incomplete (for instance, one of the original bills of lading issued by the shipping company may be missing). In such instances the importer may request its bank to issue a letter, known as a *steamship guaranty*, on the basis of which the merchandise can be moved off the docks in order to avoid costly charges and other risks. Since this letter functions as a third-party guaranty, its issuance is conditional upon prior indemnification of the bank by its customer.

FINANCING IMPORTS

Issuance of a letter of credit by a bank may or may not entail extensions of credit. As indicated earlier, when the importer makes a cash deposit or maintains adequate balances in its bank account, issuance of a letter of credit entails no bank financing. The bank issuing the letter of credit will be paid in cash by charging the customer's account. By contrast, if the importer does not have all or part of the funds for the transaction, it will have to negotiate a loan from the bank. If the importer has sufficient creditworthiness, the bank will extend it an unsecured loan. Otherwise, the bank will extend it credit only through a security agreement that enables the bank to perfect a lien on a particular asset or assets of the importer. Both unsecured and secured financing are considered below.

Unsecured Financing

Unsecured bank credit or working capital loans are the most conventional source of short-term accommodation for U.S. business firms. The importer that can obtain its cash requirements through properly priced unsecured bank borrowing has adequate capital and net worth, competent management, stable earnings, a record of prompt payment of obligations, and a bright business future. An importing firm that meets these criteria will have little trouble obtaining a short-term unsecured loan through the signing of a promissory note.

Importers that qualify to borrow on an unsecured basis are generally few in number. A typical firm in the import trade is relatively small, and its capital investment is almost entirely in trading assets— that is, in working capital. To a banker accustomed to traditional liquidity levels (a current ratio of 2:1) or leverage ratios (debt/ equity ratio of 1:1), a typical importing firm constitutes a major deviation from such standards. For example, it is not unusual for importing firms to have less than acceptable liquidity (such as 1.25:1) and/or quite excessive leverage (for instance, 5:1 or even higher).

Another decisive factor weighting heavily against unsecured financing is the vulnerability of the import business. An importing firm usually has as its outlets businesses that are far larger than itself. For example, import companies include among their clients large tire companies, coffee roasting companies, chain stores, and department stores. This inequality in size increases the dependency of the importing firms upon their customers, and tends to create problems when business conditions are slack. Specifically, when the economy contracts, importing firms are faced with requests for delayed deliveries, cancellations of letters of intent, and difficulty in obtaining new orders—all resulting in shrinking backlogs and business.

Importing firms are also vulnerable vis-à-vis their suppliers. In periods of increased tightness in foreign suppliers' markets, contract prices are reopened for negotiation, and deliveries are delayed or rationed. Such a development could prevent the importer from honoring customer orders, leading to loss of reputation and, in turn, income.

Secured Financing

In secured financing a bank relies not only on the moral and financial integrity of the importer but also on the possession of, or title to, an asset as additional protection for its repayment. In many instances the merchandise being imported may qualify as collateral for bank financing, depending upon the nature of the merchandise and how much margin is required. The suitability of the goods imported as collateral will significantly influence lending terms.

A bank will be more liberal in its terms if the commodity being imported is readily salable and standard in nature, and if hedging facilities exist on a recognized commodity exchange. Coffee, for example, is excellent collateral for bank loans. Such a commodity allows the importer to command greater bank credit, thus leveraging its own capital to a greater extent. A bank will be less inclined to extend generous terms if the commodity is subject to spoilage (for instance, seafood), style factors (for instance, shoes or textiles), or, in the opinion of the bank, to a decreasing demand because of oversupply or a change in buying habits.

Another asset that can qualify as collateral for import financing is the accounts receivable arising from the sale of the merchandise. Accounts receivable are one of the oldest types of collateral available to banks.

Use of the imported merchandise or of the accounts receivable arising from the sale of this merchandise as collateral entails different financial arrangements between the borrower and the bank. The forms of import financing arrangements related to each type of asset are discussed below.

Assignment of Accounts Receivable

Borrowing secured by the assignment of accounts receivable and the pledging of inventory normally provides enough cash flow for the importer to meet his current obligations. Accounts receivable fre-

FIGURE 12.3: Schedule of Assigned Accounts Receivable

Walter E. Heller & Company
Southeast

Heller Building
4500 Biscayne Boulevard, Miami, Florida 33137, (305) 576-4800

EQUIPMENT FINANCING • WAREHOUSE LOANS • EQUIPMENT LEASING

SCHEDULE OF ASSIGNED RECEIVABLES

ASSIGNED BY

TOTAL ACCOUNTS ASSIGNED_____

TRADE DISCOUNT OR CREDITS ISSUED

NET ACCOUNTS   02 _____

DATE _____

RESERVE   12X _____

SCHED.NO. _____

NET ADVANCE _____

CLIENT NO. _____

AUDITED	SIGNATURE OK	CHECK NUMBER	BANK	DATE	ENTERED	APPROVED

KNOW ALL MEN BY THESE PRESENTS that for value received, the undersigned does hereby pledge, deliver, bargain, sell, transfer, assign and set over unto WALTER E. HELLER & COMPANY SOUTHEAST, its successors and assigns (herein collectively called HELLER) the accounts receivable listed hereon, and all property, rights to property, title, and interest of the undersigned therein, and in the merchandise represented thereby, to have and to hold the said accounts and merchandise (if returned or rejected) unto HELLER for its own use and benefit, the intent and effect hereof being to vest HELLER with and subrogate HELLER to, all property and other rights, custody, security, and guaranties possessed by the undersigned with respect thereto, including the right of stoppage in transit. The undersigned irrevocably constitutes HELLER as pledgee, or its designee, as attorneys in fact for and in the name of the undersigned or otherwise to sell, assign, transfer, compromise, pledge, discharge and collect said accounts, to demand, sue for, and receive all moneys due or to become due thereon, to receipt for and endorse in the name of the undersigned any and all checks or other media of payment pertaining thereto, and to take, hold, transfer, assign, sell, and receive the proceeds of sale of any merchandise returned, rerouted, reconsigned or rejected at public or private sales without notice and with authority in HELLER to be the purchaser at such sales, whether public or private, and for said purposes to do all acts and things necessary or proper in the premises, hereby ratifying and confirming all that said attorneys-in-fact or their substitutes shall lawfully do by virtue hereof.

We hereby certify and covenant that the said accounts and the invoices representing the same are each a true and correct statement of a bona fide indebtedness incurred by the debtor therein named upon the terms therein stated, now outstanding and owing to the full amount thereof for merchandise actually sold and delivered or services actually rendered to and accepted by the debtor, that no payment has been made thereon, that there are no defenses, offsets or counterclaims thereto, that said merchandise was, at the time of sale, owned by the undersigned free from lien or encumbrance, that none of said accounts represents a consignment or sale on condition, that said accounts are free from all encumbrances except as granted to HELLER hereby and that the same will be duly paid in full in accordance with their tenor.

This instrument is made in accordance with the terms, provisions and conditions, and is entitled to the benefits, of the existing agreement between the undersigned and HELLER.

We hereby agree that if the said accounts are not paid by each debtor when due we will pay the amount or any part thereof that remains unpaid whether or not the failure of the debtor to pay shall be for credit or any other reasons, and that HELLER at its option may charge the part remaining unpaid against our account with HELLER and that any or all of said merchandise that may be returned, rejected or reconsigned will be held by us as the property of HELLER and upon demand at once delivered to HELLER until and unless the invoice value of the said merchandise and any and all other indebtedness of the undersigned to HELLER present or future shall have been paid to HELLER and we further agree promptly to make payment for said returned, rejected or reconsigned merchandise or in the event of a resale by HELLER we will promptly pay to them the difference between the amount realized from such resale and the invoice value of said merchandise as set forth in the statement above. All representations, warranties and agreements anywhere herein contained are made to induce HELLER to accept said accounts or claims so assigned by us and to accept transfer of our rights, titles and interest as herein provided. The rights and remedies of the Company under this assignment and the existing agreement shall be cumulative.

Whenever the words "accounts receivable" are referred to above, it shall also mean third party notes receivables, security agreements, chattel mortgages, mortgages on real property and all collateral and security thereto appertaining.

In accordance with all the terms of the formal assignments stated hereinabove, we hereby assign all accounts, notes, bills, acceptances, installment paper, or other forms of obligations which are acquired by us in the normal course of our business, evidenced by said instruments numbered from

_____

_____

_____

_____

_____

which are attached hereto and made a part hereof, and as shown on the attached, initialed, and dated adding machine tape or other data attached hereto in the aggregate amount of

$_____

together with all contracts and/or notes and other evidences of indebtedness pertaining to the foregoing all with the same force and effect as though detailed hereon. For additional details as to the names and addresses of each debtor, the unpaid balances owing by each debtor therefore, and other particulars, reference is hereby made to the books of account, statements, and other records kept at the First Party's place of business, all of which are likewise hereby assigned to you.

IN WITNESS WHEREOF, we have hereunto set our hand and seal this _____ day of _____ 19_____

Firm Name _____

Source: Walter E. Heller and Company Southeast.

quently make up the largest portion of an importer's current assets, providing his inventory is turning over at a normal rate, and usually provide the primary collateral for secured short-term borrowing. Importers usually have little in the form of fixed assets that can be used as collateral. To assure proper cash flow and to be able to fund the drafts when they are presented, as well as to meet normal operating expenses, the importer must be able to pledge and borrow secured by his accounts receivable (see Figure 12.3).

The receivable loan may be short-term or on a revolving basis, and the amount of credit available tends to increase as the need for credit grows. The importer may use his accounts receivable line to fund a large shipment, and then, since receivables are collateral, the line will be reduced. Or the line may be on a revolving basis, depending on the borrower's needs.

Usually the financing is done on a nonnotification basis, with the customers of the importer not being notified that their accounts are being pledged as collateral for a loan. The importer collects all payments, and forwards the collections to the lender. In notification financing the lender advises all account debtors to send their checks directly to the lender, who credits the loan account on receipt. The lender usually makes the decision as to notification or nonnotification. Notification may help in the collections of accounts by virtue of the borrower's customers' desire not to become delinquent with a large lending institution. Another theory is that the lender shows more confidence by nonnotification financing.

The lender looks not only to the integrity and creditworthiness of the borrower but also to the collateral or the receivables themselves. The type of merchandise being sold is a factor, as is the demand for it. The amount of returns in relation to sales is one of the determining factors in arriving at the percentage of advance. The lender also must review carefully the aging of accounts receivable to determine the paying habits of the debtors of the importer. Depending on the custom in the trade, accounts delinquent beyond a certain period are ineligible for advance. Accounts that also may be considered ineligible are those to affiliated companies or those in which there is a high degree of concentration to any one customer, usually 25 percent of the total receivables. When 50 percent of the total receivables is delinquent, the balance, or the current portion, may be considered ineligible.

A prudent lender, depending on the collateral, will take means to ascertain that the receivables actually do exist by confirming with the debtor that the merchandise was received and that there is a valid trade debt that conforms to the collateral. Internal controls dictate that the lender conduct field examinations of the books and records of the client and, each month, reconcile agings with the past month after taking into account sales represented by assigned accounts and collections.

The percentage of advance is determined by an analysis of the foregoing factors, and usually ranges from 75 to 80 percent of the total receivables pledged, less those considered ineligible or not worthy of advance.

An accounts receivable security agreement is entered into, and is a contract between the lender and the importer imposing obligations on both. As long as the importer meets all the requirements called for in the contract, the lender has the obligation to lend. Since the document is a loan agreement, certain convenants protect the lender:

• Requirements for timely financing information
• Submission of agings on a monthly basis
• Responsibility to forward all payments received directly to the lender
• Availability of books and records for inspection by the lender
• Right of the lender to determine the eligibility of collateral
• Dollar amount of line of credit
• Duration of contract
• Percentage of advance.

The prudent lender will build credit files on the larger customers of the importer and be prepared to cut back on the percentage of advance, thus warning the importer of "danger ahead." Slow accounts receivable constitute a "red flag" to the credit grantor.

Factoring

A factor (from the Latin "he who does things") was originally a business, not a financier. It originally referred to an agent for a property owner, following the Roman practice of entrusting property management to others. It was in connection with the growth of the wool industry in England, beginning in the late fourteenth century, that the commercial factor was developed as an institution. The factor served as a commission merchant or selling agent for the mill. Because of the slowness of transportation and communication in those days, geographical distances were cumbersome obstacles to business transactions. The factor would, therefore, advise the mill of the styles and merchandise most popular in the local market. The mills would ship merchandise in bulk to the factor, who would sell it in his area and assume the responsibility for the creditworthiness of his customers.

Typically the factor buys the accounts of his clients on a non-recourse basis and provides credit analysis, bookkeeping, the collection of accounts, and the assumption of the credit risk. The importer submits a list of his customers/prospective customers to the factor, who establishes credit limits in advance. The customers of the importer are instructed that the invoice has been purchased by the factor, and are instructed to remit directly to him. Prior to the maturity date of the invoice or prior to the agreed-upon date that the factor will remit to the importer, the latter may request an advance, which the factor may make, up to 90 percent of the invoice value. A reserve is maintained to cover shortages in goods shipped, returns, and disputes.

The factors charge a commission, based on the invoice value, that covers the assumption of the credit risk, bookkeeping, and collection of the accounts. Commission charges usually run from 1 to 2 percent, and interest is charged only when collections are anticipated.

Factoring, which lends itself to repeat transactions, had been confined to the textile and furniture industries, but lately it has spread to toys, shoes, and floor coverings, to name a few. It does not lend itself to a single sale, such as equipping a building with machinery.

Warehouse Receipts

The underlying or primary collateral for the importer is the merchandise being imported. To protect the lender and to control the collateral, the services of a warehouse company are enlisted and warehouse receipts are issued as collateral for the loan. These warehouse receipts may be either negotiable or nonnegotiable, with the latter the more desirable because the former are transferable and must be presented to the warehouse company each time a release is made. Nonnegotiable warehouse receipts are issued in the name of the lender, and describe in detail the merchandise being stored (see Figure 12.4).

FIGURE 12.4: Nonnegotiable Warehouse Receipt

GENERAL OFFICES

NATIONAL FREEZERS, INC.
1849 N.W. FIRST AVENUE
MIAMI, FLORIDA 33136

DOCUMENT
NON NEGOTIABLE
WAREHOUSE
RECEIPT

RECEIVED ON STORAGE IN WAREHOUSE.

F/S/AM 1849 NW FIRST AVE MIAMI FLA 33136 82054-13.59

THE MERCHANDISE DESCRIBED BELOW, DELIVERABLE ON WRITTEN AUTHORITY WITHOUT THE RETURN OF THIS RECEIPT, SUBJECT TO LIEN FOR STORAGE AND OTHER CHARGES, ADVANCES, AND EXPENSES, ACCORDING TO LAW AND SUBJECT TO EXCLUSIONS BELOW AND TERMS AND CONDITIONS CONTAINED IN THE CONTRACT OF STORAGE ON THE REVERSE SIDE HEREOF.

FOR ACCOUNT OF:
WALTER E. HELLER & CO.
FOR THE ACCOUNT OF
GUAYAS SFD CO. INC.
4500 BISCAYNE BLVD.
MIAMI, FLORIDA 33137

COPY TO:
GUAYAS SEAFOOD CO. INC.
9390 NORTHWEST 13TH ST.
UNIT 67
MIAMI, FLORIDA 33172

OWNERS WEIGHTS ONLY ARE SHOWN WHEREVER WEIGHT IS LISTED HEREIN UNLESS OTHERWISE INDICATED

NO RESPONSIBILITY IS ASSUMED BY THE WAREHOUSEMAN FOR INABILITY TO MAKE DELIVERY OF THE MERCHANDISE REPRESENTED BY THIS WAREHOUSE RECEIPT BECAUSE OF ARMED ROBBERY, STRIKES, LOCKOUTS OR UNION LABOR OPPOSITION TO OR INTERFERENCE WITH SUCH DELIVERY. THIS WAREHOUSE IS NOT AN INSURER OF THE MERCHANDISE STORED THEREIN.

WHS.	ACCOUNT NO	LOT NO	STORAGE FROM	QUANTITY	UNIT	AVERAGE WEIGHT NET	AVERAGE WEIGHT GROSS	LOCATION	CC
M	72206	13840	02 16 82	1	CTN	50.0	60.0*	9L	012

STORED IN	TO BE REG. FRZN	TO BE BLAST	TO BE OTHER	BOND NO	RECEIVED VIA	
FREEZER					O/T AECA AL AWB 746-00237300	TD

SAID TO BE OR CONTAIN

ACCOUNT P.O. NO. ORDER NO.

PRODUCT CODE	PACK - SIZE - PRODUCTS - MARKINGS - EXCEPTIONS
	10/5 SHRIMP U/7 WHITE FRIGORO
	CASES RECEIVED WET TORN OPEN REPACKED 31 TEMPS 30 TO 33

THE UNDERSIGNED WAREHOUSEMAN ALSO CLAIMS A LIEN FOR ALL LIKE CHARGES AND EXPENSES IN RELATION TO OTHER GOODS WHENEVER DEPOSITED WHETHER OR NOT THEY HAVE BEEN DELIVERED BY THE WAREHOUSEMAN

NATIONAL FREEZERS, INC.

STRG. FROM	ACCT. NO.	FOR ACCOUNT OF / COPY TO	PRODUCT CODE	SAID TO BE	LOT NO
02 16 82	72206	WALTER E. HELLER & CO.	10/5 SHRIMP U/7 WHITE FRIGORO		
		GUAYAS SEAFOOD CO. INC.			13840

Source: Walter E. Heller and Company Southeast.

As the importer makes sales and notifies the lender, the latter, either by telephone followed by a letter of confirmation, or with a prior letter authorizing partial releases up to a specific dollar amount, gives instructions to the warehouse for partial releases of merchandise. The lender may require the importer to pay a percentage of the loan when releasing inventory, or may depend on the cash flow from the accounts receivable being generated to replace the collateral. The lender, therefore, is a partner in the transaction from the opening of the letter of credit to the collection of the accounts receivable generated from the sale of the imported merchandise. It therefore behooves a prudent lender to know the merchandise being imported and its salability, the market conditions, the reliability of the shipper, the character of the importer, and the ability of the importer to market and the ability of the credit department to collect.

Since it is difficult to chart the peaks and valleys of an importer's cash flow, secured financing lends itself to import financing rather than to working capital loans.

In cases where a public warehouse is not conducive to the normal conduct of a business or is too costly for the importer, the goods may be stored on the importer's premises. The storage facility can be a separate building, part of a building, an oil tank, or any kind of area on the borrower's premises where commodities such as lumber, coal, and iron bars may be stacked or stored and kept under control. This type of warehousing is called a *field warehouse* and is under the control of a person bonded and employed by the warehouse company. Actually, the individual may be an employee of the borrower who, while continuing his normal duties, goes on the payroll of the warehouse company and reports the "ins and outs" as the goods are moved.

When a loan is made on the security of field warehouse receipts, great reliance is placed on the integrity and the competence of the warehouse company. Signs are posted around the collateral area to show that the goods, although on the premises of the importer, are under the control of the warehouse company. The lender is furnished inventory certificates, such as the one in Figure 12.5, that state the present inventory value at a specific date below the dollar amounts received and shipped. In order to preserve the proper collateral balance and loan amount, the field warehousing company is given a "hold" figure beyond which they must not release goods. The amount of advance is negotiated between the lender and the importer, and will usually be about 50 percent of the cost.

This type of financing requires a little more of the "C" represented by character than do nonnegotiable warehouse receipts because there is little to separate the importer from the goods except, in most cases, a flimsy participation. Also, the warehouse receipt is only as good as the issuing company. How long has the warehousing company been around? What is its reputation? Its net worth? (A lender should not be afraid to ask for a financial statement.) Remember the salad oil scandal of the early 1960s when "Tino" De Angelis cost the most sophisticated banks in New York City well over $100

FIGURE 12.5: Inventory Certificate

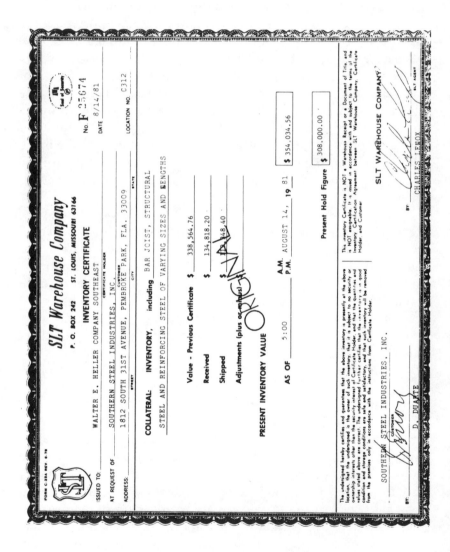

Source: Walter E. Heller and Company Southeast.

FORM C-234 REV 8-78

SLT Warehouse Company
P. O. BOX 242   ST. LOUIS, MISSOURI 63166

INVENTORY CERTIFICATE

No. F 25674

DATE 8/14/81

ISSUED TO: WALTER E. HELLER COMPANY SOUTHEAST

AT REQUEST OF: SOUTHERN STEEL INDUSTRIES, INC.

ADDRESS: 1812 SOUTH 31ST AVENUE, PEMBROKE PARK, FLA. 33009

LOCATION NO. C312

COLLATERAL: INVENTORY, including BAR JOIST, STRUCTURAL STEEL AND REINFORCING STEEL OF VARYING SIZES AND LENGTHS

Value - Previous Certificate	$	338,564.76
Received	$	134,818.20
Shipped	$	119,348.40
Adjustments (plus or minus)		

PRESENT INVENTORY VALUE

AS OF 5:00 A.M. / P.M. AUGUST 14, 19 81 $ 354,034.56

Present Hold Figure $ 308,000.00

The undersigned hereby certifies and guarantees that the above inventory is presently at the above location, that the undersigned is the owner of such inventory, that it is subject to no security or ownership interests other than the security interest of Certificate Holder, and that the quantities and values stated above are correct. The undersigned further certifies that the inventory is in good condition and storage conditions are safe and satisfactory, and that such inventory will be removed from the premises only in accordance with the instructions from Certificate Holder.

This inventory Certificate is NOT a Warehouse Receipt or a Document of Title and is NOT assignable. It is issued in accordance with and subject to the terms of the Inventory Certification Agreement between SLT Warehouse Company, Certificate Holder and Customer.

SLT WAREHOUSE COMPANY

BY _____ CHARLES LENOX   SLT AGENT

SOUTHERN STEEL INDUSTRIES, INC.

BY _____ D. DUARTE   CUSTOMER

million, bankrupted two brokerage companies, and sent reeling American Express Field Warehousing Company, a subsidiary of American Express Company, because field warehouse receipts had been issued against salad oil that existed only in Tino's fertile mind. Loans were based on a reasonable percentage of the market value of the salad oil, as shown in the warehouse receipts, that proved to be stored in tanks in New Jersey that were as hard to locate as the salad oil.

The prudent lender visits the premises, locates the tanks and peers into them, opens the boxes where the goods are stored, and, if the collateral is perishable, sees that it is stored under proper conditions.

Trust Receipts

Providing the importer is a retailer or wholesaler who must have the goods in his possession to sell, trust receipts or floor planning is appropriate where the importer holds the goods in trust for the lender. The lender holds legal title to each item being financed until it is sold, at which time the borrower is obligated to remit the amount owing and represented by the item. Trust receipts are used extensively in financing the inventories of automobile dealers, heavy equipment dealers, and retailers of major appliances. This type of inventory can be identified by serial numbers as well as by physical descriptions, both of which are outlined in the financing agreement. The prudent lender will make spot checks on his importer to be sure items are not sold "out of trust"—that is, without the funds being remitted to the lender. Trust receipts imply "trust" in the importer, and are close to being unsecured financing because the lender does not have physical control of his collateral.

Security Agreement

The adoption of the Uniform Commercial Code by all of the states except Louisiana, which still clings to the Napoleonic Code, gives a lender a security interest by the execution of a security agreement and by complying with the statutes of the state as to proper filing.

The security agreement gives the lender a security interest in the borrower's changing assets, for a specified period of time, whatever

FIGURE 12.6: Inventory Computation

Walter E. Heller & Company
Southeast

Heller Building
4500 Biscayne Boulevard, Miami, Florida 33137, (305) 576-4800

INVENTORY COMPUTATION

NAME AND ADDRESS OF CLIENT   LOCATION OF PROPERTY

American Importer

INVENTORY PER REPORT # __1__ DATED __December 31, 1981__ $ __1,000,000.00__

PURCHASES FROM __January 1, 1982__ TO __January 31, 1982__

AS EVIDENCED BY CONSIGNMENT # __2__ BELOW. $ __200,000.00__

SALES FROM __January 1, 1982__ TO __January 31, 1982__

AS EVIDENCED BY ASSIGNMENT SCHEDULES # __50__ TO __55__

$ __500,000.00__

COST OF SALES AT __70__ % OF SALES.   ($ __350,000.00__)

TOTAL INVENTORY AS OF __January 31, 1982__ $ __850,000.00__

AVAILABILITY COMPUTATION

PROPER ADVANCE AT __30__ % $ __255,000.00__

ACTUAL LOAN BALANCE $ __50,000.00__

NET FUNDS AVAILABLE OR OVER $ __205,000.00__

Date __January 31, 1982__   Consignment No. __2__   Location __same as above__

The undersigned does hereby consign to Walter E. Heller & Co. Southeast (Heller) all of the merchandise inventory purchased by the undersigned for the period commencing Jan. 1, 1982 and terminating Jan. 31, 1982, which said merchandise is more particularly described on invoices retained by the undersigned in trust for Heller or held in trust by a custodian appointed by Heller, which invoices reflect in detail the merchandise purchased; the unit price; the total cost; and the terms of sale; and all of which invoices are referred to in the undersigned's purchase journal and other records of the undersigned, all of which are held in trust for Heller by the undersigned or by a custodian appointed by Heller, all of which are made a part hereof as if set forth in detail herein in order to determine the inventory merchandise and other personal property made a part of this consignment and all of which is consigned to Heller pursuant to the terms and conditions of an Inventory Loan Security Agreement dated Nov. 21, 1971 between the undersigned, as Borrower, and Heller.

The consignment is in addition to and not in lieu of any and all previous consignments heretofore executed and delivered by the undersigned to Heller, and the undersigned hereby warrants and represents that the values set forth herein are true and correct and said consignment accurately and fully itemizes the value of the undersigned's merchandise inventory and other personal property purchased during the period indicated above and added to the existing merchandise inventory and other personal property previously consigned. This consignment is executed pursuant to the provisions of the Uniform Commercial Code of the State of Florida.

The merchandise described on the invoices, purchase journal, and other records of the undersigned or by a custodian appointed by Heller as referred to above is hereby consigned to Heller to be held by Heller subject to the terms and conditions of the Inventory Loan Security Agreement dated Nov. 21, 1971 as security for any and all loans, and all charges or debts due Heller and any and all advances made by Heller to the undersigned (whether or not said loans and advances shall exceed the limits agreed upon) and for its expenses, commissions, discounts, court costs and reasonable counsel fees, and for all liabilities which shall be made or incurred by Heller in connection with the said merchandise or by reason of any act done or omitted by the undersigned. Heller shall have at all times a general lien upon all of the goods now or hereafter consigned to it, or held by the undersigned, or which at any time hereafter the undersigned may, in any manner, purchase, manufacture or acquire, and upon any and all accounts receivable, notes, drafts, bills receivable or evidences of debt arising from the sales of said goods. Said merchandise is hereby consigned to Heller pursuant to the terms of an Inventory Loan Security Agreement by the undersigned and Heller and such lien shall secure Heller for all of its loans and advances to or for the account of the undersigned and for any and all obligations of the undersigned to Heller, regardless of however and whenever created, together with interest thereon.

Said merchandise is to be disposed of according to the Inventory Loan Security Agreement referred to above and in addition to and supplementing such Inventory Loan Security Agreement. Heller shall have exclusive supervision and control of all such consigned goods and shall decide all questions as to the credit to be given to purchasers on sales arising from this merchandise; and the accounts, remittances, checks, bills receivable or other proceeds of the sale of said goods shall be in the exclusive possession and control of Heller; also all ledger cards, stock books, finishing books, sales books and any other books and records maintained by the undersigned to determine its inventory and its record of sales of the merchandise or other personal property covered by the lien of Heller shall be the property of Heller and its officers and representatives shall have free and uninterrupted access to all such books at all reasonable times.

If, upon termination of the Inventory Loan Security Agreement with Heller, there is any balance due Heller for advances which Heller may have made to the undersigned, Heller, at its discretion, will have the right immediately to recover such balance in full from the undersigned without first having recourse to any collateral consigned to it by the undersigned, or may proceed without further notice or advertisement of same, crediting the proceeds less costs and expenses, to the account of the undersigned and pay over to the undersigned any balance or hold the undersigned for any deficiency or for any obligation due Heller from the undersigned regardless of however or whenever created.

Value: $ __200,000.00__   American Importer

Date: __January 31, 1982__   By: (Signature)

ALL MIAMI PRESS — 794-9684

Source: Walter E. Heller and Company Southeast.

310

the value of such assets may be at the time the loan is made and afterward (floating or blanket lien). By proper filing in the county seat or the state capital, the lender gives public notice of the lien, the type of collateral, and the parties involved. The floating lien may provide security for future advances of funds and may cover the inventory itself, and/or the proceeds from the sale of such inventory—that is, the borrower's present and future accounts receivable. In order to monitor the accounts receivable at any particular time, schedules of all credit sales are prepared and presented to the lender. Once a month a complete aging of accounts receivable is given to the lender for the purpose of reconciling collections and new receivables.

Since the underlying collateral is the inventory and the consignment thereof, the importer presents, on a regular basis, a computation of inventory (see Figure 12.6). Such a computation includes the inventory from the previous schedule, purchases identified by particular consignments, sales after giving consideration to gross profit, inventory at date of computation. Using the dollar value and the rate of advance, the lender and borrower can readily see if the loan is in balance.

There are various ways a lender can obtain a security interest in at least a portion of the borrower's assets if another creditor has interest in them by means of a security agreement. If the first lender has a security interest in the inventory and proceeds thereof, he can be asked to subordinate his interest in the accounts receivable so the second lender can base a loan on accounts receivable. If the lender wants to obtain a security interest in goods coming into the possession of the borrower through a letter of credit or new items, the lender can arrange to become a purchase money financier. This can be accomplished by perfecting a security interest in new items before they are delivered to the borrower. The floating-lien holder must be notified by registered mail that these particular purchases are being financed by the lender.

A floating lien does not provide the same protection as a warehouse receipt or trust receipt, and requires diligence by the lender and the expertise expected of a commercial finance company.

SUGGESTED REFERENCES

Bureau of National Affairs. *Export Shipping Manual.* Washington, D.C.: Bureau of National Affairs, annual with periodic supplements.

Cateara, Philip, and John Hess. *International Marketing.* 4th ed. Cincinnati: South-Western Publishing Co., 1979.

Chemical Bank New York Trust Company. *Financing Imports and Exports.* New York: Chemical Bank New York Trust Company, 1981.

Kramer, Roland L. *International Marketing.* 3rd ed. Cincinnati: South-Western Publishing Co., 1970.

Mathis, F. John, ed. *Offshore Lending by U.S. Commercial Banks.* 2nd ed. Washington, D.C., and Philadelphia: Bankers' Association for Foreign Trade and Robert Morris Associates, 1981, ch. 6, pt. I.

Morgan Guaranty Trust Company. *The Financing of Exports and Imports.* New York: Morgan Guaranty Trust Company, 1977.

Oppenheim, Peter J. *International Banking.* 3rd ed. Washington, D.C.: American Institute of Banking, 1978.

Shaterian, William S. *Export-Import Banking.* New York: Ronald Press, 1947.

Wasserman, Max J., Charles W. Hultman, and Laszlo Zsoldos. *International Finance.* New York: Simmons-Boardman, 1963.

Wishner, Maynard I. *Analysis of Alternative Types of Financing.* Homewood, Ill.: Dow Jones-Irwin, 1976.

13 EXPORT FINANCING
James P. Morris

The subject of export financing must of necessity start with an understanding of the underlying trade transaction. The process begins with buyer and seller coming together to negotiate a sale. Like any negotiations, discussions involve give and take from both parties that, if done in good faith, should result in a sales contract. From these discussions, determinations are made as to type, quality, and quantity of product, shipping mode, delivery date, and, of course, price and payment terms. Several points are consciously or unconciously considered in arriving at method of payment. They include customary trade terms, exchange restrictions, import controls, the dollar value of the order, the buyer's and seller's financial conditions, and the seller's margin of profit. In the final analysis, these points are determined by the parties' relative competitive strengths and weaknesses. From conversations with the export community and from personal experience, I have formed the opinion that attractive financing is now more vital to the consummation of an export sale than ever before in recent history. When a financial institution is approached to provide financing for a viable transaction, the institution must ensure that its customer, whether buyer or seller, is presented with the best possible financing package. Domestic and foreign competition from other finance houses and other suppliers demands it.

CUSTOMARY TRADE FINANCING PRACTICE

Good lending practice dictates that the repayment terms granted for international trade financing not exceed those customarily given for similar international transactions. In other words, a bank should not deviate from industry practice. All short-term trade financing (maximum 180 days) should be tied to the normal trade cycle, which covers the shipping period, the inventory period, and the collection period. If longer-than-normal repayment terms are given, the lender is providing working capital facilities and violating the self-liquidating objective of export financing. For example, a buyer of fresh fruits and vegetables should be given a maximum of 30 days. Because of the perishable nature of the product, its quick sale, and the finality of its consumption, a longer financing period would result in a working capital facility used for general funding purposes. This violation of trade practice would surely cause serious collection problems. This rule is not limited to the financing of consumables; it must also be applied to the financing of raw materials, small manufactured items, and spare parts. Trade lines of credit are by their nature evergreen (they will be always in use); consequently, all borrowings under them must be tied to specific, self-liquidating transactions. On the other hand, working capital lines are not evergreen, and by their nature require annual cleanup.

As can be imagined, there are exceptions to every rule. For example, spare parts financing is usually done for a maximum of 180 days; however, when an end user finances a capital equipment purchase over an extended period of time, he may include a normal complement of spare parts as part of the financing package. Industry practice sometimes allows one-year financing of spare parts to a newly appointed distributor for the initial stocking order, or to an established distributor for the initial stocking of parts needed to service a newly introduced equipment or machinery line.

Medium-term financing (181 days to 5 years) is granted to overseas buyers to enable them to purchase capital equipment. In most cases normal trade terms, coupled with the buyer's ability to repay (the capital asset's ability to earn), are the standards used for setting repayment terms. A rule of thumb long followed by the Export-Import Bank of the United States (Eximbank) relates repayment term to sale price.

Sale Price	Repayment Term
$0–50,000	2 year maximum
$50,001–100,000	3 year maximum
$100,001–200,000	4 year maximum
Over $200,001	5 year maximum

These guidelines are of course arbitrary. Some U.S. lenders consider them to be too liberal, especially in cases involving larger and financially stronger buyers. Nevertheless, lenders should not lose sight of the fact that these guidelines were established, in part, to accommodate the realistic needs of the small buyer.

The normal frequency of repayment for commercial installment debt in the United States is level monthly payments of principal and interest. Over the years monthly repayments on international, medium-term trade credits have fallen out of favor because of the administrative cost associated with processing such loans. Repayments are now made quarterly or semiannually, with interest calculated on the declining principal balance. I sometimes feel that the international lending fraternity, when financing small buyers' capital equipment purchases, has performed a disservice to these buyers by not requiring monthly repayment terms, thereby imposing the repayment discipline needed by this segment of the market. Lenders should ask themselves whether the cost savings attributable to quarterly and semiannual loan repayments offset the costs associated with the collection of these loans. If monthly installments were the norm, lenders would learn about problem loans earlier and take the corrective action necessary to salvage them. Although not fully comparable, we can just imagine the collection problems that would occur with quarterly or semiannual car and mortgage payments.

Sometimes annual repayment terms become necessary when financing sales to government bodies subject to annual appropriations and to that part of the agricultural sector dependent on a yearly harvest. Grace periods are sometimes given by lenders, thereby delaying the repayment of the first installment until sometime after the completion of the installation of the equipment. These grace periods provide the time necessary for the capital good to become a productive, earning asset.

One positive development since the 1970s in medium-term trade financing has been the increase in the down payment requirement from a minimum of 10 percent to a minimum of 15 percent of the contract price. This development can be attributed directly to Eximbank, which changed the cash payment requirement of its Bank Guarantee Program (to be covered later in this chapter). Nevertheless, there are occasions when 100 percent financing is granted to a buyer. This practice normally does not result in a serious reduction of credit standards, because the underlying transaction usually bears the guarantee of a local financial institution or is the obligation of a full-faith-and-credit borrower or guarantor.

Long-term financing (over five years) of export trade usually involves the sale of "big-ticket" products, such as locomotives, commercial airplanes, and large draglines used for strip mining, and "big ticket" turnkey projects, such as power and fertilizer plants. Because of tenor (to 15 years or more), product or project cost (to $1 billion), and fierce worldwide, government-supported finance competition, private lenders alone cannot provide the necessary funds at attractive enough rates to compete for this business. The U.S. approach to obtaining this business for U.S. exporters is through a mixed funding facility. Typically, commercial banks fund the earlier maturities, possibly up to the first ten years of a project or product loan, at commercial interest rates. Eximbank then funds the later maturities at a beneficial fixed interest rate. Eximbank's involvement can also include the issuance of its guarantee on part of the private-sector financing package. Eximbank's support, in the form of both loans and guarantees, can reach 85 percent of the U.S. costs. This support is determined by budgetary restraints imposed by Congress, the extent of foreign-government-supported finance competition, and the credit and term limitations of the private sector lenders.

In 1970, Eximbank and the Bankers' Association for Foreign Trade were instrumental in the creation of the Private Export Funding Corporation (PEFCO). PEFCO's principal purpose is to provide fixed-rate funding for the middle maturities of large product and project financings. All of the loans that PEFCO makes must be unconditionally guaranteed by Eximbank. PEFCO in turn funds its loan portfolio by issuing its own debt obligations in the public market or through private placements. PEFCO issues are secured by a pledge of its Eximbank-guaranteed loan portfolio.

The end result of a product or project financed through private financial institutions, PEFCO, and Eximbank will be the lending of floating-rate, private-sector funds, fixed-rate PEFCO funds, and fixed-rate Eximbank funds, with the private sector repaid from the early maturities, PEFCO from the middle maturities, and Eximbank from the later maturities.

POLITICAL, TRANSFER, AND COMMERCIAL RISKS

Once the underlying trade transaction is understood, the provider of export credit must analyze three risks—political, transfer, and commercial—whereas his domestic lending counterpart need analyze only one risk: commercial.

Broad definitions of these three risks are as follows:

- Political risk—Loss resulting from war, civil war, rebellion, license cancellation, or other politically related occurrences.
- Commercial risk—Loss resulting from the inability or unwillingness of the buyer to repay.
- Transfer risk—Loss resulting from the inability of the buyer to exchange local currency for U.S. dollars or another hard currency in a lawful market of the buyer's country.

Since the 1970s serious debt servicing difficulties (transfer risk) have surfaced in Turkey, Zaire, Peru, Chile, Bolivia, Poland, Pakistan, the Dominican Republic, and Costa Rica. Add to this the revolutions (political risk) in Iran and Nicaragua. Sudden maxi currency devaluations in Argentina and Mexico caused serious cash-flow problems (commercial risk) for unhedged, private-sector, and hard-currency borrowers, many of whom went bankrupt or required debt rescheduling. One of the results of Argentina's lowering its tariff barriers was the bankruptcy (commercial risk) of many private-sector companies. As can be seen, these three risks are real. (Political and transfer risks are analyzed in chapters 9 and 10, and commercial risk is analyzed in chapters 11 and 14.)

As stated earlier, an exporter, or a financial institution providing export finance, must weigh these commercial, political, and transfer risks, and do its utmost, in the light of competitive pressure, to minimize them. In analyzing these risks, the lender must not lose sight of the fact that the longer the financing term, the higher the risk. Some lenders feel relatively comfortable in taking a short-term risk (180 days or less) in a market such as Guatemala, yet refuse to take a medium-term risk (181 days to 5 years) in the same market because of the continuing political deterioration in the region.

SHORT-TERM TRADE FINANCING

Payment methods for short-term trade traditionally fall into three broad classifications or categories: open account, trade draft (collections), and letter of credit. The trade draft classification has two subcategories, time draft collection and sight draft collection. The letter of credit classification also has two subcategories, confirmed and unconfirmed, which in turn are subdivided into sight payment and time payment.

Open Account

The seller finances the transaction for the buyer on terms of up to 180 days. Shipping (title) documents are sent directly to the buyer, which results in the seller's relying solely on the buyer's ability (financial strength) and willingness (moral strength) to pay for the goods. The buyer is not required to execute a debt instrument acknowledging his obligation to the seller. The seller faces all three risks: commercial, political, and transfer.

Time Draft Collection

The seller finances the transaction for the buyer on terms of up to 180 days. In contrast with an open account sale, the seller sends the shipping (title) documents through banking channels. To receive the documents, the buyer must accept the draft that the seller has drawn on it. The accepted instrument is called a trade acceptance, and it matures on a certain date. In comparison with open account terms, the seller gains a small advantage because he has in his possession the buyer's written promise to pay. The seller again faces commercial, political, and transfer risks.

Sight Draft Collection

The seller forwards shipping (title) documents, accompanied by a sight draft drawn on the buyer, through banking channels for collection. The sight draft is not a necessary part of the collection process, and in shipping to some markets it is not used, thereby avoiding stamp taxes. With or without a sight draft, the documents are released to the buyer at the time of payment. If the buyer refuses the merchandise, the seller's commercial loss is usually limited to shipping, storage, financing, and reselling costs. If the goods were made to buyer's specifications, the loss could be total—for example, a sale of jackets that have the buyer's name and logo woven into the material. Political and transfer risks are present. Imagine a situation in which the buyer pays in local currency, his government does not have the hard currency to exchange for it, and, during the waiting period, a civil war occurs.

Unconfirmed Letter of Credit

As indicated in chapter 12, a letter of credit is a financial instrument through which a bank substitutes its credit for that of its client. The unconfirmed letter of credit is sent through a correspondent bank (the advising bank) in the seller's country for forwarding to the seller. A letter of credit calling for the presentation of a time draft will instruct the seller to draw the draft on either the buyer, the issuing bank, or the advising bank. If the buyer or issuing bank is the acceptor, the seller is faced with political and transfer risks. The commercial risk is that of the issuing bank. If the draft is accepted by the advising bank, the seller receives the advising bank's promise to pay, which removes transfer and political risks, and shifts commercial risk to the advising bank.

Confirmed Letter of Credit

The buyer's bank (the issuing bank) has a bank in the seller's country (the confirming bank) substitute its credit for that of the issuing bank. The confirming bank then forwards (advises) the credit with its promise to pay to the seller. When the credit calls for a time draft as part of the documentation, the seller will receive the confirming bank's promise to pay at maturity. If the seller needs funds, he of course has the ability to discount the underlying time draft. Because the credit is confirmed by a bank in the seller's country, both transfer and political risks are eliminated, and the commercial risk belongs to the confirming bank. A sample export letter of credit

FIGURE 13.1: Export Letter of Credit

Southeast First National Bank of Miami, P.O. Box 012500 Miami, Florida, 33101. USA
LETTERS OF CREDIT DEPARTMENT CABLE ADDRESS: FIRNATBANK, MIAMI

SAMPLE - Unconfirmed or Confirmed Export Letter of Credit

Documentary Letter of Credit - Irrevocable   Date: **February 8, 1982**

    Issuing Bank's ref. no.: 0123   Our ref. no.: ELC-724

For Account of   **Issuing Bank**

    Foreign Buyer, S.A.   Buyer's Bank
    Apartado 8240   Caracas, Venezuela
    Caracas, Venezuela

Beneficiary   Amount

    U.S. Exporter, Inc.   US $100,000.00
    275 N.W. Pebble Street   (One hundred thousand and
    Miami, FL 33987   no/100 U.S. Dollars)

                                       Expiry Date

                                      March 31, 1982

Gentlemen:

We have received a __X__ letter ____ cable from the Issuing Bank dated
February 2, 1982 requesting us to inform you that they have opened their
Irrevocable Credit in your favor, particulars are as follows:
    Available by your draft(s) at 180 days sight on us, accompanied
    by the following documents:

    1. Signed Commercial invoice in duplicate.
    2. Packing list in duplicate.
    3. Insurance Policy or Certificate in duplicate covering
       Marine and War Risks.
    4. Full set of clean on board ocean bills of lading
       issued to order of shipper, blank endorsed, marked
       "Freight Prepaid" and notify Foreign Buyer, S.A.,
       Caracas, Venezuela

    Covering shipment from Miami of 200 T.V. sets C.I.F.
    La Guaira

    Partial shipments permitted. Transshipments prohibited.

☐   This Letter of Credit is advised to you without engagement on
    our part.

☐   This Letter of Credit is confirmed by us and we hereby undertake
    that all drafts drawn and presented as specified above will be
    duly honored by us.

The Issuing Bank engages with you that all drafts drawn and presented in
accordance with the terms of this Letter of Credit will be duly honored on
presentation against delivery of documents at our office together with
this Letter of Credit on or before the Expiry Date.

Drafts must be marked "Drawn under Southeast First National Bank of Miami
Letter of Credit No. ELC-724."

                                        Sincerely yours,

           Authorized Signer   *Authorized Signer*
           For Cashier   For Cashier

(Left margin, vertical text: "UNLESS OTHERWISE EXPRESSLY STATED, THIS CREDIT IS SUBJECT TO THE UNIFORM CUSTOMS AND PRACTICE FOR DOCUMENTARY CREDITS (1974 REVISION), INTERNATIONAL CHAMBER OF COMMERCE PUBLICATION NO. 290.")

Source: Southeast Bank, N.A.

FIGURE 13.2: Banker's Acceptance Created
Under A Letter of Credit

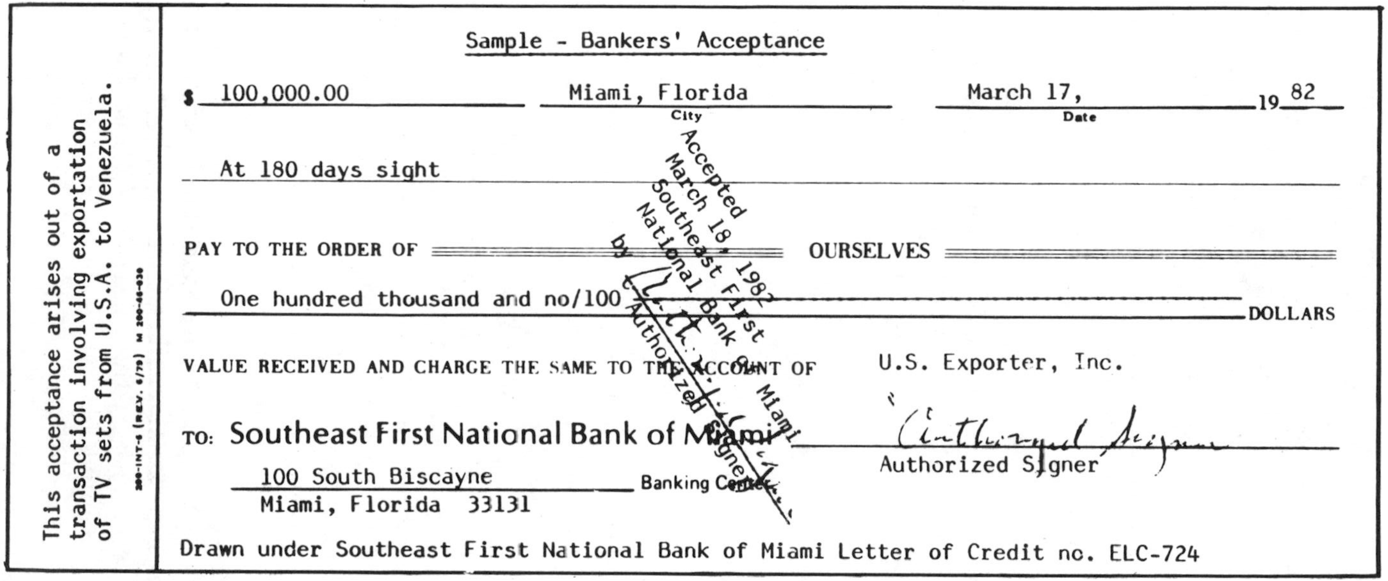

Sample - Bankers' Acceptance

$ 100,000.00   Miami, Florida   March 17,   19 82
                                  City   Date

At 180 days sight

PAY TO THE ORDER OF ═══════ OURSELVES ═══════

One hundred thousand and no/100 ═══════════════════════ DOLLARS

VALUE RECEIVED AND CHARGE THE SAME TO THE ACCOUNT OF   U.S. Exporter, Inc.

TO: Southeast First National Bank of Miami

100 South Biscayne   Banking Center
Miami, Florida 33131

Accepted
March 18, 1982
Southeast First
National Bank, Miami

by _____
      Authorized Signer

_____
Authorized Signer

Drawn under Southeast First National Bank of Miami Letter of Credit no. ELC-724

This acceptance arises out of a
transaction involving exportation
of TV sets from U.S.A. to Venezuela.

200-INT-6 (REV. 6/79) M 200-46-030

Source: Southeast Bank, N.A.

(for either unconfirmed or confirmed use) calling for the drawing of a time draft on the advising bank appears in Figure 13.1.

In the United States, when an advising or confirming bank accepts a time draft drawn on it, it creates an instrument called a banker's acceptance (see Figure 13.2). There are other ways to create this very important instrument, and they will be explored later in this chapter. To recap, a time draft accepted by a buyer is a trade acceptance, and a time draft accepted by a bank is a banker's acceptance.

Financing Options

In analyzing the exporter's creditworthiness, a prudent financial institution must also look closely at the transfer, political, and foreign commercial risks that face its borrower. Since spread of risk is very important, a large per-country or per-buyer exposure should be studied carefully.

An exporter who sells his product or service on repayment terms of 180 days or less has several options available for the financing of his export trade.

Option I

An exporter can approach a financial institution for a line of credit to finance each individual export through the sale of the underlying receivable on a full recourse basis. The financed amount of each receivable would normally be in the 50–80 percent range. The repayment term of each sale corresponds to the repayment term of the underlying receivable. This procedure is expensive because of the administrative costs associated with the booking, collecting, and policing of each sale, especially when the dollar value per transaction is small and the volume of transactions is large. Interest is normally paid by the exporter. Because of the high administrative costs, rates charged will be similar to those charged by commercial finance companies.

Open account, draft (sight and time), and letter of credit (sight and time) shipments can all be financed under this option. A banker's acceptance originating from a letter of credit should be discounted with the accepting institution. Because of the favorable rate differential, the proceeds are used to retire the corresponding receivable sale.

An exception occurs when an exporter who has a few relatively strong buyers endorses these buyer obligations over to a financial institution with minimal or no recourse.

Option II

An exporter can approach a financial institution for a line of credit to finance export sales by batching a number of export receivables, and either selling these receivables on a full recourse basis or using them as evidence to support a loan made directly to the exporter. The selling or borrowing can be done on a periodic basis (such as weekly or monthly), or on an as-needed basis, based on a minimum dollar volume (such as $100,000 or $500,000). Repayment terms on batched sales or borrowings normally correspond to either the repayment term of the underlying package of receivables or to the average yearly turnover of the export portfolio.

Because a batched sale or borrowing is for a large amount, the financial institution quotes a better rate. In some cases competitive pressure requires a bank to quote a rate based on the banker's acceptance rate. To create the banker's acceptance, the exporter simply draws a draft on the financing bank. To ensure the best rate possible, a financially strong exporter may accept banker's acceptance lines from several banks and get competitive quotes each time a borrowing is planned. The batching option is usually granted on an unsecured basis to strong exporters, who may borrow up to 100 percent of the value of the underlying batching. Again, the analysis done on the exporter should include a study of the spread of transfer, political, and foreign commercial risks.

Option III

A financial institution, through its own calling efforts, or through introductions provided by its exporter prospects and customers, can establish lines of credit directly to foreign buyers to finance their imports. These buyer credit lines can be restrictive and finance only purchases from a named supplier, or they can be quite liberal and finance all imports. Most lines probably fall between these two extremes and allow financings of purchases from suppliers located in the financial institution's major marketing region. Repayment terms are dictated by the product being financed, and usually do not exceed 180 days. Interest rate quotations depend on credit (transfer, political, and commercial risks) and competitive considerations. It is not uncommon for banker's acceptance rates to be quoted to the strongest buyers.

Almost all short-term export financing is done under the three options discussed above. To my knowledge, there are only three exceptions to this rule. First, the exporter provides financing direct to his customers, without the assistance of a financial institution. Second, financial institutions in the buyer's country, the seller's country, or a third country provide the financing on a "bank to bank" or "institution to institution" basis. Third, governments provide the financing through their loan programs.

To minimize foreign commercial risk and to eliminate political and transfer risks, many U.S. exporters and financial institutions, sophisticated and unsophisticated alike, have placed an insurance umbrella over their short-term export trading operations by obtaining credit insurance from the Foreign Credit Insurance Association (FCIA).

FCIA is an association of 50 of the largest insurance companies in the United States. Besides the profit motive, its main purpose is to insure exporters of U.S. goods and services, and the financial institutions serving this trade, against losses caused by political, transfer, and foreign commercial risks. FCIA works closely with the Export-Import Bank of the United States (Eximbank), a U.S. government agency that bears the "full faith and credit" of the United States. Eximbank assumes all FCIA-insured losses resulting from defined transfer and political risks. FCIA assumes the losses caused by commercial risks, with Eximbank reinsuring all excess commercial losses suffered by FCIA.

Before obtaining FCIA coverage on a short-term export portfolio, an exporter should, in keeping with good insurance practice, review his portfolio in terms of spread of risk by country and by buyer. The exporter must remember that the purpose of all insurance coverage is to avoid a catastrophic loss—a loss that will cause the exporter extreme hardship. For example, a financially strong exporter selling on 180-day terms or less to the West European, Japanese, and Canadian markets faces little, if any, political and transfer risk. In our example he also has sold to the same buyers for over ten years without a significant loss. Each buyer's purchases are a negligible part of our exporter's total sales. This exporter probably does not need credit insurance at this time. If he decides to expand his export efforts to the Middle East and South America, or one or two of his buyers decide to substantially increase their purchases, his risk changes dramatically, and he should give serious consideration to FCIA credit insurance. From this scenario we should be able to appreciate FCIA's major requirement for issuing a short-term policy: the receipt of whole turnover or a satisfactory spread of risk. In the vernacular, FCIA wants an exporter's good risks, if the exporter expects FCIA to insure its less favorable ones.

Typically an exporter who sells on terms of 180 days or less obtains a short-term deductible policy from FCIA. This policy gives the exporter a discretionary credit limit (DCL) that is large enough for him to make 70 percent of his own credit decisions. In exchange for granting the DCL, FCIA requires the exporter to assume a first-loss, commercial-risk deductible per policy year. FCIA thus delegates substantial credit authority to the exporter in return for the deductible. FCIA benefits because of the savings in administrative cost (fewer small credits to review and approve). The exporter benefits from lower premiums because of FCIA's reduced administrative burden, and from the time he saves by making the majority of his own credit decisions. The policy does not cover interest loss, but it does provide 100 percent coverage against principal losses caused by transfer and political risks. Coverage on commercial losses is 90 percent after the exhaustion of the deductible. For example, if the first-loss commercial-risk deductible is $50,000 and the insured suffers $100,000 in commercial losses during the policy year, the insured receives $40,000 from FCIA (the 10 percent exporter's retention is applied first).

Under Option I an exporter with a FCIA short-term deductible policy can enter into an agreement with a lender under which the exporter assigns the proceeds of the policy to the lender. The exporter then endorses (sells) each insured receivable to the lender on a without-recourse basis except for the uninsured part of each sold receivable. Negotiations between exporter and lender determine if the uninsured amount will be sold without, with partial, or with full recourse, or will be held by the exporter. Under this arrangement the lender assumes the primary collection responsibility. Because of the FCIA insurance at least 90 percent of the CIF value of a shipment can be financed by the lender without violating good lending practices.

Again under Option I the exporter can enter into a slightly different agreement with the lender (probably on a secured basis), whereby the exporter borrows against each individual receivable. The proceeds of the policy again are assigned to the lender; however, the exporter does the collecting. When the payment is received, it is turned over to the lender. Again a lender can feel comfortable in financing at least 90 percent of the CIF value.

In analyzing creditworthiness the prudent lender's main concern is the exporter's ability to reimburse the lender for the first-loss, commercial-risk deductible and the uninsured 10 percent, if the lender purchases the 10 percent on a with-recourse basis.

In addition to the obvious advantage of protection against credit loss, other advantages accruing to the FCIA-insured exporter are a reduction in borrowing cost and the ability to finance at least 90 percent of the invoice value of each piece of equipment. The disadvantages, as enumerated under Option I, remain the same.

Under Option II (batching receivables) an exporter with FCIA coverage can assign the proceeds of the policy to a lender and, on either a periodic or a minimum-dollar-volume basis, batch and sell the insured receivables. Even though the agreement considers the sale or endorsement of the insured receivables to be without recourse or with minimum recourse (the 10 percent uninsured commercial risk and the first-loss commercial-risk deductible), the exporter must make certain that each batching is paid on its maturity date. This is mandatory if he is to keep his lender's costs and his resulting borrowing costs as low as possible. The insurance coverage reduces the credit risk, and consequently should reduce the borrowing cost. It is not uncommon to see quotations based on the banker's acceptance rate.

Under Option III a bank or other financial institution can obtain its own FCIA short-term comprehensive policy to insure the direct lines of credit it has established for foreign buyers of U.S. products (buyer credit). A bank or financial institution can also use its policy on a supplier (exporter) credit basis. To make certain that FCIA receives a fair spread of risk on supplier credits, the insured financial institution is required by policy endorsement to enter into an agreement in which the supplier agrees to offer all insurable indebtedness to the insured. The financial institution must maintain its insurable interest either by providing without-recourse financing on the insured amounts or by guaranteeing payment of the insured amounts.

Coverage is voided if the financial institution has recourse to the supplier for any part of the insured amount.

Under a supplier credit arrangement the financial institution establishes a line of credit for each buyer. The underlying agreement calls for either the supplier or the financial institution to do all collecting. If the latter approach is followed, the financial institution takes the responsibility of notifying the buyer to make payments directly to it. The agreement also states if interest and other charges (finance fees, FCIA premiums) are for the buyer's or the seller's account. If they are for the buyer's account, the buyer must be made aware of, and must accept, this fact. To avoid misunderstandings, the interest rate should always be reflected on the buyer's debt instrument.

At the time of this writing (January 1982) a short-term FCIA policy issued to a bank does not include a first-loss, commercial-risk deductible, even though most banks have been given a discretionary credit limit of up to $200,000. In my view the lack of a first-loss deductible provision is questionable underwriting procedure. I feel that the policy issued to banks may soon be changed to correct this deficiency. The current bank policy provides 100 percent transfer and political risk principal coverage, 90 percent commercial risk coverage, and no coverage for interest loss. As it does with its exporter insureds, FCIA requests bank insureds to offer it a reasonable spread of risk.

MEDIUM-TERM TRADE FINANCING

The vast majority of exporters who sell on terms of 180 days or less carry the resulting receivables on their own books, whereas the vast majority who sell on terms of 181 days or more sell the resulting medium- or long-term paper to financial institutions. Mainly as a result of the longer financing terms and larger per-unit values of capital goods, exporters of this type of product try to arrange a financing package that provides them with minimum or no recourse. And yet, because of strong domestic and foreign competition, these same exporters, even as they try to eliminate their own exposure on medium-term financings, must also provide a potential customer with an attractive, low-cost financing option.

Financial institutions that are contemplating entering or are already active in financing medium- or long-term capital good exports have their own dilemma: Do the rewards of assisting a customer or prospect, or do the realities of losing a good customer, outweigh the risks associated with granting term export credit to foreign buyers?

In the United States the dilemmas encountered by the export and financial communities can be lessened by the role played by the U.S. government through the Eximbank and the FCIA. These two institutions offer several programs that can greatly reduce the credit and interest rate risks associated with export term lending.

In the final analysis, however, the granting of medium-term export finance, like the granting of short-term export finance, depends on the willingness of, and the degree to which, the ultimate lender will accept the commercial, political, and transfer risks inherent in international lending. If the lender is not willing to accept these risks completely, he must turn to the guarantee and insurance programs of Eximbank and FCIA. Of course, Eximbank and FCIA charge for their protection and, in most cases, these costs are not completely recovered through a reduction in some other charge levied by the lender (for example, a lower interest rate).

To better understand medium-term export finance, let us return to the negotiation between buyer and seller. During negotiations with an end user on the purchase of capital goods, the exporter should determine the role, if any, that financing will play in finalizing the sale. On one extreme the buyer may have his own source of finance, and the subject never surfaces during the negotiation. On the other extreme, financing could be a very important factor because of fierce competition in which other purchase considerations, such as price, quality, and delivery, are nearly equal.

Take, for example, an invitation to bid that is issued by a Colombian municipality for the purchase of ten trucks. The tender calls for the best financing terms, and mentions that the financing will be guaranteed by a prime Colombian private-sector bank. To simplify our example, only two U.S. companies submit bids for approximately $1 million each. For some reason the first company's lender does not feel completely comfortable with some aspect of the commercial, political, or transfer risk. This lender's quotation requires the guarantee of Eximbank, which for a five-year financing costs $2.80 per $100 of the note value. The second company's lender feels comfortable with these same risks, and quotes a financing without this added cost. If other considerations are basically equal, the second company should be the low bidder and receive the award. In this example, as with most opportunities that are presented, a potential lender must also make judgments on several other points. Should the lender require a minimum cash payment of 15 percent, or should this requirement be waived? Should the lender quote a fixed or an adjustable rate? Should the lender require quarterly, semiannual, or annual repayments? Are the repayment terms sufficient? too long? too short? Should the lender require the exporter to share in a portion of the risk?

Because of these variables, most stronger exporters usually obtain quotations from two or more sources. A strong exporter can be defined as one whose business is solicited by several lenders. Many small and/or financially weak exporters are limited, at best, to a single quotation because of the financial community's reluctance to work with marginal names. In the negotiation stage the marginal exporter is placed at a serious disadvantage because the potential buyer may be forced to arrange his own credit.

Typically, capital goods are sold in one of two ways: directly from the manufacturer to the end user, or from the manufacturer to a stocking distributor who, in turn, resells to the end user. Examples of products sold directly to end users are machine tools, communications systems, and corporate aircraft. Examples of products sold through stocking distributors are cars, trucks, agricultural equipment, and construction equipment. Depending on the size of the foreign market, the distribution chain for many of these stock products can include a network of dealers buying from the distributor.

As mentioned previously, direct negotiations between an exporter and an end user will determine whether financing will be an integral part of the sale. If it is, the exporter must gather the financial information necessary to make a credit decision. Good credit practice dictates that the exporter make the first credit decision by thoroughly analyzing political, transfer, and commercial risks. If, after this analysis, the exporter finds the package to be unattractive, he should renegotiate with the buyer and structure a package that he feels will prove acceptable to a lender. This salable package should then be presented to one or more lending institutions. These lenders are usually the seller's banks, banks that are "prospecting" him, or banks referred to him by the buyer.

Exporters who mainly sell their capital goods through distributors historically have introduced these distributors to lenders who have established revolving lines of credit to finance their imports. Over time the distributor-lender relationship becomes a valued one, whereas the end user-lender relationship usually remains impersonal and lasts only until the repayment of the "one shot" term loan. In many cases the end user and the lender never meet each other.

In the past, U.S. capital equipment exporters, and the lenders who serve them, have looked at medium-term trade financing (single sale or revolving line) on a case-by-case basis. With the advent of FCIA's master policy, many of these exporters have elected to insure their exports (both short- and medium-term) on a spread-of-risk basis under the master policy umbrella. As with its short-term deductible counterpart (discussed earlier), the master policy provides 100 percent principal coverage against political and transfer risk loss and, after a first loss per policy year deductible, 90 percent principal coverage against commercial risk loss. Interest loss on medium-term transactions is covered to 6 percent per annum. In exchange for accepting the deductible, the exporter receives a discretionary credit limit, which is large enough for him to make the majority of his own credit decisions.

Once an exporter who mainly sells directly to end users has obtained or renewed his FCIA master policy, it is customary for him to approach several potential lenders for quotations to finance all of his insured business for the ensuing policy year. From these quotes the exporter may choose one or more lenders as participants. Besides the lowest interest rate quotation, the exporter will also look for a financial institution willing to accept all or a part of the 10 percent foreign commercial risk exposure. To my knowledge the first-loss, commercial-risk deductible has always been for the account of the exporter.

An exporter covered by a master policy who mainly sells through stocking distributors tries to follow the relationship concept (discussed earlier) by having his distributors work with the same lenders on a continuing basis. To facilitate and develop these relationships, it is ideal to use lenders located near the exporter's credit office, or near the distributor's normal point of entry into the United States. For example, an Illinois manufacturer tends to rely on Chicago- and Miami-area banks for the credit needs of its South American distributors.

Even if an exporter has credit insurance, a lender to one or more of the exporter's distributors will not, in most cases, be completely covered against political, transfer, and commercial risk. Historically, Eximbank and FCIA have followed the policy of limiting their combined commercial exposure to any one buyer, whether the buyer is an end user or a distributor, to the buyer's net worth. To maximize profits for themselves and their suppliers, distributors must have credit far in excess of their net worth. It is not uncommon to see debt-to-equity ratios of more than 3:1. Additionally, multinational manufacturers selling from non-U.S. plants are not protected by FCIA or Eximbank coverage. Nowadays a financial institution that actively participates in the export financing of capital equipment sales to distributors must be prepared to grant five-year amortizing term facilities to leveraged obligors. In return they will receive 50 percent loss protection at best. Remarkably, the U.S. financial community is so competitive that a sought-after exporter does not have a problem arranging credit for this "risky" type of lending, as long as the buyer and his country are the least bit stable.

During this discussion of medium-term export credit, mention was made of the fact that both Eximbank and FCIA have loss protection programs. Their standard medium-term programs will now be analyzed to point out similarities and differences.

	Eximbank	FCIA
Coverage provided by	guarantee	insurance
Applicant	commercial bank	exporter or financial institution
Cash payment	15%[a]	15%[a]
Term	181 days–5 years[b, c]	181 days–5 years[b, c]
Repayment	monthly, quarterly, or semiannually[d]	monthly, quarterly, or semiannually[d]
Risk coverage (principal)		
Political	100%	100%
Transfer	100%	100%
Commercial	76.5 or 85.5%[e, f, g]	90%[f, g]
Risk coverage (interest)	6% p.a.	6% p.a.
Fee	same as FCIA[h]	same as Eximbank

[a] May be financed by using a separate promissory note.

[b] See informal table under "Customary Trade Financing Practice" for further breakdown.

ᶜFive-year terms can be exceeded on a case-by-case basis. For example, a seven-year term is sometimes granted for executive jets and turboprop aircraft.

ᵈAnnual repayments are sometimes granted on sales to government bodies subject to annual appropriations and to agricultural buyers dependent on a yearly harvest.

ᵉIf a bank exercises its delegated (discretionary) authority of up to $750,000, it must accept the lower coverage. A bank may also elect the lower coverage and in return retain a higher percentage of the guarantee fee for its account (see footnote h).

ᶠ100 percent coverage is available on financing of three years or more, if the first half of the installments have been paid in a prompt manner.

ᵍGenerally Eximbank and FCIA require the exporter to retain 10 percent of the note value for his own risk.

ʰA bank retains either 15 percent or 25 percent of the guarantee fee (see footnote e).

Until now our discussions have mostly centered on trading with private buyers. Whenever a sale is made to this sector on other than confirmed letter of credit terms, the exporter or lending institution faces commercial, political, and transfer risk. The commercial risk aspect of international lending disappears when a sale is made to a sovereign public buyer or is guaranteed by a sovereign public entity. A sovereign public buyer or guarantor can be defined as a country's ministry of finance, central bank, or a similar entity carrying the full faith and credit of its government. There is a third type of buyer—the nonsovereign public buyer. Into this classification fall government-owned development banks, government-owned corporations (such as utilities or steel companies), and state and local governments, their agencies, and their departments. Typically, lenders to nonsovereign public buyers require a full-faith-and-credit guarantee, or a guarantee from a commercial bank. If the nonsovereign public buyer generates its own revenues, and is not dependent on public funds, a lender may very well waive the normal guarantee requirement. Eximbank and FCIA recognize these differences in risk in their guarantee fee and premium schedules. The cost of their coverage is lowest for sovereign public buyer risk and highest for private buyer risk. Coverage on sales to nonsovereign public buyers and to private buyers guaranteed by commercial banks falls in the middle.

We learned from our discussion of Eximbank's direct funding of large product and project sales that the percentage of funds that it will lend is directly related to the amount of foreign-government-supported finance competition encountered by the U.S. supplier. In the medium-term arena, fixed-rate, low-cost financing can also be crucial to obtaining a sale. Many foreign buyers prefer to buy from suppliers who provide fixed-rate financing, simply because they can compute their borrowing cost. Because of volatile rate fluctuations and the inability to obtain a steady supply of fixed-rate, medium-term money from the marketplace, most financial institutions will not finance this fixed-rate export trade unless they are provided a source of fixed-rate money. In order to satisfy this need, Eximbank makes available a pool of fixed-rate money to the U.S. commercial banking community, from which the latter can borrow to support its financing of fixed-rate, medium-term trade. Eximbank has named this program its *Medium-Term Discount Loan Program.*

Mainly because of budgetary restraints placed on it, Eximbank is forced to control the use of this pool of funds by varying the maximum amount of funds available to a particular foreign buyer (currently $10 million per year), by varying the maximum value of an individual sale (currently $5 million CIF), and by varying the maximum amount of discount loan funds available to support a particular sale (currently 65 percent of the contract price for large manufacturers and 85 percent for small manufacturers). By Eximbank's definition a small manufacturer is one with gross annual sales of $25 million or less.

The interest rate that Eximbank charges a commercial bank for a discount loan is 1 percent below the fixed rate on the note that the commercial bank receives from the foreign buyer. Eximbank of course has "floor" rates on the discount loans it makes in support of the exports of both small and large manufacturers. As of January 1982 both of these rates have a floor of 12 percent per annum.

To obtain a discount loan, it is not necessary to have the foreign buyer's loan guaranteed by Eximbank or insured by FCIA. Generally speaking, the criteria to qualify for a discount loan are the same criteria required by Eximbank to qualify for its medium-term guarantee. For example, all discount loan commitments require the buyer to make a 15 percent cash payment at the time of shipment. This payment may be financed by a separate note. Discount loan repayments are usually made on a quarterly or semiannual basis, and correspond to the repayment terms of the underlying buyer obligation. A discount loan can be prepaid, even though the underlying buyer obligation remains outstanding; however, the commercial bank cannot borrow again under the same commitment. The term of the discount loan is dictated by the contract value of the sale and customary international trade terms—and, again, corresponds to the term of the underlying buyer obligation.

REVIEW OF MEDIUM-TERM TRADE FINANCING

To give the reader a better understanding of medium-term export lending, it is appropriate at this time to review the credit needs of a typical heavy equipment distributor located in a developing country. As we will see, his needs are varied. For lenders to service his needs in particular, or the needs of the export community and their customers in general, it is necessary that lenders understand the underlying trade transaction, the recurring theme of this chapter.

A distributor of heavy equipment needs revolving short-term lines of credit for the 180-day financing of his spare parts purchases. These lines should allow the distributor to carry a sufficient parts inventory to service the machine population in his market area. At times these lines can be used to finance the emergency shipment of parts needed to repair inoperative machines. A lender does not require a down payment, and finances up to 100 percent of the invoiced value of the shipment. U.S.-manufactured spare parts can be insured by FCIA.

A heavy equipment distributor needs revolving short-term lines of credit for the 270-day (maximum) floor plan financing of his capital equipment inventory. These lines ensure the distributor of having a wide range of fast-selling equipment in his inventory. Take, for example, a small contractor who has just won a bid. To start work on the project, he must have several new pieces of equipment. If his preferred brand is not in stock, he most probably will buy from a competitor that can fill his immediate needs. With today's high interest rates, a distributor must carefully plan his stocking strategy, and weigh the advantages of having a large inventory against the realities of borrowing expensive money. Floor plan (inventory) financing is done without a down payment. The lender advances 100 percent of the invoice value of the equipment. If desired, FCIA insurance coverage is available on U.S.-produced goods. As an alternative to FCIA coverage, the lender (commercial banks only) may use Eximbank's Bank Guarantee Program to obtain protection.

Most developing countries do not have sufficient sources of

medium-term funds. For a heavy equipment distributor to be successful in this type of market, it is mandatory for him to provide his buyer with the necessary financing. Normally this is accomplished by the distributor's receiving a down payment from the buyer and taking his note (five years maximum) for the balance. The lender, in turn, receives a cash payment (15 percent minimum) from the distributor and his note (five years maximum) for the balance of the original invoice price. The distributor's cash payment and his new note are used to pay the floor plan note. The distributor takes a lien on the equipment. The export lender remains unsecured, and usually receives a written promise from the distributor not to double-finance the sale. On rare occasions the export lender may take the end user's note as collateral. If the distributor has not sold a piece of equipment by the end of the floor plan (inventory) period, his options are limited and, in most instances, number only two: pay for the equipment, or make a 15 percent down payment and finance the balance through a term borrowing from the export lender. When the products are of U.S. origin, Eximbank or FCIA coverage can be obtained against political, transfer, and commercial risks.

Depending on the market, a large portion of a heavy equipment distributor's business can be the rental and leasing of equipment. The distributor therefore needs revolving lines of credit for the medium-term financing of products purchased specifically for use in his rental fleet. Export lenders require a minimum down payment of 15 percent, with the balance financed for up to five years. Loans can be insured by FCIA or guaranteed by Eximbank, if the products are U.S.-made.

It is possible for the typical heavy equipment distributor to have up to eight separate credit lines from a lender bank: two spare parts lines, two floor plan lines, two retail lines, and two rental fleet lines. One group of lines finances U.S. products and is covered by FCIA and/or Eximbank. Borrowings under the second group finance non-U.S. products, or U.S. products that are over FCIA and Eximbank's maximum commercial exposure comfort level.

EXPORT FINANCING TRENDS

It is my feeling that U.S. exporters, and the lenders who service their needs, can expect continued pressure from buyers for longer and longer terms. In addition, strong interest rate competition can be expected to continue. From the exporter's viewpoint this competition can be a mixed blessing—good because his lenders will bid down rates when competing for the same export business, and bad because foreign suppliers will be competing against him with rates subsidized by their governments at a time when Eximbank will be forced, for budgetary reasons, to cut back on its direct lending and discount loan programs. Because of mixed sourcing (supplying a buyer from both U.S. and foreign plants) and Eximbank's and FCIA's maximum per-buyer commercial credit limits, private credit insurance carriers will play an ever increasing role in insuring exports. Eximbank and FCIA will become more attuned to the needs of small manufacturers, and encourage them to become involved and stay involved in exporting. Eximbank and FCIA have already established meaningful programs for the small exporter. These programs offer credit protection on their short- and medium-term sales and a source of low-interest, fixed-rate funds to finance their medium-term sales. For the next few years Eximbank's and FCIA's challenge will be to market their programs to small businesses and, more important, to encourage the financial community to provide financing to these small businesses and their foreign buyers once Eximbank and FCIA credit protection is in place.

SUGGESTED REFERENCES

Export-Import Bank of the United States. *Commercial Bank Guarantee Program—Instructions to Banks*. Revised 11/1/79. Washington, D.C.: Export-Import Bank.

———. *Medium Term Discount Loan Program—Instructions to Banks*. Revised 10/1/80. Washington, D.C.: Export-Import Bank.

14 LOANS TO FOREIGN CORPORATIONS

Richard L. Heilman

Foreign lending is a very complex operation, and varies considerably from country to country. It is not the simple embracing of the "five Cs" of commercial lending but, rather, the analysis of a broad array of matrixed factors. To assess that matrix, this chapter will first provide a history and background of U.S. loans to foreign corporations. Then it will consider the rationale behind making such loans and the associated risks, the regulatory factors to be considered, issues in evaluating financial statements, direct lending considerations, some of the various types of credit facilities, and the profitability of foreign corporate financing.

In viewing loan opportunities abroad from the perspective of a U.S. bank, it is important to understand the impact of long-standing domestic U.S. banking policies and practices on decisions to lend to companies abroad, and how the sometimes significant difference can be reconciled to permit profitable international corporate lending. This is not an insular attitude or a declaration that U.S. lending practices are inviolate or etched in stone, but it is a fact that U.S. banks are major factors in most foreign corporate marketplaces, and their policies and practices tend to have an impact on corporate lending patterns.

HISTORY AND BACKGROUND

Essential Elements of U.S. Lending Policies

Primarily as a function of considerable federal banking regulation on their consolidated worldwide position, U.S. banks enter the marketplace with certain competitive disadvantages that are almost universally unique. These are summarized as follows:

- 10 percent of the bank's capital, surplus, and retained earnings is the maximum that may be lent to any one borrower
- Prohibition against equity ownership of industrial clients
- Prohibition against underwriting and distributing corporate stocks and bonds
- Restricted leverage ratios
- Strict capital adequacy requirements
- Prohibition against hidden or undeclared reserves
- Voluminous and open financial reporting
- In-depth examination by federal bank examiners
- Restricted branching possibilities.

In addition, U.S. banks broadly enjoy a vibrant and profitable home market, and therefore do not have the compulsion to expand abroad. Sustained growth of both assets and profits has been historically possible with little or no international involvement.

Finally, U.S. banks domestically are cash-flow lenders, and go to great analytical lengths to assess the wealth of financial data generally available to them. Significant importance and virtually total reliance is placed on audited financial statements with detailed supporting schedules and cash flow and other projections. Extensive use is made of a variety of credit agency reports, industry analyses, and filings with the Securities and Exchange Commission.

The Move Abroad

A small number of U.S. banks started developing their international business and branches after the turn of the twentieth century, but the real growth did not begin until the middle 1960s. The oft-stated rationale was "to follow our customers abroad to serve their ever-increasing international needs." There certainly was a degree of validity to this argument, but for more than just a few years the profits from these offices did not come from U.S.-owned companies. Actually the motivating factor contained a large element of "metooism"—maintaining a competitive balance with domestic U.S. competitors.

The first years of the move abroad involved progress up the learning curve that was generally supported by earnings from foreign exchange dealing, money market arbitrage, and syndicated loan activity. Ascending the learning curve meant a high degree of sovereign risk and bank-guaranteed lending. Private-sector corporate lending typically was not in the forefront.

Having done the necessary homework on the foreign legal, tax, accounting, banking, and fiscal systems, and having assessed the intermediate and longer-term political and economic pictures, thereby gaining a measure of head office comfort, banks started turning with increasing pace to the foreign corporate marketplace. The measure of head office comfort frequently bore a direct correlation to the depth and breadth of analyses sent from the field officers.

The complexion and makeup of the foreign corporate marketplace do not readily lend themselves to generalizations, since each country is obviously distinctive, but a few overviews are possible. There is, broadly, a greater degree of government ownership and involvement in corporations overseas than in the United States, which has resulted from forced nationalizations to prevent bankruptcies and loss of jobs, or from pursuit of socialist policies, as is currently being witnessed in France. There is also a fairly widespread involvement of government in keeping ailing companies afloat, purely to avoid the unpalatable social and political consequences of increased unemployment. Nationalization does, however, tend to be somewhat like haute couture, and can come and go, depending on the orientation of the government in power. The Thatcher government in Great Britain has pursued a reversal of the public ownership trend embarked upon by the previous Labour government. The present Trudeau government is emphasizing Canadianization in its economic policies.

Next in importance are the large, locally headquartered conglomerates, which frequently are family-controlled, and with which banks are firmly connected through equity holdings and board memberships. Since the early 1970s these companies have become increasingly multinational in order to expand beyond limited home markets, as well as to diversify their assets and to come under more lenient regulatory environments abroad. Equally important are large, publicly traded companies with broad domestic sales networks or large market share.

The United States and other countries' multinational corporations typically are next on the ladder, with large capital investment plants producing for that country's home market or for export to surrounding regional markets—or occasionally to economic blocs not readily receptive to or able to purchase U.S.-produced goods.

The vast middle market, which classically is the backbone of many countries' economies (of which no more pronounced case exists than in Italy), has increasingly become the focus of the major international banks.

The Business Development Effort

The obvious prerequisite to meaningful penetration of the foreign corporate market is a direct lending capability through a branch, subsidiary, or affiliate. It is possible, through periodic business development trips, to lend Eurocurrencies without an operating vehicle in a country, but this "paratrooper" approach of dropping in several times a year does not readily lend itself to development of ongoing, broader banking relationships. This approach is put at a disadvantage by geographic distances, cost, and the wear and tear on the traveling banker. It does not afford the opportunity to easily build the confidence and rapport necessary to obtain a more lasting and in-depth banking relationship—particularly in competition with bankers who are on the spot day in and day out and have the capability to deliver locally. It is undeniably important to have the relationship banker become part of the environment in which he is expected to operate. Following up is one of the critical success factors, and it is greatly facilitated by being on the spot rather than trying to do so on the airplane while returning home or via telephone or postal communications.

Being on the spot also affords the opportunity to assess more fully the borrower's operations and management, the latter being another of the critical success factors that will be discussed later. Proper analysis of the political and economic scene is also made possible by being part of the environment.

The advent of foreign banks, and particularly American banks, on the business development scene in the 1960s and early 1970s revolutionized the banking interface in many countries. This was illustrated in Great Britain, where, as recently as the early 1970s, a great many finance directors were quite used to being summoned once a year to the local branch of their bankers to explain their credit needs. This was the way things had been for the full 200 or more years of the relationship, so it is easy to imagine the quizzical responses to direct solicitation efforts by scores of bankers from unfamiliar banks at distant points in "the colonies." The response of "what do you want to talk about?" was frequently given, and many of the first series of business development calls flowed in "yes/no" dialogues.

Gradually, through a systematic and programmed calling effort keyed to introduction of new ideas, inroads were made into local corporate banking. Today most finance directors or corporate treasurers are besieged by bank calling officers, for the competition is fierce in all of the creditworthy countries. In London, for example, there are over 400 banks, and more on the way.

Success in developing corporate borrowing relationships abroad requires innovation, flexibility, competitive pricing, large lending capacity, and timely follow-up—the critical success factors of business development. It should be clearly recognized that there are only so many hours in the business day for the treasurer, and there are only X number of banks manageable in his banking array. So precious is this finite time that some treasurers have developed a rating system for both the calling bank officer and his bank, based on delivery of the above critical success factors. The treasurer wants to hear things from his banker (or prospective banker) that will make his job easier and his results better. Thus, there is a real premium on knowing the company and the industry and environment in which it operates, and then targeting market-specific financial products and services to accomplish the above objective. This approach, consistently applied, will likely lead to effective penetration of most companies. There is no specific magic formula, but a hands-on approach to the problems and opportunities offered by the client, executed by properly trained and motivated bankers who are thoroughly knowledgeable about the company and its operating environment, is a good way to start.

Local Banking Practices

Returning to the opening comments covering domestic U.S. lending policies, it must be recognized that foreign-based treasurers generally are not compelled to accept the consequences of such policies because of the great wealth of other foreign bank competition as well as local lending practices. These practices can be summarized as follows:

1. Preponderance of asset-based lending—that is, the taking of a chattel or a fixed and floating registered charge over all the assets of a company, including unissued capital. This obviously places any subsequent lender in an inferior position vis-à-vis asset protection for the loan.
2. The asset-oriented lending means that very little, if any, analysis is done of the financial statements, nor is any demand made for projections.
3. Absence of any limit on the amount of credit accommodation to any one customer—only a "prudent" self-imposed limit—offers significant latitude as well as the ability to convincingly "lockup" a customer in the face of competition: "Why go to another bank when we can take care of all your needs?" This policy produces a good revenue stream and requires no incremental effort—until the company gets into financial difficulties. It then becomes a question of how many eggs you can get into one basket. It doesn't take many such large nonperforming assets to impair the earnings stream and capital position.
4. Existence of "universal" banks that can provide both commercial and investment banking services—again the ability to provide one-stop financial services. North American banks, prevented in their own countries from doing so, have this capacity abroad through merchant banking subsidiaries.
5. Relatively little reliance on or demand for CPA-prepared financial statements because they are not available or are deemed unimportant.
6. Lack of generally accepted accounting principles.
7. Profit is not the motivating factor for banks, as it is in the United States.
8. Abbreviated loan agreements—a handshake and long-standing personal contacts are deemed adequate.

9. Lack of a broad capital market to supply long-term financing or equity in sufficient amounts. Thus high short-term debt accumulation and high debt-to-worth ratios.

RATIONALE FOR BANKING RELATIONSHIP AND ASSOCIATED RISKS

Rationale

Why would a foreign-based corporation bank with a nonindigenous bank? The answers combine both subjective and objective reasons. A discussion will be made according to the sector of the borrower.

Public Sector

The government-owned companies normally are world scale and have large, sometimes insatiable, appetites for credit. This is based on their high capital intensity, resulting from industrial reorganization or expansion on a national scale or the need to develop the natural resource base. Alternatively, the company could be used by the government as a borrowing vehicle essentially for coverage of balance-of-payments deficits. In either case the borrowing usually is denominated in U.S. dollars and the bias is toward large international banks with unlimited access to dollars; this naturally includes U.S. banks, since it is their currency of operation. They have the added feature of being able to source the dollars from the domestic home market in the event of interference with the workings of the Eurodollar market. In turn, U.S. banks generally feel more comfortable with these "full faith and credit" (of the government) borrowers, and frequently solicit their business.

Thus, there is a high measure of compatibility, since the borrowers' needs far outstrip the domestic banks' lending capacity, which is characterized by large local currency loan exposures or restricted access to dollars. There is also a compatible personal fit, since the finance directors of these enterprises are highly visible internationally and develop a number of long-standing friends in the international banking community. Last, the borrower may well be obtaining capital equipment from abroad and will want to take advantage of the exporting countries' attractive incentive financing schemes, which are usually combined with a commercial bank portion.

Large Indigenous Corporations

Diversification of sources of financing is a strong motivation, as is the ability to provide Eurocurrency financing, which is generally cheaper than local currency borrowings. Inclusion of one or more foreign banks also offers a buffer against unreasonable charges by the domestic bank as well as a comparison for performance and a motive to continued good service and attention. The foreign banker frequently brings new ideas and approaches learned in other marketplaces. Very competitive quotes for surplus funds and on foreign exchange transactions also are a factor. Finally, the charisma of the calling officer and the personal rapport he/she establishes are strong subjective swing factors.

Multinational Corporations

In addition to the above, a foreign multinational corporation (MNC) will have a degree of loyalty to a core group of banks, but it is the treasurer's task to find the best services available to make his job easier and to borrow the required amounts of funds at the lowest cost. No one bank is ever able to serve an MNC's multiplicity of needs. A core group of relationship banks will be selected and will be given the opportunity to provide the required services (beyond the provision of loan funds), which include foreign exchange trading and advice, funds transfers, letters of credit, collections, cash management, and pension and profit-sharing funds management. If a core group member(s) fails to perform, banks that have professionally solicited the business will be given the chance to perform in selected areas. If successful, they will likely replace one of the core banks. Nothing should be taken for granted, and attentive and professional service is always required. A premium is always attached to the generation of new ideas.

Risk

As was mentioned at the outset, the decision to make a corporate loan abroad depends on a full and comprehensive assembly of the myriad impactive factors either absent from or less important to the domestic U.S. corporate lending situation. An experience-based professional assessment of these intertwined considerations is mandatory. The first and foremost consideration in processing a foreign loan request is assessing country risk. Since this subject is very capably covered in chapter 9, this discussion is not meant to be a discourse; rather, it provides a few pertinent comments in relation to private-sector lending.

The undertaking of granting loans to private-sector companies abroad must empirically start with a full and knowledgeable assessment of the country risk, since that is the ultimate risk. The corporate borrower can be of sterling quality, but the country in which it is located can be in total shambles and myriad government sanctions can be imposed to prevent the company's proper continued functioning, as well as to hinder its ability to obtain and/or transfer foreign currency abroad.

There are two basic questions to be answered by the country risk analysis, from a corporate lending viewpoint.

Marketing Priority

Is the medium- and long-term profile of the country synchronized with the marketing and/or investment strategies of the bank and its clients? This pragmatic question is important, for the bank must have demonstrated reasons for incurring country risk beyond the desire for short-term profits, which may become Pyrrhic if the principal subsequently proves to be uncollectible. Valid reasons certainly include servicing multinational clients' needs on a global basis and pursuing the bank's established areas of expertise.

Repayment Capacity

This consideration entails assessment of the borrower's credit character and credit capacity.

Credit Character. The willingness to repay a foreign loan is, in the final analysis, essentially a political variable. This is illustrated by the cases of Iran and Argentina. Iran's obvious reluctance to repay debts owed to U.S. sources reflects the weight of political considerations on debt servicing. So, too, does Argentina's unwillingness to repay its debts to United Kingdom lenders on a timely basis.

Credit Capacity. The ability to repay is a function of the interaction of economic factors, such as level of debt, maturity profile, international reserves, foreign exchange earnings, and management.

After completing the country analysis, the setting of a dollar amount of country risk exposure is customarily made in relationship to the bank's shareholders' equity—a certain percent of capital as the criterion for maximum international exposure. The resulting amount is small enough to permit management and the board of directors a level of comfort and security, yet large enough to permit business to be done.

Once limits have been established, there are several factors that can serve to reduce the risk in a particular country:

- Guarantees. Partial or full guarantees from supranational organizations such as the World Bank, International Finance Corporation (IFC), and Inter-American Development Bank (IDB) should always be sought. The covering guarantee for project or general purpose borrowing should in all cases be obtained from the government, the central bank, or a wholly government-owned development bank. Loans to subsidiaries of MNCs should be covered by a parent guarantee or letter of awareness.
- Self-payout transactions. Risk is always reduced when financing is keyed to a self-liquidating transaction.
- Access to capital markets. The maintenance of an acceptable international borrowing stance is important for providing the continued access to the various money markets, thereby permitting the continuance of the country's development and the proper servicing of its debt.
- Maturity distribution. A proper balance in the maturity profile of the bank's exposure is mandatory, since risk is partially a function of time. Shorter maturities and a low average life of the loan portfolio permit the advantage of loan portfolio liquidity in the event of unsettled conditions.
- Geographic and industry diversification. Dispersal of the risk assets over a manageable geographical and industrial plane helps avoid catastrophic results—which are often due to purely external, noncredit circumstances. The British property market and shipping are two prime examples, as are the copper-producing countries of Zaire and Peru.

Industry Review

It is most important to have thorough knowledge and understanding of the industry group in which a particular borrower operates. This involves not only the industry within the borrower's country, but also the surrounding region, any economic bloc to which the country belongs, and the global situation.

In a particular country there are likely to be cartel-type arrangements for price setting, and even tacit agreements as to market share and privileged channels for sales to the government and for receiving preferential financing or grants. The key question is where the borrower fits into this matrix. What barriers exist to fair competition for competing imports? Is there a nationalistic trend to "buy locally"? Does such a trend include joint ventures with foreign ownership? How secure are sources of raw material?

On a regional basis is there domestic saturation that could lead to "dumping," which could undercut the borrower's sales prices? A good example is the excess capacity that has developed in Eastern Europe in electric motors, petrochemicals, and machine tools. East European countries sell these goods to capitalist countries at break-even prices, which they can fully document as not being "dumped" because their costs are not in synchronization with world prices. Other questions a lender must ask about the industry concern the general terms of sale and the possibilities of foreign currency sales to surrounding countries, a natural focus due to shorter lines of transport. If the country is a member of an economic bloc such as the EEC or EFTA, what obligations or restrictions are imposed? Does this free movement of trade mean competition from higher quality and/or lower priced goods, or does it offer a much larger and more dynamic market than at home?

On the world scale the macro questions of supply and demand must be fully understood. What is the cyclical nature of the demand, and what are leads/lags in various countries, which permit counter-cyclical export opportunities? Good visibility should be gained on present and projected worldwide supply versus worldwide demand. All of these factors affect the capacity of a borrower to sell its products.

ROLE OF THE GOVERNMENT
AND REGULATORY ENVIRONMENT

The policy as well as the de facto position of the government should be well understood, with particular emphasis on attitudes toward competition, foreign investment, tariff setting, importation of capital equipment, exchange control (free flow of capital, foreign currency holdings, borrowing abroad, and such), authorizations for borrowing foreign currency within the country, availability of guarantees, potential for nationalization/denationalization, fiscal control, and conducive monetary policy.

Frequently, government policy or attitudes will favor indigenous companies, and place certain tangible or intangible hurdles in the path of joint ventures or foreign-owned corporations. This policy can become manifest through the favoring of local companies for procurements, import licenses, preferential development or export finance, tax incentives, price increases, and access to capital markets.

A good case to illustrate the impact of government actions is that of a Spanish manufacturer that had excellent management and traditionally enjoyed healthy domestic and international markets. Projecting the favorable sales trend lines of the last two decades, the company committed several hundred million dollars to a five-year capital investment program for new plant construction at 12 locations in the country, equipping the plants with modern production lines. Having completed the program within the originally projected time frame and reasonably within budget, the company almost immediately started to encounter a number of problems, all beyond their control. To start, the country began relaxing import controls and tariffs on foreign manufactured parts—this gradual relaxation of years of protectionism followed the passing of General Franco and was in anticipation of admission to the European Economic Community. An economic downturn occurred while the country's leaders were busy focusing on more pressing political and constitutional tasks, and the home demand weakened. The company's exports (some 40 percent of sales) were denominated in U.S. dollars and deutsche marks, but the peseta was held artificially high, thus making imports of materials more expensive while keeping export earnings low. Then price controls were imposed on the domestic selling prices, but were not accompanied by controls over domestic wages, which spiraled at a rate of 28–30 percent per annum. It was also virtually impossible to lay off redundant workers, for layoffs would undoubtedly have caused crippling strikes by the emerging unions, anxious to show their muscle after being banned for more than 40 years.

This web of events outside the control of management need not be described further, but it obviously prevented the company from meeting its substantial foreign debt. It became clear that no improvement of the situation was on the horizon, and the bank lenders had to act. In friendly and cooperative fashion the banks were able to facilitate the injection of foreign capital and a wider foreign distribution network, and the company survived.

There are also examples of government policy working in a positive manner for foreign banks. One such case was a syndicated Euroloan arranged through a European government-owned bank for a corporate borrower located in an African colony. Revolution came to both the colonial power and its colony, and the private-sector company ceased to operate because its technicians left and the company was damaged in the fighting. However, the new government in the European country felt at least a moral obligation, and continued to service the corporate debt to the full terms of the loan agreement.

The lending and deposit-gathering operations of foreign banks in a host country are generally affected by local banking regulations that can have a material impact on corporate lending. Factors with a role in the lending decision include total asset ceilings on the foreign banks, which naturally limit the size of a loan to any one customer; reserve requirements, which make foreign banks' loans more expensive because of lack of access to local demand or lower-cost funds; prohibition of deposit instruments or bankers' acceptances being guaranteed by the parent bank, again making them uncompetitive; and leverage constraints, which force injection of new capital in an environment less than conducive to realistic returns on assets and equity.

In making foreign currency loans to companies within the country, as is frequently done because of lower rates of interest than on domestic currency borrowings, it is necessary to fully understand all applicable regulations attached to such loans. It is a broad policy in most countries that foreign currency loans must be approved in advance by the central bank or the ministry of finance, and the loan agreement must be officially filed and registered. This action is necessary in order to get subsequent approval to buy the required foreign currency and to "export" it to repay the loan. There can also be stipulations as to the margin that may be charged over LIBOR or cost, as well as to a minimum dollar amount and minimum grace period before amortization may commence. The purpose of the borrowing can also be restricted—particularly for acquisition of a local company. During times of monetary restraint, a portion of the loan proceeds may have to be placed in a noninterest-bearing deposit with the central bank—this is a tool periodically used in Italy, and also has been used in Great Britain and Germany.

EVALUATING FINANCIAL STATEMENTS OF FOREIGN CORPORATIONS

Analyzing the financial statements of foreign corporate entities calls first for understanding the basis on which these statements were prepared. What follows is a brief discussion of some of the variables frequently encountered in looking at foreign financial statements.

Accounting

There should be early recognition of the fact that considerable diversity of accounting principles and reporting practices exists, owing in part to each country's stage of economic development and to different national cultural influences. There is a growing awareness of the desirability of eliminating unnecessary differences and moving toward a greater harmonization of international accounting, but that harmony is still far in the future. In the interim the lender must have a keen awareness of the national accounting principles, as well as those that may exist for the public sector as opposed to the private sector, and of those for specialized industries such as construction, toll highways, utilities, and shipping. Some countries require that certain information be disclosed in documents other than financial statements. As an example, in the United Kingdom the Companies Act requires that a breakdown of sales and profits (loss) between various categories of a company's business be disclosed in the directors' report that is filed with the Companies' House. It is important to know of the existence of these other sources of financial information. Many foreign stock exchange commissions require additional financial information similar to the 10K and other reports required by the Securities and Exchange Commission in the United States.

To provide insight into some of the more prominent areas of divergence, the following areas are discussed.

Fixed Asset Revaluation

In countries with continuing high inflation and/or essentially dormant stock markets, the upward valuation of fixed assets is an expedient to increasing net worth. In Spain and France, for example, government decrees require the increase of fixed asset value by application of specified indices at fixed intervals, while in Great Britain management exercises discretion at irregular intervals. The valuation method varies: by independent third-party appraisal, management appraisal, or legislated indices.

Revaluation Reserve

The reserve or surplus created from the above fixed asset revaluation is variously handled on the other side of the balance sheet. In virtually all but four countries, it is credited to a revaluation reserve or surplus account within the stockholders' equity section; in Spain and Italy this exercise helps bring down companies' debt-to-worth ratios, for the availability of additional equity through new stock offerings is limited by the relative inactivity of the stock exchanges. In Sweden and Greece the adjustment is credited to the common stock account.

Consolidated Statements

Preparation of consolidated statements is axiomatic in many countries, while in others the practice is totally unknown. This is because in some countries the concept of parent-subsidiary relationship simply does not exist, or because of legislative prohibitions on intercompany holdings, or because the usefulness of consolidated statements is not appreciated, or because corporate lenders wish to avoid full disclosure on the total holdings out of fear of nationalization, kidnapping, or the tax authorities. Variations on consolidated statements may occur—as in Germany, where only domestic operations are consolidated.

However, as companies grow and have to tap international capital markets, they are being forced by the lenders or the foreign regulatory agencies to present their total financial picture.

Foreign Currency Translation

This topic evokes the most emotion and controversy, and international harmonization is hopelessly out of sight. Nevertheless, the two main aspects—accounting for foreign currency transactions and translating the financial statements of a foreign company—must be examined to determine the method used. Almost all companies are concerned with these questions. For the former the two main approaches for setting the rate of exchange to be used are "time of transaction" and "time of settlement." Gains or losses on exchange when these dates are in the same accounting period are generally viewed as being realized, and are recognized in the profit and loss statement (P & L). Gains or losses from the translation of receivables or payables at statement date are unrealized, and the practice of charging unrealized losses to the P & L is widespread (but not so with gains). Consideration of nontrading transactions is another topic, particularly for medium-term loans. The unrealized gains or losses relating to these loans are variously included in the P & L, taken directly to the net worth section, or deferred or deferred and amortized. Thus, it is obvious that the method used must be determined and recognition must be made of the total lack of uniformity—thus inhibiting straightforward comparisons.

DIRECT LENDING CONSIDERATIONS

Apart from the variables associated with foreign financial statements reviewed in the preceding section, lending to foreign corporations involves a number of additional considerations. What follows highlights some of the most important considerations encountered in making loans to foreign companies.

Quality of Management

Quality of management is probably the most important and the most difficult factor in international credit analysis. Management has a dynamic quality because it combines perspective, order, power, and timing. In a sense it synthesizes human beings, raw materials, and capital into a stream of goods and services. It is a faculty that some men possess, enabling them to expunge waste from industry, increase production, facilitate distribution, and at the same time reduce costs. In simple terms, it is the principal differentiating factor between economic success and failure.

If the borrowing corporation's management factor is positive—that is, if it has the "know-how" and is thoroughly trustworthy—special arrangements for a loan will sometimes be made when other factors, financial and economic, are not altogether propitious. On the other hand, given favorable financial and economic conditions, but management of a questionable character, a bank is likely to be reluctant to extend credit accommodations.

Prior to entering any credit arrangements, it is most important to have a good knowledge and understanding of the quality and character of the corporation's management. An interesting illustration of this is provided by a European appliances manufacturer that had been built to national proportions by a single strong-willed man who personally ran the company as would the captain of a ship. He had all the attributes of good management: a definite program, control of inventory, efficiency of operations, alertness to developments and change, ability to utilize cost figures, good distribution system, and good personnel relations. He viewed this company as his whole life, and was totally dedicated to its continuing success. Upon investigation, however, it became known that he kept a revolver in his desk and appeared to have no hesitation about using it if his company ever faced severe difficulties. Moral of the example: get to know the borrowers' management, for they are frequently the best assurance of repayment of the loan. The lender must have an appreciation of how management will react under a number of different economic and financial scenarios.

Plant Visit

There is absolutely no substitute for going out to "kick the tires" and actually seeing the physical plant firsthand. The plant visit is obviously another factor in the evaluation of the management factor, and a face-to-face dialogue with the managers of the major functional areas can be most revealing. A background summary on each should be developed.

The product lines, competition (both present and anticipated), and the R & D effort should be examined, as should the condition of the equipment producing these goods. Is the equipment old and fully depreciated, without automation, and subject to frequent downtime for repairs, or is it state of the art, automated, and cost-efficient? How does the company ensure uniformity of quality? This is very important if the goods are to compete on world markets, for there are frequently stigmas attached to goods from industrializing countries. The goods may be of acceptable quality, but the marketing, advertising, distribution, and after-sales service systems may not be fully supportive—the lender should inquire closely into each of these areas because they are the means of selling the goods to repay the loan.

While on the plant tour, the bank officer should acquire a good feeling for the role and involvement of the board of directors—do they provide an independent and persuasive voice, or are they a rubber stamp for management's actions? Finally, the financial management and controllership should be familiar to the lender.

Purpose of the Loan

A clear understanding should always be gained of the purpose of the borrowing. This is necessary not only to permit the lender to be sure that the loan proceeds will be utilized for a productive purpose to help assure repayment, but also to provide the background necessary for the proper structuring of the credit facility.

If the purpose is to bridge very short-term gaps in the flow of revenue and demands for disbursement of payables, the tenor of the loan and the matched currency is obvious, but for virtually all other purposes, including restructuring of a debt maturity profile, indeterminate-period working capital, capital equipment investment, acquisitions, or major development, it becomes necessary to consider the customer's overall financing picture and to formulate the most appropriate credit facilities (discussed below under "Types of Credit Facilities").

Currency of the Loan

The choice of currency of a lending arrangement, if different from the currency of the borrower, must reflect the export earnings of the customer, a swapped coverage, or an open foreign exchange position.

The customer frequently will opt for the currency that bears the lowest rate of interest as the denomination of the loan. Historically, the Swiss franc has been a favored currency for borrowing because of its lower rate of per annum interest vis-à-vis the U.S. dollar. In the lending equation analysis should be made of the ability of the borrower to repay in the currency of the borrowing if the company does not have a natural income stream from exports, investment income, or dividends in that currency, or coverage through a swap or forward purchase.

Since the departure from fixed exchange rates under the Bretton Woods Agreement, it has been the maxim that every investment or borrowing decision has been a foreign exchange decision. In recent years the appreciation or depreciation of the major currencies has, in large measure, far outweighed the difference between the rates of interest on the currencies. It is, therefore, necessary to try to quantify the degree of foreign exchange risk implied by prevailing borrowing rates of interest on the major currencies. This involves the determination of the points of no return or break-even exchange rates where the interest savings meets possible appreciation/depreciation of the currency principal.

The choice of currency may also be subject to availability. In Spain, for example, the peseta has in recent years been under severe availability constraint and the only viable borrowing option has been the U.S. dollar. In certain public sectors the government provided exchange rate guarantees while the private sector was left at the mercy of market movements, without the benefit of swap coverage or natural sources of currency.

In periods of widespread anticipation of a currency devaluation, companies will build up liabilities in the subject currency so they will, ideally, be able to repay the devaluated currency of the loan with the appreciated natural currency of the company.

Cash Flow Analysis

For varying historic or socioeconomic reasons, banks in many countries lend solely on the premise of taking security in the assets of the company while giving little or no regard to cash flow. Loan structuring and documentation then tend to be short and simple, and the lending philosophy seems to extend into perpetuity. The premise that pledged assets can be liquidated to repay loans must be questioned, since asset values realized at a distress sale or "firesale" seldom bear correlation at par to market values.

It is contended that cash-flow-based lending affords greater protection for the lender and its depositors and shareholders, because it involves all of the above analytical factors concerning the borrower, and the repayment terms are geared to the ability of the borrower to generate cash. Ultimately it is hard cash that repays loans. Cash flow lending is differently premised: it advocates the capacity of an ongoing company to generate cash from its operations to repay debt. It imposes a certain discipline upon the company to accurately plan and forecast cash flows and to provide the supporting rationale. The benefit is that it may provide the supportive basis for a lender's extending medium-term credit accommodations keyed to cash inflows. This is contrasted with the typically on-demand or short-term renewable credit facilities associated with the asset-based approach.

Availability of Added Credit Support

The question of the need to look beyond the financial standing of the direct borrower obviously depends upon the company's corporate format. Starting with indigenous companies with no foreign parentage, the only available means of added credit support would be to obtain export credit insurance for their foreign sales or to avail themselves of buyer credit facilities abroad.

For subsidiaries of foreign companies, it should be taken as axiomatic that the parent wishes to commit as little of its capital funds as possible to achieve desirable leverage or to lessen the exchange risk. Nevertheless, the country risk or market conditions or the perilous state of the borrower may dictate that the parent guarantee the obligations of the foreign subsidiary if financing is to be obtained at all. This was more prevalent in the 1960s and early

1970s, but less so since about 1975, years due to competitive pressure and the tendency to greater leniency toward lending documentation and covenants. If a guarantee is indeed taken, it should always be approved by local in-house or outside counsel, and should contemplate multicurrency denomination of the loan facility. In many countries central bank or ministerial approval is required in order to exercise control over potential outflows of foreign exchange.

More often than not in the late 1970s and early 1980s, parent guarantees were not available, and lenders had to rely solely on the financial strength of the borrower or on some indirect or esoteric obligation of the foreign parent. The parent guarantee is becoming increasingly rare because parent companies wish to avoid additional contingent liabilities that must be noted in financial statements and that will affect leverage ratios, capital adequacy, loan covenants, or bond indentures. This has forced the move toward a document known variously as a comfort letter, parent support, letter of awareness, or Oklahoma letter (the origin of the latter totally obscured). It should be recognized that these expressions of involvement are not legally enforceable guarantees, and many times are drafted by lawyers instructed to make them anything but enforceable. For a lender it thus becomes incumbent to evaluate a number of subjective factors associated with the situation, which include the following considerations:

1. The international reputation of the parent and what damage would be done if it let a subsidiary default
2. Whether the subsidiary is wholly owned and whether it carries or incorporates the parent's name
3. Whether the wording implies a guarantee obligation
4. Potential for shareholder blockage of performance
5. Guarantee limitations
6. What parental action is stated or implied
7. Whether the initial investment in the subsidiary has been fully recouped through dividends, depreciation benefit, or transfer pricing
8. What direct parent supervision over, or management injection into, the subsidiary has taken place
9. What parent sales and advertising support takes place
10. Magnitude of parent company loans, subordinated or otherwise
11. Undertaking to maintain majority ownership position.

In the final analysis, if the parent intends to honor the debt of its subsidiary, then the debt will be serviced properly. If not, the piece of paper is worthless. Thus, we come back to the character of management.

Added credit support may also take the following forms:

• Take or pay or off-take agreements. The parent or independent third parties may undertake to buy a specified amount of the borrower's production each year or to pay the associated amount. This is usually done in connection with refineries or pipelines, but could be extended to mine production, petrochemicals, and oil or natural gas production.

• Foreign receivables insurance. Programs whereby government or privately sponsored agencies provide insurance against commercial and political risks of selling abroad. The Export Development Corporation of Canada and the Export Credit Guarantee Department of Great Britain are two prime examples.

• Political risk insurance. An investment abroad by a U.S. company, for example, may be insured by the Overseas Private Investment Corporation (OPIC), a self-sustaining U.S. government agency, against specified political risks.

• Long-term sales contracts. The lending bank could look to firm long-term supply/sales contracts as a source of repayment, whereby the proceeds could be paid into an account at the bank, with the bank holding an assignment of proceeds.

• Third-party guarantees. This type of guarantee can be secured by a supranational agency, such as the Inter-American Development Bank or the European Investment Bank (EIB), national development agencies, or export-import agencies.

TYPES OF CREDIT FACILITIES

The purpose of the loan and the particular financial market(s) to which the bank has access, as well as exchange control, foreign exchange exposure, and banking regulations, all contribute to determining the type or combination of credit facilities made available to a client.

In today's market "financial engineering" has become a commonplace term, and embodies the structuring of financial facilities to meet the specific needs of the customer. It thus becomes particularly important for the lending officer to be totally familiar and comfortable with a broad array of international financial products and services. The mere provision of loan funds is not what today's treasurer or finance director wants from his relationship bank or banks—that generally takes only several hours a year of the borrower's time, while the remainder of the time is spent on a vast number of financial problems and opportunities.

Rather than provide a detailed discussion of a few of the more prominent lending forms, the following delineates the broad spectrum of international financial products and services that most world-class banks make available to multinational corporations.

International Trade Financing Facilities

One of the most important functions performed by U.S. banks engaged in international banking is to finance international trade activity. There are several ways through which U.S. banks finance the import and export activities of their clients: letters of credit, advances, bankers' acceptances, and medium-term credits. (Because of the great variety exhibited by each of these financial methods, a detailed account of the different services appears in the appendix to this chapter.)

Facilities for Foreign Subsidiaries

In addition to the products/services under "International Trade Financing Facilities" above, the following are typically required by foreign subsidiaries of MNCs:

1. Local currency of Eurocurrency short-term finance for carrying receivables/inventory, tax or dividend payments, bridging to a term debt or equity issue, swing between parent company advances, foreign securities purchase, or dealer/distributor loans
2. Local currency or Eurocurrency medium-term finance for plant expansion, equipment purchase, acquisitions, debt consolidation, or joint-venture funding
3. Personal or real estate loans for executives.

Project Bid Financing

In the 1980s natural resource and energy development, as well as infrastructure development around the world, will be a vital area of focus for a bank's key clients/prospects. In their tender offers, contractors and major equipment suppliers typically must incorporate an offer of medium-term financing along with their straight cash-price quotation for the equipment or services. This represents a good opportunity for a bank to work closely with a client to submit a joint (equipment price/financing offer) bid on a project. If successful, it provides a bank with the mandate for a club or open syndication loan and other ancilliary benefits, such as the letter of credit's (L/Cs) project accounts.

Project Financing

This can be the financing of projects abroad or in the United States for foreign multinationals. There are obviously a great variety of projects, but the principal areas include construction and equipment financing for LNG plants and carriers, hydroelectric utility facilities, and coal-, nuclear-, or oil-fired utilities. The range of financial services related to project financing includes the following:

1. Project loan. Generally a syndicated loan that looks directly to the project for its security and source of repayment
2. Bridge financing. Interim bank credit to the project during the time required for the start-up of operations, building the required infrastructure, construction and installation of processing equipment, or construction of storage and shipping facilities
3. Merchant banking. Capability to arrange equity placement and the nontraditional debt financing needed for various types of new projects
4. Leasing. Arranging the leasing of capital equipment on a straight or leveraged basis
5. Equipment financing. Variety of commercial bank financing arrangements, involving various private and government export credit institutions, and agencies in the United States as well as their counterparts abroad
6. Local and multicurrency financing.

Foreign Buyer Finance

This is an area of frequent requests by MNCs, and involves shifting the buyer risk from the MNC to a bank, with the usual comment that the MNC is in the manufacturing business—not banking. Providing financing to foreign buyers generally takes the following forms:

- Purchase or discounting of notes or bills of exchange
- Purchase of book receivables with recourse
- Direct short- or medium-term loans to buyer
- Use of the Loan Discount Program of the Export-Import Bank (Eximbank) of the United States
- Buyer credits insured by the Foreign Credit Insurance Association (FCIA) of the United States
- Eximbank-guaranteed or directly funded loans
- Eximbank Cooperative Finance Facility
- Private Export Funding Corporation (PEFCO) fixed-rate loan
- Loans through Canada's Export Development Corporation (EDC)
- Loans guaranteed by Italy's government-backed SACE Program (Sezione per l'Assicurazione del Credito all'Esportazione)
- Loans guaranteed by the United Kingdom's Export Credits Guarantee Department (ECGD)
- Funding loans under the FOMEX Program of the Mexican government (Fondo para el Fomento de las Exportaciones de Productos Manufacturados).

Specialized Arrangements

Syndicated Guarantee Facilities

For major project construction in the Middle East, it is almost always required that the contractor provide certain tangible assurances to the purchaser. The various requirements and the bank-provided instruments are delineated below. Typically, the sums involved are very large and a number of banks can be involved to spread the risk. Hence, the need to syndicate the risk.

Bid Bonds. Bid bonds are usually required of a contractor/supplier by a buyer (which is frequently a government or government procurement agency) when the contractor/supplier tenders a bid. The bid bond ensures the buyer of some compensation for the time and money lost if a bidder, having won the award, decides to withdraw. The bid bond is usually for a small percentage of the total bid, typically 1-3 percent for large contracts and up to 5 percent for smaller contracts. These are normally issued for short periods only, because they are replaced by performance bonds by the winning bidder within 10-20 days. They can also be required in the bidding for commodities.

Performance Guarantees. A performance guarantee is one placed by the successful bidder indemnifying the buyer in the event the bidder does not supply the specified goods or properly execute the contract. It is usually 5 percent of larger contracts and up to 10 percent of smaller contracts. Validity is commonly for periods of up to one year from completion.

An aspect of a performance guarantee of which the account officer should be aware is the "on demand" feature prevalent in certain parts of the world, particularly in the Arab countries. The "on demand" clause allows the buyer to "call" the guarantee (in essence, declare default) at any time, regardless of reason and without arbitration. While this appears extremely risky for the bidder/contractor, in practice it apparently has rarely been utilized. The purpose of the "on demand" clause is to enable the buyer to exercise full control over the project.

In some cases the prime contractor may require performance guarantees from his subcontractors, thus reducing his risk and that of his banks. Performance guarantees are frequently required to ensure performance under commodity purchase contracts, particularly in Latin America.

Advance Payment Guarantee. The successful bidder may receive a payment of up to 20-25 percent of the total contract amount just prior to commencing work. The payment enables the contractor to start the project. Suitable guarantees must be arranged to protect the buyer, typically for the same amount as the advance payment. This guarantee is reduced over the life of the contract as the buyer withholds the 20-25 percent from each progress payment made.

Retention Money Guarantee. The contractor is generally responsible for ensuring the project's proper functioning for up to one year after the completion date. Guaranteeing this (usually 10 percent) can take two forms: a certain portion of the final payment can be withheld, or a guarantee can be issued in favor of the buyer, whereby a certain amount will be paid to the beneficiary in the event of the project's not performing up to standards. It is not widely used, because the performance guarantee features cover this aspect.

Progress Payment Guarantees. Standby L/Cs are issued to guarantee progress payments (payments made when various stages of the project are completed).

Standby L/C as Commercial Paper Back-up

Foreign corporations seeking alternative money markets (and lower cost of funds) can tap the domestic U.S. commercial paper market and obtain the highest credit rating if they obtain a letter of credit from a first-class group of commercial banks. The letter of credit is an irrevocable undertaking to provide financing to the issuer if it is unable to renew its paper in the market. The L/C can be attached to the commercial paper, or it can be in a "submerged" form whereby a trustee is created and the L/C is not attached to the commercial paper. The bank L/C backing of the commercial paper helps reduce the rate on the paper sold, and helps keep the company's access to the market open during times of market turbulence or fluctuations in the company's earnings pattern.

Nuclear Fuel Financing

Similar to the commercial paper back-up facilities, a syndicate of banks can be arranged to issue a submerged letter of credit to a special-purpose trust created for financing the ownership of nuclear fuel intended for use by an electric utility company. The trust, created by the utility but trusteed by a bank, purchases the nuclear fuel and leases it to the utility on a heat supply basis. The trust finances the purchase of the uranium and the costs of enrichment, transportation, fabrication, insurance, and financing with the issuance of commercial paper. By this means the financing is off the utility's balance sheet.

Note Purchase Syndication

One of the most frequent requests from corporations is for a bank to purchase or discount medium-term notes, stating that banks are in the business of risk-taking, whereas the corporation simply manufactures items. Translation: the corporation wants to rid itself of the foreign buyer risk and liquidize the ill-liquid, medium-term receivable.

This can take the form of a single bank's involvement or that of a syndicate, depending on the size and nature of the underlying transaction and the availability of country limit. It could involve one supplier/contractor or a group of suppliers. The purchase or discount usually must involve an adjustment to current market yields for the country. This can be accomplished by acquiring the notes on a discount-to-yield basis, by applying a margin or an interest basis such as LIBOR or prime and having the purchaser pay the interest, or by having the contractor/supplier pay an interest rate on the notes to equate the overall yield to market.

Other

The list is almost endless, bound only by limitations of bankers' inventiveness and creation of new financial structures. Other specialized arrangements include the following:

- Syndicated L/C backing industrial development bonds
- Leveraged buy-out financing
- L/C covering margin deposit requirements for commodity hedging operations
- Ship mortgage finance
- Railway equipment collateral trust financing
- Royalty anticipation financing
- Medium-term committed loan available by syndicated short-term notes
- Gold price-indexed short-term notes.

International Services

Some of the more important international services that multinational banks extend to their clientele include the following:

International cash management
Eurobond underwriting

Eurobond trading
Eurocommercial paper placement
Corporate financial consulting
Forfaiting
Europrivate placements;
Lead management of true project financings.

THE PROFITABILITY OF
FOREIGN CORPORATE FINANCING

International corporate lending has, since the 1960s, been like religion, in that it has had blind faith followers and profitability was deemed obviously to have been attached to it. Banks with globe-girdling reaches were the envy of all, but now banks are increasingly taking a new look at their worldwide positioning, motives, strategies, and the illusive profits therefrom. By any measure, whether it be return on assets, return on equity, or return on effort, the profits from international corporate lending have proved to be surprisingly sparse. The business of serving corporations internationally has become a hotly contested arena and perhaps has become overly competitive and only marginally profitable. The key problem is measuring the profitability. The accurate gauging of international profitability of a corporate relationship has totally eluded the vast majority of the world's major banks.

I would like to end this discourse on international corporate lending with two unresolved questions: is it profitable, and if it is not, what alternatives exist?

APPENDIX: INTERNATIONAL TRADE
FINANCING FACILITIES

A. Import Transactions
   1. Letters of Credit
      a. Issuance of sight L/Cs
      b. Issuance of up to 180-day usance L/Cs
      c. Deferred sight L/C
      d. Deferred-payment L/C

2. Advances
   a. Financing payments on trust receipt basis of payment made under sight L/Cs up to one year; in essence, this is "flooring" of merchandise until sold and collected
   b. Financing payments on incoming documentary or cash collections on full or marginal basis
   c. Unsecured advances
   d. Secured advance against accounts receivable and/or inventory
   e. Financing against warehouse receipt for goods in warehouse
   f. Participation in financing by another bank, secured by share in trust receipt or warehouse receipt held by agent bank
   g. Unsecured advances for payment of freight and customs duty charges
3. Bankers' Acceptances
   a. Financing on trust receipt basis of payments made under sight L/Cs up to 180 days
   b. Financing payments on trust receipt basis of payments made on incoming documentary collections
4. Miscellaneous
   a. Issuance of shipside bonds or guarantees for missing shipping documents
   b. Issuance of airway release to allow importer to obtain goods shipped by air prior to receipt of title documents
5. Medium-Term Loans
   a. Euro or U.S./Canadian prime-quoted loans for import of capital equipment, for plant expansion, or acquisitions
   b. Fixed-rate ECGD-guaranteed term loans in dollars, sterling, or any freely convertible currency for purchase of British capital equipment
   c. Fixed-rate financing of imports from Mexico under FOMEX Program of Mexican government
   d. Financing, on floating rate, imports of Italian goods under the government-backed SACE Program—same for Canada under EDC
6. Foreign Exchange
   a. Purchase of spot exchange to pay for drafts or foreign remittances in foreign currency
   b. Purchase of forward exchange to fix the rate of exchange for future payment of drafts or foreign remittances

      c. Purchase of spot exchange and investment of foreign currency in interest-bearing foreign debt instruments with maturities coinciding with future payment dates of foreign obligations

B. Export Transactions

   1. Letters of Credit

      a. Confirmation of another bank's L/C in favor of exporter

      b. Back-to-back L/C—the exporter uses the L/C in its favor as back-up for the issuance of an L/C in favor of his supplier, the only changes between the two being beneficiary's name, account party, amount, and validity reduced a few days for substitution; this is one of several methods of financing for purchase of goods for onward sale by a middleman

      c. Transferable L/C, which allows the beneficiary of an L/C to request the negotiating or paying bank to transfer all or a portion of the proceeds to one or more parties

      d. Red clause, which allows the negotiating bank of an L/C to make advance payment to the exporter prior to receiving conforming documents

      e. Support, an L/C issued on the strength of another L/C involving a related transaction and identical terms except that the evidence of shipment will differ between the two L/Cs

   2. Advances

      a. Financing on full or marginal basis on outgoing documentary or cash collection

      b. Advances up to 100 percent of invoice value of export sales insured by FCIA to a minimum of 70 percent of commercial risks

      c. Financing of outgoing documentary collections insured by FCIA

      d. Financing under deferred-payment L/C

   3. Acceptances

      a. Preexport financing based on firm foreign purchase order or another bank's L/C

      b. Financing of commodities or staple goods warehoused in the United States or foreign countries, secured by warehouse receipt, and subsequently released against trust receipt

      c. Financing of exportation based on outgoing documentary collections secured by title to goods on order bill of lading

    d. Financing of goods in transit in United States, provided a bank holds title documents

    e. Financing up to 180 days under deferred-payment L/C

    f. Discounting of time drafts under usance L/C

    g. Export financing up to 180 days

    h. Ineligible acceptance (finance bills) may be created against shipments within the United States where title documents are not available to a bank or against the warehousing of manufactured goods in the bank's possession (may also be created for up to 360 days)—there is a limited market, and reserves must be maintained

4. Foreign Exchange

    a. Sale of spot exchange for foreign currency received for exports

    b. Forward sale of foreign currency to be received at future date

    c. Advisory services

5. Medium-Term Loans

    a. Euro, Asian, or local currency loans to foreign buyers of exporting client

    b. Case-by-case FCIA insurance loans for individual transactions covering 90 percent of commercial risk and 100 percent of political risk up to five years

    c. Purchase or discount of medium-term notes/receivables with or without recourse/guarantees

    d. Eximbank Exporter Guarantee Program, wherein foreign buyer's debt obligation is guaranteed to the commercial bank financing the export

    e. Eximbank Discount Program, whereby Eximbank will discount a commercial bank's loan to finance a U.S. export of goods/services

    f. Eximbank will participate in the export financing with a commercial bank

6. Miscellaneous

    a. Purchase or discount of foreign notes receivable or of trade acceptances with or without recourse or FCIA insurance

    b. Foreign collections

    c. Incoming/outgoing remittances

    d. Credit information service

7. Deposit Services
   a. U.S. dollar demand accounts for international purposes
   b. Dollar time deposits, certificates of deposit, bankers' acceptances, or purchase of treasury bills at prevailing interest rates in the United States
   c. International placement capability in all major money markets, such as Nassau, London, Tokyo, Frankfurt, Singapore, and Toronto

SUGGESTED REFERENCES

Angelini, Anthony, Maximo Eng, and Francis A. Lees. *International Lending, Risk and the Euromarkets.* Ch. 2. New York: John Wiley and Sons, 1979.

Donaldson, T. H. *Lending in International Commercial Banking.* Chs. 2 and 4. New York: John Wiley and Sons, 1979.

Mathis, F. John, ed. *Offshore Lending by U.S. Commercial Banks.* 2nd ed. Chs. 7 and 8. Washington, D.C., and Philadelphia: Bankers' Association for Foreign Trade and Robert Morris Associates, 1981.

15 SYNDICATED LOANS
Andrew M. MacLaren

WHAT IS SYNDICATION?

Syndication is the technique adopted by bankers to solve the problem of how to lend or provide other credit facilities to a borrower who needs far more than one bank is able or willing to supply. If a private-sector or government borrower wishes to obtain credit facilities in large amounts, all but the very largest of banks will be unwilling to provide them on their own. In the United States there are statutory prohibitions[1] against banks lending more than 10 percent of capital funds to one borrower; there are similar prohibitions, whether statutory or regulatory, in many other countries. And, most important, there are few cases when, as a matter of banking practice, it is prudent for a banker to commit as much as 10 percent of his capital to the risk of one borrower. On the other hand, large amounts are sought by borrowers for matters as diverse as trade financing, project financing, debt rescheduling, and the funding of balance-of-payments deficits.

In theory it would be possible for a large borrower to take out a number of small loans from different banks, but the costs of negotiating different sets of documentation and the risks involved in monitoring payments under so many loans are extremely high. A syndication solves this problem by providing for a number of banks each to make part of a large loan in such a way that they all sign the same loan agreement and stand equally with each other in right of repayment.

HISTORY AND BACKGROUND

There are many conflicting accounts as to when the first syndicated international loan was made. Suffice it to say, however, that in the London market (which in 1980 retained its place at the top of the league—34.7 percent in amount, 32.7 percent in number of loans[2]) syndicated loans have been made since about 1970, and new techniques are continuously being developed. In the last few years we have seen syndicated letter of credit and guarantee facilities, particularly in connection with trade financing in the Middle East. Many of the observations in this chapter concerning syndicated loans apply to these other facilities, but great care should be taken when considering these credits, because their essential nature has important differences from the structure of a syndicated loan (as discussed below). In 1980 borrowers raised over $88 billion[3] in syndicated credits. Although this was lower than the corresponding figure for 1979 ($99 billion[4]), early figures for 1981 imply a further rise. This represents an impressive growth trend when one considers that 15 years previously this market barely existed. It is now an established market enabling large borrowers to raise medium-term funds from a number of banks at a minimum of expense.

Most of the loans with which this chapter is concerned are medium-term (generally three to ten years), and the interest rate is quoted as a spread over the London Interbank Offered Rate (LIBOR) for successive three- or six-month periods. Prime-based loans have been seen, but since most of the loans are funded in interbank markets such as London, rather than in domestic U.S. dollar markets, an interest rate relating to the domestic prime rate will not accurately reflect the cost of funding. For the most part, such syndicated lending is in U.S. dollars or Eurodollars, but other Eurocurrencies are also used. Such Eurocurrencies are simply credit balances in banks or branches of banks outside the country whose government issued such currency. Ironically, some of the earlier Eurodollar deposits were made by Communist and other governments that needed to trade in U.S. dollars but did not feel happy holding credit balances in U.S. accounts. They were also considered to be a safe haven for the dollars being spent abroad by the U.S. government in the postwar period. They could be traded free of the fiscal and regulatory controls imposed in the United States. Since 1950 these offshore balances in U.S. dollars in particular have grown so that their size today, although difficult to measure, is sufficiently large to fund outstanding Euro-dollar lending and Eurobond indebtedness. One estimate is that at the end of 1979, the size of the market was in excess of $400 billion, net of interbank deposits.[5]

SYNDICATION AND PARTICIPATION

The type of syndication most frequently encountered in the Euromarkets is the "true syndication." In this a syndicate of banks is assembled by a manager (syndicate manager or lead bank), and they simultaneously make several loans to the borrower pursuant to the terms of the same agreement. In normal circumstances they will rank equally with each other as creditors of the borrower, and each of them enjoys a direct contractual relationship with him. The effect of this is that, subject to any agreements it may have reached with the other members of the syndicate, any one of the banks may sue the borrower if he is in default.

Members of a syndicate are often described as participants. This is unfortunate, because it often leads to confusion with those who hold a participation in a loan. If a lender decides, after having made a loan, that his exposure to the borrower is too great, he may decide to sell part of his exposure to another bank. This is often done when, for example, the selling bank has reached its internally set lending limit for the country where the borrower is based, but wishes to make other loans in that country. While it may technically be feasible for the lender to assign all or part of his interest in the loan to a purchaser, so that the purchaser stands in the same relationship to the borrower as that previously enjoyed by the selling bank, this course is not always followed, for a number of reasons. In England the document effecting the transaction attracts stamp duty at 2 percent; the borrower, particularly if the selling bank is a member of a syndicate, may not be interested in the administrative technicalities involved in registering another lender; but, most important, the selling bank will wish to preserve the appearance of being a direct lender to the borrower.

In circumstances such as this, the selling bank grants a subparticipation to the purchasing bank. This is essentially a subloan between bank and participant that is governed by many of the terms of the main loan between bank and borrower. For the selling bank this preserves the relationship with the borrower, but for the purchasing bank there are a number of pitfalls. A subparticipant has no direct contractual relationship with a borrower, and consequently may not exercise a right of setoff. He normally will not have the benefit or protection of indemnities or yield protection clauses contained in the main agreement between the borrower and the lender. In addition, all repayments of principal or interest on the loan are due to the original lender, who has a duty under his subparticipation arrangement to pass on such sums to the purchaser of the subparticipation. Should the original lender go into liquidation, the liquidator would be entitled to the repayments, and the purchaser would be a mere creditor of the original lender. Some participation agreements are so structured as to constitute a sale of a right to receive payment—in essence an assignment, but one where the selling bank acts as a collecting agent or trustee for the purchasing bank. There are few decided cases on this arrangement. At first sight it appears to offer a way for a subparticipant to be protected, but if the selling bank adopts the procedure common to most banks and mixes funds received by it in respect of loans, then the benefit of a trust or agency will be lost and, again, the purchasing bank will simply have the status of a creditor in the liquidation.

Occasionally a syndicated loan may be structured as a loan by the lead bank, subparticipated to members of a syndicate. This may enable the banks to take advantage of a particularly favorable withholding tax arrangement (or, conversely, avoid a penalizing one) between the country of the borrower and that of the lead bank. Again, it may be advantageous to follow this procedure if one bank is to hold collateral security in cases where it would be impracticable for all members of the syndicate to hold it. In these cases the subparticipant banks should take especial care to see that the documentation is structured to avoid the problems mentioned above.

PARTIES TO A SYNDICATED LOAN

The Borrower

The borrower wishes to raise a large amount of money in an efficient and inexpensive manner. He therefore prefers to deal with one bank. At the same time, however, he sees a benefit in developing relationships with other banks, perhaps over a wide geographical area so that he may become better known and his credit reputation enhanced.

The Syndicate Manager

The syndicate manager or lead bank is the bank that originates the transaction, structures it, assembles the syndicate, supervises the documentation, and, in most cases, services the loan after signing. Its position is the most crucial and, from a legal viewpoint, the most exposed. It owes a duty to the borrower to arrange a syndication, and a duty to the other banks not to mislead or misrepresent any aspect of the credit. It will also be a lender. (These problems are considered in more detail under "Legal Problems," below.)

It is possible for more than one bank to perform the duties of a syndicate manager, and in such cases marketing, publicity, organization of the signing ceremony, and other functions will be divided as agreed among the managing group.

Syndicate Members

Each member of the syndicate will be a direct lender to the borrower and, as such, will need to check and analyze the credit independently. Typically, some of these will be large banks in the same marketplace as the lead bank. Others may be relatively small regional and/or correspondent banks. These latter banks, in particular, need to take great care. While a regional bank will benefit from spreading its exposure among various syndicates in the international arena, it should seriously consider whether it is adequately staffed with bankers of sufficient international experience to judge credits that may be proposed to it.

The Agent

In most cases the syndicate manager performs the functions of agent, but occasionally an affiliate of the manager or another member of the syndicate may do this. Essentially, the agent services the loan from the moment it has been signed until the moment it is repaid. Its responsibilities will be set out in the loan agreement, and include collecting interest and principal on the loan from the borrower and disbursing the same to the syndicate members, distributing information to the syndicate members, and generally acting as their agent. This is a fiduciary relationship.

FIGURE 15.1: Example of a Tombstone Announcement of a Syndicated Eurocredit

This advertisement appears as a matter of record only.

Hellenic Aerospace Industry Limited

U.S. $100,000,000

Medium Term Loan

guaranteed by

The Greek State

managed by

Manufacturers Hanover Limited   The Bank of Nova Scotia Group
Girozentrale und Bank der österreichischen Sparkassen Aktiengesellschaft
Republic National Bank of New York

co-managed by

Banco di Roma   Bankers Trust International Limited
Continental Bank of Canada

provided by

The Bank of Nova Scotia Channel Islands Limited
Girozentrale und Bank der österreichischen Sparkassen Aktiengesellschaft
Manufacturers Hanover Bank (Guernsey) Limited
Republic National Bank of New York
Banco di Roma (Caribbean) Co. Ltd.
Bankers Trust Company
Continental Bank of Canada
County Bank Limited
Irving Trust Company
Österreichische Volksbanken Aktiengesellschaft

Agent Bank

The Bank of Nova Scotia

March, 1981

Source: Reprinted from *Euromoney*, April 1981, p. 83, by permission of the publisher.

The Guarantor

Some agreements rely upon the credit of a guarantor—for instance, a parent company, if the borrower is an offshore financing subsidiary with a nominal capital structure. In these cases the guarantor is included in the main loan agreement, and the guarantee section will usually be drafted so that the guarantor is primarily liable under the loan. This facilitates enforcement against a guarantor with a minimum of formalities.

The parties to a syndicated loan can be readily identified in a "tombstone," such as the one shown in Figure 15.1, which is a public announcement of the details of a Eurocredit.

ORIGINATING A LOAN

A lead bank's objective is, in a nutshell, to find a creditworthy borrower and a group of banks willing to lend, and to "assemble" a loan between those parties. First, it must be sure that the borrower really requires a syndicated Eurocurrency loan and not, for example, domestic finance or funding by means of the issue of bonds or commercial paper. Second, it must thoroughly satisfy itself as to the creditworthiness of the borrower. The lead bank should bear in mind that other members of the prospective syndicate will also be analyzing the credit, and if it is below an acceptable standard, the lead bank's reputation will be damaged. Third, it must propose and agree upon terms with the borrower that it will be able to sell to a syndicate. The lead bank must have a fine knowledge of the types of risks and the spreads over LIBOR for which the market has appetites. Its reputation will be jeopardized if it obtains a mandate from a borrower that it is then unable to syndicate.

Prospective borrowers will be large corporations, governments, or governmental agencies, and it is a matter of marketing skill for a prospective lead manager to attract such a borrower. Sometimes potential borrowers will be referred to a lead manager by affiliate banks that do not operate in the Euromarkets. European and Japanese banks often hold equity stakes in client corporations, and may refer those to branch or affiliate banks active in the Euromarkets. A bank that has already successfully managed a number of Euromarket credits will find it relatively easy to attract prospective borrowers. As always, it is most difficult to find a borrower for the first transaction, which normally results only from a combination of persistence and professionalism tempered by luck.

STRUCTURING A LOAN

Before it begins to think of assembling a syndicate, the prospective syndicate manager must develop with the borrower a clear idea of the purpose and structure of the loan. The purpose must be clearly stated, even if it does not relate to any fresh investment but, rather, to the refinancing of existing debt, working capital finance, or, in the case of a government, balance-of-payments financing. This should be balanced against the capacity of the borrower to repay in a timely fashion. In the case of private sector borrowers, detailed cash flow projections must be prepared and consideration taken of any extraneous factors that may affect the fortunes of the borrower during the term of the proposed loan. A public sector borrower such as a government may not normally go into liquidation, so that questions of sovereign immunity, future political stability of the country in question, the likelihood of its government keeping control over the balance of payments, and the size of its current and future debt in proportion to its gross national product must all be considered.

All of this information is normally presented in an information memorandum that will be circulated among prospective banks. Great care must be taken in the preparation of this document and the way in which it is circulated. (Some of the potential problems are mentioned under "Legal Problems," below.)

Important components in a credit decision made by prospective syndicate members are term, spread (or price), fees, and documentation (or "How effective is the small print?").

Term

It is not possible to say in general terms what is an acceptable tenor for a particular loan. This depends upon what the market is currently accepting, how the country of the borrower is viewed in political and economic terms (whether or not it is a public sector risk), and the financial strength of the borrower as evaluated by the manager and analyzed by prospective syndicate members. At the beginning of 1974, some loans in excess of 12 years were being granted. These terms shrank after the Herstatt crisis in 1974, but have recently been lengthening again. Acceptable maturities are essentially a combination of what might objectively be considered to be financially prudent and what one bank thinks its competitors might accept.

Spread

Loans in the Euromarket are normally made at a margin or spread over LIBOR (or the offered rate in another appropriate market, such as Singapore or Bahrain). This spread depends upon the quality of the risk and the current market assessment of the country concerned. When the demand for funds is high, spreads will also be high. Since 1965 they have varied between 0.375 and 3.0 percent. Average spreads in 1979 and 1980 were 0.76 percent and 0.79 percent, respectively.[6] A borrower will argue strongly to reduce the spread being charged to him. Partly this is to improve his credit rating, but often it is also done in the belief that he is saving himself money by reducing the spread. Although this is perfectly true, a number of borrowers began to realize in 1979, as dollar rates began to rise dramatically, that a matter of 0.25 percent was immaterial when the underlying LIBOR rate had itself risen by, say, 5 percent. It is the total amount of interest to be paid that will affect the borrower.

Fees

If a bank calculates the time costs to it of maintaining credit and syndication departments, it is unlikely that it will make profits on spreads of less than 1 percent. Naturally, some institutions are more efficiently managed than others, and for some banks this break-even point may be higher; for some banks it will be lower. In order to ensure profitability, a structure of fees, often elaborate, is imposed at the time of signing or drawdown of the loan. Management fees of up to 2 percent may be payable to the syndicate manager by the borrower, and participation fees of lesser amounts will be paid, normally by the manager out of the total fee, to members of the syndicate. These participation fees may vary in accordance with the amount to be lent. They are calculated so that in any event the syndicate manager is properly rewarded for its work in assembling the syndicate and managing the transaction.

Other fees may include commitment fees and agency fees. Commitment fees are normally a percentage figure slightly less than the appropriate spread on any amount undrawn under the loan agreement. Many borrowers prefer not to take all the funds to which they may be entitled under an agreement until they need to use them. So that the banks do not suffer by committing a portion of their lending limit without profit, most agreements provide for the borrower to pay a commitment fee to compensate them.

Agency fees are specific amounts that may be provided to compensate the manager or whichever other bank acts as agent during the course of the loan.

Documentation

The basic documentation for a Eurocurrency loan will be a loan agreement. For the most part this will be governed by the law of England or of the state of New York, even though the participants may have little connection with either jurisdiction. These two systems of law have historically been used, and have the advantages of familiarity, the presence of a large pool of legal talent in London and New York, and a more developed body of case law on these financial topics than most other jurisdictions. In many transactions, particularly loans governed by New York law, promissory notes will also be signed. Depending upon the complexity of the transaction, other documents, such as guarantees and security documents, will be used. The loan agreement will normally contain, *inter alia*, the following:

1. Provisions concerning tenor, interest, drawdown, and repayment.
2. Prepayment clause, which will specify the situations where early repayment is required or permitted. It will normally be required in some events of default if funding becomes impossible, if political or other risks adversely affect the market (as specifically

defined in the loan agreement), or if withholding taxes are imposed so as to make the continuation of the loan uneconomic for the borrower. It may be permitted upon due notice or upon payment of a fee, although care must always be taken to see that the fee does not amount to a penalty in law.

3. Representations and warranties. Representations and warranties are statements by the borrower about its condition (such as ability to carry on a business, title to its assets, absence of material litigation or default under other debt arrangements). They normally apply only at the time of signing and/or drawdown, but may be expressed as having to be repeated at intervals throughout the term of the loan. Breach of any of these will constitute an event of default, whereupon the lenders, if they so decide, will be entitled to call the loan.

4. Conditions precedent. Before any drawdown may be made under the loan, the lenders will need to be satisfied in a number of respects. They will need to see the borrower's constitutional documents, copies of necessary exchange control and other government consents, registrations, legal opinions on the legal ability of the borrower to perform under the agreement, the enforceability of the agreement and any supporting documentation, and such other matters as may be required.

5. Covenants. These, in contrast with representations and warranties, constitute promises made by the borrower about his future condition during the course of the loan. They cover such matters as obeying laws and regulations, maintaining government approvals, and paying taxes. Most agreements also contain financial covenants, such as a promise not to exceed a prescribed debt: equity ratio. Negative pledges or prohibitions on liens, mortgages, or encumbrances are contained here, and it is very important to consider exceptions to this in the form of security interests that may arise in some jurisdictions without the deliberate action of the borrower. Breaches of covenants will constitute an event of default enabling the lenders to call the loan.

6. Withholding tax clause. A cardinal principle of the Euromarkets is that interest on loans or bonds should be payable free of withholding tax. In the case of bonds, this attracts more investors, and lending banks have followed the same principle. Accordingly, a clause will be included in the document to ensure that the lending banks receive the interest they expect to receive in full, even if this means that the borrower will have to gross up the net payment and

hand over some withholding tax on the payment to a taxing authority. Should this situation occur, there may be scope for some or all of the paying banks to obtain a credit against their own domestic tax payments. This will depend upon the terms of relevant double taxation treaties, and is a situation that has to be examined very carefully.

7. Government law and jurisdiction. Clauses clarifying these matters are extremely important, and the legal implications have already been considered (see chapter 7).

8. Increased costs and availability of funds. To a lender these clauses, while complicated, are of great importance because they ensure that any increased costs (such as reserve requirements) or risk of underlying funds being available are borne by the borrower. A borrower who thinks he has a term loan of several years may, under the operation of one of these clauses, discover that his loan will be due at the end of the current funding period.

9. Events of default. The clause usually referred to as an "events of default clause" is unfortunately named. It is really a list of events that will enable the banks to accelerate the payment date of the loan, and therefore turn it into a demand facility. The clause is essentially the trigger that enables all the lending banks to terminate the loan and to declare all amounts immediately due. On the occurrence of any of these events (which will usually include failure to pay interest or principal when due), the banks will have the power to call the loan. The mechanism usually provided is that the agent is bound to take such action as banks holding the majority amount of the outstanding debt shall direct. This has the effect that if a minority of banks wish to accelerate the loan, they cannot do so on their own and are precluded from taking any action against the agent bank so long as it has complied with the terms of the agency as set out in the loan agreement. Such minority dissenting banks will normally be able to proceed only for such amounts of interest and principal as are past due. They cannot unilaterally accelerate the debt.

10. Agency clause. This attempts to absolve the agent from breach of any duty to the borrower or, more important, to the other banks. It also sets out the duties of the agent in servicing the loan, and will provide that the agent may have other financial transactions with the borrower without prejudice to the loan in question.

ASSEMBLING THE SYNDICATE

First, the prospective syndicate manager will decide which banks it would like to invite into a syndicate. There will be some who may offer participation in their loans if the prospective manager makes similar offers to them. There will be some correspondent banks and other banks with whom the prospective manager maintains a close relationship—often a syndications officer in Bank A knows, and in the past has worked well with, his counterpart in Bank B. The borrower may suggest to the prospective manager that it include some banks, often in different regional markets, with whom the borrower already maintains a good relationship.

How does the prospective syndicate manager approach the syndicate? The practice is to send an offering telex to those banks it wishes to invite. Some of them may decline. It may then send it to a wider circle of banks. The offering telex will ask for an indication of interest within a specified period. It will contain enough information for banks to be able to decide whether they have an interest in principle in making this type of loan before carrying out any credit analysis. This information will include the amount, maturity, interest rate, purpose, fees, a very brief description of the principal terms of the documentation, the identity of the lawyers who will prepare the loan document, and any other relevant information.

The syndicate manager will then supply such supplementary information as may be necessary to assist in the credit decision. This will initially include the provision of an information memorandum describing the borrower, his financial history and prospects, and other helpful information. On occasions a draft loan agreement is supplied at this stage. However, comments on the drafting are not normally dealt with until banks have indicated firm interest to the manager. Even at this stage they are free to drop out, because they are not committed until the loan agreement is actually signed.

The syndicate manager, on the other hand, may be committed. This depends upon the terms of the mandate document it has secured from the borrower. It may have made a firm commitment, which means that it will be obliged to proceed with the transaction even if it has been unable to find any syndicate banks, and therefore has to take the entire transaction on its own account. It may proceed on a best-efforts basis, which obliges it only to try to put a syndicate together. If it fails, the loan is not made. Obviously this latter method may be embarrassing for both the borrower and the manager. In practice, syndicate managers will often make firm commitments for a relatively small amount, in the hope that a greater amount of interest may be shown; the total proposed loan may then be raised to accommodate this extra interest—subject, of course, to the dictates of prudent credit requirements.

SERVICING THE LOAN

Once the loan agreement has been signed, the agent bank takes over the center of the stage from the syndicate manager. In many cases these are one and the same institution, but now a different function is being performed. The agent's responsibilities include the collection of funds from the banks at drawdown and the distribution of interest and principal to the banks when such payments are due. These are the simple mechanical duties. Its function is also, however, to take steps to enforce the loan, distribute information about the borrower to the other banks, and generally to act in accordance with the wishes of the banks holding a majority amount of the outstanding loan. These duties are normally spelled out in the loan agreement or a separate interbank agreement. In any event, an agent must act strictly in accordance with this document and with the duties of a fiduciary in order to avoid legal liability. In practice an agent must have first-class legal advice, since the most difficult situations tend to arise when a borrower is about to default or has just done so. Then the agent has to see that all banks have as much information as is available, and as promptly as possible.

LEGAL PROBLEMS

When one considers the volume and complexity of transactions in the Eurocurrency markets, it is surprising that there are few reported cases arising out of syndicated loan transactions. One reason for this is that the market, as it is known today, has been in existence only since about 1970. Another is that many of the banks in the market are well-known to each other and to large borrowers, and when problems have arisen, many of them have been settled without recourse to litigation. However, in the light of market history to date and of potential litigation, some problems need to be mentioned.

These arise out of the conduct and duties of a syndicate manager, and are as follows:

1. Securities legislation. It is possible that the syndication of a loan falls within the purview of the U.S. Securities Act of 1933. Thus, if syndication takes place within the United States or if the Securities Act is considered to have jurisdiction over a transaction, the syndicate manager may be liable to the syndicate members under the antifraud provisions of that act. Rule 10b-5(b) of the rules made under that act provides that "It shall be unlawful to make any untrue statements of a material fact or to omit to state a material fact necessary in order to make the statements made in the light of the circumstances under which they were made not misleading." This is a very heavy burden to place on the shoulders of a syndicate manager engaged in preparing an information memorandum and trying to encourage other banks to participate in its loan. Under this standard anything stated or omitted, whether orally or in writing, could involve a liability. This extends to matters that the syndicate manager knows or, with the exercise of due diligence, could know.

The courts have not ruled definitively as to whether a participation in a syndicated loan is a security demanding this high standard of care. A liberal reading of the act indicates that it is a security, but court decisions exist both ways. It is probably a question of fact depending upon the degree to which the syndicate manager interposes itself between the borrower and the syndicate member. The Colocotronis suit[7] was brought against a U.S. syndicate manager in 1976 for allegedly making untrue and incomplete statements concerning the Colocotronis group, and the antifraud provisions were cited. The actions were, however, settled and the courts did not pronounce.

In order to avoid this potential liability, there are a number of steps that a prudent syndicate manager will take. First, it will arrange for the borrower to confirm that the information memorandum is true, correct, and complete, and that the borrower authorizes the distribution of the document. Second, it must be careful to send the memorandum only to banks that are considered to have the experience and expertise to make a good credit judgment. Next, it will be careful to ensure that its own syndication department is aware of all the information that the bank has (other branches or other departments may have information about which the syndication department knows nothing). It will also advise all syndicate members of any conflicts of interest that it may have as a lead bank (such as enjoying security under another loan or being an agent under another Eurocurrency credit agreement).

2. Misrepresentation. Avoidance of liability here is more than adequately covered by the precautions desirable to avoid securities legislation liability.

3. Common law fraud. It should not be necessary to consider this, since it involves an intention to deceive, and if any bank attempts to syndicate a credit on this basis, it deserves to suffer all the penalties of the law that are available. In practice, banks prefer to deal with other banks that they know, and if they follow this precept, the chances of participating in a fraudulently induced credit are minimal.

4. Negligent misstatement. This is another potential source of liability that is more than covered by the precautions taken to minimize liability under the securities legislation. If a statement is made negligently, and a syndicate member relies on that statement, thereby suffering loss, then a breach of duty will have taken place, and in some jurisdictions damages will be awarded.

Since syndication takes place on an international basis, and much of it is outside the borders of the United States, the securities acts will not apply in every case. When they do not apply, the potential sources of liability for a syndicate manager will be misrepresentation, common law fraud, and negligent misstatement, together with any other locally effective sources of liability. It is submitted, however, that if a syndicate manager takes the precautions listed above to minimize liability under the securities acts, in addition to any local requirements, it will not only have taken the correct legal steps but also have acted with a high degree of commercial prudence.

The position of the agent in a syndicate has already been described, and it is worth dwelling for a moment on its legal predicament. Since it has to act in accordance with its mandate as set out in the loan agreement, it should make sure that the agency clause and any other clauses affecting its function are as explicit as possible. Even so, after the loan has been signed, the agent will be the conduit between the borrower and the banks and, as their agent, will be liable for any breach of the terms of that agency. It will owe a duty of care and diligence, and in order to perform this, it must make all information that it has available about the borrower to the banks at all times. This applies even if the information is deliberately or inadvertently made available to a department of the agent bank other than the syndication or agency department.

Some of these duties appear to be simple enough at face value, but if disclosure of information will involve the agent in a conflict of interest, it will have to tread very carefully indeed. For example, the disclosure of some information about the borrower may be harmful to the borrower. In this case the agent should persuade the borrower to make the disclosure. The agent may have lent to the borrower under other facilities or may be an agent under other facilities, and it may therefore have a conflict when it comes to recovery of money from a borrower who has insufficient funds. This type of conflict should always be provided for in the agency clause.

In the event of a default, the agent may need to act very quickly, and should always have first-class legal counsel available. Any delay may involve the risk of liability.

The best protection available to an agent is to ensure an explicit agency clause, to obtain in the loan agreement an indemnity from the other banks for all operations it may perform or omit (other than cases of gross negligence or willful default), to act promptly, and to retain first-class legal counsel.

CURRENT TRENDS IN THE SYNDICATED EUROLOAN MARKET

The Euromarkets in all their forms (and syndicated loans are merely one form) grew and developed to accommodate various demands. Currently there are many holders of offshore currencies, principally U.S. dollars, and many prospective takers, whether issuers of bonds or borrowers under loan transactions.

Loans have increased in amount (albeit without allowing for inflation) at a very high rate since 1970. However, as the old loans are repaid, there are new borrowers and other transactions coming along to take their place.

It is impossible to make any valid predictions about the future of these markets and transactions, since they are a function of demand for and availability of funds created by political and financial forces. Without the ability to predict interest rates in the future—or, indeed, the next Iran, Afghanistan, or Poland—categorical pronouncements on the future of the market are worthless. That having been said, there are some pointers.

1. As the market has developed in the past in response to demand, so it will in the future. Banks that have lent to Iran and Poland are spending more effort on analyzing country risk and spreading their portfolio. Accordingly, some countries that have borrowed heavily will find it difficult to raise further Euromarket funds, except from those institutions that have already lent heavily and will advance more funds as part of rescue packages.

2. There have been suggestions that regulatory controls should be imposed on the Euromarkets. This is not considered to be an effective measure, since controls would have to be imposed in individual geographic markets, and if any market were so controlled, the deposits and other transactions would simply move to another venue. However, that is not to say that there is no control even today. Many countries keep a close watch over the operations of their own banks anywhere in the world, and these banks will therefore have to observe their own capital ratio requirements even when lending out of a foreign center. Such controls, even operated from the home base, will help to prevent a bank from imprudently overreaching itself.

3. Many of the transactions proposed in 1980 and 1981 have been project finance transactions or loans made for the purpose of a particular construction or other development. Documentation for this type of transaction, which includes syndicated guarantee and letter of credit facilities, is constantly being developed and improved.

4. The center of the Euromarket is still in London, but more syndications are taking place in Hong Kong, Bahrain, Singapore, and other centers. The decision by the Board of Governors of the Federal Reserve System on June 9, 1981, to make the appropriate regulatory amendments (Regulations D and Q) in order to permit the establishment of international banking facilities in the United States may lead to syndication centers emerging in New York, Miami, Los Angeles, San Francisco, Chicago, and other cities. One fact that has to be remembered is that syndicate managers must be able to meet and talk regularly. If London and Hong Kong are already established centers for this, it is very expensive to set up further offices, staffed with expensive personnel, in other centers, unless there is clearly syndication business there waiting to be done. It is possible that a

small number of major centers will continue to develop, together with a few smaller ones (such as Bahrain) dealing with regional syndications of lower amounts.

The Euromarkets are already developed and well known, and afford a structure to provide investing and financing opportunities in the future. They grew initially because the demand was there, and they will adapt as demand changes. While the syndication market of the 1990s may bear little resemblance to the one known in the 1980s, it is hard to believe that such a market will decline into obscurity. The inventive spirit of the Euromarkets is too resilient.

NOTES

1. National Banking Act, 12 U.S.C. 84.
2. *Euromoney Annual Financing Report, 1981*, supplement to *Euromoney*, March 1981, p. 20.
3. Ibid., p. 22.
4. Ibid.
5. "Survey on Money and Finance," *The Economist*, November 29, 1980, p. 24.
6. *Euromoney Annual Financing Report*, op. cit., p. 16.
7. *In re Colocotronis Tanker* Sec. Litigation, 420 F. Supp. 998 (JPMDL 1976).

SUGGESTED REFERENCES

Mathis, F. John, ed. *Offshore Lending by U.S. Commercial Banks*. 2nd ed. Ch. 9. Washington, D.C., and Philadelphia: Bankers' Association for Foreign Trade and Robert Morris Associates, 1981.

Rendell, Robert S., ed. *International Financial Law*. London: Euromoney Publications, 1980.

16 LOANS AND PLACEMENTS TO FOREIGN BANKS

Robert S. Damerjian

Extension of credit between banks in different countries is not significantly different from credit extended between banks in the United States. In either case a credit risk must be assumed, although it is always more difficult to analyze offshore credits because of differences in governments and accounting, as well as in other foreign practices. International extension of credit takes place in many forms: notable loans, interbank deposits, purchase of negotiable Eurodollar CDs and Yankee CDs, foreign exchange, acceptances, letters of credit, and overdraft facilities.

Most credit extensions in international banking are basically used to finance some form of international trade, although leakage does occur with the funds converted for domestic use. Regardless of the form that credit extension has taken, once it has been determined that the repayment ability of the borrower is in jeopardy, it is generally too late for the lending institution to take steps to secure its credit. In the modern world of international banking, a lending institution may not fully recognize the exposure it may have with other institutions at any one time. The ability of even the best banks to fully recognize their exposure in various credits at any one time is limited. While an institution may extend a firm lending line, the various areas of the organization may also be extending credits that in the aggregate exceed the confirmed line. The possibility that the foreign exchange area, CD trading, interbank placements, and accept-portfolio, in addition to the loan extension, all combined at any one time, may exceed the credit line should not be dismissed. More than one bank has discovered such overextensions when it became known that a credit was in difficulty and it was too late for recovery.

Bank-to-bank international business takes two basic forms: deposits and loans. In both instances extension of credit is involved. In recent years the growth of the Eurodollar interbank market (both negotiable CDs and nonnegotiable deposits) and of loans has been substantial.

The sheer size of individual transactions in both categories clearly indicates the need for credit review and market knowledge of the reputation of the borrowing banks. Knowledge of domestic banks, while helpful, cannot alone be relied upon to measure international credit risks. The participants are a rapidly growing list domiciled in a number of countries, each possessing its own economic, financial, and political considerations.

While the credit record with respect to international bank depositing and lending has been good, risks are still inherent, particularly as the number of participants increases and international credit conditions begin, possibly, to experience strain. The volatility in interest rates and foreign exchange alone can create great uncertainty for individual banks with respect to their creditworthiness.

USE OF CREDIT FACILITIES

Because money is fungible once it is lent or deposited with another bank, its final use is lost. Interbank credit facilities are obtained for many uses, ranging from a back-up facility for credit crises to supplying foreign exchange. The maturity and terms for the various types of facilities vary almost as much as the underlying reasons for the credit requests. In the lending area the most significant need for the borrowing bank generally is to relend the funds to its own clients for the financing of imports of goods or capital equipment. The longer the term of the transaction, the greater the need to "front" the transaction to refinance the local borrower. Interbank correspondent relationships are in many instances used to finance the latter type of transaction. Although many are self-liquidating, many are for longer-term capital items, which means that terms are longer than in the past.

Regardless of the original purpose of the loan (or deposit), it is all but impossible in most instances to trace the extended funds or to seek specific collateral should a default occur. In the event of a default, the maturity question becomes almost academic.

Not in any order of importance, the following cover probably 90 percent of the proceeds of interbank loans and deposits:

1. Acquiring of interbank deposits to redeposit with other banks in the interbank market. While the business is marginal on a matched book basis, on a mismatched book it can be very profitable, although funding risks for the deposit-taking bank are real. In early 1981 several banks, both domestically and in their international operations, had mismatches that resulted in sizable interest losses completely unrelated to any credit risk. It is difficult (until too late) to discover if the borrowing bank has a mismatched book, even if it is known that the purpose of the borrowing is for interbank placements. The credit risk in this activity is the redepositing in a poorer credit risk bank for an increase in spread, even where the bank is engaged in matched book redepositing. The volatility of interest rates and foreign exchange since 1980 has caused some concern among banks lending interbank deposits where the proceeds are being used for "interbank trading."

2. To provide foreign exchange. The purpose is not to allow the borrowing banks to obtain exchange for open market trading, but to provide exchange to finance general imports to the country through importing clients. This type of loan may be seasonal, short-term, or long-term. In any case, the general credit of the bank must be relied upon for repayment, since it is all but impossible to obtain specific collateral for this type of borrowing.

3. Loans to government-owned banks, government agencies, or the government. While the loan is made to the bank, if the latter is government-owned or -controlled, the lending institution must basically look to the government in measuring credit risk. This does not mean the individual bank should not be reviewed from a credit point of view. In these instances the banks are the conduit through which the borrowings are channeled.

4. Collateralized interbank loans. This type of loan is highly unusual, and means the borrowing bank cannot borrow on its own credit. When a bank must secure its interbank borrowing, it usually means noncollateralized borrowing is not available through the normal channels. A growing number of foreign banks have issued short-to-intermediate-term notes (three to seven years) in recent

years. These have been both fixed-rate and floating-rate obligations, and in some cases have been purchased by other banks. They have almost all been negotiable, and a secondary market exists. These are, however, not secured, and are basically no different from debentures of the borrowing institution. That a lending bank will have the ability to obtain collateral after an interbank loan has been executed is unlikely, unless special provisions have been written into the loan agreement.

5. General funding loan. Loans made for the general use of the bank for internal purposes usually take the form of short-to-intermediate-term notes, as described elsewhere. Very short-term funds are usually obtained in the interbank market for periods ranging from overnight to one year. These borrowings are almost exclusively unsecured if and when they are booked. In most instances such borrowings, in contrast with deposits of the same maturity, are more expensive and more difficult to execute. They do not originate (as do CDs) through the interbank market, but through negotiations with underwriting and investment firms.

6. Standby facility loans. Such loans are rare because they will most likely be activated when conditions in the marketplace are unsettled, with the result that the granting institution may also be facing difficulties. These facilities can take the form of either a deposit or a loan, and usually are paid for through a fee arrangement. These standby credits are generally sought by smaller banks that from time to time may find their name unacceptable in the marketplace because of uncertain or abnormal conditions. This "back-up" facility is also used by banks entering the international money markets as a source of funding until their name is established. These credit agreements also specify a rate usually based at something over LIBOR.

USE OF LINES

Foreign banks that use credit lines in either a loan or an interbank deposit form basically are not concerned with the source of funds. The actual funds may come from either the head office or a branch of the lending institution. In many cases the loans or deposits are made from London, or from Nassau, Grand Cayman, or another offshore branch. Regardless of the source of lending, a credit exposure exists that requires proper credit reviews and approvals. The fact that a loan or interbank deposit is made from a U.S. branch to a foreign bank in the same country adds little to its collectibility should the borrower default.

Occasionally, less well-known banks may obtain guarantees from larger banks (for loans rather than interbank deposits) for a fee. The value of the guarantee must, therefore, be measured by the credit standing of the guaranteeing bank, although to some extent the lender has "two-named paper." In case of default, many types of legal complications should be expected as a result of local laws and regulations.

Generally in the event of default a depositor ranks ahead of a lender. However, different countries have different laws, with the result that it may be possible that the two parties are equal. Should a bank that has outstanding foreign exchange contracts, loans, deposits, acceptances, guarantees, and other liabilities default, the "lineup" of creditors in a foreign country may be very difficult to assess without substantial legal research and cost. These hazards are nevertheless real. It is very possible for one bank to be holding all of the latter liabilities if the failing bank was a close international correspondent.

INTERBANK DEPOSITS

The placement of interbank deposits, both negotiable and non-negotiable, cannot be ignored as a credit risk. The amounts are enormous, with the minimum transactions approaching $5.0 million. While the maturity in most instances is shorter than that of the inter-bank loan, the credit risk nevertheless is present. In view of the fact that the negotiable Eurodollar CD gives the depositor greater flexi-bility (at some concession in rate), by possibly allowing a sale should the credit of the bank come under suspicion, the market may already have recognized the deteriorating credit situation, with the result that no bids may exist.

Most interbank time deposit placements have maturities of 90 days or less, although maturities of up to 5 years are not uncommon. Floating-rate, longer-term negotiable Eurodollar CDs have also in-creased substantially, with the result that credit extension periods have been lengthened. Interbank commitments such as "Rolly Pollys" pose a new type of credit extension heretofore not witnessed. Under the latter arrangement, the placing bank under contract must roll over a CD every three months for a given period, which may extend up to three years, at the prevailing LIBOR rate plus some prefixed spread. Should the accepting bank encounter financial stress at the time of a rollover, the depositing institution may attempt to refuse to refund. The major credit problem in this situation continues to be the period between the refundings when no market may exist and the depositing bank is holding the CD of the failed or failing institution.

The interbank market, while very sizable and broad-based, nevertheless is very sensitive to credit conditions that affect the name of an individual bank operating in the market. Generally, well before a particular bank's name is tarnished in the market, the dealer fraternity and participants have already recognized the problem. While it is not the purpose of this chapter to examine the complexities of interbank trading, traders are keenly aware of increasing premiums paid by deposit-seeking banks because of individual financial difficulties or of higher rates due to increases in paper outstanding.

The fact that the interbank deposit market is largely one in which contracts are arranged through brokers rather than directly tends to make most of the transactions impersonal. Those operating the individual trading (placement) desks are, therefore, largely guided by internal lines established by various credit committees. When a particular credit has begun to deteriorate in the interbank market, the traders, because of their daily contact with the market, are generally the first to recognize the problem. Deposits with various branches besides head offices must also be considered in any overall exposure assessment.

The ability of a bank to fund or refund liabilities under various market conditions in most maturity sectors is the supreme test of strength. In times of financial stress, such as was experienced during the Bankhaus D. I. Herstatt affair, a rush to quality becomes evident, with the less-than-prime names either unable to fund themselves comfortably or forced to pay substantial premiums.

The fact that in the interbank dealing function, interbank deposits between two organizations may exist concurrently should not cause relaxation of credit qualifications. Differences in maturities may exist in addition to the question of "right of offset" and the problems associated with explaining a position to the market.

RISK EXPOSURE

All international lending and depositing entails risk. In lending to and depositing with foreign banks, there is an omnipresent risk of bank failure in addition to country risk. The overall risk range extends from complete loss to partial loss or a long delay in repayment. Repayment, but at a reduced interest rate, is also a reality. Rescheduling of credits in many instances means longer terms and further credit problems.

Bank Failures

Complete bank failures, both domestic and international, are rare. In many cases, while the stockholders may eventually receive nothing, the depositors eventually receive all or most of their funds. Lenders (bondholders), who rank behind depositors, may have a partial recovery, depending on the seriousness of the failure. Because banks are examined and are involved with the public's funds, governments tend to work closely with institutions in difficulty, in order to prevent their failure. The spillover or secondary negative impact on a country's internal and external financial stability, and the confidence it may undermine, are too great to be treated lightly.

Before a bank is allowed to fail, with possible losses to depositors, government, central bank, or other bank support (through merger or guarantees) is generally arranged. While these arrangements may secure all depositors, others, such as noteholders and foreign exchange and acceptance beneficiaries, may not be as fortunate.

Because international bank failures are rare, there is no general statement of how, or in what order, creditors are paid. Each case is different, for many reasons. Two identical conditions may be handled differently, depending on the nation in which the failed institution is incorporated. While it is difficult to generalize in an area where failures are few and far between, it would appear that deposit obligations (particularly short-term) are paid first, so as to maintain some form of financial confidence in the marketplace. Restructuring of longer obligations, particularly loans at reduced interest rates or reduced amounts, generally are sought concurrently, as part of a stabilization or reorganization plan.

The longer the term of the obligation, the greater the potential risk. The ability of the borrowing institution to service and repay long-term debt is always difficult to predict, regardless of the original purpose of the loan. Because it is virtually impossible to trace the flow of funds through the bank, the original purpose of a note issue generally is lost quickly, with the result that lenders must have confidence in the overall ability of the institution to generate earnings to repay all deposits and debts as they mature. In any case, depositing or lending to foreign banks should not be done on the theory that some form of government or other official aid will be forthcoming, should the borrowing institution fall into difficult times.

Country Risk

Overshadowing individual bank credit analysis is the question of country risk. Regardless of the quality of an individual foreign bank, the government of the country in question ultimately will determine the fate of all payments should an economic or financial crisis occur. Therefore, the risk a bank assumes in lending to foreign banks—or, for that matter, to any foreign concern—constitutes its foreign risk exposure.

The risk exposure assumed by a bank in dealing with foreign banks is a product of a wide spectrum of activities, and is defined by the extent of the institution's involvement. The principal areas of "hidden" exposure are the following:

- Acceptances owned
- Letters of credit purchased or confirmed
- Foreign exchange contracts
- Federal funds sold
- Interbank deposits or negotiable CDs owned
- Clearing payments (direct or through Edge corporations)
- Commercial paper or notes issued by bank, subsidiaries, and affiliates
- Current accounts (working balances).

It is substantially easier for a bank to capture the various exposures from the home office than from banks with a worldwide network of international operations and various time zones. The ability to collect this information at a central point is still questionable, although a number of banks appear to have a system that is achieving this goal.

Not only is total exposure important to recognize, but information about the maturity distribution of such exposure should be immediately available. Offsetting balances and safekeeping items should be noted and recorded.

In addition, the role of the central bank and its relationship to the government must be considered. In the long run, both economic and political stability must be present for the banking system to function effectively and for the country's foreign exchange rates to maintain a reasonable parity with those of other countries. Anyone not believing country risk is real in recent times need only examine the multitude of financial and banking problems that arose from the Iranian situation in 1980–81. This situation tested many aspects of international banking, ranging from payments under letters of credit to the freezing of assets by both official and private sectors of more than one country. The problems that arose from this episode are too numerous to note, except to say that as late as 1981, many claims and counterclaims were still unresolved. Despite the fact that no bank failed, government directives appear to overrule normal banking law.

The role of the central bank and regulatory authorities should not be underestimated. While it is no guarantee that official aid will be provided in times of stress, countries with well-developed internal banking systems generally have reasonably good examination procedures and strong central banks that aid in the early detection of banking problems.

TYPES OF FOREIGN BANKS

Foreign banking institutions can be categorized into five main groups:

1. Government banks that are completely government-owned and service most of the government's financial needs
2. Government agency banks that are government-owned and service particular areas of the economy, such as agriculture or export

3. Banks of national status and importance that are government-owned or owned by the private sector of the country
4. Commercial banks operating within the country, many of which are well known but do not have "international status" as viewed by the market
5. Noncommercial bank institutions, such as merchant banks and discount houses.

Government Banks

It is safe to say that a government-owned bank is probably a better credit risk than a privately owned bank in the same country, although it is possible that both could fail or temporarily not meet their internal and external obligations. Government-owned banks are basically only as good as the government itself. This is not to say that a new government will accept the liabilities of the prior administration. On the other hand, a stable government does not "turn over." Government-owned banks created by "new" governments need careful scrutiny. Their ability to repay is based on factors well beyond financial analysis. Their livelihood depends on politics and the health of the local economy. Because government banks perform many tasks for the government, their statements are somewhat different from those of the normal commercial bank. The problem in such an analysis is the lack of comparison. Attempting to compare government-owned banks in one country with those in another country is less than fruitful.

Information on government-owned banks can be obtained from the IMF and the World Bank, since both of these institutions deal largely through government-owned banks. The real ability to service and repay debt must depend on the government, the economy, and the management of the bank itself. Moreover, politics cannot be ignored.

Nongovernment Banks

These banks may range in size from those that rank as the largest in a country (or possibly the world) to those that are small, independent operations. The factors that should be analyzed for this category of banks are noted later in this chapter. In some instances nongovernment banks are so large that the banking system of a country could not operate without their survival. In such cases the likelihood of official government intervention to assure their continuance is extremely high. Where the cutoff between major and nonmajor banks lies is difficult to assess. At what level or size the government or other banks would step in to offer financial aid cannot be easily defined. Needless to say, however, somewhere in the analysis this should be noted.

For obvious reasons the medium-size-to-smaller bank needs greater screening. Problems associated with such institutions can be solved only by the banks themselves. They have limited resources both domestically and internationally. Their funding ability under adversity is rapidly diminished. This is true even for those banks which under normal conditions are active participants in global funding.

In the medium-to-smaller institution, management's reputation becomes increasingly important in the analysis. Their limited resources mean that management's skills must make up for the lack of capital or for smaller size. As will be described later, a full analysis of the financial statements must be completed in order to properly evaluate the ability of the bank to meet its liabilities and to withstand reasonably negative news.

Specialized Banks

In the case of specialized banks, such as merchant banks or discount houses, the same problems exist as in the case of medium-to-smaller banks, except that they are greater. Each firm's business is slightly different from the other's. By most standards they are highly leveraged. Their earnings tend to fluctuate more than those of a commercial bank. Turnover in personnel is somewhat higher. Earnings projections are more difficult to make. Both contingent liabilities and inner reserves are more difficult to establish. Obtaining new capital in times of stress is more difficult for them. Their earnings and financial reporting are more complicated, making analysis more challenging. Their businesses are less understood. Their earnings in some cases are based on factors beyond their control, such as interest rates or foreign exchange movements. One bad decision, because of the impact it may have on the business, can severely affect earnings.

BANK CREDIT REVIEW

Because of foreign accounting and other customs, foreign bank balance sheets and income statements tend to be somewhat difficult for the inexperienced credit analyst to analyze. Banks active in the international markets generally use their senior credit analysts to research foreign bank statements. Because foreign bank credits are less well understood than those of domestic banks, a somewhat more conservative posture toward the foreign credit should be taken.

Generally it is more difficult to obtain as much data on foreign bank operations as on those of domestic banks—hence, the need for greater detail. In many instances supplementary inquiries will be required, such as those directed to bank management and competitor banks, as well as to correspondents.

The major areas of investigation are listed below. They are not in order of importance.

• Earnings record and reason for any major deviations
• Growth in assets, deposits, borrowings, and capital, and reason for any unusual deviation
• Quality of income
• Loan losses and/or other major losses
• Reputation of bank in both local market and international money markets
• Level at which bank's obligations trade in local and international markets
• Type of general banking the institution is engaged in, including major areas of loan and investment concentration
• Ownership of institution
• Major subsidiaries and their earnings contribution and risks
• Lines or back-up credits, both domestic and international
• Trends in foreign exchange earnings
• Management changes
• Liquidity position
• Contingent liabilities
• Balance sheet compared with those of other local banks
• Funding sources, including foreign network
• Unrealized gains or losses not shown on balance sheet
• Gap analysis (sensitivity ratio), particularly if bank is active in interbank market

- Nature of hidden reserves
- Expansion plans of bank.

Ownership and Management

Both ownership and management are important in the analysis of foreign banks. From time to time, in both the domestic and the international markets, individual names or families become associated with particular banks. Depending on the name(s), the reputation may range from unacceptable to first-class. Most lenders do not basically desire to deal with another bank if there is questionable ownership, even if the earnings or financial conditions appear adequate. It is difficult to describe the "financial uneasiness" that exists when the latter situation is present.

In any analysis of ownership, careful checking with local competition and well-regarded individuals will generally give the first clues of undesirables taking a position directly or indirectly in the institution.

The ability to measure management is difficult by itself. Management's success or failure must ultimately be the financial result over a reasonable period of time. A consistent upward earning pattern, coupled with reasonable ratios and small turnover in management, is basically a good sign. In most cases it is impossible to know management in the interbank deposit market unless the depositing bank restricts itself to a very small list. One must depend on the financial numbers and information gathered from all other sources regarding the owners and the management. While knowledge of the board of directors is helpful, it should not be relied on alone. Even the best boards are not made up entirely of individuals who remain informed about current practices and events. Some boards still have members who are figureheads. A large turnover of directors or key officers should be carefully screened. A bank cannot have high turnover without some deterioration in its basic fabric.

Banks that show large swings in foreign exchange or securities trading profits should be carefully analyzed. Managements that allow nontraditional, nonrecurring types of income to become significant may not be completely acceptable, viewed in terms of conservative management.

Early Signs of Problems

In many cases the early signs of problems are reflected in the marketplace, the borrowing institution paying over the market to attract deposit or loan funds. Traders and participants in the market are quick to observe growing rate differentials between institutions that result from market knowledge that a particular institution may be facing difficult times. Banks' financial conditions do not deteriorate overnight. Bank creditworthiness is judged by both the price of a bank's stock (if publicly owned) and the rate the bank pays for overnight or term funds. The collective judgment of the marketplace is difficult to escape in terms of the cost of money reflecting the creditworthiness of individual banks.

Capital and Ultimate Strength

The traditional role of capital for both domestic and international banks is the cushion between deposits and assets. It is there to support the deposit or other liability levels of the bank. It is limited, except possibly for foreign banks that are fully or partially government-owned. The degree of ownership by other major institutions can also mean that additional capital may be available should the bank's own capital be impaired. The degree of "back-up" capital is difficult to assess unless it is clearly defined. While support may be forthcoming from other owner-banks in times of difficulty, the degree of financial support should be viewed on a conservative basis.

An examination of foreign bank capital should be done against competing institutions. The major problem, however, is the measuring of inner or hidden reserves. The amount may be significant, yet substantially different in percentage terms, between competing local institutions. The capital accounts should be reviewed, and "guarantees" of items that may not appear on the balance sheet ("contingent liabilities") should be closely examined. In many instances they are difficult to detect.

The question of capital should not be viewed lightly. Once it becomes known that an institution is in difficulty, the drain of deposits that generally occurs is swift and the question of capital becomes paramount.

Evaluating a Bank's Financial Condition

Ultimately, someone must analyze the bank statements and inquire about loans and deposits. Regardless of the bank's size or reputation, the periodic review must be performed. The major problem in this analysis, of course, is the differences in the reporting between U.S. banks and those in foreign countries. Compounding this problem is the fact that each country has its own accounting practices, which makes comparable analysis very difficult but not impossible. Only the best and senior financial analysts should be given this assignment. As with domestic banks, foreign banks' accounting and reporting are undergoing substantial change, with the result that up-to-date accounting and reporting news for each country must be known.

To some extent the financial condition of individual banks depends on the central bank, its method of operation, and the role it plays in the banking system. Factors such as ease or difficulty in rediscounting, government-guaranteed loans, and foreign exchange control directly or indirectly influence the statement of the bank over a period of time.

Individual bank analysis should take into consideration earning trends, deposit growth, capital, losses, return on assets, leverage, and other ratios or percentages that appear reasonable. The ratios or percentages should, however, be measured against banks operating in their own country, rather than against banks in the United States. Any bank that stands out from others in a comparison year after year should be further analyzed for specific reasons. What may at first appear to be an asset could quickly become a liability or negative factor. What is acceptable in a foreign country may not be acceptable in the United States.

Directly influencing individual banks in a foreign country is the government's role in the financial market through subsidiaries, grants, guarantees, or partial ownership positions. Other areas of investigation are government deposit guarantees, foreign exchange profits, government or government agency deposits, types of deposit growth (or no growth), and types of business in which the bank is directly or indirectly engaged.

Equally important in any analysis is the country risk exposure that individual banks have in their loan portfolios. The impact of this surfaced during the Polish situation in late 1981, when a number of German commercial banks revealed their individual Polish loan exposures. These exposures overshadow any and all other factors concerning the banks' finances. This type of unexpected development clearly indicates the risks that must be considered in the individual analysis.

The volatility of both interest and foreign exchange rates has brought to the surface another dimension in bank analysis: gap analysis or interest sensitivity. Basically this analysis attempts to measure the profile of the bank's interest-sensitive liabilities versus its interest-sensitive assets. The balance of the sensitivity becomes pronounced when interest rates rise or decline sharply over the interest cycle and quickly impair the earnings of the bank. During the volatile interest rate period of 1980-81, a number of banks found themselves either liability-sensitive or asset-sensitive at the wrong time, or found substantial maturity mismatches of assets and liabilities. In some instances both conditions prevailed, resulting in a severe earnings squeeze. The latter conditions are completely separate from any loan and credit problems. In those instances where substantial swings in earnings result from the various mismatches, bank management has generally adhered to a firm position on interest rates. Absolute, firm views on interest rates should be avoided by bank managements. The more conservative approach is to have a more balanced book or one that is moderately unbalanced in either direction.

The major problem in attempting to measure the sensitivity is obtaining sufficient and accurate data. U.S. banks are only now publishing some information that can aid in this type of analysis. In the case of foreign banks, this information probably can be obtained only through conversations with bank management.

Lending banks are interested in relationships that shed light on the direction in which a foreign bank appears to be moving. In identifying relationships and analyzing trends, a lending bank will make use of ratio analysis. While a detailed analysis of individual bank ratios should be kept and updated, only a certain number of them need be closely monitored, with the other ratios used as supporting data. The data should be viewed over a period of time and, as noted elsewhere, should be compared with those of other banks operating in the same country.

The following ratios should be noted, analyzed, and considered as major factors:

Deposits to capital
Loans to deposit
Liquid assets to deposits
Inner reserves (if obtainable) to total capital
Growth of published capital
Deposit growth
Contingent liability growth
Trend in foreign exchange profits
Trend in reported earnings
Loan or asset concentration to one country, borrower, or industry.

An analyst should look for balanced growth in earnings as well as total asset growth. At the same time the sources of earnings and their vulnerability to various influences should be noted. Over time the major ratios noted above should promote sufficient insight into any bank's financial condition. No one ratio is more important than another; hence, each must be reviewed in the context of the total. Significant alterations should be noted and explained.

SUGGESTED REFERENCES

Angelini, Anthony, Maximo Eng, and Francis A. Lees. *International Lending, Risk and the Euromarket.* New York: John Wiley and Sons, 1979.

Association of Reserve City Bankers. *Country Exposure Measurement and Reporting Practices of Member Banks.* New York: ARCB, 1977.

Brackenridge, A. Bruce. "Country Exposure, Country Limits, and Lending to LDC's." *Journal of Commercial Bank Lending,* July 1977, pp. 3-13.

Field, Peter. "Meet the New Breed of Banker: The Political Risk Expert." *Euromoney,* July 1980, pp. 9-10, 12-13, 15, 18-19, 21.

International Monetary Fund. *International Capital Markets: Recent Developments and Short Term Prospects.* Washington, D.C.: IMF, 1980.

Johnson, Howard. "Assessing Risks in Foreign Lending." *Burroughs Clearing House,* June 1980, pp. 12-13, 43-45.

Mathis, John, ed. *Offshore Lending by U.S. Commercial Banks.* 2nd ed. Washington, D.C., and Philadelphia: Bankers' Association for Foreign Trade and Robert Morris Associates, 1981.

Nagy, Pancras J. "Country Risk—A Quality Indicator for the International Loan Portfolio." *Euromoney*, April 1980, pp. 165–66, 169.

Riley, William H. "How Regional Banks Approach Country Exposure and Country Risk." *Journal of Commercial Bank Lending*, March 1980, pp. 33–44.

Sofia, A. Zuheir. "Sovereign Borrowing—How to Rationalize Country Risk Ratios." *Euromoney*, September 1979, pp. 76, 79, 81–82, 85.

17 FINANCING FOREIGN GOVERNMENTS

Anthony Angelini

Why do commercial banks lend to foreign governments? How different is lending to these borrowers, compared with lending to domestic borrowers? Why do foreign governments borrow? What are their characteristics? What are the various sources and forms of borrowing? Do commercial banks ignore domestic borrowing needs in favor of lending to foreign governments, including loans to Eastern bloc countries? Who are the leading borrowers? Who are the leading lenders? In this chapter we shall answer these questions by surveying lending to foreign governments.

CHARACTERISTICS OF LENDING TO FOREIGN GOVERNMENTS

Since industrialized countries have access to funds in their domestic markets, have established creditworthiness internationally, and therefore may borrow abroad, our study of lending to foreign governments is confined to those countries designated as less developed (LDCs). There are two types: oil-exporting and nonoil-exporting. The World Bank divides the latter into five categories, classified in terms of per capita income: high-income (over $2,500), upper middle-income ($1,136–2,500), intermediate middle-income ($551–1,135), lower middle-income ($281–550), and low-income ($280 or less). This classification divides LDCs according to borrowing status.[1] The poorest LDCs seek aid from such agencies as the World Bank and the

407

International Development Agency (IDA), in some cases borrowing at zero interest cost. In short, it is the commercially developed countries that are eligible for loans from commercial banks, and lenders specify factors used in evaluating the creditworthiness of the borrowing countries. The Morgan Guaranty Trust Company of New York looks at 14 factors divided into 4 groups (see Table 17.1).

Another characteristic of lending to foreign governments is the assessment of country risk and the setting of limits on the amount of country borrowing based on this assessment. (This has been discussed in chapter 9.)

A third characteristic is sovereign risk and immunity. Tracing the history of international lending since the early 1960s reveals that commercial banks literally followed their private domestic corporate customers abroad by lending short term to help them finance trade and investment. With the skyrocketing fuel prices during the 1970s, attention in international lending shifted to financing foreign governments' energy needs as OPEC drained financial resources from oil-consuming countries. Corporate borrowing diminished in importance, and the commercial bankers were faced with a different set of factors in making loans to LDCs. Commercial bankers had established new evaluation standards in lending to these countries compared with private corporate borrowers, for in addition to looking at economic data, an evaluation of political and social factors had to be made. Some countries, such as Poland, did not even have data on their balance of payments.

Expert credit evaluation is essential for lending to LDCs. The skill required exceeds that necessary in making loans to domestic borrowers. If sovereign governments default on their loans, they cannot be sued without their permission. The courts of the lending bank's country cannot give judgment on loans made to foreign borrowers. For example, one of Costa Rica's creditors, Libra Bank, was granted an attachment order by the New York State Supreme Court against Costa Rica's Banco Nacional's account in the Bank of America in New York City. The order proved worthless because Costa Rica had withdrawn the funds from its account. Usually, instead of resorting to a drastic action, like declaring default by a borrower, lenders agree to a rescheduling of the debt, which may have to be worked out with as many as 100 banks. Depending on the type of loan made, some of the lending banks may be difficult or even impossible to contact. Had the loan been made to a private corporate

TABLE 17.1. Creditworthiness: Some Factors to be Taken into Account

A. Policy factors
  1. quality of economic team; strength of central bank; impact on political leadership
  2. monetary/budget policies; wage/price policies
  3. current-account adjustment policies; exchange rate policies; import restraint policies
  4. relations with IMF; willingness to cooperate with international banking community in providing necessary data, projections and other information

B. Basic economic factors
  5. growth strategy: is it balanced; policy toward agriculture; appropriateness and efficiency of industrial investment
  6. natural resource base
  7. human resource base: population growth, educational level, entrepreneurial ability
  8. financial resource base: policy toward stimulating domestic savings; financial market development; relative importance of foreign capital in total domestic investment
  9. export diversification by commodity and region

C. External finances
  10. external debt, level and maturity structure; and debt service burden
  11. reserves
  12. potential access to medium-term official finance, e.g. IMF
  13. balance-of-payments prospects and outlook for external debt service burden

D. Politics
  14. domestic and regional political stability

Source: Morgan Guaranty Trust Company, New York.

borrower, the lead bank in the syndicated loan would have been knowledgeable enough to work out a plan to help the borrower comply with the loan agreement.

In short, it is easier to work out a rescheduling for corporate borrowers than for government borrowers. In practice, most government borrowers waive sovereign immunity and thereby give the lender permission to take the necessary action to satisfy the loan. The Foreign Sovereign Immunities Act of 1976 provides for the waiver of sovereign immunity by foreign governments, which is binding in U.S. courts and any courts of the states. In effect, it makes foreign states subject to the jurisdiction of the U.S. courts. Periodically commercial bank lenders are warned that too much lending to LDCs will eventually expose them to too much risk. So far this has not happened, but it is not precluded from happening in the future.

Commercial bank lenders consider lending to LDCs as a submarket of a total market for loans. When there is a recession in the domestic economy, a slowdown from loans ensues, so banks will solicit new foreign customers or renegotiate existing loans with old customers. This trend was particularly apparent during 1977–79, and is likely to continue through the 1980s, when many LDCs are given an opportunity to lower their annual debt service and lengthen their average maturity schedule. This has the effect of increasing the volume of borrowing by LDCs. Many of the loans made to LDCs to finance foreign trade were given to countries that had already established a good credit reputation. With the exception of Iran's default on its loans, some problem with Zaire, and the present Polish debt situation, LDCs generally have met their debts on time, even though debt rollovers and reschedulings have played important roles in avoiding default.

SOURCES OF LDC BORROWINGS

Commercial bank lending to LDCs receives a tremendous amount of publicity. Unless LDCs have established creditworthiness, they have to rely on official flows and other noncommercial bank flows. The Development Assistance Committee (DAC) of the Organization for Economic Cooperation and Development emphasizes lower interest rates and longer-term loans to LDCs. DAC comprises 17 major industrialized Western countries. It makes official development assistance (ODA) grants or concessional loans containing a grant element of at least 25 percent. These loans are expected to decrease as DAC countries experience recessions or other economic problems. Most of the loans are nonconcessional when they are on commercial terms and the grant element is less than 25 percent. Private flows include direct investment, portfolio lending (purchasing bonds issued by LDCs and multilateral developing agencies), and export credits. LDCs will have to rely more on nonconcessional flows of the private type. This will increase the need for them to borrow to meet debt service requirements. DAC and ODA loans are channeled through United Nations agencies, the World Bank, and regional development banks. Since we are mainly concerned with LDC borrowing in the international financial markets, we shall concentrate on the gross amounts borrowed through syndicated lending, international bonds, and foreign bonds.

Table 17.2 shows that, as a percentage of total market borrowing, syndicated bank credits (medium- and long-term) varied from 28.1 percent in 1974 to 57 percent in 1979. The importance of this type of borrowing is exhibited by the third section of the table, where, as a percentage of total developing country borrowing, it varied from 82.4 percent in 1977 to 96 percent in 1974, averaging some 90 percent during 1973–79. In contrast, the external bond market was a relatively unimportant source, and many of the new bond issues of LDCs took the form of floating interest-rate notes that were really another form of syndicated lending. Since the data in Table 17.2 are not adjusted for inflation, the amount of syndicated lending is somewhat lower than that indicated, depending upon the inflation rate selected.

Table 17.2 indicates that there are two types of bond issues: international and foreign. The former are those that are simultaneously underwritten and sold in several national markets, usually through international bank syndicates. The latter are those issued in a single national market, sold and written by a group of banks of the market country, and denominated in that country's currency. Since foreign bond issues are extensions of the respective bond markets, they are subject to the regulation of the national authorities. With a projected U.S. federal budget deficit of $150 billion for fiscal 1983, it does not appear that LDCs will be using this market during the early 1980s. Private and institutional borrowers will prefer domestic government debt, judging it to be safer and more marketable than foreign govern-

TABLE 17.2. Total Gross Amounts Raised by Developing Countries on International Financial Markets

Year	International Bond Issues	Foreign Bond Issues	Medium- and Long-Term Syndicated Bank Credits	Total
		Millions of U.S. Dollars		
1973	471.9	282.5	7,271.3	8,025.7
1974	96.2	233.8	8,029.6	8,359.6
1975	240.5	305.0	10,972.3	11,517.8
1976	1,046.4	587.1	14,226.1	15,859.6
1977	2,473.4	1,328.5	17,803.5	21,605.4
1978	2,919.3	1,940.0	31,802.4	36,661.7
1979	1,691.9	1,242.6	44,677.0	47,611.5
		As Percentage of Total Market Borrowing		
1973	10.0	5.3	34.8	26.0
1974	2.1	3.0	28.1	20.5
1975	2.3	2.5	53.3	26.5
1976	6.8	3.1	52.7	25.5
1977	12.7	8.0	52.4	30.9
1978	18.3	9.0	48.2	35.4
1979	9.4	6.4	57.0	40.6
		As Percentage of Total Developing Country Borrowing		
1973	5.9	3.5	90.6	100.0
1974	1.2	2.8	96.0	100.0
1975	2.1	2.6	95.3	100.0
1976	6.6	3.7	89.7	100.0
1977	11.5	6.1	82.4	100.0
1978	8.0	5.3	86.7	100.0
1979	3.5	2.6	93.9	100.0

Source: Organization for Economic Cooperation and Development, *Financial Market Trends*, February 1980, p. 92.

ment debt. Institutional investors already have an established relationship with domestic borrowers, and therefore will want to continue the relationship unless the borrower's credit rating deteriorates. Regulatory authorities may make it impossible for institutional investors to hold foreign government debt in their portfolios.

For these reasons the foreign bond market does not look promising for LDC borrowers, since it is mainly for conservative investors, who do not rate LDC borrowers high on their investment list. Borrowing in the international bond market, on the other hand, looks more encouraging for three reasons: investors are less risk-averse, they are more receptive to innovative investment ideas and proposals, and government regulation is more limited than in the foreign bond market.

Although we have indicated the size and scope of syndicated lending, it is necessary to review some of the major advantages that this form of financing offers to both borrowers and lenders as against bond issuing. One major advantage of syndicated lending is that it contributes to the development of a permanent relationship between borrower and lender. The lending bank (or banks) continues to lend so long as funds are available, and the borrower abides by the terms of the loan agreement. By contrast, when a bond is issued, the loan is a one-time affair whereby the bondholders lend and, once the bond matures, there is no obligation to buy any more bonds. So the bond relationship is a transient one. Also, lenders may sell their bonds prior to maturity, and bondholders may not be known if the bond is of the bearer type. Another advantage to syndicated lending is its greater flexibility, compared with bonds. Most bonds and notes do contain provisions in which a change in the agreement can be negotiated through a trustee who represents the bondholders, after they have met and agreed unanimously to changes in any of the provisions. In syndicated loans nonmaterial loan provisions can be altered by a designated majority (say 70 percent) of the participating banks; therefore, commercial bank lenders enjoy an advantage over bondholders and noteholders in this respect. However, a rescheduling of a loan normally requires the unanimous consent of all the lenders.

Most of the floating-rate notes issued by LDCs are held by commercial banks. The majority of international securities are cleared through either Cedel or Euroclear, which present the securities to paying agents.[2] Neither Cedel nor Euroclear supplies the identity of the owner of the securities, since this would violate the laws of the

TABLE 17.3. Top Lead Managers to the Top 20 Borrowers in the Syndicated Loan Market, 1979–80

	Borrowers	Volume (in thousands of dollars)	Lead Managers	Volume (in thousands of dollars)
1	Bank of China	9,075.0	Bank of Tokyo	8,000.0
2	Petróleos Mexicanos (Pemex)	5,084.3	Bank of America	2,500.0
3	Kingdom of Belgium	3,800.0	Société Générale de Banque	875.0
			Banque de Paris et des Pays-Bas Belgique	875.0
			Kredietbank	875.0
4	Ente Nazionale per l'Energia Elettrica (ENEL)	3,300.0	Banca Commerciale Italiana	618.1
5	Joseph E. Seagram & Sons	3,000.0	Citibank	1,000.0
			Bank of Montreal	1,000.0
			Manufacturers Hanover	1,000.0
6	Electricité de France (EDF)	2,726.0	Crédit Lyonnais	742.8
7	Petroleo Brasileiro (Petrobras)	2,597.9	Wells Fargo	1,133.7
8	United States of Mexico	2,380.0	Société Générale de Banque	624.9
9	Republic of Venezuela	2,138.8	WestLB	251.8
10	Comisión Federal de Electricidad	2,135.0	Bank of Tokyo	220.0
11	Kingdom of Sweden	2,096.1	WestLB	633.5
12	Bank Handlowy w Warsawie	1,985.3	Commerzbank	213.0
13	Kingdom of Denmark	1,974.3	Citicorp	600.0
14	Federal Republic of Nigeria	1,940.0	Deutsche Bank	585.6
15	Instituto Nacional de Obras Sanitarias	1,887.0	Credit Suisse First Boston	1,587.0
16	Republic of Ecuador	1,777.0	Shearson Loeb Rhoades	650.0
17	Kernridge Oil Company	1,750.0	Chase Manhattan	1,750.0
18	Instituto Nacional de la Vivienda	1,717.0	Orion Bank	480.0
19	Province of Quebec	1,709.0	Bank of Nova Scotia	633.0
20	Sonatrach	1,598.6	Dai-Ichi Kangyo Bank	150.3

Note: Sole lead managers receive full amounts; colead managers, apportioned amounts.
Source: Annual Financing Report, *Euromoney*, March 1981, p. 5.

country in which they operate and the customs of the trade. Since bondholders should have a say in any alteration of a bond agreement, bearer bonds may be prohibited as a condition of a syndicated loan. Debt rescheduling will become a more important problem if more LDCs experience debt servicing problems.[3]

Loan-Signing Centers

Bank lenders and borrowers select loan-signing centers according to the jurisdiction of the loan, the nation where the bank lender is located, or the country of the borrower. London is the most popular site and the center of the syndicated loan market. Borrowers prefer the use of English law for loan agreements, and most banks syndicate loans out of London. Most of the loans signed in New York are U.S. bank loans to Latin American borrowers. Even though the loan may have been signed in New York for the benefit of Chile, the Chilean government considers it to have been made in Chile by what is known as force of attraction.[4]

Top Lead Managers and Top Borrowers

Table 17.3 shows the top 20 borrowers and lead managers in the syndicated loan market. For our purposes it should be noted that among the top 20 borrowers are the governments of Mexico, Brazil, Venezuela, the Federal Republic of Nigeria, and Ecuador. The U.S. lead managers include Bank of America, Citibank, Manufacturers Hanover, Wells Fargo, Citicorp. Shearson Loeb Rhoades, Chase Manhattan, and Credit Suisse First Boston.

WHY LDCs BORROW

There are five major reasons why LDCs borrow:

1. To meet large and rising deficits on the current account of their balance of payments
2. To finance long-term investment plans
3. To deliberately increase foreign exchange reserves in order to cope better with future adverse balance-of-payments problems

4. To purchase high-interest-earning assets
5. To meet interest payments on current outstanding debt.

Current account positions improve or deteriorate, depending on the terms of trade. During 1973–77, for example, the terms of trade for LDCs improved, but for the rest of the 1970s there was a deterioration and, with it, rising current account deficits as export prices softened on the major export commodities for these countries. In an attempt to increase their foreign exchange reserves, LDCs increased their exports, causing a further price decline in their primary export commodities that only aggravated their balance-of-payments problem. The International Monetary Fund has tried to get some countries to diversify their economies, Bolivia being a prime example. But this has met with limited success.

In order to finance long-term investment plans, many LDCs resort to project finance. In the petroleum industry project finance refers to financing capital requirements for petroleum production. It is expected that the sale of petroleum will provide the basis for the payment of the interest and principal on the loan. Project finance techniques are used in the exploitation of natural resources. This type of financing is especially difficult to evaluate because an assessment must be made of the amount of oil in the ground and of the future price of oil. Therefore, project finance does not really depend on the credit status of the LDC, but on the type of facility being financed. Project financing also gives rise to alternative financing arrangements giving the bank lender reinforced leverage in the form of partnership creditor status with prestigious lending institutions. One of these alternative financing arrangements is cofinancing, which at the end of 1980 amounted to $6.5 billion (see Table 17.4).

Cofinancing is an arrangement under which funds from the World Bank and other lenders are brought together in project financing. Participation by private lenders may be required to complete project financing before a World Bank loan is finalized. The largest element of cofinancing is official source aid, in which the World Bank provides loan funds in partnership with countries supplying bilateral funds, with export credit agencies, and with private lenders. The World Bank works closely with colenders in preparing and appraising projects, negotiating loans, and even administering loans.

The arrangement is present in both joint and parallel financing. In the former there is a common list of goods and services in which

TABLE 17.4. World Bank Cofinancing Operations, Fiscal Years 1973–80 (amounts in millions of U.S. dollars)

| Fiscal Year | Projects with Cofinancing | | Sources of Cofinancing | | | | | | World Bank Group Contribution | | Total Project Cost |
| | | | Official | | Export Credit | | Private | | | | |
	No.	Amount	No.	Amount	No.	Amount	No.	Amount	IBRD	IDA	
1973	37	496.2	30	313.0	10	183.2	0	.0	478.9	308.0	2,813.1
1974	48	1,463.0	44	788.8	11	589.5	2	84.7	1,092.6	184.3	5,446.0
1975	53	1,940.3	48	923.3	10	962.0	1	55.0	1,033.6	346.1	8,817.4
1976	73	2,255.1	61	1,079.7	16	902.9	5	272.5	1,583.3	403.1	9,620.3
1977	81	2,289.1	72	1,547.9	9	191.3	9	549.9	1,866.2	698.0	9,916.5
1978	87	2,426.4	77	1,756.7	15	539.3	7	129.9	1,827.5	798.8	11,730.0
1979	109	3,149.4	88	1,976.3	16	659.2	13	513.9	2,993.3	1,146.2	14,004.8
1980	93	6,516.3	68	2,458.6	23	2,282.3	21	1,775.4	3,192.9	1,605.2	21,535.5

Notes: The information provided on private cofinancing is tentative, since private loan arrangements are usually completed when funds are required, which may be as long as one to two years after approval of a project by the World Bank's Board of Executive Directors. Data on private cofinancing include all external private loans that assist in financing World Bank operations, whether or not formal cofinancing arrangements are concluded.

Since this table reflects adjustments in cofinancing data for fiscal years 1973–79, the statistics for those years differ from tables published earlier.

Source: World Bank, *Co-Financing*, September 1980, p. 20.

financing is shared by the World Bank and other lenders, whereas in the latter the World Bank and lenders finance different goods and services or parts of a project in which flexible financing arrangements are available. Colenders in joint financing have the World Bank assume the primary responsibility for day-to-day supervision. Consultation between colenders and the World Bank is regular, so that both parties agree to avoid drastic action, such as suspension of the loan, without consultation. The advantage of joint financing is the avoidance of duplication of effort in loan administration and related functions. Parallel financing has grown more acceptable among official lenders in cases where each colender administers its own part of the project. During the period of implementation, there are agreements and memoranda of understanding providing for consultation and joint action.

The World Bank enters into cooperative agreements with lenders in prospective cofinancing arrangements with LDC governments and their agencies. In addition it has played a dominant role in helping newly organized Arab investment funds begin lending operations. These funds include the Arab Fund for Economic and Social Development, the Abu Dhabi Fund for Economic Development, the Islamic Development Bank, and the Saudi Fund for Development.

In 1975 the World Bank entered into cofinancing arrangements with a group of 16 private banks to finance a steel plant in Brazil. In this project financing, the private banks' medium-term Eurocurrency loan was $55 million, the World Bank provided $95 million, the Inter-American Development Bank supplied $63 million, and other lenders provided $490 million in export credits. In this and similar loans private lending institutions negotiate and enter into separate loan contracts with the borrower. The World Bank provides the private lenders with credit information on the borrowing country and the project because the World Bank is better able to conduct a comprehensive credit analysis than the private borrower. The World Bank assumes the administrative responsibilities of the private loan, including the disbursement of funds and receipt of debt service payments. There is also a cross-default clause in the loan agreement in which the World Bank is given the option to suspend disbursement or accelerate repayment of the loan if the borrower fails to meet scheduled payments.

Cofinancing extends many advantages to commercial banks. First, the World Bank assumes administrative responsibilities associated with the loan. Second, the banks have better access to World Bank knowledge and information on credit evaluation, a broader range of loan opportunities, and reduction of risk. Risk is reduced because large project loans are better planned and administered with the World Bank as a participating lender.[5]

Cofinancing loans can be structured so as to afford participants maximum protection and selection of risk and return in a loan package. The presence of the World Bank and other official lenders adds prestige to a loan. LDCs have given repayment and servicing of World Bank loans top priority because they want to establish a favorable credit rating. With increasing financial resources for the IMF and development banks, country risk climate should improve, paving the way for more participation in cofinancing arrangements.

CREDIT TERMS

The interest rates LDCs pay on their loans depend upon the type of loan, the credit standing of the borrower, and the state of the capital and money markets. The latter is the most important factor. Most syndicated loans carry floating interest rates based on a fixed margin over the three-month London Interbank Offer Rate (LIBOR). Sometimes the rate may use Singapore (SIBOR) or even Madrid (MIBOR). Or part of the loan may be based on the U.S. prime rate or the Spanish preferential rate. There are different rates within a given loan agreement. For example, a loan package in the fall of 1981 was designed to finance Spanish government-owned steel companies as well as private companies. Part A of the package consisted of a dollar Eurocredit loan for eight years with a four-year grace period at 0.50 percent over LIBOR. Part B consisted of domestic credit for six years with a three-year grace period at 0.875 percent over MIBOR, and Part C consisted of a six-year domestic credit with a three-year grace period tied to the then preferential rate of 17 percent.[6] The parts are referred to as tranches.

Table 17.5 gives the average maturity and rate above LIBOR available to public-sector borrowers in Brazil, Mexico, and France during 1974–79. In 1974 prime borrowers from LDCs paid slightly more than a prime OECD country like France, and maturities were generally longer. During 1975–77 maturities were generally shorter for Brazil and Mexico. In 1978–79 maturities for Brazil were in-

TABLE 17.5. Best Loan Conditions Available to Public-Sector Borrowers: Brazil, Mexico, and France, 1974-79

	Brazil		Mexico		France	
	Maturity (yrs.)	Spread (%)	Maturity (yrs.)	Spread (%)	Maturity (yrs.)	Spread (%)
1974	12	0.625-0.75	10 12	0.50 0.50-0.75	10	0.375-0.625
1975	7	1.75	5	1.50	5	1.25
1976	7	1.875	5 7	1.50 1.75	7	1.0-1.125
1977	5 8	1.875 2.125	5 10	1.50 1.50-1.75	5 8	0.625 0.875-1.0
1978	10 12	1.0 1.25	8 10	0.75 0.875-1.0	10	0.50
1979	12	0.625-0.75	6 12	0.50 0.625	15	0.375-0.50

Source: OECD, *Financial Market Trends*, February 1980, p. 92.

creased. Note also that spreads for LDCs were higher than for OECD borrowers for much of the period under review. The differential between LDCs and industrial countries fell in 1978 and 1979 to less than 0.25 percent in some cases. This trend continued during 1980–81 as banks competed in the international market to make loans to LDCs.

While it would appear that banks would consider such spreads to be hardly profitable, it must be remembered that many fees are charged in addition to the interest rate. Banks also require compensating balances from borrowers. In addition, in the case of project financing, supplies have to be imported, and commercial banks make additional funds on the issuance of letters of credit. All of these factors increase the yield on an LDC loan. Likewise, many lenders consider where to "park" their loans, depending upon the tax rate of the borrowing country, which is used as a foreign tax credit in filing U.S. federal income tax returns. This too influences the net yield on a loan. So one must be cautious in using only the spread in making loans to LDCs.

BALANCE-OF-PAYMENTS DEVELOPMENTS OF NONOIL DEVELOPING COUNTRIES

LDCs do not produce goods needed by oil-exporting countries, so they cannot pay for their oil imports. In addition, they export primary commodities, for which there may be periods of weak demand. Yet these nonoil developing countries have been able, on the whole, to sustain economic growth and avoid excessive increases in their ratio of debt or debt service payments to exports of goods and services. Some countries have experienced difficulties in financing their current-account deficits. As indicated earlier, the major reason why the debt ratio of these countries was generally manageable through the end of 1980 was that they experienced large negative interest rates during the several preceding years. For example, during 1974–79 low-income countries as a whole had an average nominal interest rate of 2.5 percent on their external debt, yet their export prices rose at an annual rate of 13 percent during the same period. Another factor that assisted these developing countries was that a large part of their financing was supplied at concessionary rates. The honeymoon for these LDCs is over, and in the future they will face

market-related interest rates and the debt service burden will grow
more rapidly.

Since these LDCs rely on the export of primary products that
tend to have an inelastic demand, it is usually thought that devaluation will not improve their balance-of-payments position. It should
be remembered that these products compete with goods produced in
the industrial world, so the elasticity of demand is not necessarily
less than 1. For LDCs it is important to allocate imports through the
price mechanism by exchange rate devaluation rather than by using a
system of import quotas. LDCs must make more frequent use of devaluations. In addition, they must do a better job of restricting
aggregate demand growth in order to avoid inflation. And if they are
to increase their exports of agrobusiness products and manufactured
goods, industrial countries are asked to remove protective tariffs. The
alternative would be for industrial countries and oil-exporting surplus
countries to increase their direct investment in LDCs.

During the 1970s average interest rates on fixed-rate loans were
in the range of 4.2–5.5 percent, compared with 7.9–12 percent on
floating-rate loans. Preliminary estimates for 1980 and 1981 on floating rates are 15.3 percent and 18 percent, respectively. Much of the
rise in the floating-rate market was attributable to tight monetary
policy in lending countries that were attempting to restrain inflation.
Inflation was a double-edged sword for LDCs. On the one hand, they
benefited from a lowering of the real cost of the interest, but on the
other hand, their terms of trade worsened. Fixed-interest rates cover
merchandise flows that are subsidized through aid loans and export
credits. During the 1970s real interest rates were actually negative,
whereas floating interest rates rose and were positive. The bulk of
developing countries' net debt is still on fixed-interest loans. The
share of floating-interest loans rose from 16 percent in 1979 to 24
percent in 1981. Brazil and Mexico accounted for most of the net
floating-interest loans in 1981. With the rising interest rates in 1980
and 1981, LDCs received more export credits from the World Bank,
the IMF, and short-term bank financing.

By the end of the 1970s and the early 1980s, it became apparent
that bank lenders were insisting that they would not commit long-
term capital at fixed nominal interest rates. Lenders have imperfect
knowledge of future interest rate developments, so they insist on
receiving a premium for this uncertainty in the form of higher interest rates even from LDCs. Higher interest rates and a strong U.S.

dollar have discouraged consumers of commodities from LDCs and speculators from holding inventories of primary goods.

Table 17.6 indicates that in 1973 the current-account deficit of nonoil developing countries stood at $11.5 billion, which was 2 percent of their gross domestic product (GDP). By 1980 the deficit grew to $82.1 billion (4.8 percent of their GDP). In 1981 the estimated deficit was $97 billion (over 6 percent of GDP). Three factors are responsible for the rise in the current account deficits since 1978: a slowing down in the rate of growth in exports, the deterioration in the terms of trade, and an increase in interest rates on external debt. The depressed world demand for rice, rubber, tapioca, and corn was a major factor responsible for Thailand's $1.6 billion trade deficit as of June 30, 1981. The recession in the automobile industry in the United States and Western Europe led to a softening in the demand for rubber. Record U.S. corn crops in 1981 caused corn prices to soften worldwide.

The deterioration in the terms of trade can be explained partly by the drop in the prices of primary commodities exported and the rise in prices of oil imports, and has been particularly severe for nonoil LDCs of Africa. Many countries tried to avoid curtailment of imports by borrowing heavily, but import prices for these countries rose more rapidly than export prices for their goods, so that in real terms they imported less in 1980. And with a tightening of credit markets as well as the limited growth of official development assistance, import growth is not likely to increase in the early 1980s and some development plans will have to be curtailed or scrapped.

Higher interest rates on external debt will absorb a larger part of these LDCs' receipts from exports of goods and services. For example, interest payments by nonoil developing countries on medium-term and long-term external debt more than doubled from 1978 to 1980, and absorbed about 7.5 percent of the earnings from goods and services in 1980, compared with 5.5 percent in 1978. Interest on short-term external debt also accounted for additional absorption of export earnings. This was especially burdensome for the middle-income exporters of primary products because they receive a smaller amount of credit from private financial institutions. When viewed in absolute terms, the major exporters of manufactures were most affected by the rise in interest rates. Although this is a small subgroup, they account for a large share of the total external indebted-

TABLE 17.6. Nonoil Developing Countries: Current-Account Deficits as Percentage of Gross Domestic Product, 1973–80

	1973	1974	1975	1976	1977	1978	1979	1980
Weighted averages*								
Nonoil developing countries	2.0	5.0	5.8	3.7	3.0	3.2	4.0	4.8
Net oil exporters	2.9	4.5	7.3	5.3	4.4	4.3	3.8	3.8
Net oil importers	1.8	5.1	5.5	3.4	2.7	3.0	4.0	4.9
Major exporters of manufactures	1.5	6.2	6.0	3.2	1.9	2.0	3.5	4.3
Low-income countries	3.1	4.9	4.7	2.6	1.8	3.1	4.0	4.7
Other net oil importers	0.9	3.1	5.3	4.3	4.8	4.8	5.0	6.5
Medians								
Nonoil developing countries	4.1	6.0	8.9	6.7	6.4	7.4	7.6	10.1
Net oil exporters	3.1	1.9	7.0	6.7	5.9	6.9	5.8	3.4
Net oil importers	4.2	6.2	9.1	6.7	6.6	7.4	7.7	10.6
Major exporters of manufactures	0.4	6.2	4.9	4.0	3.0	3.0	4.8	4.2
Low-income countries	7.9	10.1	11.8	9.4	8.6	13.9	11.2	13.9
Other net oil importers	2.6	3.6	7.4	6.4	5.9	6.7	7.2	10.1
Memorandum item								
Weighted averages (including People's Republic of China)								
Nonoil developing countries	—	—	—	—	2.5	2.7	3.5	4.2
Low-income countries	—	—	—	—	0.7	1.7	2.2	2.8

Note: Excludes data for the People's Republic of China, except where otherwise noted.
*Ratios of current account balances to GDP for individual countries, averaged on the basis of current GDP weights. Such estimates correspond exactly to those obtained through calculation for any particular grouping of countries of the ratio of the sum of the current account balances to the corresponding sum of GDP values.

Source: International Monetary Fund, *Annual Report*, 1981, p. 30.

ness of nonoil developing countries and debt owed to private foreign financial institutions.

Figure 17.1 depicts the ratios of debt to exports of goods and services and of debt to domestic output for all nonoil developing countries and for other major subgroups used by the IMF. During 1974–78 the magnitude of debt to both exports of goods and services and domestic output rose, while in 1979 and 1980 it declined

FIGURE 17.1: Nonoil Developing Countries: Ratios of Debt to Exports of Goods and Services and to Domestic Output, 1974–80
(percent)

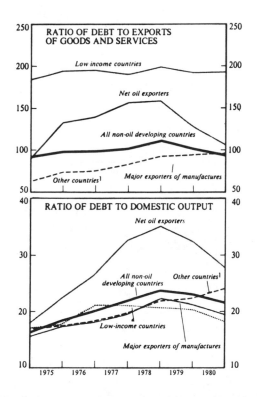

[1] Consisting of middle-income countries that, in general, export mainly primary products.

Source: IMF, *Annual Report*, 1981, p. 35. Reprinted by permission of IMF.

for nonoil developing countries. This reflected the substitution of short-term debt for long-term debt in the latter two years, the reduction in the reserve account accumulation, and the fact that a given year's inflation, while fully reflected in that year's exports or domestic output, affected only the newly incurred part of the year-end debt.

FIGURE 17.2: Nonoil Developing Countries: External Debt Service Payments, 1973–80 (percent)

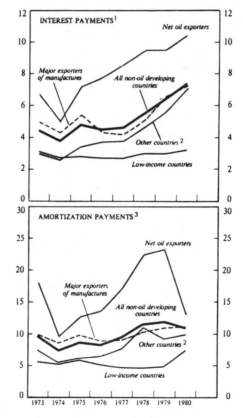

[1] Annual interest payments as percentage of annual exports of goods and services.

[2] Consisting of middle-income countries that, in general, export mainly primary products.

[3] Annual amortization payments as percentage of annual exports of goods and services.

Source: IMF, Annual Report, 1981, p. 35. Reprinted by permission of IMF.

TABLE 17.7. Nonoil Developing Countries: Current-Account Financing, 1973–80 (billions of U.S. dollars)

	1973	1974	1975	1976	1977	1978	1979	1980
Current-account deficit[a]	11.5	36.8	46.5	32.9	28.6	37.5	57.6	82.1
Financing through transactions that do not affect net debt positions	10.4	12.8[b]	12.0	11.9	14.6	15.3	21.6	20.6
Net unrequited transfers received by governments of nonoil developing countries	5.6	6.9[b]	7.3	7.4	8.2	7.8	10.4	10.6
SDR allocations, valuation adjustments, and gold moretization	0.4	0.5	-0.7	-0.3	1.0	1.2	3.0	2.1
Direct investment flows, net	4.4	5.4	5.3	4.8	5.4	6.2	8.2	7.9
Net borrowing and use of reserves[c]	1.1	24.0[b]	34.6	21.0	14.0	22.2	36.1	61.5
Reduction of reserve assets (accumulation)	-9.9	-1.4	2.5	-12.5	-12.1	-15.8	-10.1	-1.2
Net external borrowing[d]	11.0	25.4[b]	32.1	33.5	26.1	38.0	46.2	62.7
Long-term borrowing	11.4	19.8[b]	26.7	28.2	27.7	35.1	44.7	48.1
From official sources	5.7	9.9[b]	11.7	10.8	12.5	14.3	14.5	21.0
From private sources	10.4	13.5	14.9	19.0	21.3	27.0	33.1	27.2
From financial institutions	9.0	12.3	13.2	16.1	17.6	23.0	32.1	24.2
From other lenders	1.4	1.2	1.8	2.9	3.6	4.0	1.0	3.0
Residual flows, net[e]	-4.7	-3.6	0.1	-1.6	-6.1	-6.1	-2.9	-0.1
Use of reserve-related credit facilities[f]	—	1.5	2.3	3.7	-0.6	-0.5	0.2	3.0
Other short-term borrowing, net	—	5.1	7.8	4.9	-0.5	2.2	7.6	11.6
Residual errors and omissions[g]	-0.4	-1.0	-4.7	-3.3	-0.5	1.2	-6.3	

Note: Excludes data for the People's Republic of China prior to 1977.

[a] Net total of balances on goods, services, and private transfers, as defined for IMF's *Balance of Payments Statistics* purposes (with sign reversed).

[b] Excludes the effect of a revision of the terms of the disposition of economic assistance loans made by the United States to India and repayable in rupees, and of rupees already acquired by the U.S. government in repayment of such loans. The revision has the effect of increasing government transfers by about U.S. $2 billion, with an offset in net official loans.

[c] That is, financing through changes in net debt positions (net borrowing, less net accumulation—or plus net liquidation—of official reserve assets).

[d] Includes any net use of nonreserve claims on nonresidents, errors and omissions in reported balance-of-payments statements for individual countries, and minor deficiencies in coverage.

[e] These residual flows comprise two elements: net changes in long-term external assets of nonoil developing countries, and residuals and discrepancies that arise from the mismatching of creditor source data, taken from debt records, with capital flow data taken from national balance-of-payments records.

[f] Comprises use of IMF credit and short-term borrowing by monetary authorities from other monetary authorities.

[g] Errors and omissions in reported balance-of-payments statements for individual countries, and minor omissions in coverage.

Source: IMF, *Annual Report,* 1981, p. 32.

Figure 17.2 shows the interest and amortization payments of nonoil developing countries for 1973–80. It will be observed that the increase in the long-term interest payments since 1975 has averaged about three percentage points, placing a burden on the export payments of all subgroups except low-income countries. Furthermore, the ratio of debt amortization payments to export earnings has substantially increased since 1976. Higher amortization payments will become a serious problem for those countries that are unable to refinance maturing debt.

Table 17.7 shows how nonoil developing countries financed their current-account deficits during 1973–80. Between 1979 and 1980 their net external borrowing rose and their reserve assets were reduced, and some countries had to increase their official borrowing in order to sustain their imports and maintain their liquidity position. It will be noted that net direct investment fell slightly between 1979 and 1980, reflecting reluctance of some private financial institutions to commit any more funds in developing countries, as well as borrowers' reluctance to pay higher interest rates. Use of reserve-related credit facilities, which comprises use of IMF credit and short-term borrowing by monetary authorities from other monetary authorities, rose from $0.2 billion to $3.0 billion between 1979 and 1980. There was a sharp increase in use of short-term credits in financing the 1980 current-account deficit. This was considered to be a temporary situation after which the short-term credits would be replaced by longer-term credits. Finally, it should be noted that whenever there is a decrease in private source financing, as there was in 1979–80, official financing will increase. This happened during that same period, when private financing declined from $33.1 billion to $27.2 billion and official sources increased from $14.5 billion to $21.0 billion.

THE IMF OIL FACILITY SUBSIDY ACCOUNT

This account was established on August 1, 1975, by the Executive Board of the IMF to assist members of the IMF that were seriously affected by oil price increases. The amount of the subsidy payments is computed as a percentage per annum of the average daily balances, subject to charges, of the IMF's holdings of eligible members' currency outstanding under the 1975 oil facility. As indicated in Table 17.8,

TABLE 17.8. Oil Facility Subsidy Account: Total Use of 1975 Oil Facility by Beneficiaries, and Subsidy Payments for Financial Year Ended April 30, 1981[a] (millions of SDRs)

	Total Use of 1975 Oil Facility	Subsidy at 5 Percent	
		Amount	Cumulative to date
Original beneficiaries: Subsidy for financial year ended April 30, 1981			
Bangladesh	40.47	1.17	9.52
Cameroon	11.79	0.35	2.75
Central African Republic	2.66	0.07	0.63
Egypt	31.68	1.00	7.30
Haiti	4.14	0.12	0.98
India	201.34	–	26.95
Ivory Coast	10.35	–	1.42
Kenya	27.93	0.75	6.68
Mali	3.99	0.13	0.92
Mauritania	5.32	0.16	1.24
Pakistan	111.01	2.98	26.47
Senegal	9.91	0.25	2.40
Sierra Leone	4.97	0.16	1.15
Sri Lanka	34.13	1.00	8.01
Sudan	18.30	0.51	4.36
Tanzania	20.61	0.50	5.00
Western Samoa	0.42	0.01	0.10
Yemen, People's Democratic Republic of	12.02	0.35	2.82
Subtotal	551.03	9.51	108.68
Additional beneficiaries: Subsidy for financial years ended April 30, 1978–81			
Grenada	0.49	0.08	0.12
Malawi	3.73	0.64	0.87
Morocco	18.00	3.21	4.10
Papua New Guinea	14.80	1.93	2.73
Philippines	152.03	25.49	35.93
Zaire	32.53	5.81	7.40
Zambia[b]	29.72	3.37	3.37
Subtotal	251.30	40.54	54.52
Total	802.33	50.05	163.20

Note: Columns do not necessarily add to totals.

[a]Purchases began in July 1975 and continued until May 1976. The subsidy amounts shown are calculated as a percentage per annum of the average daily balances, subject to charges, of the IMF's holdings of each eligible member's currency outstanding under the 1975 oil facility during the year.

[b]Zambia received a subsidy only for the period July 1, 1978–April 30, 1981.

Source: IMF, *Annual Report*, 1981, p. 101.

the subsidy payments totaled SDR 50 million as of April 1981 and were made to 23 eligible beneficiaries. These countries had two common characteristics qualifying them for subsidies: their export growth declined because of slackened demand from industrial countries, and their terms of trade deteriorated. While this facility is of some help, it is small in relation to the amount of external credit granted by the private international banking sector.

DEBT RESCHEDULING

In 1981 the Group of 30 established a study group dealing with all the major aspects of international lending. Of especial interest is a consideration of the important aspects of rescheduling, which at times are the same for both private and sovereign borrowers but, at other times, differ. Questionnaires were distributed to about 200 banks, and the response rate was 50 percent. The important aspects dealing with debt rescheduling are summarized below.

1. Among European and American banks there was a fear of the possibility of an increasing number of debt reschedulings involving larger sums in the future, and that these reschedulings would be at increasingly less favorable terms for the lenders. Asian banks, being more pessimistic, feared a greater chain of defaults through sovereign debt repudiation.

2. Fifty percent of the respondents thought that existing arrangements were adequate to deal with frequent debt rescheduling. Forty percent voiced uncertainty, and the remaining 10 percent, comprising mainly Asian banks, felt the present system was inadequate to deal with more frequent debt rescheduling.

3. In an attempt to avoid an increasing number of reschedulings, the IMF, the World Bank, and the International Finance Corporation should be called upon to initiate an early warning system and to address themselves to the rescheduling problem. In short, there should be continuous contact between these international agencies and lending banks. These institutions should also communicate with each other regarding any change in the credit status of the borrowers. About two-thirds of the respondents thought that a jointly organized private international "safety net" would be an effective tool for supporting individual banks in the event of a liquidity crisis.

4. Important indirect costs involved in debt reschedulings were emphasized and evaluated. These costs involved the time devoted by management to working out the reschedulings and the reduced present value of the loans. In some cases it may pay for the bankers to declare default rather than reschedule the loan.

5. Banks that were surveyed were more concerned with country debt rescheduling than with private debt rescheduling, although the increased incidence of the latter is leading to the same apprehension. This is of particular concern to the smaller banks with minuscule international banking departments that lack experience and expertise in debt reschedulings.

6. When a country reschedules its debts, foreign banks are involved, and the availability of hard currency becomes a crucial problem. This is in contrast with private corporate rescheduling, in which both local and foreign banks, having diverse interests and operating procedures, are involved. The local and foreign bank loans may or may not be secured. Both local and foreign banks may be persuaded by governments to help bail out a failing company or sovereign government.

7. Fortunes of private corporations and sovereign governments change, and with them their credit ratings may change appreciably within a short period of time. The consensus among respondent banks was that there will be a modest increase in risks involved with lending to foreign governments.

8. While there have been some banks participating in syndicated loans that are unwilling to agree to debt rescheduling, the presence of uncooperative banks in a rescheduling is likely to increase in the future and to become a real problem.[7]

Polish Debt Rescheduling

Poland is cited as a case study of the principles and problems relating to lending to foreign countries. As of December 31, 1981, $500 million was due on a total outstanding debt of $16 billion. More than 500 Western creditor banks had extended loans to Poland. Creditors agreed to postpone for several years the payment of $2.4 billion in principal due in 1981, providing Poland could meet its 1981 interest payments. Some Western banks insisted on the interest payment even if the Soviet Union was to rescue Poland, presumably through gold sales. They preferred this method of payment to making additional loans to meet the interest payment. The Soviets were pressured to pay the interest so as not to cause any further deterioration in the creditworthiness of Eastern bloc countries.

Since a consortium of banks was involved, the major Western banks hoped that smaller creditor banks would not claim that Poland was in default. Indeed, there was even a suggestion made by Polish officials that payment to the smaller banks be made first, because they were more vulnerable to nonpayment of interest than the larger banks. Creditors could obtain court attachment orders against Polish assets (such as ships and aircraft located in the West). This action would force other banks to declare Poland in default, thus causing the losses to be written off against profits. In effect, Polish debt default would have a domino effect, in that other countries that could not meet their interest payments (such as Brazil, Yugoslavia, and Zaire) would be declared in default.

Had the Polish debt been declared to be in default, what could be realized from the sale or lease of Polish assets? And what would have prevented Poland from moving those assets out of the West? Default would not have been in the interests of the lenders, who preferred getting full payment.

Of course there were political aspects of the Polish debt situation. Solidarity blamed the Soviet Union for Poland's economic problems. According to that labor organization, in 1976 the Soviet Union and Poland began transacting trade in a specially created accounting system in which the unit of exchange was the transferable ruble used in settling trade accounts among Comecon partners. In effect the transferable ruble was neither transferable nor liquid. Poland borrowed in the West when it needed hard currencies to buy raw materials, semi-finished goods, and food. It sold finished goods to the Soviet Union and, for accounting purposes, these transactions were designed to favor the Soviet Union. For example, suppose the Poles sold $1 million worth of finished products to the Soviets at an exchange rate of 68 kopecks. Poland would receive 68 million kopecks in the transactions. But if the rate fell to 60 kopecks, Poland would receive only 60 million kopecks. Clearly, the Soviet Union would profit from such a transaction. The Soviets were buying coal, chemical fertilizers, drugs, grains, and meat in such quantities that not enough was left for the Polish domestic market. This necessitated getting hard currency loans from the West in order to purchase these products from other countries.

Poland was also selling the Soviets such finished goods as computers, shipbuilding machinery, and airplane engines, items geared for Soviet export markets and necessitating investment in high technology available only in the West, largely in exchange for hard currency. This helps to explain why Poland has had to borrow in the West, where its indebtedness, which stood at $3.8 billion in 1976, grew to a staggering $27 billion by 1981.

Some began wondering how Poland was able to incur such a sizable debt for such a long period of time. In November 1981 a consortium of banks finally started asking Poland many questions, including the contents of once-secret bank accounts in Soviet rubles, and requested an estimate of Poland's personal income for 1982. How could so many prominent lending institutions make loans on inadequate credit information supplied by Poland? Western bankers still do not know the amount of Poland's external reserve holdings.

In January 1982 the U.S. press reported that Poland had raised $350 million in interest that was due in 1981, although the source of the funds was not known. Later the report proved to be false. In February 1982, Secretary of Defense Caspar Weinberger was pressing to have Poland declared in default of its debts to the West. At the same time, on the recommendation of the State, Treasury, and Agriculture departments, President Reagan agreed to have the administration pay American banks the $71 million owed them by Poland in order to forestall a declaration of default as well as a possible disruption of East-West economic relations. On February 11, 1982, a business-oriented legal foundation (the Capital Legal Foundation) filed papers requesting a temporary restraining order against the Agriculture Department to stop payment of $71 million to American banks. The foundation wanted Poland declared in default. Apparently the Commodity Credit Corporation, a division of the Agriculture Department, had guaranteed $800 million worth of private bank loans to Poland to finance purchases of American grain. Not even the House of Representatives would have voted in favor of barring the $71 million payment.

The Soviets have been accused of using their satellites to support the Soviet economy (as was explained in the case of the transferable ruble). Poland has the highest debt service ratio of all East European countries: .19 in 1970, .32 in 1975, and .87 in 1981, according to the Wharton Forecast. However, the authenticity of the latter figure is highly questionable, since data from Poland are scarce.

West German bankers, who hold about 20 percent of Poland's outstanding debt, were extremely sensitive to any talk of default on the Polish debt. German banks had experienced depressed earnings during 1980–81, and if any of the banks had failed for lack of repayment, foreign banks with Eurodeposits would have found it difficult to withdraw their funds or might not have been able to withdraw funds at all. The German banks' exposure to the risk of nonrepayment of the Polish debt was greater than for U.S. banks, partly because American banks had not made any new loans to Poland since 1976. The Soviets were expected to cover the debts of Comecon countries under what is known as the umbrella theory. Otherwise, any further credits to Comecon countries would have been sharply curtailed.

Many conservative economists wanted the Polish debt declared in default so that any future borrowing by East European countries would prove very costly and the Soviet Union would no longer be able to spend so much on its defense budget. In short, what should be an economic matter turned into a political football.

Early in 1982 serious consideration was given to the economic rather than to the political consequences of the default on the Polish debt. Politically, default would have placed a large burden on the Soviets, who would be expected to assume the debt and would thus be compelled to curtail their own military spending. With the declaration of martial law in Poland, default advocates hoped that default would punish the Polish government. However, the economic consequences would have been far more serious for the U.S. taxpayers, who would have to pay a bill amounting to $2.4 billion: $1.9 billion in government-guaranteed credits to Poland and $500 million in tax write-off claims of U.S. commercial banks.

West European bankers, who held most of the Polish debt, expected U.S. commercial banks to be more sympathetic to their viewpoint. If there had been default, West European bankers would not be sympathetic if, in the future, Brazil were to be in default and U.S. banks held most of that debt. This may have been a factor explaining the more sympathetic attitude on the part of the United States in early 1982. Yet one cannot eradicate the predominant political overtones of Polish default, since many Western financial analysts feel that the United States could lose an important pressure on Poland in the future. Had the U.S. banks declared default, Poland in all probability would have little incentive to service its debt and to liberalize its economy. Without default there is more room for negotiation and flexibility in Poland, and the hope that Poland will not be driven totally toward the Soviet Union.

It appears that the storm over the Polish debt rescheduling is over, since Polish bank officials announced on March 16, 1982, that the unpaid interest of $80 million due at the end of 1981 had been paid, and the debt rescheduling of some $2.4 billion was completed in the spring of 1982. There are 500 banks involved in the rescheduling of the principal, which involves a complex payment system entailing many currencies.

The 1982 rescheduling presented a formidable task as renewed pressure for a default surfaced in the Reagan administration. Default would symbolize and accentuate the failure of the Communist economic system and would nudge the Soviets into assuming a greater proportion of the Polish debt burden. Credit to Communist countries would be a strategic weapon to be used in case of a rise in Soviet militarism in a satellite country. As of mid-August 1982, the Polish government had, in effect, a de facto debt moratorium.

PROSPECTS FOR THE FINANCING OF
FOREIGN GOVERNMENTS

More international lending will go to natural resource development projects in the 1980s. Project financing and direct investment are expected to account for a greater proportion of investment in LDCs, but will not be able to meet all LDC needs. The IMF and World Bank must play a greater role in financing LDCs, and they will insist on sound monetary and fiscal policies in the borrowing countries. Almost three-quarters of the loans made by the IMF in 1980 were made available under programs with high conditionality. The IMF has attempted to enlarge its lending by raising members' quotas to reflect member countries' proportions of world trade— and thus to increase lending to the poorer LDCs that do not qualify for private loans. World trade during the 1980s will grow at a faster rate than during the 1970s.

Additional sources of lending might very well include trust funds managed by U.S. banks that are currently entering the international markets. Chase Manhattan, for example, has established an international monetary operation outside the United States. Even pension funds might tap this market for their investment portfolios.

We are currently witnessing a decline in oil dependence internationally. Higher oil prices have caused conservation of this form of energy and have led to the exploration of alternative sources that had been considered too expensive. The 1980s will see an expansion in the development of nuclear, coal, and non-OPEC oil; this expansion will involve tremendous need for capital. One nuclear plant may cost as much as $3 billion and involve financing for seven years. There will be more oil exploration outside the OPEC area, especially in India, Malaysia, and the Atlantic off Ireland and the United Kingdom. Coal facilities located mainly in the United States, China, and Australia will require about $60 billion for the construction of ships and port facilities.

By March 15, 1982, the OPEC surplus totaled $360 billion. The countries continuing to enjoy this surplus are Kuwait, Libya, Qatar, Saudi Arabia, and United Arab Emirates. The oil glut that emerged early in 1982 has prompted some of the OPEC countries to scale down grandiose development plans. Indonesia, Iraq, Iran, Nigeria, and Venezuela showed deficits ranging from $2 billion to $9 billion. Algeria, on the other hand, was in balance. During 1982 revenue from oil sales declined about $25 billion for OPEC.

An emergency meeting held by OPEC in mid-March 1982 imposed quotas on members for the first time, in an attempt to hold the price on oil. Even Saudi Arabia, which cut production to 7.5 million barrels per day, was not able to sell that amount. There is considerable speculation as to whether the OPEC quotas will be honored. Many of these countries have made promises to their citizens regarding development, and it would be unpopular politically to reverse their plans. If the world economy revives, there will be an increased demand for oil and OPEC may be able to maintain its price, but there is considerable speculation as to when the worldwide recession will end. Likewise, economists, citing a cartel model, contend that it pays for some members to cheat on their agreements. This is a complex problem that is best discussed in a microeconomic theory course.

Other future developments include changes of an institutional nature. The Arabs will increase the management of their own assets, so Western bankers can expect a decline in the share of international banking. Greater Arab bank influence will evolve and, correspondingly, diminished Western bank influence is expected. Arabs will increase their real investment in LDCs, which will be motivated by both political and economic considerations.

LDCs, especially the low- and middle-income developing countries, can expect greater attention from bank lenders as uranium and other strategic materials for high technology are located in their regions, and this lending will be financed by Western and Arab bankers. Despite warnings given earlier about banks having to finance current-account deficits in LDCs, a conservative estimate is that the financing requirements during the 1980s will be in the vicinity of $700–$750 billion.

NOTES

1. Developing countries are further classified by income groups as defined by the World Bank in the 1981 *World Development Report*: capital-surplus oil exporters, middle-income countries (over $370 per capita), and low-income countries ($370 or less per capita), based on 1979 GNP per capita in 1979 U.S. dollars. A fourth group, "other developing," which includes countries for which 1979 GNP per capita data are unavailable, has been added.

2. Cedel (Centrale de Livraison), one of the Eurobond market's two main clearing systems, is owned by several European banks. Euroclear, the other main clearing system in the Eurobond market, is operated by Morgan Guaranty for more than 100 banks that own the system.

3. S. M. Yassukovich, "Eurobonds and Debt Rescheduling," *Euromoney*, January 1982, pp. 60, 62.

4. Annual Financing Report, *Euromoney*, March 1981, pp. 20, 22.

5. Anthony Angelini, Maximo Eng, and Francis Lees, *International Lending, Risk and the Euromarkets* (New York: John Wiley and Sons, 1979), pp. 178–82.

6. See "Euromarket Letter," *Financial Times*, October 30, 1981. This is a weekly report on international money and capital market developments.

7. Geoffrey Bell, "Debt Rescheduling—Can the Banking System Cope?" *The Banker*, February 1982, pp. 17–24.

SUGGESTED REFERENCES

Annual Survey of International Banking. *The Banker*. Various issues.

"Euromarket Letter." *Financial Times*. Various issues.

International Bank for Reconstruction and Development. *Annual Report.* Washington, D.C.: International Bank for Reconstruction and Development, various years.

——. *Borrowing in International Capital Markets.* Washington, D.C.: International Bank for Reconstruction and Development, various issues.

——. *World Debt Tables.* Washington, D.C.: International Bank for Reconstruction and Development, various issues.

——. *World Development Report.* Washington, D.C.: International Bank for Reconstruction and Development, various issues.

International Monetary Fund. *Annual Report.* Washington, D.C.: International Monetary Fund, various years.

——. *World Economic Outlook.* Washington, D.C.: International Monetary Fund, various issues.

Morgan Guaranty Trust Company. *World Financial Markets.* New York: Morgan Guaranty Trust Company, various issues.

Organization for Economic Cooperation and Development. *Development Cooperation Efforts and Policies of the Members of the Development Assistance Committee.* Paris: Organization for Economic Cooperation and Development, various issues.

——. *Economic Outlook.* Paris: Organization for Economic Cooperation and Development, various issues.

——. *Financial Market Trends.* Paris: Organization for Economic Cooperation and Development, various issues.

——. *Financial Statistics.* Paris: Organization for Economic Cooperation and Development, various issues.

"A Survey of Nigeria." *Economist*, January 23, 1982.

18 INTERNATIONAL AND U.S. FINANCING AGENCIES

Christopher M. Korth

As has been seen in earlier chapters, the international financial arena is not monopolized by commercial banks. Both government and intergovernment agencies are very active, both as partners and as competitors of commercial banks. This chapter will examine the major examples of these institutions. They will be examined in the following order:

International Monetary Fund
International Bank for Reconstruction and Development
Regional development banks
Programs of the U.S. government.

THE INTERNATIONAL MONETARY FUND

Once the tides of World War II had been reversed, the Allied governments turned their attention to the postwar world. Representatives of many of the Allied nations met in 1944 at Bretton Woods, New Hampshire, in order to plan and control the international financial and trading relations of the postwar world.

The planning at Bretton Woods addressed three major areas: monetary problems, financing problems, and trade problems. Correspondingly, three international bodies were designed to deal with these problems. Two of them are of interest to us: the International Monetary Fund (IMF) and International Bank for Reconstruction and Development (IBRD).[1]

Goals of the IMF

The International Monetary Fund was designed to accomplish the following:

1. Promote international monetary cooperation
2. Facilitate international trade as a means of raising employment and incomes
3. Promote exchange stability, maintain orderly exchange arrangements, and avoid competitive exchange depreciation
4. Assist in the establishment of a multilateral system of payments without foreign exchange restrictions
5. Make the general resources of the IMF available as loans to help countries adjust to temporary international payments problems
6. Shorten the duration and severity of international payments disequilibrium.[2]

It is the fifth of these goals that is of primary concern to us.

Membership in the IMF

In order to oversee the efforts to pursue these goals, the IMF was designed as a formal and permanent organization with headquarters in Washington, D.C. Membership is open to any country willing to abide by its regulations. Only national governments can be members or take advantage of its resources. More than 140 countries are members. Most non-Communist countries, as well as Yugoslavia, Romania, Vietnam, and the People's Republic of China, belong.

All member countries must buy into the IMF. They do this by paying their subscription quota. Prior to the 1970s this quota was to be paid 25 percent in gold and 75 percent in the country's own currency; the gold contribution has since been replaced by a 25 percent contribution in reserve currencies. The quota is determined by each country's relative economic strength and importance in world trade and finance; the United States has by far the largest quota. The subscription quotas do the following:

- Provide the resources for IMF loans to member countries
- Constitute the major factor in determining how much a member can borrow from the IMF

- Determine the member's voting strength
- Serve as the basis for the allocation of special drawing rights (SDRs).

The funds provided by member governments in compliance with these subscription quotas are the primary financial resources of the IMF. However, as will be seen below, there are other funds that some member governments have contributed but that can be used only for special purposes.

Loans from the IMF

Governments need international financial resources in order to pay their obligations, to intervene in the foreign exchange markets, and to otherwise help finance balance-of-payments imbalances. Some of these resources come from the governments' own international monetary reserves. Also, as has been seen earlier in this book, governments can borrow from commercial banks. In addition, any member government can borrow from the IMF.

The function of most of the loan facilities of the IMF is to "buy time" so that the government can take the necessary steps to end a "temporary" payments imbalance. The resources that the IMF has available to lend to its member countries come primarily from the members' subscription quotas. These quotas are increased periodically; as a result the IMF's resources have grown substantially since its inception (see Figure 18.1). As can be seen, starting with initial quotas of $8 billion in 1947, the IMF found it unnecessary to increase its assessment of its members until 1959. Since then, quotas have been increased four times; with the 1980 increase they totaled more than $70 billion (59 billion SDRs).

Tranches

When a member country borrows from the IMF, it must offer an equivalent amount of its own currency as collateral. Thus, the IMF's holdings of that currency will rise. It will automatically lend to a member until its holdings of that country's currency equal 100 percent of the nation's subscription quota. When the country first joined the IMF, this line of credit was equal to 25 percent of its

FIGURE 18.1: Contributions Paid In to the IMF, 1947–80
(subscription quotas)

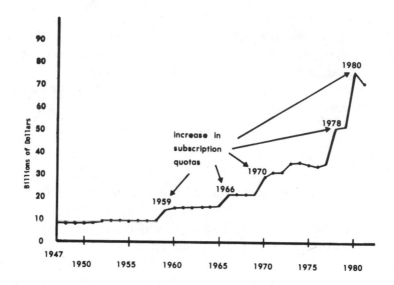

Note: Subscription quotas are denominated in SDRs. The volatility of quotas in the years since 1970 (including the decline in 1981) is the result of fluctuations in the value of the SDR.

Source: International Monetary Fund, *International Financial Statistics*, various monthly issues.

quota, since originally the quota was paid 75 percent in its own currency and 25 percent in gold. As a result that 25 percent of automatic credit line was formerly referred to as the *gold tranche*, but is now called its *reserve tranche*. (Tranche means a portion or share.) Borrowing against this line of credit is automatic—as long as the country can demonstrate balance-of-payments need.

Even if a country's reserve tranche becomes exhausted, the IMF will provide further assistance. The next category of loans is called the credit tranche. This occurs when the IMF's holdings of the country's currency exceed 100 percent of the member's quota but are less than 200 percent; it is divided into four credit tranches of 25 percent each. This portion of credit is not automatic. Generally, the more credit tranches a country has borrowed, the more stringent the demands placed by the IMF upon the borrower in terms of monetary and fiscal action expected. The terms for drawing against the tranches are shown in Table 18.1.

TABLE 18.1. IMF Policies for Utilization of Borrowing Tranches

Reserve tranche
Condition: Balance-of-payments need must be demonstrated.

First credit tranche
Condition: Country must offer a program representing reasonable efforts to overcome balance-of-payments difficulties.

Second, third, and fourth credit tranches
Condition: Country must offer a program giving substantial justification of its efforts to overcome balance-of-payments difficulties; resources are normally provided in the form of stand-by arrangements that include performance criteria and drawings in installments.

Source: IMF Survey: Supplement, September 1979, p. 7.

Remember that these loans are made to help shore up a nation's currency temporarily, until corrective action can be taken. If the country will not or cannot take the necessary steps, the IMF may be unwilling to help maintain the present value of a currency.

Other IMF Credit Facilities

The IMF has devised additional channels for providing funds for countries that are experiencing difficulties in maintaining exchange rate stability. These special facilities are listed in Table 18.2. As can be seen, funds are available from these financial facilities only for special purposes (such as unexpected export shortfall, participation in an international commodity buffer stock, and concessionary trust-fund loans to very poor countries).

The IMF's influence has been greatly enhanced by its increased resources and greater flexibility, which have been made possible by the wider variety of lending facilities and by some new policies regarding the manner in which the facilities may be employed. It has acquired much more self-confidence in its relations with members. As a result the IMF has made strong demands for internal monetary and fiscal adjustment upon many borrowers, including such industrialized countries as Italy and the United Kingdom.

TABLE 18.2. Financial Facilities of the IMF and the Conditions of Their Use

---

Compensatory financing facility (1963)

Condition: Existence of temporary export shortfall for reasons beyond the member country's control. Member cooperates with IMF in an effort to find appropriate solutions for any balance-of-payments difficulties.

Buffer stock financing facility (1969)

Condition: Participation in an international buffer stock accepted as suitable by IMF. Member is expected to cooperate as in the case of compensatory financing.

Extended fund facility (1974)

Condition: Structural balance-of-payments difficulties. Medium-term program for up to three years. Detailed statement of policies and measures is required. Resources are provided in the form of extended arrangements that include performance criteria and drawings in installments.

Trust fund (1976)

Condition: Available to low-income developing countries only. Provides balance-of-payments loans on very concessionary terms.

Supplemental financing facility (1979)

Condition: For use when credit tranches are insufficient, in support of programs under stand-by arrangements reaching into the upper credit tranche or beyond, or under extended arrangements. Subject to relevant policies on conditionality, phasing, and performance criteria.

Source: *IMF Survey: Supplement*, September 1979, p. 7.

INTERNATIONAL BANK FOR RECONSTRUCTION AND DEVELOPMENT

One of the major concerns of the Bretton Woods conferees was the very serious problem of the reconstruction of war-ravaged Europe and Asia. Coupled with this was the compelling need to aid in the economic and social development of less-developed countries (LDCs). The International Bank for Reconstruction and Development (IBRD) was designed to fill these needs.

Any member of the IMF may elect to join the IBRD. The basic function of the IBRD (or World Bank, as it is misleadingly called) is to make loans to its needy members.

The financial resources come partially from members' contributions (quotas), but primarily from borrowing in private capital markets. Since the majority of the World Bank's resources depend upon its borrowing capacity, it is critical that the organization maintain a prime credit rating. It does this in the following ways:

- By extending loans only—it makes no equity investments
- By charging rates of interest that will fully cover both its borrowing and its administrative costs
- By lending only to countries with reasonable credit ratings (although it does not lend to developed countries)
- By extending loans only for economically attractive and self-financing projects
- By requiring guarantees from the government of the country to which the loan is being extended
- By financing only part of any project
- By insisting upon repayment only in hard currencies
- By having limited recourse to its members for additional contributions as part of their membership quotas.

The IBRD has been very successful in maintaining its prime credit rating. Furthermore, it has been able to do this without ever having to call for the supplemental contributions of its members.

Although the IBRD had as its primary initial objective the reconstruction of the war-ravaged countries, its resources proved very inadequate for the task. Accordingly, when the U.S. government introduced the Marshall Plan, with its significantly greater resources, the IBRD shifted its activities almost totally to the economic and social development of the LDCs. Now its loans go only to developing countries—not to the industrialized countries, which have the capacity to finance their needs by alternative means, or to the poorest countries, which generally do not qualify because of their poor credit ratings.

The IBRD is careful to avoid competing with private-sector lenders. Not only might competition lead to antagonism, but it might discourage direct private-sector financial flows to developing countries—something the IBRD is anxious to promote. Moreover, in order to encourage loans from commercial banks, the IBRD will often offer guarantees to banks on part of some bank loans.

Because of the need to maintain its credit rating, the World Bank is very restricted in the type of projects it can finance. There are many worthwhile projects that its charter or prudence will not allow it to finance. In order to surmount these limitations and to increase its contribution to economic and social development, two subsidiary organizations have been created.

International Finance Corporation

Early experience at the World Bank indicated that, because of the stringency of the conditions under which loans could be made, the IBRD was not able to offer financial help for many worthy investments. Therefore, in 1956 a sister organization, the International Finance Corporation (IFC), was created. The IFC is designed to make loans without government guarantees (and therefore for investments only in the private sector), and even to make equity investments (to have partial ownership rather than simply to make loans); in fact, its loans may even have provisions for profit sharing.

As in the case of the IBRD, the fostering of private money and capital markets is of paramount importance. Toward this end the IFC is anxious to sell its investment when a venture becomes successful enough to attract private investors.

However, since the IFC makes nonguaranteed loans and equity investments, its risks are greater than are those of the IBRD. As a result its credit rating does not permit it to borrow in the private capital markets. Accordingly, all of the institution's resources must come from member-government contributions. This, of course, makes the IFC much more dependent upon the generosity of member governments than is the parent organization. However, it also allows the IFC to be more flexible in credit terms or currency of repayment.

International Development Association

Even the IFC had certain limitations regarding the variety and stipulations of its loans. Therefore, in 1960 the third organization of the World Bank Group was created. The International Development Association (IDA, sometimes called the "soft-loan window" of the World Bank) provides money for "nonproductive" loans, such as housing and sanitation projects. Also, the stipulations can be very generous—no interest charges, 10-year "periods of grace" (no repayment of principal for the first 10 years), and up to 50 years for repayment. The IDA is even less creditworthy than the IFC. Therefore, all of its resources must also come directly from member-government contributions.

REGIONAL DEVELOPMENT BANKS

The job of financing international economic and social development is so immense that even the extensive resources of the World Bank Group are inadequate. To help meet the tremendous demands for assistance, a number of other international financing organizations, mostly public but some private, have been created. Although they are not part of the World Bank Group, many of them are somewhat similar and, at least indirectly, they owe their existence to the example set by the IBRD. These organizations are called development banks; like the IBRD, they receive their funds primarily from contributions by member countries, but also from debt financing—not from deposits.

The goals and method of operations of the development banks are generally comparable with those of the World Bank, but they each have a much more limited geographical focus. The major development banks are Inter-American Development Bank, Asian Development Bank, and African Development Bank. (These will be discussed individually below.) Three European development banks also exist. The European Investment Bank is a unit of the European Economic Community. Two development banks exist in Eastern Europe, primarily to aid countries in that region: the International Bank for Economic Cooperation and the International Investment Bank.

The Inter-American Development Bank

The largest and most prominent of the international development banks is the Inter-American Development Bank (IDB). The IDB is a regional bank that seeks to accelerate economic and social development in the developing countries of the western hemisphere. In addition to the potential borrowing countries, the United States, Canada, and many developed countries outside the western hemisphere are capital-contributing (but not borrowing) members.

The IDB makes two different types of loans, each of which comes from a different "fund": the ordinary capital resources fund and the Fund for Special Operations.

The ordinary capital resources fund is used to make productive loans at conventional terms to governments or private organizations capable of bearing the debt. Such loans must be repaid in the currency in which the loans were made, and guaranteed by the government of the recipient nation. These loans are similar in many respects to IBRD loans. The funds for the ordinary capital resources fund are provided by member-country quotas. Also, the ordinary capital resources are buttressed by an additional, and much larger, amount of "callable" capital that is used as security for borrowing in world capital markets.

The Fund for Special Operations (FSO) provides funds on a less stringent basis than that associated with ordinary capital funds. Loans are not restricted to directly productive employment—for instance, housing and improvement of water and sewage facilities are legitimate purposes. Also, these long-term, relatively low-interest loans are often repayable in the currency of the borrower. The FSO receives its resources from member-country contributions. This fund is similar in activity to the IDA, which it antedates.

Asian Development Bank

The Far Eastern counterpart to the IDB is the Asian Development Bank (AsDB), which was opened in 1966. Its members include not only Asian countries, which can be both contributing and borrowing members, but also non-Asian countries, which can be contributing members only. The United States, Canada, Great Britain, and many West European countries are among the nonregional members. Its headquarters is in Manila.

The AsDB's financial resources come primarily from member-country contributions, plus borrowings from money and capital markets. Although its loans can extend for as long as 30 years and grace periods on the repayment of principal can be as long as 7 years, the interest rates and credit record of the organization, as well as the backing of its member governments, have allowed the AsDB to maintain a strong credit rating. Most of the loans are extended to governments or government agencies. Much of the AsDB's lending involves cofinancing with commercial banks. Technical assistance is also an important service of the organization.

The AsDB has a "soft-loan window," the Asian Development Fund (AsDF), which is analogous to the Fund for Special Operations of the IDB. The AsDF extends loans for as long as 40 years with a 10-year grace period and a very nominal 1 percent interest. Obviously, the credit rating of the AsDB would be impaired with such loans in its portfolio. However, the AsDF's funds come from special contributions of its members; it cannot borrow from private markets.

African Development Bank

In the same year as the initiation of the AsDB, a similar organization was begun in Africa. In that year the Organization of African Unity created the African Development Bank (AfDB), which is headquartered in Abidjan, Ivory Coast. The AfDB, like the IDB and the AsDB, was designed to provide financial and technical assistance to member countries. The AfDB was, until the early 1980s, more restrictive than either of the other two development banks: only African countries (and only independent African countries at that) could be members. The organization is now willing to accept non-African countries as contributing, but not borrowing, members.

The AfDB receives its funds both from its members' subscribed capital contributions and from private-sector borrowings. It has a good credit rating that qualifies it for commercial credits. In order to qualify for commercial bank funds and public debt offerings, the AfDB maintains conservative lending policies and interest rates. Loans are made only to governments or their agencies. Interest rates are close to commercial rates. Loans can be for as long as 20 years, and grace periods of 3 to 5 years are common. In addition to the loans, the AfDB also provides guarantees and technical assistance.

The AfDB also has its own "soft-loan window" analogous to the Fund for Special Operations of the IDB and the Asian Development Fund of the AsDB. The African Development Fund (AfDF) was founded in 1972. Unlike the parent organization, the AfDF has from its beginning included as members many non-African countries, such as Great Britain, the United States, Germany, Brazil, Japan, and South Korea. Its soft loans can be for as long as 50 years, include 10 years of grace, and be repaid at interest rates of 1 percent in the 10 years after the grace period and 3 percent after that.

GOVERNMENT PROGRAMS

In addition to the funding programs provided by the above international agencies, most national governments and some private-sector companies or associations have their own unilateral programs as well. Several of the major ones of the United States are discussed below.

The U.S. Export-Import Bank

The U.S. Export-Import Bank (Eximbank) is the major U.S. agency for providing financial support for exports. Most other countries have analogous agencies (for instance, the Export Credits Guarantee Department in the United Kingdom, COFACE in France, and the Export-Import Bank of Japan).

The Eximbank is a U.S. government agency that was set up in 1934 to finance both exports and imports. When it was organized, it was specifically intended to promote trade with the Soviet Union. However, no trade with the Soviet Union has ever been financed by Eximbank. An act of the U.S. Congress forbids the extension of government credit to any country that is not satisfactorily paying the U.S. government for past loans. Since the Soviet Union is in default on a significant amount of such credits, it has been, and continues to be, ineligible for Eximbank trade credits. However, several other Communist countries are eligible.

The title Export-Import Bank implies that imports as well as exports will be financed, and this was the original intention. However, no imports have ever been financed. The agency supports the purchases abroad of American-made products, whether the purchasers are foreign governments or U.S. companies abroad.

The Eximbank has a wide range of authority to help it foster U.S. exports. First, it can extend loans with its own funds, either directly to importers abroad, through the buyer-credit program, or to foreign banks or other foreign financial institutions (the Cooperative Financing Facility) that will combine the funds with their own resources to finance U.S. exports. It will sometimes buy bankers' acceptances that were used to finance U.S. exports. Second, it can issue guarantees against both political and commercial risk on the loans made by commercial banks. Third, it can issue insurance on the trade credits extended by exporters. These are part of the supplier-credit program.

The Eximbank wishes to encourage as much export financing as possible. Therefore, it is careful to avoid disrupting the private sources of trade financing. Indeed, the Eximbank works very closely with such institutions. When it extends loans directly, it is only on condition that part of the funds must come from the private sector. The Eximbank's share is never more than 85 percent—and often much less; the buyer must make at least a 15 percent down payment (although such funds could be borrowed from another source).

These direct Eximbank loans are generally for the financing of long-term trade credits—longer maturities than commercial banks generally will issue. The bank is also a strong proponent of cofinancing with commercial banks. Under this arrangement the commercial bank lends the short- and medium-term funds (the first five years) while the Eximbank lends the long-term portion. In addition, the Eximbank may extend a guarantee for the commercial bank's share of the loan. The latter will be at standard commercial loan rates, while the Eximbank loan will be at a subsidized rate.

The Commodity Credit Corporation

Another agency of the U.S. government that finances American exports is the Commodity Credit Corporation (CCC) of the U.S. Department of Agriculture. As the name and parentage of the CCC suggest, this agency exists for the purpose of promoting the export of American agricultural commodities.

The CCC extends its credit to export firms in the United States. The credits are provided through the purchase of the exporter's accounts receivable. The financing cannot exceed three years, and the total amount of the discount is limited to the export value of the commodities without any allowance for shipping, insurance, and financial charges. An irrevocable standby letter of credit must back all of the discounted trade credits.

In conjunction with the Eximbank, the CCC also helps to finance the export of agricultural storage and processing facilities. It is felt that the increase of such facilities abroad will encourage the export of U.S. agricultural products.

The Foreign Credit Insurance Association

The Eximbank has always been anxious to cooperate with private-sector companies to promote exports by American companies. In 1961 it cooperated with a large group of insurance companies to create the Foreign Credit Insurance Association (FCIA). The FCIA is a voluntary association, not a corporation. Its basic function is to provide political and commercial risk insurance for American exporters, and sometimes for banks. The exporter will thus be protected against nonpayment for a wide variety of reasons within these general categories. With such insurance the exporter will likely find it easier to obtain export financing; the proceeds from an FCIA insurance policy can be assigned to the bank that provides the financing. The FCIA does not make loans.

The basic coverage of FCIA assistance includes a short-term policy (up to six months) and a medium-term policy (six months to five years). The short-term policy is generally available only to an exporter who will insure all or a well-diversified group of his receivables. Such insurance is limited to 95 percent of the value for political risk and to 90 percent or less for commercial risk. With medium-term policies both the political and the commercial risk coverage can vary between 70 and 90 percent, depending upon the country.

Special insurance packages can be obtained for some specific cases. For businesses that have done little exporting, short-term and medium-term insurance can be obtained on a case-by-case basis. Alternatively, a master policy can be obtained for all of a company's short- and medium-term credit risks; thus, FCIA approval is not necessary on a case-by-case basis. Insurance against only political risk is available at a lower cost than combined commercial and political risk. A special policy for the export of services is also available; this is attractive to management consultants, engineering companies, transportation companies, and oil drillers.

FCIA insurance is available for any exporter in the United States under certain conditions. Specifically, at least half of the exports, valuewise, must have been from the United States, the export must be payable in dollars, and the payment terms must be normal for that particular type of export. The existence of such insurance protection enables the exporter to offer better credit terms to foreign customers. The company therefore should be able to compete more successfully in export markets than would otherwise be the case.

The Private Export Funding Corporation

There is another special organization that provides loans to assist U.S. exports. The Private Export Funding Corporation (PEFCO) is, as its name suggests, a private company. It was established in 1970 under the initiative of the Bankers' Association for Foreign Trade and with the encouragement of the Eximbank. It is owned by a large group of banks and some major exporters.

PEFCO's principal focus is upon the extension of medium- and long-term credit to foreign purchasers of U.S. capital goods such as aircraft, power plants, railroad equipment, and mining and industrial installations. Although a private-sector company, PEFCO is designed to supplement other private-sector sources of financing—including, but not limited to, loans from the banks and companies that own it. If alternative funding sources are available, PEFCO ordinarily will not loan. However, when credit conditions are tight or when the project is large and the financing period is long, PEFCO can play a very major role.

PEFCO never extends loans without significant participation from commercial banks. Very often the Eximbank is also a lender. If the Eximbank is lending, then it will take the long-term maturity share of the loan, PEFCO will take the middle range, and the commercial banks will take the shorter term. If Eximbank is not a lender, PEFCO will take the long-term portion and the banks will take the shorter-term share.

Both principal and interest on all of PEFCO's loans are unconditionally guaranteed by the Eximbank. This is true whether or not the Eximbank is sharing in the project as a lender. The majority of the funds of PEFCO come from borrowings in the private money and capital markets. With the Eximbank guarantee of all of its lending, PEFCO's credit rating is very strong.

SUMMARY

There are many international, government, and private-sector organizations with which commercial banks come in contact in international markets. Many of these institutions can assist and supplement the international financial efforts of commercial banks. The international intergovernment organizations are the IMF and a group of development banks: the IBRD, the IDB, the AsDB, and the AfDB. All of the development banks provide technical and financial assistance (via loans, guarantees, or insurance) for developing countries. The American organizations that are described herein include government institutions (the Eximbank and the CCC) and private institutions (the FCIA and the PEFCO). They are all oriented toward promoting the international trade of the United States through the provision of loans and guarantees or insurance. These organizations and some of the more important aspects of their operations were discussed in this chapter.

NOTES

1. The third organization that was planned at Bretton Woods was the International Trade Organization. However, it was never ratified. It was supplanted by the General Agreement on Tariffs and Trade (GATT).

2. Articles of Agreement, International Monetary Fund, art. 1.

Part VI
CONCLUSION

19 THE INTERNATIONAL ROLE OF U.S. BANKS IN PERSPECTIVE

Dwight B. Crane and
Samuel L. Hayes III

The competitive fabric of international banking at the beginning of the 1980s is much changed from two decades earlier. U.S. financial institutions have been significant agents in the evolution of the international banking industry that has occurred, and they are important industry leaders, but their market position has shifted. While still very important, U.S. banking firms have moved from a position of preeminence to one in which they represent only a subset of a growing number of strong competitors.

While the evolution observed over this period was spurred by such factors as the growing strength of other economies and the further development of the Euromarkets, perhaps the single most important influence on international banking in recent years has been the quantum jump in oil prices beginning in 1973–74. In this chapter the contemporary competitive structure of international banking will be described, some of the capital market repercussions of the oil price rises will be explored, and their impact on U.S. banking will be examined.

FACTORS IN INTERNATIONAL BANKING COMPETITION

In describing the competitive environment of international banking within which OPEC-related developments took place, it is helpful to utilize concepts drawn from industrial organization theory. In the extensive body of literature on this approach to the analysis of competitive structure,[1] we find the framework devised by Michael E. Porter to be particularly useful in articulating the topography of these financial markets.[2]

Porter envisions a competitive structure that is multidimensional. That is, while the degree of competition or rivalry among firms within an industry is indeed an important component of that structure, it is only one of five principal forces at work. Other factors in the competitive structure include the relative bargaining power of suppliers to the industry, the bargaining power of buyers from the industry, the threat of substitute products, and the threat of new entrants. The interplay of these factors makes up the "extended rivalry" that determines the relative profitability of an industry.

Porter's comprehensive competitive framework is readily applicable to the international banking industry if one makes modest adjustments in his terminology. Banking institutions, of course, represent the competing firms in his model. Depositors at financial institutions are both suppliers and customers, in that they both supply funds and purchase banking services. Therefore, to reduce confusion, this exposition will replace Porter's terms "customers" and "suppliers" with two new terms. His term "suppliers" will be replaced by the term "suppliers of funds" to the banking industry, and his "buyers" will be taken to mean "users of funds." Porter's framework, adapted to the banking industry, is shown in Figure 19.1.

In the present focus on international banking, "users of funds" include primarily governments, government agencies, and corporations that borrow or obtain funds in a foreign currency or from a foreign-headquartered institution. It would include, for example, a German corporation borrowing French francs from a bank to build a plant in France, or the government of Spain issuing U.S. dollar-denominated bonds for a development project. The "suppliers of funds" category would include purchasers of financial securities issued by foreign entities or securities denominated in a foreign currency. Depositors at internationally oriented commercial banks also would be important suppliers of funds.

The principal competitors in the international banking industry include the relatively large commercial banks that actively engage in international lending from their home country and/or foreign-based locations, plus merchant/investment banks that underwrite or place foreign securities.

FIGURE 19.1: Forces Driving Banking Competition

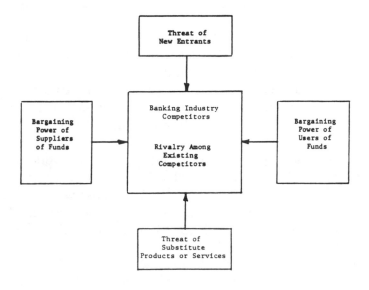

Source: From Michael E. Porter, *Competitive Strategy: Techniques for Analyzing Industries and Competitors* (New York: The Free Press), 1980, p. 4.

INTERNATIONAL BANKING AT THE BEGINNING OF THE 1970S

Historically, the competitive structure of "international banking" has been a series of bilateral financial relationships between parties in separate countries. Much of the international financial activity emanated from the European colonial expansion, and banking networks subsequently were established in those possessions, as well as in other countries, to handle important commercial intercourse with the home country. The expansion of French banks into French-speaking Africa is a typical example.

Europe was the source of much of the world's excess capital, and thus the banking houses on the Continent and in Great Britain exercised great power in their dealings with borrowers in other countries, for which alternative means of obtaining capital outside their home countries were severely limited. Even the modest amount of public foreign bond financings undertaken by capital users tended to concentrate in those capital-surplus countries where the borrower had close ties stemming from a common language, culture, or other relationship.

After World War II the United States assumed the role of principal capital exporter, and U.S.-based corporations gained preeminence in many export markets. Large money center banks in the United States followed their corporate and commercial customers abroad, much as the Europeans had done a generation or two earlier. However, there was an important difference. U.S. banks were following their customers into industrialized countries as well as into developing countries, so that a more truly international network of banking relationships and competition was beginning to develop.

By the beginning of the 1960s, the U.S. banks were clearly major factors in across-national-boundaries financial services. In the early days of the Eurobond market, for example, the majority of leading bond underwriters were U.S.-owned commercial and merchant/investment banks. The rebounding European and Japanese economies began to generate increased international banking activity among the banking houses of those countries, but competition was still quite muted. In the industrial organization terms articulated earlier, the capital users had few options for foreign financing; the capital suppliers were similarly limited to the traditional banking institutions present in their home markets; and threats of new entrants or substitute products were not important enough to pose a real threat to the preeminent position held by a relatively small number of commercial and merchant banks. Furthermore, these financial institutions were somewhat segmented by geographic boundaries, and by a separation of commercial and merchant/investment banking activities in some key countries, so that profit margins were generally conceded to be quite robust.

Subsequent developments substantially altered this competitive picture by the early 1970s. These included the continued resurgence of other Western industrial and Japanese economies relative to that of the United States, the formation and subsequent growth of the Eurodollar markets, and the spectacular advances in electronic communications and transportation. Thus, by the early 1970s there was a true "international" capital market rather than the previous series of bilateral capital intercourses.

Rivalry among primary participants was greatly increased as the number of players grew and as the physical and communications barriers that had previously separated markets fell. In contrast with the earlier, relatively modest competition across country boundaries, by the early 1970s U.S. commercial banks had moved aggressively into European and other financial centers, competing directly with domestic banks in those locations. The large European banks had also moved out to foreign financial centers, but to a lesser extent and frequently only as part of a joint venture, such as a consortium bank, or as a member of a "banking club" (a group of banks working together). Major international commercial banks were in active competition, not only among themselves but also with merchant/ investment banks in loan syndications and in Eurobond underwriting.

In addition to the increased number of competitors, two other factors increased the rivalry among financial institutions at the beginning of the 1970s. For one thing, competitors came to the market with different objectives and backgrounds. Some banks, for example, were willing to cut prices and take lower profits in the short run in order to gain market position. Another factor was the relatively high level of fixed costs incurred to maintain branches in London and other European centers. In these circumstances banks were tempted to cut margins in order to maintain volume and thus cover overhead costs.

Barriers to entry were also breaking down, particularly in terms of access to funds. The development of the certificate of deposit market in the United States, and the Eurodollar market internationally, made it possible, for example, for regional banks in the United States to aspire to a larger size and to a greater position in the international lending community. A total of 61 U.S. banks had established a branch or representative office in London by 1974. In addition, access to Eurocurrency funds encouraged the expansion of bank branches in other countries. Even if local currency was difficult to obtain in some of these countries, the Eurocurrency market made it possible to engage in international banking activities, including syndicated lending of U.S. dollars or other foreign currencies to government agencies.

The decision by President Nixon to unfreeze the relationship between the U.S. dollar and gold in 1971 was essentially a decision to "devalue" the dollar in relation to a number of other currencies. This action was taken in the face of mounting U.S. balance-of-payments deficits and the strong international payments positions of Japan and several European countries.

One consequence of the weakening of the U.S. dollar, and a contributor to its fall in value as well, was that some dollar holders shifted into other currencies. The Swiss franc had for some time been a secondary reserve currency. Now the West German deutsche mark and Japanese yen were sought as well. Although these countries did not desire to assume a reserve currency role, as the influx of capital continued, they became somewhat more relaxed about the creation of foreign holdings of their currency. This whole process led to a growing pool of Eurofunds in stronger currencies of select industrialized countries. It also led to increased use of these countries as sources of international finance and, relatedly, it enhanced the position of their banks in such international financing activities as loan syndication and bond underwriting.

The Eurocurrency markets loosened the ties between suppliers of funds and banks, and increased the amount of product substitution, both of which had the effect of increasing international banking competition by the early 1970s. This source of funds provided a new supply of "cold-nose" money that essentially went to the highest bidder rather than to institutions that had historical ties to the depositor. In addition, if a depositor did not like the dollar interest rate quoted in New York City, it was possible to deposit dollars in London and other financial centers. It was similarly possible to borrow dollars and other currencies outside the home country of the currency. Thus, depositors and borrowers were able to arbitrage markets across country boundaries. There was also more choice of financial instruments as competition in the Eurocurrency markets pushed maturities on syndicated loans to periods almost as long as those of Eurobonds.

In sum, the international banking markets were clearly much more competitive in the early 1970s than they had been a decade earlier. The degree of competition was increased by the substantial rise in the number and variety of banking firms in the marketplace, by the growth of substitute products, and by the related increase in bargaining power of both suppliers and users of funds. Furthermore, there was a continuing threat of new entrants. Major banks in some countries still had a strong domestic orientation, and had not yet started to expand their international activity aggressively.

Thus, when producing countries raised their oil prices threefold in late 1973 and early 1974, the international banking industry had already undergone substantial recent change and the role of the U.S.

banks within this industry structure was being challenged by the resurging banks of other thriving Western and Japanese economies.

AFTERMATH OF OIL PRICE HIKES

In order to understand the impact that the oil-related shift in spending power was to have on the international banking system and, ultimately, on U.S. financial institutions, one must understand some important dimensions of the OPEC capital flow. These include the growth in the pool of investable funds, the repercussions it had on the Euromarkets and other geographic markets, and the competitive implications of the investment patterns of various investing units within the OPEC group.

As a result of the 1973–74 price increases, the oil-exporting countries' (OEC) current-account surplus of $67 billion for 1974 represented an income many times greater than in any previous year. (Data for OEC include the 13 members of OPEC plus Bahrain, Brunei, Oman, and Trinidad and Tobago, as reported by the Bank of England.) The surpluses continued, though less dramatically, for the next three years, but by 1978 the positive flow of funds had diminished to almost nothing (see Figure 19.2).

FIGURE 19.2: OEC Current-Account Surpluses, 1973–80

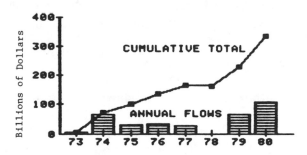

Annual and Cumulative
Current-Account Surpluses
of Oil-Exporting Countries

Source: Bank of England, *Quarterly Bulletin*, various issues.

This gradual erosion of OEC's surplus spending power was due to a drop in the price of oil relative to the price of world exports during this period, as shown in the table below. Thus, as the cost of the imported goods and services used for the internal development of the OEC countries caught up to the level of oil revenues earned, the current-account surpluses were erased.

Comparison of Oil Prices with Export Prices of Industrial Countries

	1972	1973	1974	1975	1976	1977	1978	1979	1980
Oil prices	18	25	91	100	107	116	119	158	271
Export prices	60	72	90	100	104	114	123	143	166

Source: Susan Bluff, "OPEC's $350 Billion Balance Sheet," Euromoney, September 1980, p. 110.

After 1978 leaders in the OECs became more concerned about the erosive effects of inflation, and began adjusting the price of oil to maintain its real value. Saudi Arabian prices, for example, were raised from $12.70 per barrel in 1978 to $16.97 in 1979, and to an average of $29.00 in 1980.[3] Such rises led to a 1979 OEC surplus of $67 billion and to a 1980 record surplus of $106 billion.

By the end of 1980, balance-of-payments statistics suggested that the OECs held financial assets amounting to some $335 billion. As one illustration of the relative magnitude of this pool of funds, the total Eurocurrency deposits of nonbank institutions at this point was $270 billion.[4] Clearly the OEC pool represented a large source of funds capable of influencing the pattern of international financial flows.

CONCENTRATION OF FINANCIAL ASSETS

The concentration of OECs' financial resources is even more dramatic when one examines more closely the actual control of the funds. Four of the seventeen oil exporters—Saudi Arabia, Kuwait, the United Arab Emirates (especially Abu Dhabi), and Qatar—controlled 69 percent of the accumulated assets at the end of 1979 (see Figure 19.3). Data were not yet available, but if this share continued in 1980, their year-end holdings would be $230 billion. Saudi Arabia alone, which was pumping 40 percent of OPEC's daily oil output in early 1981, was estimated to hold almost half of this capital.[5]

FIGURE 19.3: Cumulative Current-Account Surpluses, 1973–80

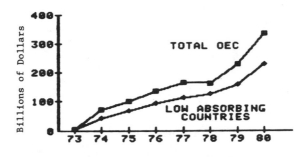

Cumulative Current-Account
Surpluses of all OEC and
Low-Absorbing Countries

Note: Low-absorbing OEC countries are Saudi Arabia, Kuwait, United Arab
Emirates, and Qatar.
Source: Bank of England, *Quarterly Bulletin*, various issues.

These countries have large surpluses because their internal
economies can absorb only a relatively modest proportion of their oil
revenues as investments in their infrastructures. Figure 19.4 illustrates
that the four "low-absorbing" countries have disproportionately high
oil revenues in relation to their sparse populations, a rough measure
of absorptive capacity.

The Bank of England characterizes Libya, Iraq, Iran, Oman,
Trinidad and Tobago, and Brunei as middle-absorbing oil exporters.
Together these six nations held most of the approximately $105 bil-
lion of surplus not held by the low absorbers at the end of 1980.
Nigeria, Algeria, Gabon, Venezuela, Ecuador, Indonesia, and Bahrain,
which have large populations to support relative to their revenues,
are classified as "high-absorbing" countries. These countries recorded
surpluses in their current account during the years of the largest price
increases, such as 1974 and 1979, but their accumulated balance over
that six year period was slightly negative, suggesting a nominal
accumulated pool of funds at best.

The irregularity with which the high-absorbing countries earn
surpluses is in contrast with the low absorbers' continuing earnings.
Figure 19.5 shows that the current-account surpluses of the three

FIGURE 19.4: Pattern of Oil Revenues Per Capita

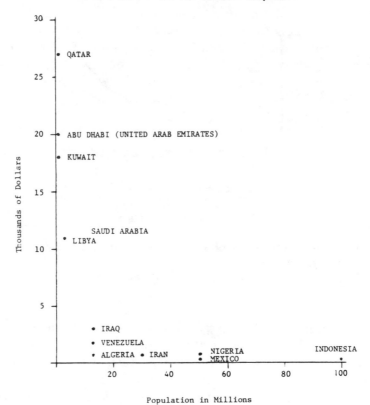

Source: Bruce R. Scott, "OPEC, the American Scapegoat," *Harvard Business Review*, January–February 1981, p. 8.

groups tend to move together in direction but to differ in order of magnitude. Although the low absorbers experienced a decline in the annual volume of surplus funds from 1976 to 1978, they continued to have a considerable amount of new funds to place each year. In the case of the high absorbers, however, the fluctuations meant the difference between being a placer of funds or a borrower of funds.

These differences in the patterns of earnings have further enhanced the relative financial power of the low absorbers, particularly Saudi Arabia and Kuwait. They are consistent investors in the financial markets both because of the natural turnover in their large in-place pool of capital and because of a continuing stream of new surplus money. They have therefore developed relatively sophisticated systems and institutions for handling this wealth, and have accumulated considerable experience in operating in a variety of financial market settings as they have sought to diversify the types and maturities of their portfolio holdings.

By contrast, because the high absorbers experience surplus earnings only sporadically, their surplus funds typically are held in an investment account only briefly, until they are committed to infrastructure development projects. Thus, these countries tend to rely on highly liquid investment alternatives, such as Eurodeposits, which require a less sophisticated investment management.

FIGURE 19.5: Current-Account Surpluses, 1973-79

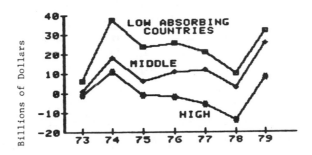

Annual Current-Account Surpluses
of Low-, Middle-, and High-
Absorbing OEC Countries

Note: Middle-absorbing countries include Brunei, Iran, Iraq, Libya, Oman, and Trinidad and Tobago. The high-absorbing countries include Algeria, Bahrain, Ecuador, Gabon, Indonesia, Nigeria, and Venezuela.

Source: Bank of England, *Quarterly Bulletin*, various issues.

OEC FUNDS: IMPACT ON CAPITAL MARKETS

The capital-surplus accumulation of oil exporters brought a dramatic change in the size and level of activity in the international capital markets with respect to deposits, loans, publicly underwritten bonds, and a variety of other investment activities. These, in turn, have had an impact on the competitive structure of the international financial industry.

Deposits, for instance, took a sharp upward turn in the period following the first oil price increase. Data from the Bank for International Settlements (BIS) illustrate the growth. Eurocurrency deposits at the international banks that report to the BIS almost tripled from $205 billion at the end of 1975 to $575 billion at the end of 1980. As might be expected, a substantial part of that growth is attributable to OECs. From a base of $5.3 billion in 1975, OEC Eurocurrency deposits at these banks grew to nearly $110 billion in 1980.[6] As a percentage of the total, they rose from 2.6 percent of the Eurocurrency deposits in 1975 to 19.1 percent in 1980.

As the Eurocurrency market grew, the nature of this international banking market changed. In 1974 the major foreign borrowers from banks reporting to the BIS were from East European and other developed economies. Many banks and other borrowers from the United States, for example, relied heavily on the Eurodollar market in 1974 because of the credit crunch and shortage of funds at home. Thus, as shown in Figure 19.6, in 1974 the international banks were recycling funds primarily from some developed and oil-exporting countries to other developed countries. This changed dramatically after the oil price increases. As illustrated by the 1980 numbers in Figure 19.6, the major suppliers of funds to the international banks were still oil-exporting and developed economies, but East European and nonoil-exporting developing countries had become substantial net users.

The use of Eurocurrency markets to fund country deficits, induced in large part by oil price increases, shows up clearly in the growth of Eurocurrency bank credits and the international bond market, including both Eurobonds and other foreign bond issues. Figure 19.7 shows that Eurocurrency loans rose from an annual volume of under $10 billion in the early 1970s to approximately $80 billion at the end of the decade. Nonoil developing countries accounted for a significant share of this growth in bank loans, because they were less able to obtain longer-term funds in the international bond market. Industrialized countries, however, turned to the bond market for substantial amounts of borrowing. The $42 billion of international bonds issued in 1980 was six times the level in 1974, as shown in Figure 19.8.

This quantum jump in international capital markets activity quite naturally spurred a number of entrants to establish a position in the competitive arena. Foreign commercial bank representation in Lon-

FIGURE 19.6: Net Foreign Deposits/Loans Outstanding at Banks Reporting to the BIS, 1974 and 1980 (billions of dollars)

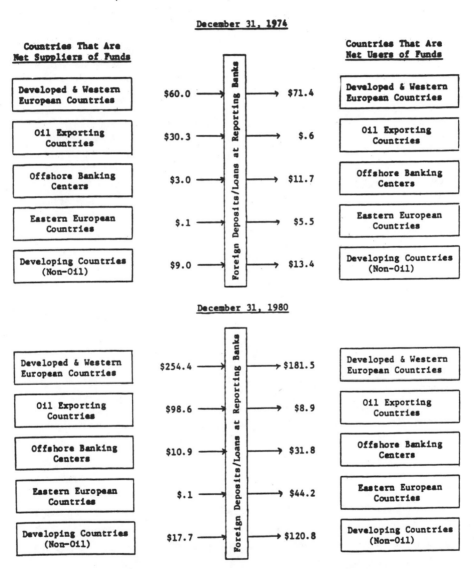

Source: Derived from data provided by Bank for International Settlements, *Quarterly Reports*, fourth quarter 1974 and fourth quarter 1980.

FIGURE 19.7: New Eurocurrency Bank Credits, 1970–80

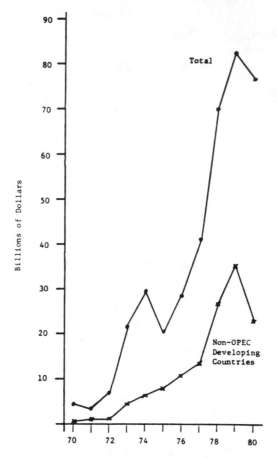

Source: Morgan Guaranty Trust Company, *World Financial Markets*, various issues.

don, a geographic focus of these markets, grew even larger after the 1973-74 oil price hike; foreign banks with branches or representative offices there increased from 230 in 1973 to 351 by the end of 1980. The number of U.S. banks in London remained at about the level reached in 1974, 61 banks.[7]

While many of these banks engaged in securities-related activities, in addition to deposit-taking and lending, the number of firms represented in London with principally a securities orientation also grew during this period. The number of securities firms reached 72 in 1980, with more than one-third having arrived after 1973. U.S. firms were prominent among both the established firms and the new arrivals, accounting for about half of each group.

The growth of the Eurocurrency markets and international lending in general is a visible and important manifestation of the oil price increases. However, there are other results that have significant implications for international banking. These include the placement of OEC funds directly in foreign economies, the development of domestic banking markets in OECs, and the growing outreach of banks in the Persian Gulf region.

FIGURE 19.8: Annual Volume of International Bond Issues, 1963–80

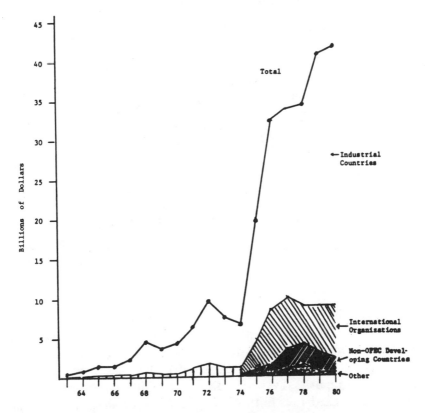

Note: Data include foreign bonds sold in the United States.
Source: Morgan Guaranty Trust Company, *World Financial Markets*, various issues.

PATTERNS OF OEC INVESTMENTS

Jumps in oil prices have, as noted, provided huge increases in investable funds to OECs. A large share of these funds were placed in readily available short-term assets, such as Eurodollar and other bank deposits, and Treasury bills. This was done partly because of the conservative investment strategy of these countries, but it was also because moving funds into more permanent investments, either the international financial markets or their domestic economic development, takes time. As shown in Figure 19.9, there has been a substantial movement into longer-term financial assets, but only with some lag after the oil price jumps.

FIGURE 19.9: OEC Maturity Patterns, 1974–80

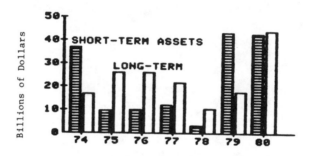

Annual Flow of OEC Funds to Short-
Term (Deposits and T-Bills)
and Long-Term Assets (Loans and Investments)

Source: Bank of England, *Quarterly Bulletin*, various issues.

The bulk of OEC funds in bank deposits is placed in Eurocurrency deposits in London and other major financial centers. However, in 1979 and 1980 a substantial amount of funds were placed in domestic currency deposits, such as a deutsche mark deposit in a domestic German bank (see Figure 19.10). One reason for this flow into domestic deposits, averaging about $12 billion per year in 1979 and 1980, was that banks in the Euromarkets were already flush with OEC and other funds, and thus they were bidding more eagerly for local currency deposits in their own domestic markets. In addition,

FIGURE 19.10: Flow of OEC Funds into Deposits, 1974–80

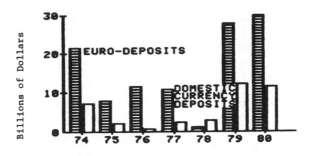

Annual Flow of OEC Funds into
Eurocurrency Deposits and Domestic
Deposits in Industrialized Countries

Source: Bank of England, *Quarterly Bulletin*, various issues; Bank for International Settlements, *Quarterly Report*, various issues; and authors' estimates.

the OECs began a program of diversifying their holdings away from U.S. dollar assets, the major denomination of the Eurodeposit market. As a result of this shift, U.S. dollar deposits owned by the OEC in the United States decreased somewhat in 1980.[8] This may also have resulted in part from concerns about President Carter's decision to freeze Iranian assets, but OEC dollar deposits in foreign branches of U.S. banks increased in 1980, even though they represented a declining share of OEC holdings.[9]

In spite of this shift to other currencies, the U.S. dollar is still the major denomination of OEC assets. The importance of U.S. dollars in the Eurocurrency markets contributes to this situation, as does the fact that the United States provides a major investment outlet for long-term OEC funds. In 1980, OECs placed $44 billion in long-term foreign assets, including government bonds, corporate debt and equity investments, real estate investments, and loans to the international organizations and developing countries. Of this amount, $14.3 billion has been identified as flowing into U.S. assets (see Table 19.1). The actual amount invested in U.S. financial securities and other assets was actually larger, probably much larger, because of indirect investments that were not traced back to the ultimate owner. Funds used to acquire a Netherlands corporation that in turn invests

TABLE 19.1. 1980 Flows from Oil Exporting Countries into Long-Term Assets

Country	Amount
United States	
Treasury bonds	$ 8.3
Portfolio investments	4.6
Direct and other investments	1.4
	14.3
United Kingdom	
Treasury bonds	1.9
Other investments	-.4
	1.5
Other industrialized countries	
All investments	16.7
Loans and contributions to IMF, World Bank, and developing countries	11.5
Total	$44.0

Source: Bank of England, *Quarterly Bulletin*, June 1981, p. 185.

in a U.S. firm, a procedure that reduces shareholder taxes, would show up in U.S. data as an investment from the Netherlands. Similarly, a substantial amount of OEC funds are managed by Swiss and other banks. When these funds are invested in the United States by a foreign bank, they appear as an inflow from the bank's country, not from the OEC.

U.S. banks and securities firms are also actively involved in providing international banking services to OECs. For example, they manage investment portfolios, they privately place corporate debt issues with OEC investors, and they seek out acquisition candidates and other investment opportunities. Competition for this business is quite keen, however, and a number of foreign institutions have established excellent relationships with OEC investors. Furthermore, countries with the largest investment pools, such as Saudi Arabia and Kuwait, have become sophisticated enough to undertake financial transactions that bypass financial intermediaries. The Saudi Arabian Monetary Authority, for example, has entered into programs with the governments of the United States, West Germany, and Japan to purchase government securities directly. U.S. financial institutions cannot compete in such government-to-government transactions, but they do have an important edge when competing with banking firms of other countries. The U.S. economy remains a very large, attractive investment outlet, and U.S. financial firms are closest to the public securities market and private opportunities that might be available in the United States.

BANKING ACTIVITY IN THE PERSIAN GULF

The increased level of financial activity after 1973 was not limited to financial centers and industrialized countries. Western and other banks came to the Persian Gulf, both to compete for OPEC's international financial business and to participate in domestic activity in the region. Even though funds could be collected through London banking outlets, many banks believed they could gain preferential access if they established a branch in the Middle East as evidence of their dedication to Middle Eastern clients. Securities firms also came to establish contacts with Middle Eastern government institutions and individuals in order to market securities and investment advice.

The pace of economic growth and accompanying commercial and financial opportunities within the Persian Gulf area also drew the attention of Western banks. Some had already established a presence by virtue of commercial relationships or historical accident. In Saudi Arabia, for instance, approximately ten foreign banks that had established themselves prior to 1960 were permitted to operate. These included Citibank, Banque de l'Indochine et de Suez, Algamene Bank Nederland, Banque de Caire, and the British Bank of the Middle East. But no others were allowed to enter, and after 1976 those already in the kingdom were required to sell 60 percent of their equity to Saudi citizens, even though the management of the banks effectively remained in the hands of the foreign minority holders. Thus, for example, Citibank became a 40 percent owner of the newly reorganized Saudi American Bank.

For a period the United Arab Emirates had the most liberal laws, with almost no special restrictions placed on foreign banks. However, the country subsequently perceived itself to be "overbanked," suffered some bank failures in 1977, and since then has closely regulated growth in the banking sector. In Kuwait and Iraq no foreign banks were allowed to operate. However, many of the existing domestic Arab banks were former colonial banks that had been nationalized after the countries became fully independent. Most still had expatriate managers, as in Kuwait, where British managers ran some of the domestic institutions.

Most Western and Japanese banks without a beachhead in the individual Persian Gulf economies eatablished their offshore offices in Bahrain, where the government had enacted laws and regulations favorable to foreign banks. From this base they sought to generate business in the various sovereignties in the region.

There are a number of important domestic banks in the Persian Gulf countries, some dating back many years, such as the National Commercial Bank, established in Saudi Arabia in 1938, and Jordan's Arab Bank, established in 1930. These local banks have grown rapidly in recent years, but most have retained a strong domestic orientation. The international banking expansion has been undertaken primarily by consortia or joint-venture banks (although Arab Bank is an important exception). Saudi International Bank, for instance, is partly owned by Morgan Guaranty Trust, and Banque Nationale de Paris is a joint owner of Banque Arabe et Internationale d'Investissement. These joint ventures have served as an important way for Middle Eastern countries to acquire international banking talent and expertise. A different kind of joint venture is represented by international banks that are jointly owned by Middle Eastern governments. Gulf International Bank, owned by all the Arab Persian Gulf governments, and the Arab Banking Corporation, owned by Kuwait, Libya, and Abu Dhabi, are prominent examples.

These Arab banking firms began an aggressive push in international banking at the start of the 1980s. The rankings of managers of Eurocurrency syndicated loans give some indication of this effort. In the 1980 rankings only one Arab bank was included in the top 50 syndication leaders (the Gulf International Bank, rated number 34). In the first nine months of 1981, four Arab banks had moved into the top 50, led by the Arab Banking Corporation (ABC) at number 21.[10] This was particularly noteworthy because ABC had been formed only a year earlier. As the Middle Eastern banks continue their move into international banking, they clearly will not be constrained by a lack of capital. The most limiting resource for them has been their lack of indigenous banking talent, which can be developed only over time.

THE SHIFTING COMPETITIVE STRUCTURE

The picture of the competitive relationships within the international banking community in the wake of the price hikes by the major oil producers is thus quite different from the situation at the beginning of the 1960s. One major change is the number and diversity of competitors within the industry. Banking firms from Western Europe and Japan have extended their international outreach, and, more recently, institutions from the Middle East and other regions have begun to compete for market position. This competition shows up both in the extended foreign branching in the United States and other countries, and in the Eurocurrency markets. As shown in Table 19.2, U.S. and British commercial and merchant/investment banks dominated the early years of the Eurobond and loan syndication markets. More recently the leadership has been spread across a much wider array of countries as other banks have acquired the necessary skills and competed for market position.

Looking at other parts of the multidimensional competitive structure presented at the beginning of this chapter, there has been an increase in product substitution, which has heightened the overall level of competition. The development of Eurocurrency markets in numerous locations, for example, has provided a set of integrated financial markets around the world. Thus, a depositor of U.S. dollars can arbitrage across national boundaries rather than be limited to products sold in the United States by U.S. financial institutions. Similarly, there has been growth in new products that bypass banks. The commercial paper market in the United States is a major example; others are large financial transactions negotiated directly between "suppliers" and "users." The concentration of financial

TABLE 19.2. Leading Managers of International Financings

Country of Ownership of Banking Firm	Eurobond Managers Share of Volume of Top 12 Managers		
	1963–65	1970–71	1980
United States	43% (7 banks)	34% (3 banks)	24% (3 banks)
United Kingdom	38 (3)	13 (2)	8 (1)
Germany	13 (1)	35 (4)	28 (3)
Belgium	6 (1)	5 (1)	—
Netherlands	—	13 (2)	—
Multinational	—	—	23 (2)
France	—	—	13 (2)
Japan	—	—	4 (1)

Country of Ownership of Banking Firm	Syndicated Loan Managers Share of Volume of Top 20 Managers	
	1973	1980
United States	54% (10 banks)	44% (7 banks)
United Kingdom	22 (5)	14 (3)
Japan	13 (3)	—
Multinational	7 (1)	4 (1)
France	4 (1)	12 (3)
Canada	—	15 (3)
Germany	—	8 (2)
Belgium	—	3 (1)

Source: *Euromoney*, February 1981, pp. 38–39, 85–86; data provided by Inter-bond Services, Ltd., and the World Bank.

resources in the hands of a relatively small number of oil-producing countries has also helped to strengthen the bargaining power of the "suppliers of funds" in the extended rivalry of the international financial industry. As a result, the influence and power of these capital holders has been much enhanced, and, given the inevitability that much of their remaining oil assets will eventually be transformed into monetary assets, they can be expected to become increasingly preoccupied with exerting their financial market influence in the most effective ways possible.

Last, the power of "users of funds" has grown in recent years vis-à-vis the financial institutions. This has resulted partly from the ability of borrowers to arbitrage across national boundaries, just as depositors do. In addition, the growth in international deposits has strengthened the hand of quality borrowers, which are in relatively short supply. Even weak credits have a kind of bargaining power, given the predisposition of lenders to keep borrowers viable after large sums of money have already been lent.

IMPLICATIONS FOR U.S. BANKING FIRMS

The natural consequence of this evolution of the competitive structure is a significant reduction of profit margins in many areas of international banking. There may be some maturing of the industry in the future as, for example, potential new entrants decide the profit opportunities are too small. However, there is little hope of a return to the "good old days." The increased integration and efficiency of the international banking market are here to stay.

U.S. commercial and investment banks have a number of important strengths upon which they can draw as they develop a strategy for international banking in the 1980s and beyond. Several have established positions in key market areas that will be an ongoing resource. These and other firms have strong management, along with organizational and decision-making structures that help make them effective competitors internationally. Furthermore, they have the powerful U.S. economy as a home base.

It is important to recognize, though, that foreign institutions also have some important strengths to bring to bear in the struggle for competitive position. For one thing, some of these banking firms have built strength by adopting U.S. management innovations and have established a significant position in the attractive U.S. market. They and others also have important competitive advantages stemming from their home country environment and regulation. For instance, "universal banking" is permitted in several key countries, so that major financial institutions can offer a full range of well-developed commercial and investment banking services to corporate clients around the world. U.S. institutions can act as universal banks outside the United States, but the Glass-Steagall Act has prohibited the development of a full array of services in their home market. A second important difference is that many international banking competitors have a large, stable source of relatively low-cost retail or consumer deposits at home, which adds to their aggregate profitability in high-interest environments. However, retail checking accounts and low-interest savings accounts were never an important source of funds for the big New York City and Chicago banks, and they have generally become even less available to U.S. banks as the interest rate and regulatory environments have changed.

Perhaps the most important difference is that non-U.S. institutions are less responsive to short-term profit pressures than are U.S. banking firms. This is partly a matter of management style, in that non-U.S. managers are more willing to take a longer-term, "strategic" perspective, and not be concerned about immediate profit problems with a foreign branch, for example. They often have the latitude to adopt this approach because they feel less need to be responsive to external capital markets. In some countries, such as France, major institutions are owned by the government, but even when the banks are privately owned, non-U.S. equity markets exert little short-term pressure on bank managers.

This poses an important dilemma for U.S. financial institutions. There is substantial evidence that the developments in the international capital markets during the 1970s—particularly those related to OECs' capital flows—have substantially changed the competitive structure and prospects of these markets from the perspective of banks around the world. The growth of international markets relative to that of individual national markets suggests that the former will be a principal focus of banking activity for the foreseeable future. Thus, banks that aspire to status as leading institutions within their home markets and abroad will find it hard to abandon their international banking positions even in the face of short- and intermediate-term profit pressures.

For many U.S. banks to rationalize "staying the course," it may be necessary to place more emphasis on strategic position decisions and less on the more conventional "return on investment" criteria. Representation in the international marketplace will not be viewed simply in discretionary profit-center terms. Some form of effective continuing presence will be seen as a competitive necessity, and the specific strategy adopted, whether it be a full range of service activities or a specialized niche approach, will depend on the banks' available resources and historical international business activity.

NOTES

1. See, for example, Richard Caves, *American Industry: Structure, Conduct, Performance*, 4th ed. (Englewood Cliffs, N.J.: Prentice-Hall, 1977).

2. Michael E. Porter, *Competitive Strategy: Techniques for Analyzing Industries and Competitors* (New York: Free Press, 1980), esp. ch. 1.

3. Susan Bluff, "OPEC's $350 Billion Balance Sheet," *Euromoney*, September 1980, p. 110.

4. Morgan Guaranty Trust Company, *World Financial Markets*, May 1981, p. 13.

5. "Saudis Pressed to Lift Oil Price, Cut Output as OPEC Convenes," *International Herald Tribune*, May 25, 1981; Morgan Guaranty Trust Company, *World Financial Markets*, January 1981, p. 7.

6. Bank for International Settlements, *Quarterly Reports*, various issues.

7. *The Banker*, various issues.

8. Bank of England, *Quarterly Bulletin*, June 1981.

9. *U.S. Treasury Bulletin*, March 1981, p. 78, reports a 1980 increase in total dollar deposits of the OEC.

10. *Euromoney*, February 1981, pp. 38–39, and November 1981, pp. 144, 151.

20 TRENDS IN INTERNATIONAL BANKING AND IMPLICATIONS FOR REGULATION

Gunter Dufey and
Ian H. Giddy

This chapter summarizes significant patterns of change in world banking by identifying competitive and structural changes and their implications for regulatory change in the offshore markets. These trends, the authors argue, call for a distinctly more circumspect role for prudent regulation in domestic and international banking.

TWO DECADES OF CHANGE IN INTERNATIONAL BANKING

From a historical perspective it is evident that the 1960s and 1970s were characterized by an erosion of the dominance of many domestic markets by a few large banks as these markets became integrated into the international financial system. This erosion was the result of two developments.

First, there was the emergence of the Euromarkets during the early 1960s. These markets, in which financial intermediation is performed outside the country of the currency being borrowed or deposited, developed and thrived largely because international banks are not subject to certain domestic banking regulations, such as

Some of the material in this article was published by the authors in "Alternative Approaches to the Regulation of International Banking," in *Singapore Banking and Finance, 1979* (Singapore: Institute of Banking and Finance, 1979), pp. 120–24.

reserve requirements and interest rate restrictions, and because the market facilitated the circumvention of capital controls. These features enable Eurobanks—banks that take and lend Eurocurrencies—of almost any nationality to operate more efficiently, cheaply, and competitively than their domestic counterparts—and, hence, to attract banking business away from domestic markets. Competitiveness and the absence of regulation, in other words, form the basis for the growth of what can be called an external market from U.S. $14 billion in 1964 to U.S. $65 billion in 1970, and to its net size of over U.S. $800 billion at the end of 1981.

The second major development was the international penetration of domestic wholesale markets. American, and subsequently other, international banks at first pursued the banking business of their own multinational firms; later they found themselves able to offer their services to domestic firms, particularly where a well-developed money market already existed in the country (that is, where banks were able to obtain funds easily from other banks).

The United States and the United Kingdom constitute the prime examples of such internationalization of the banking system. According to a survey by *The Economist*, at the end of 1978 foreign banks had about 30 percent of loans to British manufacturing companies and 25 percent of all bank loans to British companies and banks. In the United States, by one calculation, foreign banks now account for approximately 20 percent of all domestic commercial and industrial loans extended by the 300 largest banks in the United States. At the end of 1981, there were over 300 foreign banks with offices in the United States.

As banks acquire experience with the financial systems of a wider range of countries, they are increasingly gaining a foothold in the domestic wholesale (and possibly retail) banking markets of countries without well-developed interbank markets. Three major changes in the competitive environment that accompany this international banking expansion are reviewed below.

Breakdown of Geographical Barriers

The first is the breakdown of geographical barriers to entry—specifically, those associated with national boundaries. Custom, the administration of regulations and licenses, and economic factors had

long maintained domestic banking cartels even in the major countries. Now, however, the aggressive entry of foreign banks (particularly American and Japanese) has given domestic wholesale banking
clients a distinctly wider range of choice. U.S. banks' branches
abroad grew from 577 in 1970 to 623 in 1976, while the foreign
affiliates of the world's 50 largest banks (excluding American ones)
grew from 997 to 1,847 in the same period.

Financial Service Innovations

The second feature of heightened competition is the erosion of
product boundaries in international financial markets. Many of the
most important innovations in international finance have involved
services, such as the issuing of bonds, that were once tied to particular countries, or to particular groups of banks. Now, in contrast,
financial services available in the Euromarkets allow customers to
choose between banks of different nationalities and in different
locations. Eurobonds allow placements to be made simultaneously
in a variety of countries where they are not subject to traditional
regulations governing bond issues. Parallel loans, in which two firms
lend to one another simultaneously in two different countries, allow
corporations to obtain funds even in countries with constraining
credit and capital controls. Sears, Roebuck and Company broke new
ground in 1978 by being the first corporation, Japanese or foreign,
to offer unsecured bonds to the Japanese public.

Some new products, such as rollover credits, multicurrency
option loans, and currency combination bonds, have been developed
to provide flexible means of coping with fluctuating interest rates
and exchange rates, as well as with regulatory constraints. Where the
scale or complexity of financial needs necessitates cooperation, international banks have created consortia, syndications, and project
financing deals that readily provide larger loans, at longer maturities,
to a wider range of corporations and governments.

Certain financial service innovations, such as automatic overnight depositing of excess funds, have been facilitated by the increasing cost effectiveness of electronic banking. The wider adoption
of banking by wire and banking by computer has, in turn, motivated
cooperation among banks within and across countries. Automation
speeds international transactions, currency conversions, and transfers

of information, and forges tighter linkages among banks of all kinds and nationalities. In a sense, then, increased product competition has resulted in greater institutional cooperation.

Shifts in the Use of Currencies

The third aspect of heightened competition has been the decline in the dominance of particular banks and countries in the use of their currencies to denominate assets and transactions. The removal of constraints on capital movements and the growth of Euromarkets in most of the major currencies allow banks of almost any nation to conduct business outside the jurisdiction of national banking authorities. Approximately two-thirds of all deposits in banks in Britain are denominated in currencies other than the pound sterling.

The result of these developments has been, of course, a distinctly altered pattern of market shares. First, banking in certain currencies has gained at the expense of that conducted in other currencies. The U.S. dollar is the basis for the vast majority of international transactions. The dollar's share of the total Eurocurrency market fell from 81 percent in 1970 to 72 percent in 1979, although its share subsequently rose again. Despite the dollar's fluctuations in value, it has retained a primary role as a reserve currency. According to estimates by the German Bundesbank,[1] the share of foreign exchange reserves held by central banks in dollars was 78 percent in 1976, down only slightly from 82 percent in 1970. In contrast, the pound sterling fell from 9 percent to less than 2 percent during this period, while the deutsche mark rose from 2 percent to almost 15 percent. Even more dramatic was the shift in the share of Eurobonds denominated in deutsche marks, up from about 20 percent in 1976 to over 30 percent in 1978.

Another manifestation of this changing pattern lies in the location of banking. Eurodollar banking is now a ready substitute for domestic banking: at the end of 1981, the dollar assets in foreign branches of U.S. banks constituted 20 percent of their assets, up from 2 percent in 1970. The deposits of American banks' branches in the Caribbean now amount to almost as much as American banks have in the London Eurocurrency market. The recent shift in new offshore banking business from London to the Caribbean testifies to the fact that changes can occur within the Euromarkets, as well as between the offshore and the domestic banking markets.[2]

A third reallocation is that of the share of banking done by banks of various nationalities. Among the 100 largest banks in the world, the U.S. banks' share declined from 29 percent in 1971 to 20 percent in 1977. This drop was associated with an increase in the shares of Japanese banks from 20 to 23.5 percent, and of German banks from 11 to 15 percent.

Small increases occurred in the share of other countries. While these changes may be due in part to U.S. regulatory and legal constraints, more salient reasons appear to be the recent growth of foreign economies and banking systems, the international expansion of non-American multinational firms, and the increase in U.S. domestic loan demand.

While this reallocation of banking business has largely involved international wholesale lending, a more recent phenomenon is the incursion of foreign banks into domestic markets, both wholesale and retail. Rather than opening new offices all over the globe, the large banks are beginning to seek a more effective penetration of a few selected countries, such as the United States, Japan, and the United Kingdom. Foreign banks now control approximately 6 percent of the commercial banking market in America, as against 3 percent in 1972. If the Bank of Tokyo were an American bank, its consolidated holdings in the United States would make it number 30 in the country. Similarly, in the United Kingdom foreign banks own credit finance companies controlling 3 percent of consumer credit and 1 percent of mortgage loans, categories formerly eschewed by banks operating in foreign markets.

IMPLICATIONS FOR REGULATION: OFFSHORE BANKING

From its earliest beginnings the growth of the Eurocurrency market has been accompanied by criticism and calls for its control. As world inflation rates have risen, so has the intensity of the demands that restraints be placed on the expansion of "stateless money."

As long as these calls were restricted to the general press, they could simply be dismissed by knowledgeable observers as "loose talk about loose money." Now, however, a new fact gives rise to concern not only by those in the financial community who make a living in these markets but also by policy makers in the jurisdictions in which Eurocurrency activities are concentrated, and by those economists who believe that these markets have significantly contributed to the efficiency and stability of the international economic system. The fact is that, according to indications, the governments of both the United States and West Germany are seriously considering measures that might severely limit the future expansion of external inter-mediation.

While this does not necessarily mean that such restrictions will actually be implemented, the probability of such an event has in-creased. Faced with the apparent ineffectiveness of traditional monetary and fiscal tools for fine-tuning their economies, govern-ments everywhere tend to feel compelled to try to remedy perceived problems by curing the symptoms instead of confronting the under-lying causes. In the context of the international financial markets, it is possible that the major governments may attempt to control the expansion of international credit, regardless of the fact that inflation and rapid expansion of credit volumes, both domestic and interna-tional, have the same root cause: the overly expansive monetary policy of the major countries.

CONTROL MECHANISMS

How could controls on Eurocurrency activities be implemented? A functioning market for externally intermediated funds, as the Eurocurrency market should be properly called, depends on three necessary conditions:

1. The ultimate providers (depositors) and takers (borrowers) of funds must have sufficient freedom to move these funds across borders.
2. There must be free access to clearing balances for nonresidents in those countries whose currencies are used to denominate the external credit transactions.
3. There must be a system of profitable and sound external finan-cial intermediaries (Eurobanks).

These conditions provide the "leverage points" for controlling the growth of the Eurocurrency market. First, worldwide exchange controls would certainly slow the growth of external financial inter-mediation by making it difficult for borrowers and depositors to move funds across borders. Such exchange controls, however, would slow world trade and investment, and of course be accompanied by all the other evils of controls on international transactions, such as costly administration and complex enforcement problems.

Second, countries could control the working balances through which nonresidents clear external credit transactions. But such balances do not serve only to execute payments connected with external deposits and loans; the very same balances are used for international trade and traditional international financial transactions. Restricting nonresident convertibility of major currencies would do serious damage to the international economy. Indeed, these constraints on nonresident convertibility, if imposed by the United States, would be the equivalent of an atomic war on the world's financial system, as one observer has put it.

A THIRD ALTERNATIVE

As a practical matter, therefore, this leaves governments with the third alternative: direct control of external financial intermediaries. For many years proponents of Euromarket controls have suggested that the jurisdictions in which such institutions operate might be persuaded to impose reserve requirements on what is typically nonresident, third-currency business. For obvious reasons these suggestions have not been well received by the governments of the offshore centers. If properly insulated, these activities do not interfere with the domestic monetary policies of such governments, which derive evident benefits in the form of taxes, franchise fees, employment, and secondary economic activity.

One set of proposals to control the markets took a different tack. The overwhelming majority of Eurocurrency credits are on the books of wholly owned affiliates of banks headquartered in relatively few industrial countries (United States, Canada, West Germany, United Kingdom, Japan, France, the Netherlands, Switzerland, Italy, and Sweden). Given this structure, the proposals indicate that the governments of the parent banks might compel the institutions under their jurisdiction to extend domestic reserve requirements to foreign branches and subsidiaries.

This proposal might have been hatched somewhere in the U.S. bureaucracy; after all, there has been a precedent. From 1969 to

1978 the foreign branches and subsidiaries of U.S.-headquartered banks were, in effect, subject to reserve requirements, under Federal Reserve Regulation M, on loans made to their parents or to other U.S. resident borrowers. Impartial observers consider Regulation M (now subsumed under Regulation D) a complete failure. Originally imposed to prevent a flow of dollars into the United States, the reserve requirement was subsequently raised to prevent an outflow of dollars. It did neither; what it accomplished instead was to force many U.S. borrowers to acquaint themselves much sooner than otherwise with foreign banks and their affiliates outside the United States, which were only too happy to provide external dollar credits.

REGULATORY DILEMMAS

There have been repeated attempts to solve such competitive problems through international cooperation to ensure that the affiliates of German, Japanese, and other banks will not be subject to reserve requirements. Undoubtedly, reserve requirements, imposed in such a way, might make external intermediation less profitable and slow the growth of the Eurocurrency market. It is conceivable that such measures might even drive a significant portion of credit volume that is now on the books in Eurobanks back to intermediaries operating in national markets. However, such predictions are completely founded on the present international banking structure: one that is based on wholly owned affiliates. Although such a structure is advantageous for safety reasons, it is very likely that controls on such affiliates would produce restructuring of international banking, potential profit being the mother of circumvention. Consortium banks and "independents," headquartered in offshore centers that are not subject to pressures imposed on parents and their affiliates, would be able to perform external intermediation cheaply and efficiently.

However, such a restructuring raises some new and challenging problems for the authorities of the offshore centers. Until now, all they have had to do to attract international banking business is to create a laissez-faire regulatory environment and maintain reasonable levels of taxation. Safety and prudent supervision have been a burden that the management of the parent banks has had to bear because, in practice, the risk of the offshore affiliate—the branch or wholly owned subsidiary—was inseparable from that of the parent bank. Obviously, once external banking relies on financial intermediaries established as consortium banks and independents, the authorities of the banking center wishing to maintain an offshore industry must squarely confront the traditional regulatory dilemma: how to create an environment that minimizes the cost of regulation, yet assures banking customers of the soundness and safety of the institutions operating in a given jurisdiction. This challenge calls for a systematic review of alternative approaches to the regulation of international banking, both offshore and onshore.

IMPLICATIONS FOR BANKING REGULATION: ONSHORE

The emphasis of prudent bank regulation has necessarily changed in the face of the new, competitive banking environment. First, the banking authorities of the world have had to adapt to the blurring of the boundaries of regulatory influence and responsibility that followed from the greatly increased degree of institutional and capital mobility among national banking markets. They have sought to adapt traditional domestic regulation to the new entry by foreign banks into domestic markets, and to the expansion of their own banks abroad. In some nations new conditions of entry and operation have been adopted—not necessarily to make it more difficult to enter (although some have done this), but to make policies more explicit. The United States, for example, adopted more specific regulation of domestic banks' international activities, and Congress has passed the International Banking Act, governing the activities of foreign banks in the United States.

Some countries have responded to banks' greater mobility through legislative reform favoring foreign banks, as in the case of the Caribbean offshore centers and certain Far East countries. In the United States, on the whole, an open attitude has been maintained to the great fungibility of the banking business: several states, including New York, Illinois, and Florida, have adopted legislation favoring foreign bank entry.

Regulators also have found themselves forced to respond to new risks associated with the more competitive environment of the 1970s. On the one hand, the international money market, increasingly a single world market consisting of the Eurocurrency market and its linkages with domestic banking systems, has proved itself able to absorb much greater shocks than any individual system could have taken in the past. The financing of balance-of-payments deficits resulting from OPEC's oil price rise is an example of the system's present resilience.

BANK FAILURES

On the other hand, individual markets are no longer insulated from foreign competition, and some banks have necessarily succumbed. The most significant manifestation of these risks at the international level was the 1974 banking crisis associated with the failures of the Herstatt and Franklin National banks. Eventually this resulted in a more consistent designation, among central bankers and bank supervisors, of responsibility for international banks' safety and soundness. The Basle agreement following the international banking crisis established the responsibility of home country regulators for overseas branches, and host country responsibility for subsidiaries of foreign banks. The British authorities, through requests for "letters of intent," have sought to establish proportional responsibility for consortium banks. Finally, an ongoing international consultation has occurred since that time through the Blunden Committee (and its successor, the Cooke Committee) of the major countries' national bank regulators.

The domestic counterpart of reform in international banking regulation has been the establishment of more explicit regulation and supervision, and the institution of deposit insurance systems in several countries, including the United Kingdom, Germany, and the Netherlands. In each country the broadening and opening of financial markets has implied greater vulnerability for particular segments of the financial community. Unregulated new entry into the British banking system was partly responsible for that country's secondary banking crisis of 1973-74, and unrestricted entry into the foreign exchange market provided the opportunity for the Herstatt and Franklin banks to step beyond the bounds of prudence. The more structured, formal regulation of banking that has resulted signals heightened public concern about the stability of domestic banking systems, although, upon examination, few of these reforms prove to be significantly more restrictive in effect.

REALITIES IN INTERNATIONAL BANKING

Whatever the present state of bank regulation, it is clear that the competitive environment of the wholesale banking business will never be the same again. The low cost of communications and funds-transfer technology, coupled with the ingenuity of the modern international banker, will ensure the maintenance of competition in most segments of wholesale banking. One can expect a still more diversified allocation of international banking business by location, nationality of banks, and currency of denomination. One can also expect a further erosion of barriers to entry in product, currency, and geographical markets, and the accompanying increase in interdependence. The bank regulators of tomorrow must therefore recognize three realities.

First, what banking authorities are able to do in pursuit of safety and soundness will be determined in part by the ability of banks to relocate in another jurisdiction or to escape constraints by doing some business under a different country's laws. Just as a profit-maximizing firm's freedom to impose high prices on its customers is constrained by the ease with which the customers can buy the same product from a competitor or switch to a substitute product, so is a bank regulator's liberty to impose effective regulation constrained by the ease with which banking activities outside his jurisdiction can be substituted for business within it.

It follows that while bank regulators around the world may retain their classical sway over banks or banking activities that are geographically rooted, their influence becomes tenuous, and their choice of regulation more severely restricted, in the sphere of foot-loose, wholesale international banking. Banking services that require face-to-face contact or on-the-spot knowledge will be subject to whatever constraints the regulator chooses to impose. In contrast, banking that can be done in almost any location through the remote provision of services will take place in the location that provides the most attractive banking jurisdiction in terms of cost and risk.

Second, no country that is already linked to the world economy through international trade and investment flows can realistically expect to be immune to the competitive influence of international banking. As long as money and commerce can cross national boundaries, foreign bank competition will find its way into domestic markets, in one form or another, in almost every country of the world.

Third, since each banking system of reasonable openness is by now tightly intertwined with those of other countries through the network of interbank deposits and of cross-border lending, regulatory jurisdictions overlap, conflict, and occasionally leave gaps in responsibility. If the system's stability is to be preserved, therefore, some means will have to be found for refining or reconciling the bank regulator's aegis.

FOUR CHOICES FOR BANK REGULATION

Regulators can respond to the banking markets of the 1980s as just portrayed in a variety of ways. This variety is a product of the multidimensional nature of what is often simply referred to as "regulation." Therefore, a detailed elaboration of each potential response is not possible. But this range of choices may be distilled into four basic approaches to the prudent regulation of a country's banks.

First, regulators could seek to insulate themselves and their banking market by retaining or enacting restrictive policies. They might impose capital controls or tighten regulation of both the foreign banks operating within their boundaries and the branches of their domestic banks operating abroad.

The adoption of these restrictive principles as the basis of regulation, however, would have adverse consequences of at least two types. Domestic banking consumers, most likely, would be hurt more than would foreign banks, because the system would be deprived of the fruits of the competitive process. Further, the economies of most countries today are too reliant on foreign sources of both demand for and supply of goods and services for severe curtailment of cross-border flows of any type to be politically feasible.

The second basis upon which international bank regulation may be built is international cooperation or centralization of banking regulation. In one sense it appears logical that the heightened interdependence of banking markets, and the now global definition of the products and geographical boundaries, provide a rationale for centralized or at least highly coordinated regulation. This is certainly a more rational response than would be the retreat from interdependence through isolationist regulatory policies or the abdication of responsibility inherent in competitive laxity among regulators. But one must also recognize that a global concentration of regulatory influence has ominous overtones for dictatorial power, however enlightened the initiators of such a plan might be. Monopoly of regulation is not better, and is often worse, than monopoly of industry. And the blanket transfer of regulatory powers and duties by a country to a multinational body is politically and practically infeasible.

A third maxim to which regulators might adhere in their policy formulation is that regulators seek to maximize the size of their jurisdictions. In so doing, regulators will compete with one another, reducing the severity of regulation as far as possible in order to attract as much banking into their own jurisdictions as possible. Yet this "competition in laxity" approach represents a simplistic view not only of bank regulators' behavior, but also of the rational location decisions of banks. Banks do not seek the laxest regulatory environment, but one that provides the most attractive combination of a safe and sound banking system and a relatively unconstrained and unburdensome set of regulations.

But it is not necessary to choose between total integration of regulation and autarky, or between lack of regulation and lack of regulatees. Regulators facing the competitive environment of the 1980s can, and should, choose a fourth course, that of altering regulation in such a way as to minimize the burden of banking regulation while maintaining the safety and stability of the banking system. It is, of course, the prime duty of the bank regulator to honor his charge to maintain a safe and sound banking system; at the same time the sensible response to banks' jurisdictional flexibility is to remove all regulations that do not contribute in an efficient fashion to the stability of banking.[3]

The regulatory problems posed by the disintegration of market boundaries must be handled by an open exchange of information related to cross-border ownership and branching. The issues raised by the acquisition of domestic banks by foreign banks highlight some of the supervisory problems that are best solved by cooperation. When a domestic bank is acquired by a foreign bank, the host country regulator must, in the execution of his duty, assess the riskiness of the new banking organization. It is far preferable that the information needed to assess this risk be provided by the home-country regulators of the parent bank rather than by means of direct examination of foreign banks. In the area of regulators' informational requirements, therefore, cooperation offers the path of least intrusion into others' jurisdictions.

What, specifically, does this imply for the form of international banking regulation in the 1980s? As students of banking regulation well know, the effective function of much of banking regulation differs substantially from its ostensible function. While most of the activities of banking authorities are justified in the name of bank safety and soundness, the great majority of these regulations serve, in effect, to protect certain groups, to avoid competition, or to channel credit in favored directions. An environment of ill-defined product and geographical boundaries allows competition among banks that in turn may lead to competition among bank regulators. Such an environment leaves little room for regulation that is not central to the prime function of preserving banking stability.

PROTECTING THE SYSTEM

The adaptation of bank regulation to a highly competitive and interdependent banking environment implies protecting the system, but not necessarily protecting individual banks. More competition entails both more entry and more exit. It implies serving the interests of the banking public as a whole, but not necessarily those of individual segments at the expense of other groups. It implies reliance on monetary stability, an efficient deposit insurance system, and the ready availability of information pertinent to banks' conditions.

On the other hand, regulatory change does not call for limiting the portfolios of banks to certain types of investments. It does not imply substituting a regulator's judgment of how a bank should be run for that of the bank's management, or protecting a bank's managers and shareholders (in contrast with depositors) from their own mistakes. Finally, it certainly does not require the preservation of banks' stability by imposing barriers to new competition. What it does mean is removing, or refusing to erect, all regulations that contribute to the protection of inefficient and unresponsive banking practices instead of contributing in an efficient fashion to the soundness of the system.

NOTES

1. Reported in Dresdner Bank, *Economic Quarterly*, November 1981, p. 3.

2. We remain doubtful about the success of the international banking facilities (IBFs), which, as of December 3, 1981, can be used to do "offshore" banking in the United States. These facilities are restricted in many respects so that both U.S. and foreign customers will prefer foreign banking centers.

3. For detailed proposals based on committed lines of credit, see James W. Dean and Ian H. Giddy, *Averting International Banking Crises*. New York: New York University Press, 1981.

SUGGESTED REFERENCES

Barr, Joseph W. "The Last Days of the Franklin National Bank." *Administrative Law Review*, Fall 1975, pp. 301-14.

Becker, Joseph D. "International Insolvency: The Case at Herstatt." *American Bar Association Journal*, October 1976, pp. 1290-95.

Blunden, George. "International Cooperation in Banking Supervision." Bank of England *Quarterly Bulletin* 17, no. 3 (September 1977): 325-29.

Board of Governors of the Federal Reserve System. "The Depository Institution Deregulation and Control Act of 1980." *Federal Reserve Bulletin*, June 1980, pp. 444-53.

Dean, James W., and Herbert G. Grubel. "Regulatory Issues and the Theory of Multinational Banking." In Franklin R. Edwards, ed., *Issues in Financial Regulation*. New York: McGraw-Hill, 1978.

Dresdner Bank, "Reserve and Investment Currency Role of the D-Mark," *Economic Quarterly*, November 1981, p. 3.

Dufey, Gunter, and Ian H. Giddy. *The International Money Market*. Englewood Cliffs, N.J.: Prentice-Hall, 1978.

Eizenga, W., and Ian H. Giddy. *Banking Solvency Regulation and Deposit Insurance in the U.S. and the Netherlands*. Tilburg, Netherlands: Société Universitaire Européene de Recherche Financières 1979.

Federal Reserve Bank of New York. "A New Supervisory Approach to Foreign Lending." *Quarterly Bulletin* 3, no. 1 (Spring 1978): 1-6.

Horvitz, Paul M. "Failures of Large Banks: Implications for Banking Supervision and Deposit Insurance." *Journal of Finance and Quantitative Analysis* 10, no. 4 (November 1975): 589-601.

Kareken, John H., and Neil Wallace. "Deposit Insurance and Bank Regulation: A Partial Equilibrium Exposition." *Journal of Business* 57, no. 3 (1978): 413–38.

Morgan Guaranty Trust Company. *World Financial Markets* (monthly).

Scott, Kenneth, and Thomas Mayer. "Risk and Regulation in Banking: Some Proposals for Federal Deposit Insurance Reform." *Stanford Law Review*, May 1971, pp. 857–902.

Zolotas, Xenophon. "A Proposal for a New Fund to Insure Against Euromarket Defaults." *Euromoney*, April 1978, pp. 77–83.

GLOSSARY

ACCEPTANCE. See *Banker's Acceptance.*

ADVANCE. Short-term loan—that is, maturity less than one year.

ADVISED LINE OF CREDIT. Credit facility confirmed in writing as to the terms and conditions under which the bank is prepared to grant credit. These facilities are normally of three types:

1. GOOD UNTIL CANCELLED—the bank may terminate the line of credit at will, and prior to such termination the beneficiary may draw at will.
2. ANNUAL REVIEW—the line of credit terminates one year from date of confirmation, during which period the beneficiary may draw at will.
3. AS OFFERED—the bank must be consulted prior to each drawing.

ADVISING BANK. A correspondent of an issuing bank that notifies the beneficiary of a letter of credit without adding its own engagement to that of the issuing bank.

AGENT BANK. Bank appointed by members of an international lending syndicate to protect the interests of the lenders during the life of the loan. Its duties resemble those of the trustee of a bond issue. But while a trustee is never an investor, an agent bank is often a major lender and is, moreover, usually left free to conduct other business with the borrower. The agent's role is therefore open to conflicts of interest.

AMORTIZATION. The payment of a loan in installments.

ARBITRAGE. Strictly defined, buying something where it is cheap and selling it where it is dear—for instance, a bank buys three-month CD money in the U.S. market and sells three-month money at a higher rate in the Eurodollar market. In the money market it often refers (1) to a situation in which a trader buys one security and sells a similar security in the expectation that the spread in yields between the two instruments will narrow or widen to his profit; (2) to a swap between two similar issues based on an anticipated change in yield spreads; or (3) to situations where a higher return (or lower cost) can be achieved in the money market for one currency by utilizing another currency and swapping it on a fully hedged basis through the foreign exchange market.

ARRANGED OVERDRAFT. A debit balance in the client's account arranged by the banker at the request of the client. It is a common European method of short-term lending comparable with a line of credit.

AS OFFERED. See *Advised Line of Credit*.

ASSETS. Anything owned by a bank that has commercial or exchange value. Assets usually consist of specific property or claims against others.

ASSIGNMENT OF A LOAN. A bank taking part in a syndicated loan may, with the borrower's consent, assign its share of the loan to another bank. The bank to which the loan share is assigned then assumes the relationship to the borrower that has been relinquished by the bank assigning it.

AVERAGE LIFE. The weighted average period for which a loan is outstanding, taking into account the amortization schedule. Thus, two loans with the same final maturity will have different average lives if one amortizes earlier and/or more frequently than the other.

BANK WIRE. A computer message system linking major banks. It is not used for effecting payments, but as a mechanism to advise the receiving bank of some action that has occurred—for instance, the payment by a customer of funds into that bank's account.

BANKER'S ACCEPTANCE. A time bill of exchange (frequently called a time draft) drawn on and accepted by a banking institution. By accepting the draft, the bank signifies its commitment to pay the face amount at maturity to anyone who presents it for payment at that time. In this way the bank provides its name and credit, and enables its customer, who pays a commission to the accepting bank for this accommodation, to readily secure financing. When a banker's acceptance is discounted, the discounting bank acquires a debt investment (a claim against a third party) that appears on the balance sheet. Such acceptance can subsequently be sold to another bank or investor, although the accepting bank continues to guarantee payment on maturity.

BASIS POINT. 1/100 of 1 percent.

BEST-EFFORTS SYNDICATION. A syndicated loan the amount of which is not underwritten in advance and the borrower obtains the full amount (or, sometimes, anything) only if syndication is successful. See also *Underwritten Loan*.

BILL OF LADING. A record of the shipment of goods from a transporter confirming the receipt of goods for shipment and means of transportation. The general term "bill of lading" is used for marine and surface transport. The term "airbill" is usually used for air shipments.

BILLS DISCOUNTED. Written debt instruments evidencing the obligation of one party (the drawer) to pay another a certain sum of money at a given time. Refers to written debt instruments drawn on a payer (the borrower) by a third party (the drawer), who in turn discounts the draft with a bank. The bank may discount the draft either with or without recourse to the drawer. When there is full and unconditional recourse to a drawer who is a resident of a country other than that of the payer (the ultimate obligor), country exposure is generally transferred from the country of the payer to the country of the drawer.

BRITISH CLEARERS. The large clearing banks that dominate deposit taking and short-term lending in the domestic sterling market in Great Britain.

BULLET LOAN. A bank term loan that calls for no amortization. The term is commonly used in the Euromarket.

BUY BACK. Another term for a repurchase agreement.

CALL MONEY. Interest-bearing bank deposits that can be withdrawn on 24 hours' notice. Many Eurodeposits take the form of call money.

CASH. This definition of cash is restricted to "cash on hand" and noninterest-bearing deposits held by nonaffiliated banks. More frequently, cash held by nonaffiliated banks is considered to be exposure to the country where such banks are domiciled. For the most part, given the nominal amounts, cash on hand is only infrequently tabulated as country exposure.

CASUAL OVERDRAFT. A debit balance in a client's account. An overdraft is created when checks, drafts, money transfers, or other transactions are drawn or charged against demand deposit accounts in excess of the available balance in the account. Such an overdraft is not by prearrangement.

CERTIFICATE OF DEPOSIT (CD). A time deposit with a specific maturity evidenced by a certificate. Large-denomination CDs are typically negotiable.

CHIPS. The New York Clearing House's computerized Clearing House Interbank Payments System. Most Eurotransactions are cleared and settled through CHIPS rather than over the Fed wire.

CLEARINGHOUSE FUNDS. Payments made through the New York Clearing House's computerized Clearing House Interbank Payments System. Clearinghouse debits and credits are settled in the same business day.

COLLATERALIZED LOAN. A loan granted to a customer upon the pledge of (1) liquid assets, such as registered shares of stock or bonds, or (2) illiquid assets (such as a mortgage on a building). If the borrower is unable to repay the loan, the lender can sell the security to satisfy the claim. Generally, when liquid collateral is offered to a bank, country exposure is transferred from the country of the obligor to the country where the liquid collateral is held—provided, however, the latter is denominated in the same currency as the loan.

COMANAGERS. Banks ranking next after lead managers in the arrangement of international bond issues and international bank credits (Eurocredits). They help assess the market and discuss terms with borrowers. Comanagers of international bond syndicates are often chosen for their ability to place large amounts of a new issue with investors, while the lead manager is often chosen for having brought a borrower to market. In Eurocredit syndicates, comanagers are usually chosen for their willingness to take a large part of the loan for themselves, or their ability to parcel out a large part to other banks.

COMFORT LETTER. A written instrument issued by a third party whereby that party agrees to make every effort to assure the maker's compliance with the terms of a contract in the event the maker is unable to fulfill his obligation thereunder, but by which instrument that party is not itself obligated to perform. For the most part, banks do not transfer exposure from the country of the obligor to the country of the issuer of the comfort letter, in part because of the uncertain legal status of such instruments.

COMMERCIAL PAPER. An unsecured promissory note with fixed a maturity of no more than 270 days. Commercial paper is normally sold at a discount from face value.

CONDITION PRECEDENT. A condition in a loan agreement that must be met before the first borrowing.

CONFIRMING BANK. A correspondent bank that adds its own engagement to that of the issuing bank in a letter of credit, guaranteeing that the credit will be honored by the issuer or a third bank.

CONFISCATION. Seizure of private property by a government without any compensation to the owner. Also, a seizure of assets without fair compensation.

CONSORTIUM BANK. A merchant banking subsidiary set up by several banks that may or may not be of the same nationality. Consortium banks are common in the Euromarket and are active in loan syndication.

CONTINGENT LIABILITIES. The term applies to the obligations of a bank acting as a guarantor or endorser of a negotiable instrument. The guarantor or endorser has no benefit from the negotiable instrument involved, but is required by law to make good the payment of the instrument if the maker defaults. The actual liability exists with the maker of the note (the borrower). The contingent liability exists for the duration of the instrument, and is passed to the guarantor as a primary liability only if the borrower dishonors the instrument upon presentation and request for payment. Once the guaranteeing bank meets the liability involved, it then has a claim (asset) against the borrower. Because there is the potential for an actual claim to arise from a contingent liability, banks include all contingent liabilities issued on behalf of foreign customers as exposure to the domicile of the customer—unless the transaction is fully and unconditionally counterguaranteed by an external obligor, in which case exposure is allocated to the counterguarantor. The term "contingent liabilities" also includes legal commitments to extend credit, forward exchange contracts, and guarantees, whether or not reflected in the financial statements of the bank.

CORRESPONDENT BANK. A bank that in its own country handles the business of a foreign bank. There are also domestic correspondents in different areas of the same country.

COUNTRY EXPOSURE. A term of measurement that refers to the volume of "assets" held and "off-balance sheet items" considered to be subject to the "country risk" of a given country. In practice, one important aspect of this measurement is based on identifying the country of domicile of the entity ultimately responsible for the credit risk of a particular transaction.

COUNTRY RISK. Refers to a spectrum of risks arising from the economic, social, and political environments of a given foreign country (including government policies framed in response to trends in these environments) having potential favorable or adverse consequences for foreigners' debt and/or equity investments in that country.

Events that may adversely affect profitability and/or recovery of equity investments in a given foreign country include the following:

Confiscation
Nationalization

Branching limitations
Restrictions on earnings remittances
Higher local taxes levied on earnings
Market conditions (deflation)
Devaluation.

Events that affect profitability of debt investments in a given foreign country include the following:

Withholding and other special taxes that affect existing outstandings
Interest rate controls
Government-imposed delays on the liquidation of private-and/or public-sector external obligations.

Events that often affect potential recovery of debt investments include the following:

Certain types of foreign exchange controls, including government-imposed restrictions on the liquidation of public- and/or private-sector external obligations
Domestic policies often imposed in a sudden, unpredictable manner that affect client's ability to generate the necessary cash flow to repay loans. Examples include:

Fiscal policy (such as increase in taxes)
Restrictive monetary policy
Price controls.

The above types of country risk are incurred as a result of activities undertaken in a foreign country, and are distinct from considerations relating to a given borrower's creditworthiness. In varying degrees the above examples can affect both local and foreign currency investments.

In the above context the term "investments" is often used synonymously with "exposure."

COVENANT. A clause in a loan agreement in which the borrower "covenants" that he will do or procure (or refrain from doing) certain things—such as granting security. Financial covenants (sometimes referred to as ratio covenants) involve maintaining agreed financial ratios on items such as working capital, debt-to-worth, or interest cover.

CROSS-BORDER EXPOSURE. Exists when any subsidiary or branch of the holding company/bank, irrespective of location, lends to, invests in, places with, or otherwise extends any form of credit or credit commitment to any entity (including any holding company/ other bank entity) that is located outside the booking unit's national borders, irrespective of currency.

CROSS-DEFAULT. When a default in any other loan agreement is an automatic default in your agreement, this is known as a cross-default.

CROSS RATE. A foreign exchange rate calculated from two separate quotes that contain the same currency. For example, if one has the rate of French francs per U.S. dollar and the rate of deutsche marks per U.S. dollar, one can calculate the cross rate between French francs and deutsche marks.

DEFAULT. Failure by a borrower to pay principal or interest when due, or by a borrower, guarantor, or other party to the contract to meet any other condition of the agreement, where such failure is defined in the agreement as an event of default.

DEFLATION. A reduction in the level of economic activity in an economy. Deflation will result in lower levels of national income, employment, and imports, and lower rates of increase of wages and prices. It may be brought about by monetary policies, such as increases in rates of interest and contraction of the money supply, and/or by fiscal policies, such as increases in taxation (direct and indirect) or reductions in government expenditure.

DEVALUATION. The reduction of the official rate at which one currency is exchanged for another.

DISINTERMEDIATION. The direct investing of funds, which would normally have been placed with a bank or other financial intermediary, in debt securities issued by ultimate borrowers—for instance, in bills or bonds.

DOCUMENT OF TITLE. This term includes bill of lading, dock warrant, dock receipt, warehouse receipt, order for the delivery of goods, and any other document that in the regular course of business or financing is treated as adequate evidence that the person in possession of it is entitled to receive, hold, and dispose of the document and the goods it covers.

DOCUMENTARY DRAFT. A draft the honor of which is conditioned upon the presentation of a document or documents. "Document" means any paper, including document of title, security, invoice, certificate, notice of default, and the like. Also referred to as a documentary demand for payment.

DRAFT. An order to pay. A check is one form of a draft.

DRAWDOWN. The initial borrowing, or drawing, under a facility.

DRAWEE BANK. The bank upon which a draft is drawn. Also called paying bank.

EDGE ACT CORPORATIONS. Financial institutions incorporated in the United States under the Edge Act. Edge Act corporations are owned by commercial banks, and restrict their income mostly to foreign sources. The major advantage a commercial bank achieves in establishing an Edge Act corporation is to be able to conduct abroad some activities that are forbidden to U.S. banks.

EURO CDs. CDs issued by a U.S. bank branch or foreign bank located outside the United States. Almost all Euro CDs are issued in London.

EURO-DISASTER CLAUSE. A clause in a loan agreement designed to protect lending banks from changes in the Euromarket that either make it impossible to obtain funds or drastically change the cost of obtaining funds.

EURO LINES. Lines of credit granted by banks (foreign or foreign branches of U.S. banks) for Eurocurrencies.

EUROBONDS. Bonds issued in Europe outside the confines of any national capital market. A Eurobond may or may not be denominated in the currency of the issuer.

EUROCURRENCY DEPOSITS. Deposits made in a bank or bank branch that is not located in the country in whose currency the deposit is denominated. Dollars deposited in a London bank are Eurodollars, deutsche marks deposited there are Euromarks.

EURODOLLARS. U.S. dollars deposited in a U.S. bank branch or a foreign bank located outside the United States.

EXCESS RESERVES. Balances held by a bank at the Fed in excess of those required.

EXCHANGE CONTROLS. Any regulation or action taken by a government or government agency that restricts the free flow of domestic or foreign currency into or out of its country. During recent years such regulations have taken various forms:

> BLOCKED EXCHANGE. The condition that exists when importers and others (such as borrowers) desiring to make payments abroad are prohibited from doing so by their government—that is, they are blocked from purchasing required foreign currencies. Under such conditions, deposits in local currency are sometimes made to cover the prospective remittances, but foreign creditors must wait until the block is removed, or find some way of using the local currency credited to them.
>
> MULTIPLE CURRENCY SYSTEM. Involves the establishment by law of different exchange values for the national currency, the applicable value in any exchange transaction depending upon the type of commodity or service purchased abroad for which exchange is desired.
>
> RATIONING OF FOREIGN EXCHANGE. A means of controlling foreign exchange by requiring that all holders of bills of exchange relinquish them to the government in return for domestic currency at a stipulated legal rate, and that all importers apply to the government for bills of exchange. The government then allocates such exchange to importers and/or other claimants (those with external debt commitments) whose activities it wishes to encourage, and denies it to those whose activities are considered less essential, or perhaps harmful, to the government's plan for foreign trade equilibrium.

EXCHANGE RATE. The price at which one currency trades for another.

EXPOSURE. The maximum amount a bank could lose if all its facilities to one borrower were fully utilized when the borrower failed. This assumes a nil recovery.

EXPROPRIATION. Government seizure of assets owned by a foreign entity, with or without compensation.

FACILITY FEE. Paid by borrowers on undrawn portions of bank credits, including Eurocredits, especially in the case of revolving Eurocredits.

FED WIRE. A computer system linking member banks to the Fed, used for making interbank payments of Fed funds and for making deliveries of and payments for Treasury and agency securities.

FEDERAL FUNDS RATE. The rate of interest at which Fed funds are traded. This rate is currently pegged by the Federal Reserve through open-market operations.

FEDERAL FUNDS SOLD. An amount owed to a bank for all transactions involving the disposal of immediately available funds, enabling other U.S. domestic commercial banks, including U.S. branches of foreign banks, to maintain their reserve requirements at the Federal Reserve Bank.

FEES. Front-end fees are paid by borrowers to the managing banks arranging Eurocredits, the lead managers dividing the fee among themselves. Some of the fee is also passed on to other banks in the form of participation fees for taking parts of a Eurocredit up to agreed minimum levels. In the international bond market fees are more accurately described as management, underwriting, and selling concessions or discounts, since the borrower pays the costs of distributing a new issue by making the bonds available to managing, underwriting, and selling banks at varying discounts below their face value.

FIDUCIARY ACCOUNTS. A relationship between two or more parties whereby one party, such as a bank, gives advice, manages, controls, or holds in safekeeping assets, including foreign assets, owned by another.

FINANCE LEASE. See *Lease.*

FISCAL POLICY. That part of government policy that is concerned with raising revenue through taxation and other means, and with deciding on the level and pattern of expenditure. It is through the level and pattern of budgetary surpluses or deficits (and their means of financing) that the government can control the level of demand in the economy.

FIXED ASSETS. Those assets of a permanent nature that are required for the normal conduct of a business and that normally will not be converted into cash during the ensuing fiscal period.

FIXED-RATE LOAN. A loan on which the rate paid by the borrower is fixed for the life of the loan.

FLOATING CURRENCY. A currency whose exchange rate relative to those of other currencies is allowed to fluctuate more or less freely. "Dirty floating" occurs when the central bank intervenes to keep the currency from deviating outside a desired range.

FLOATING LENDING RATE. A lending rate that is established at a fixed number of percentage points above a given rate, such as the London Interbank Offer Rate (LIBOR), and that is renegotiated periodically, often every six months. Negotiation occurs throughout the life of the loan.

FOREIGN BOND. A bond issued by a nondomestic borrower in the domestic capital market.

FOREIGN EXCHANGE RATE. The price at which one currency trades for another.

FOREIGN EXCHANGE RISK. The risk that a long or short position in a foreign currency might, through an adverse movement in the relevant exchange rate, have to be closed out at a loss. The long or short position may arise out of a financial or commercial transaction.

FORWARD EXCHANGE CONTRACT. An example of a contingent liability—that is, a contract calling for delivery at a future date of a specified amount of one currency, the exchange rate being fixed at the time the contract is made.

FORWARD FED FUNDS. Fed funds traded for future delivery.

FORWARD FORWARD CONTRACT. In Eurocurrencies, a contract under which a deposit of fixed maturity is agreed to at a fixed price for future delivery.

FORWARD RATE. The rate at which forward transactions in some specific maturity are being made—for instance, the dollar price at which deutsche marks can be bought for delivery three months hence.

GLASS-STEAGALL ACT. A 1933 act in which Congress forbade commercial banks to own, underwrite, or deal in corporate stock and corporate bonds.

GOOD UNTIL CANCELLED. See *Advised Line of Credit*.

GUARANTEE. A written promise by one party, the guarantor, to be liable for the debt of another party, the principal debtor, should the latter be unable to meet his obligations. A guarantor can be a resident of the same country as that of the debtor, or he can reside in a different country, in which case he is often referred to as an external guarantor. In the latter case, banks almost unanimously transfer country exposure from the country of the debtor to the country of the guarantor when "hard" ("full and unconditional") guarantees cover the bank against all risks—commercial and political. Less frequently, banks will transfer country exposure from the country of the debtor to the country of the guarantor when certain types of "soft" guarantees (such as keepwell arrangements) are involved. The term "soft guarantee" is generally applied to comfort letters: letters of assurance, awareness, or indemnity, or keepwell agreements.

GUIDANCE LINE OF CREDIT. Credit facility used to facilitate extension of credit to a given entity, the existence of which facility, and its terms and conditions, are not formally advised to that entity.

HEDGE. To reduce risk (1) by taking a position in futures equal and opposite to an existing or anticipated cash position or (2) by shorting a security similar to one in which a long position has been established.

HERSTATT CRISIS. The cause of the crisis was a German bank (Herstatt) that failed, and cost a number of major banks large losses when it failed to make dollar payments after receiving the deutsche mark equivalent in settlement of foreign exchange transactions. This focused the market's attention on the risk inherent in settling different parts of a transaction on opposite sides of the Atlantic, because of the time difference, and on the risk of further bank failures. Since international banking involves many large transatlantic settlements, these two risks reinforced each other, and made it difficult for many banks to obtain funds. Some could not obtain them at all; others, only at a substantial margin above the normal rate.

INDIGENIZATION. Any action by a government agency that forces the transfer of controlling interest in an entity located within that government's country from foreign to private domestic interests or individuals.

INTRABANK TRANSACTIONS. Refers to asset acquisitions that take place within a holding company/bank, its branches, subsidiaries, and affiliates, and are eliminated in consolidated financial statements.

INVESTMENT BANK. A firm that engages in the origination, underwriting, and distribution of new issues.

ISSUING BANK. The bank that issues a letter of credit—usually the buyer's bank.

ITEMS IN THE PROCESS OF COLLECTION. A payee's means of receiving payment wherein a check or clean draft is presented to a bank, and settlement is completed only when payment in full is received by said bank.

KEEPWELL. One of the stronger types of comfort letters, whereby a provision is made by a parent of a borrowing subsidiary in which the parent specifies that its subsidiary will conform to certain requirements. Generally, these requirements are stated in financial terms. Although there are numerous potential requirements, some examples are that the subsidiary will

Maintain a minimum working capital or current ratio
Maintain a minimum net worth
Restrict the amount of capital expenditures
Not increase the current dividend rate or will not increase it by some stated amount.

In addition, the parent may provide further assurances of ongoing interest in the subsidiary by incorporating the following:

Maintenance of a certain percentage of ownership of the credit taker
Undertaking to maintain the credit taker in a financial condition that will allow it to honor its debt.

A keepwell should be distinguished from a "letter of assurance," which is less specific than a keepwell and normally acknowledges only that a loan has been made to a subsidiary. The parent "assures" that its subsidiary's financial condition will meet the standards of the parent. Letters of assurance are not legally binding on the issuer, whereas keepwells, depending on their wording, may be binding on the parent. According to many banks, a strong keepwell may be justification to transfer exposure from the country of the borrower to the country of the issuer.

LEAD MANAGER. Bank with the main responsibility for arranging a bond issue or an international bank credit. It has the main responsibility for agreeing on terms and conditions with the borrower, for assessing the market, and for recruiting other banks into the selling or lending syndicate. See also *Comanagers.*

LEASE. A contract by which one (such as a bank) conveys the use of property for a period of time for a specified rent. There are two types of leases:

FINANCE LEASE. A sales and financial term designating a lease that is recognized in law as providing the lessor with full ownership rights in the underlying asset, but that for tax purposes is treated as if the lessee were "owner." In a finance lease the lessee pays the lessor, over the term of the lease, a stream of payments that cover the full cost of the asset, the cost of administering and financing the asset, and a return on investment.

OPERATING LEASE. A lease in which the lessor provides specific services, such as insurance or maintenance. The contract terms usually do not guarantee the lessor full recovery of the cost of the asset, the cost of administering and financing the asset, and a return on the investment. In such cases the lessor assumes the "economic risk" of ownership.

LEGAL COMMITMENT TO LEND. A contractual agreement that is legally binding on both lender and borrower, defining terms and conditions of a loan.

LETTER OF CREDIT. A contingent liability—that is, a written instrument issued by a bank—whereby the bank substitutes its more widely known credit for that of the lesser-known credit of a buyer— addressed to a seller (beneficiary), authorizing an individual or firm to draw drafts on the bank or one of its correspondents for its account under certain conditions stipulated in the credit.

SIGHT LETTER OF CREDIT. Letter of credit calling for drafts payable upon presentation to the drawee at sight.
STANDBY LETTER OF CREDIT. Letter of credit against which the beneficiary can draw only if another business transaction is not completed. In other words, when a promissory note is given, sometimes a letter of credit is issued to back up the note; the credit will be used only if the maker of the promissory note defaults.

LIBOR. The London Interbank Offered Rate on Eurodollar deposits traded between banks. There is a different LIBOR rate for each deposit maturity. Different banks may quote slightly different LIBOR rates because they use different reference banks.

LINE OF CREDIT. An arbitrary decision made by a bank regarding the maximum amount of credit that may be extended to a customer under an uncommitted facility, advised or unadvised. See *Advised Line of Credit*.

LOAN. See *Advance, Arranged Overdraft, Casual Overdraft, Federal Funds Sold, Loans to Multilateral Agencies*, and *Term Loan*.

LOANS TO MULTILATERAL AGENCIES. Multilateral agencies are supranational organizations such as the World Bank, International Monetary Fund, Bank for International Settlements, Comecon, and Inter-American Development Bank. For the most part, exposure to multilateral agencies is monitored separately, and is not allocated to any specific country.

LOCAL CURRENCY EXPOSURE. Refers to the level of assets and other nonbalance-sheet items that are deemed to be subject to the country risk of a given country, and are denominated in the local currency of that country. Eurocurrency assets often are not included in the measurement of local currency exposure, even when the currency in question is the Euroversion of the local currency.

LONDON DOLLAR CERTIFICATES OF DEPOSIT. Certificates of deposit introduced in London in 1966 as an international variant of the CDs introduced in the United States five years earlier. Most London dollar CDs are "tap" issues made according to market demand. They are issued in minimum amounts of $25,000, but usually in blocks of $2 million or more, and usually have maturities of three to six months. Most are issued by big banks to obtain funds at margins slightly below LIBOR from other banks or institutional investors willing to hold highly rated and highly liquid paper. A minority of London dollar CDs are issued in maturities of two to three years, some of them at floating rates of interest. See also *Certificate of Deposit*.

MAKE A MARKET. A dealer is said to make a market when he quotes bid and offered prices at which he stands ready to buy and sell.

MARKETABLE SECURITIES—TRADING ACCOUNT. Securities held by an institution as inventory for the business of trading—that is, maintaining a secondary market—in such securities. These instruments may represent claims against public- and/or private-sector issuers.

MATCH-FUND. A bank is said to match-fund a loan or other asset when it does so by buying (taking) a deposit of the same maturity. The term is commonly used in the Euromarket.

MATCHED BOOK. If the distribution of the maturities of a bank's liabilities equals that of its assets, it is said to be running a matched book. The term is commonly used in the Euromarket.

MERCHANT BANK. A British term for a bank that specializes not in lending out its own funds, but in providing various financial services, such as accepting bills arising out of trade, underwriting new issues, and providing advice on acquisitions, mergers, foreign exchange, and portfolio management.

MINIMUM RISK ASSETS. Cash or assets whose conversion to cash at a future date is virtually assured, and on which the probability of loss is virtually zero.

MONETARY POLICY. That part of economic policy that regulates the level of money or liquidity in the economy in order to achieve some desired policy objective, such as the control of inflation, an improvement in the balance of payments, a certain level of employ-ment, or growth in the gross national product. It contrasts with more direct measures of control.

MONEY MARKET TRANSACTIONS. Refers to the purchase of for-eign and/or domestic bills in a given country where the interest rate on such instruments is closely tied to prevailing, well-publicized, day-to-day domestic and international market rates.

MORATORIUM. A temporary waiver of amortization on a loan, to enable the borrower to cope more easily with a cash shortage. Interest payments may continue or may also be deferred.

MULTICURRENCY CLAUSE. Such a clause on a Euroloan permits the borrower to switch from one currency to another on a rollover date.

NATIONALIZATION. Ownership and operation by the central gov-ernment of a nation of some enterprise previously a private or local government undertaking. Also, the act of taking over assets owned by either local or foreign entities or individuals, with compensation.

NEGOTIABLE CERTIFICATE OF DEPOSIT. A large-denomination (generally $1 million) CD that can be sold but cannot be cashed in before maturity.

OPERATING LEASE. See *Lease.*

OPPORTUNITY COST. The cost of pursuing one course of action measured in terms of the foregone return offered by the most attractive alternative.

PERFORMANCE BOND. A contingent liability—that is, a written instrument that substitutes a strong financial risk (usually of an insurance, bank, or bonding company) for a lesser-known risk, and which warranties compensation for nonperformance in accordance with certain conditions stipulated in the bond.

PLACEMENT. A bank depositing Eurodollars with (selling Eurodollars to) another bank is often said to be making a placement.

PRAECIPIUM. Part of the total front-end fee paid by a Eurocredit borrower that is kept by the lead managing bank or banks after payment of participation fees to other members of the lending syndicate (from the Latin praecipere, to take a prerogative share).

PREMIUM. (1) The amount by which the price at which an issue is trading exceeds the issue's par value; (2) the amount that must be paid in excess of par to call or refund an issue before maturity; (3) in money market parlance, the fact that a particular bank's CDs trade at a rate higher than others of its class, or that a bank has to pay up to acquire funds.

PRICE CONTROL. The fixing of prices by government statute in order to prevent price rises in an inflationary situation.

PRIME RATE. The published rate at which banks lend short-term money to their strongest commercial customers; most other rates are linked to it. More generally, the best rate or margin a bank charges its customers.

PROJECT FINANCE. Specifically, finance of a project, repayment of which is expected to come wholly or largely from the project. In relation to country lending, finance provided for a specific project, even if repayment does not depend on the project, rather than for balance-of-payments or other general use.

RATE RISK. In banking, the risk that profits may decline or losses may occur because a rise in interest rates forces up the cost of funding fixed-rate loans or other fixed-rate assets.

RECAPTURE CLAUSE. A clause obliging the borrower to repay the loan more rapidly if (usually) earnings or cash flow is above agreed levels; occasionally the recapture may relate to commodity prices, or rental or charter income.

REGULATION Q. Fed regulation imposing lids on the rates that banks may pay on savings and time deposits. Currently time deposits with denominations of $10,000, $100,000, or more are exempt from Regulation Q.

REPRESENTATIONS. Statements made by a Eurocredit borrower about the state of the borrower's affairs at the time the credit is being sought (in contrast with covenants, in which the borrower gives undertakings about future behavior). Also known as "warranties." Falsifications of representations and warranties are regarded as technical defaults, but often are overlooked as long as debt service is maintained. See also *Covenant*.

REPURCHASE AGREEMENT (RP OR REPO). A holder of securities sells these securities to an investor with an agreement to repurchase them at a fixed price on a fixed date. The security "buyer" in effect lends the "seller" money for the period of the agreement, and the terms of the agreement are structured to compensate him for this. Dealers use RP extensively to finance their positions. Exception: When the Fed is said to be doing RP, it is lending money—that is, increasing bank reserves.

RESCHEDULING. A rearrangement of amortization and/or extension of the maturity of a loan caused by the borrower's inability to meet the original repayment schedule.

RESERVE REQUIREMENTS. The percentages of different types of deposits that member banks are required to hold on deposit at the Fed.

REVOLVER. See *Revolving Line of Credit.*

REVOLVING LINE OF CREDIT. A bank line of credit on which the customer pays a commitment fee, and can take down and repay funds according to his needs. Normally the line involves a firm commitment from the bank for a period of several years.

RISK. Degree of uncertainty of return on an asset.

RISK ASSETS. All assets of a bank except cash and minimum-risk items.

ROLL OVER. To reinvest funds received from a maturing security in a new issue of the same or a similar security.

ROLLOVER. Most term loans in the Euromarket are made on a rollover basis, which means that the loan is periodically repriced at an agreed spread over the appropriate, currently prevailing LIBOR rate.

RP. See *Repurchase Agreement.*

SAVINGS DEPOSIT. Interest-bearing deposit at a savings institution that has no specific maturity.

SCALE. A bank that offers to pay different rates of interest on CDs of varying maturities is said to "post a scale." Commercial paper issuers also post scales.

SDRs. Special Drawing Rights. Money created by the International Monetary Fund with the approval of a large majority of member countries and distributed among all member countries. This paper money is used only in transactions among governments and between governments and the IMF.

SELL DOWN. The process of syndicating an underwritten loan to reduce the managers' share to the amount they wish to keep.

SELLING GROUP. All banks marketing a new Eurobond issue.

SELLING PERIOD. A week or ten days during which managing banks canvass demand for a new issue among underwriters and other selling-group banks on the basis of provisionally indicated coupon rate and issuing price. These terms are formally agreed upon at the end of the selling period on the basis of demand expressed.

SIGHT LETTER OF CREDIT. See *Letter of Credit.*

SPOT MARKET. Market for immediate, as opposed to future, delivery. In the spot market for foreign exchange, settlement is two business days ahead.

SPOT RATE. The price prevailing in the spot market.

SPREAD. (1) Difference between bid and asked prices on a security; (2) difference between yields on or prices of two securities of differing sorts or differing maturities; (3) in underwriting, difference between price realized by the issuer and price paid by the investor.

STANDBY LETTER OF CREDIT. See *Letter of Credit.*

SUBROGATION. The taking over of the rights of a creditor in return for paying the obligation due to that creditor—in other words, the payer stands in the payee's shoes.

SWAP. (1) In securities, selling one issue and buying another; (2) in foreign exchange, buying a currency spot and simultaneously selling it forward.

SWAP RATE. In the foreign exchange market, the difference between the spot and forward rates at which a currency is traded.

SYNDICATION. Act of marketing a bond issue or an international bank loan through a syndicate of banks acting jointly for that special purpose (as distinct from banks permanently grouped together).

TERM FED FUNDS. Fed funds sold for a period of time longer than overnight.

TERM LOAN. Usually a long-term loan, with a maturity from one to ten years, extended by large commercial banks to large, well-established business enterprises and repayable according to a specified schedule (for the most part in periodic installments) under a legal agreement between the bank and the borrower.

TERM RP (REPO). RP borrowings for a period longer than overnight; may be 30, 60, or even 90 days.

TIGHT MARKET. A tight market, as opposed to a thin market, is one in which volume is large, trading is active and highly competitive, and spreads between bid and ask prices are narrow.

TIME DEPOSIT. Interest-bearing deposit at a savings institution that has a specific maturity.

TOM NEXT. In the interbank market in Eurodollar deposits and the foreign exchange market, the value (delivery) date on a Tom next transaction is the next business day. (Refers to "tomorrow next.")

TOMBSTONE. Advertisement placed by banks shortly after a new bond issue or syndicated credit, to record their part in its arrangement.

TRADING PAPER. CDs purchased by accounts that are likely to resell them. The term is commonly used in the Euromarket.

TRANSFER PRICING. The sale of goods or services by one company to another in the same group at a price set by the group, not by the market. Can be used to move profits or cash from one company to another.

TRUSTEES. Independent agents, often accountants or lawyers, appointed to look after the investors' interests in a bond issue. The trustee is never an actual investor. See also *Agent Bank*.

UNDERWRITER. A dealer who purchases new issues from the issuer and distributes them to investors. Underwriting is one function of an investment banker.

UNDERWRITTEN LOAN. A syndicated loan in which one or more managers undertake to provide the borrower with a specific amount, which is more than they really wish to lend, and then syndicate (sell down) the portion they do not want. See also *Best-Efforts Syndication.*

UNMATCHED BOOK. If the average maturity of a bank's liabilities is less than that of its assets, it is said to be running an unmatched book. The term is commonly used in the Euromarket. Equivalent expressions are "open book" and "short book."

UPSTREAM GUARANTEE. A guarantee by a subsidiary of amounts owed by its parent.

UPSTREAMING. The excessive withdrawal of cash from a subsidiary for the benefit of the parent, by means of loans, royalties, management fees, dividends, or leading and lagging.

VALUE DATE. In the market for Eurodollar deposits and foreign exchange, value date refers to the delivery date of funds traded. Normally, on spot transactions it is two days after a transaction is agreed upon, and in the case of a forward foreign exchange trade, it is the future date.

SOURCES

This glossary is a synthesis of terms selected from the glossaries of the following publications:

Association of Reserve City Bankers (ARCB), *Country Exposure Measurement and Reporting Practices of Member Banks* (New York: ARCB, 1977). Reprinted by permission of the publisher.

T. H. Donaldson, *Lending in International Commercial Banking* (New York: John Wiley and Sons, 1979). Reprinted by permission of the author; Macmillan, London and Basingstoke; and John Wiley and Sons, Inc. (American publishers).

Rita M. Rodriguez, E. Eugene Carter, *International Financial Management*, © 1979. Reprinted by permission of Prentice-Hall, Inc., Englewood Cliffs, NJ.

Marcia Stigum, *The Money Market: Myth, Reality and Practice* (Homewood, Ill.: Dow Jones-Irwin, 1978). Reprinted by permission of the publisher.

INDEX

Acceptance financing, 47
Accounting practices (*see also* Financial statements): auditing standards, 267; imperfections in, 267; international variation in, 267
Affiliates, foreign (*see* Subsidiaries)
African Development Bank, 449
Agreement corporations, 7, 28, 42
American Institute of Certified Public Accountants (AICPA), 124
Antwerp, 5
Arbitrage (*see* Foreign exchange)
Arthur Andersen and Company, 124
Asiadollar market, 61, 66
Asian currency market, 64-66; Asian currency unit (ACU), 66, 89
Asian Development Bank, 448-49
Asset-liability committee (*see* Sources and uses of funds committee)
Asset-liability management, integration with domestic operations, 98

Bahamas (Nassau), 12, 59, 87-88, 129
Bahrain, 86, 91-92, 476
Balance of payments, nonoil developing countries, 421-428
Banks, foreign: capital of, 402; country risk, 396-97; credit facilities to, 390-92; credit review of, 400-5; early signs of problems, 402; evaluating financial condition of, 403-5; government banks, 397-98; guarantees, 185-86, 187; interbank deposits, 393-94; lines of credit to, 392-93; loans and placements to, 179-81; measures and ratios, 404-5; nongovernment banks, 398-99; ownership and management, 401; risk exposure, 395-97; specialized banks, 399; standby loans, 392; two-named paper, 393; types of banks, 397-99
BankAmerica, 135
Bank for International Settlements (BIS), 61, 71, 129, 263, 468
Bank Holding Companies (BHCs), 35
Bankers' acceptances, 6, 101-2, 289; creation, 32, 295; definition of, 32, 179
Bankhaus D. I. Herstatt, failure of, 394, 491

Bill of lading, 297-98
Board of Governors (*see* Federal Reserve System)
Branches of U.S. banks, foreign, 14-15, 41; assets, 14-15, 20-22; location and number, 20; operations, 17

Calvo Doctrine, 147, 153
Capital: adequacy of, 110-11; sources of, 99, 110-11
Cash flow: definition of, 255; projections, 276-77; repayment approach, 255
Cayman Islands, 59, 87-88, 129
Certificate of origin, 299
Chase Manhattan Bank, 135
Chemical Bank, 133
Citicorp, 133, 135
Clearing House Interbank Payments System (CHIPS), 34
Cocktail bonds, 77-80
Collateral, 186-88, 257-58
Collections, 33-34
Commodity Credit Corporation, 451
Common Market (*see* European Economic Community)
Comptroller of the currency, U.S., 111
Consortium banking, 15, 25-27, 42-43, 484
Correspondent banks, 15, 16-17, 31, 41, 42; collection handling, 17, 33-34; funds transfer, 17, 30-31; international services, 17, 34; reciprocal relationships, 16
Country exposure and risk, 199-221, 344-45; balance of payments and, 263; data services, 263; debt-service ratio, 209; designing a rating system, 213-221; evaluating economic structure, 202-5; external economic aspects, 207-8; gross national product (GNP) as indicator, 203, 218; lending limits and sublimits, 199-200, 251, 345-46; liquidity aspects, 208-9, 218; liquidity ratios, 209; monetary aspects, 205-6, 218; policies, fiscal and monetary, 259; political aspects, internal and external, 211-13; review group, 220; sovereign immunity and risk, 146, 154-60;

ABOUT THE EDITOR
AND CONTRIBUTORS

EMMANUEL N. ROUSSAKIS is a professor of finance at Florida International University, Miami. Concurrently he is director of the Certificate in Banking Program, the Certificate in Savings and Loan Program, and the Certificate in International Bank Management Program, designed by the Finance Department of Florida International University in cooperation with Miami's financial community for the training of bank and savings and loan personnel.

Dr. Roussakis also received a Florida State Research (STAR) grant for the study of international banking legislation and taxation; study recommendations were the basis for legislative changes implemented in July 1979 and June 1980, respectively.

Dr. Roussakis has taught at American universities in the United States and Europe, worked for American and European banks, and served in an advisory capacity to government agencies, both in the United States and abroad. He participated in the negotiations for Greece's admission to the European Economic Community in the area of commercial banks and banking policy. He has published widely on banking subjects, and his articles have appeared in academic and professional journals in the United States as well as in Belgium, France, Germany, Greece, and Italy.

Dr. Roussakis is the author of *Friedrich List, the Zollverein and the Uniting of Europe* (College of Europe Press, 1968), *Managing Commercial Bank Funds* (Praeger, 1977), and *Miami's International Banking Community: Foreign Banks, Edge Act Corporations and Local Banks* (Peat, Marwick, Mitchell, 1981). He is also editor of and contributor to *International Lending by U.S. Commercial Banks: A Casebook* (Praeger, 1981).

Dr. Roussakis holds a B.A. from Athens University; an M.B.A. from Atlanta University; a Graduate Certificate in Advanced European Studies from the College of Europe, Bruges; and a Ph.D. from the Catholic University of Louvain. While pursuing his education he lived in the Middle East, in Europe, and in the United States. He speaks English, French, Greek, and Arabic.

ANTHONY ANGELINI is associate professor of economics and finance at St. John's University, New York City. He also is research analyst for the Budget Review Office, Suffolk County Legislature, New York. He received his B.S. and M.A. degrees in economics from Temple University. He did further graduate study at Columbia University, where he was a Ford Foundation fellow, and the London School of Economics. He has had consulting and professional experience with the banking industry and on Wall Street. He is coauthor of *International Lending, Risk, and the Euromarkets* (John Wiley and Sons, 1979).

KAJ ARESKOUG is senior economist, Economics-Policy Research Department, Bank of America, San Francisco. From 1979 to 1982 he was professor of finance at the Graduate School of Business, Pace University, New York City. He holds a Ph.D. from Columbia University and a law degree from the University of Lund, Sweden. He also has taught at New York University, the University of Texas, and Columbia University, and has served as a research economist at major banks and corporations. Dr. Areskoug's research has focused primarily on capital flows to developing countries, multinational enterprises, exchange-rate instability, and international capital markets. His articles have appeared in *Review of Economics and Statistics*, *Southern Economic Journal*, *Economica*, and *Economic Development and Cultural Change*. He is coauthor (with Ingo Walter) of the third edition of *International Economics* (John Wiley and Sons, 1981).

BOWMAN BROWN is a partner in the Miami law firm of Shutts and Bowen. He also serves as adjunct professor of banking law at the University of Miami School of Law. Mr. Brown is chairman of the Florida Bar Banking Law and Credit Regulation Committee, and is a member of the Florida Comptroller's International Finance Council. He is the editor of *International Banking Centres* (Euromoney, 1982) and the author of "Interstate Banking and a Report from the Test Site" (*Banking Law Journal*, August 1981). He is a frequent speaker at the Practising Law Institute, Euromoney, and other programs relating to banking law.

ROGER A. COE, president of Barco Finance Corporation, Miami, is the former president of Bishops International Bank Ltd., Nassau, Bahamas, a merchant bank with worldwide activities. Mr. Coe was graduated from St. John's University in New York City and received his LL.B. from St. John's University School of Law, New York City. He is a member of the New York State Bar and the Inter-American Bar Association.

DWIGHT B. CRANE is professor of business administration at the Harvard Business School, where he teaches courses in the management of financial institutions. Before joining the faculty in 1969, he was director of management science at Mellon Bank. His research has led to his being coauthor of two books: *NOW Accounts: Strategies for Financial Institutions* (Lexington Books, 1978) and *Management of Bank Portfolios* (John Wiley and Sons, 1975). He has also written *Management of Credit Lines and Commitments* (Association of Reserve City Bankers, 1973), and has contributed frequently to banking and finance journals. Professor Crane is a member of the Editorial Advisory Board of the *Journal of Bank Research*, and previously served as finance department editor for *Management Science*. A graduate of MIT and the University of Michigan (M.B.A.), he received his Ph.D. from Carnegie-Mellon University.

ROBERT S. DAMERJIAN is executive vice-president of the Girard Bank in Philadelphia. He was previously senior vice-president of the J. Henry Schroder Banking Corporation and the Schroder Trust Company in New York City. He is also a director of the Girard International Bank in New York City and of Lombard-Wall International Ltd., London. Mr. Damerjian received his B.S. from Temple University and the M.B.A. from the Wharton Graduate School of the University of Pennsylvania. He also attended the Graduate School of Business of New York University. He has served on the faculties of Temple University, Drexel University, and the Pennsylvania Bankers Association School of Banking. He is also a lecturer at the Federal Reserve System Examiners School in Washington. In addition to being a past president of the Greater Philadelphia Money Market Association, Mr. Damerjian was one of its founders. He served as chairman of the Bank Investment Division of the Pennsylvania

Bankers Association. He has had numerous articles published in various publications.

GUNTER DUFEY is professor of international business and finance at the Graduate School of Business Administration, University of Michigan. Dr. Dufey joined the faculty of this university in 1969. His academic interests center on international money and capital markets as well as on financial policy of multinational corporations. He teaches related courses at the graduate level, and covers these subjects in the school's Executive Development Programs. He has had visiting appointments at C.E.I. in Geneva, Switzerland; at the universities of Augsburg (1974) and Würzburg (1980), Germany; at the Cranfield Institute, Bedford, England (summers 1975 and 1976); and the University of Texas at Dallas (1979). During 1981-82 he holds appointments as national fellow at the Hoover Institution and visiting professor of finance at the Graduate School of Business, Stanford University.

DAVID K. EITEMAN is professor of finance and director of the UCLA Management in the Arts Program at the UCLA Graduate School of Management, where he teaches courses in international business finance and financial management of not-for-profit organizations.

In 1965, Dr. Eiteman served as consultant to the Ministry of Finance of the government of Chile, and in 1966-67 he was resident research professor at the Institute for the Development of Executives in Argentina, in Buenos Aires. More recently he has been a visiting faculty member at the Cranfield Institute in Bedford, England, and at the Pacific Area Management Institute of the University of Hawaii. He has made presentations to executive programs in Canada, Mexico, Japan, Venezuela, Peru, Argentina, Uruguay, and Guatemala, as well as in the United States. He serves as a board member for the Sierra Growth Fund and the California Chamber Symphony.

Dr. Eiteman's publications include *Multinational Business Finance*, 3rd ed. (Addison-Wesley, 1982), coauthored with Arthur I. Stonehill, and *Essentials of Investing* (Irwin, 1974), coauthored with

Keith V. Smith. Dr. Eiteman did his undergraduate work at the University of Michigan and received his doctorate from Northwestern University.

IAN H. GIDDY is an associate professor at Columbia University's Graduate School of Business. He has also been an assistant professor at the University of Michigan, a visiting assistant professor at the University of Chicago, and a professorial lecturer at Georgetown University. He has served in the U.S. government as financial economist at the Comptroller of the Currency and as senior financial analyst at the Board of Governors of the Federal Reserve System. During 1980–81 he was on leave as an economist at the International Monetary Fund. Presently he is a senior international economist at the Claremont Economics Institute.

Dr. Giddy's research and teaching experience reflect his interest in international finance, financial markets, and financial management. He is coauthor of *The International Money Market* (Prentice-Hall, 1978) and coeditor of the forthcoming *International Finance Handbook* (Wiley, 1982), and is currently writing a book on international banking regulation.

DOUGLAS A. HAYES has been professor of finance at the Graduate School of Business, University of Michigan, since 1955 and lecturer at the Graduate School of Bank Management, University of Michigan, since its inception in 1976. His primary research and teaching are in the fields of banking and investments. Professor Hayes's publications include *Investments: Analysis and Management*, 3rd ed. (Macmillan, 1976), *Bank Lending Policies: Domestic and International*, 3rd ed. (University of Michigan Press, 1977), and *Bank Funds Management: Issues and Practices* (University of Michigan Press, 1980), as well as numerous articles in such journals as *Financial Analysts Journal* and *The Bankers Magazine*. Since 1971 he has been chairman of the board of Security Bancorp, Southgate, Michigan. At present he is chairman of its Assets and Liability Management Committee and Senior Loan Committee. In addition he was consulting financial economist, U.S. Treasury Department, 1951-54, and lecturer, Netherlands School of Economics, 1968.

SAMUEL L. HAYES III is Jacob H. Schiff professor of investment banking at the Harvard Business School, where he teaches courses in the management of financial institutions and corporate finance. He has published a wide range of articles on investment and merchant banking, the capital markets, and corporate financial management. He is a member of the Editorial Board of the *Harvard Business Review*, is an associate editor of *The Financial Review*, and has served as an adviser to the Justice and Treasury departments and to the Securities and Exchange Commission on securities market issues. He is a graduate of Swarthmore College, and received his M.B.A. and D.B.A. from Harvard University.

RICHARD L. HEILMAN is a senior vice-president and deputy territorial administrator of the North America Territory for Security Pacific National Bank in Los Angeles. He is a graduate of the University of Southern California with an M.B.A. in finance. He has extensive domestic U.S. and international banking experience starting in 1963, after a period in Asia as a Navy officer and as a consultant to a Japanese manufacturing company. From 1969 to 1980, he was posted in London, during which time his positions included chief executive officer of a European merchant bank. He joined Security Pacific in 1977.

CHRISTOPHER M. KORTH received his doctorate in international business and finance from Indiana University in 1969. Between 1969 and 1971 he was assistant professor of international business and economics at Pennsylvania State University. In 1971–73 he was assistant professor of international business and director of research for the Institute of International Commerce at the University of Michigan. Between 1973 and 1977 he was assistant vice-president and chief international economist with the First National Bank of Chicago. Since August 1977 he has been associate professor of international business and finance at the University of South Carolina.

Dr. Korth is the coauthor of *International Business: An Introduction to the World of the Multinational Firm* (Prentice-Hall, 1972), and has written many articles for scholarly journals on such topics as the management of foreign exchange risk, the prospects for East-

West trade, international lending risk, and the impact of foreign investments upon host countries. He has been a visiting professor at colleges in England and Ecuador, and is an international financial consultant with several corporations.

BOB KURAU is a vice-president of Walter E. Heller and Company Southeast. He was formerly a vice-president of Marine Midland Grace, a New York bank involved in import/export financing. He also served as president of Bank Associates of New York and the Planning Executive Institute of Miami. He has been a guest lecturer with the Florida Department of Commerce and the U.S. Department of Commerce on export factoring. As part of his duties with Walter E. Heller, he has responsibilities for the financing of foreign trade.

ANDREW M. MACLAREN was educated at Cambridge University, where he studied economics and law, and is now vice-president and European legal adviser to Security Pacific National Bank in London. He formerly served as a vice-president, and later international counsel, of Marine Midland Bank, N.A., in New York, where he was active in the structuring and documentation of international transactions. Mr. MacLaren lectures regularly on the legal and financial aspects of international credit transactions.

LAZAROS P. MAVRIDES is vice-president of Morgan Guaranty Trust Company of New York. He holds B.A., M.A., and Ph.D. degrees in economics and administrative sciences from Yale University. He has been at the Morgan Bank since 1970. He is at present head of Financial Management Services, and secretary of the Sources and Uses of Funds Committee at the Morgan Bank. Dr. Mavrides has given a number of international banking seminars at the invitation of the American Bankers Association, the Federación Latinoamericana de Bancos, and the European Working Group on Operational Research in Banking. He has also served as chairman of the banking session at a number of conferences of the Institute of Management Sciences, the Operations Research Society of America, and the European Congress on Operational Research. He is a member of the Executive Board and chairman of the Awards Committee of the Yale

Science and Engineering Association. He has published about a dozen articles on various subjects in banking and finance.

PHILIP G. MOON is senior vice-president and officer in charge of the National Bank of Detroit's International Division. He has been head of that division since December 1973. Mr. Moon received an A.B. degree in mathematics, magna cum laude, from Dartmouth College in 1942, and attended the Amos Tuck Graduate School of Business Administration at Dartmouth from September 1941 to May 1942. Mr. Moon is a director of Lamb Technicon Corporation, the Besser Company, and the Friends of the Detroit Public Library. He is a member of the Bankers Association for Foreign Trade, past chairman and trustee of the Rehabilitation Institute, Inc., treasurer of the Michigan Chapter of the United Negro College Fund, and past president of the National Association of Credit Management, Eastern Michigan Division. He is also a visiting lecturer at the University of Michigan Graduate School of Business.

JAMES P. MORRIS is vice-president in charge of the Trade Finance Group of Southeast Bank, N.A., Miami. In this capacity he is responsible for the bank's export loan portfolio. Mr. Morris holds an M.B.A. from Marquette University, Milwaukee. The whole of his 15-year international banking career has been spent in the trade finance area.

LAUREL A. NICHOLS, a partner in the law firm of Sage Gray Todd & Sims of New York City and Miami, graduated from Pomona College (B.A. summa cum laude, 1969) and Stanford University Law School (J.D., 1972). She is a member of the bar in California, New York, and Florida. Her practice is concentrated on the representation of banks, both domestic and foreign, particularly with respect to their financing transactions.

ARTURO C. PORZECANSKI is associate economist with the International Economics Department of Morgan Guaranty Trust Company of New York, where he acts as an adviser on Latin American economic and political affairs. He holds a B.A. in economics from Whittier College, and M.A. and Ph.D. degrees in economics from the University of Pittsburgh. Dr. Porzecanksi has served with the International Monetary Fund and the Center for Latin American Monetary Studies. He has published three books and approximately a dozen articles on international and Latin American economics and politics.

INGO WALTER is professor of economics and finance, and chairman of the International Business Department at the Graduate School of Business Administration of New York University. From 1971 to 1976 he served as associate dean for academic affairs of the school. He previously taught at the University of Missouri-St. Louis, where he was chairman of the Department of Economics from 1967 to 1970. He received his A.B. and M.S. degrees from Lehigh University and his Ph.D. degree in 1966 from New York University.

Dr. Walter's principal areas of research include international trade policy, international banking, environmental economics, and economics of multinational corporate operations. He has published papers in professional journals in these fields and is the author or editor of a dozen books, including a widely used textbook. One of his recent books is *Multinationals Under Fire: Lessons in the Management of Conflict*, written with Thomas N. Gladwin (Wiley-Interscience, 1980), which deals with nonmarket factors affecting foreign direct investment. At the present time his research interests focus on the international banking industry, and risk elements relating to international trade and capital flows.

Dr. Walter has served as a consultant to a number of U.N. agencies, the U.S. Department of Commerce, the U.S. Environmental Protection Agency, the National Academy of Sciences, the Ford Foundation, and other institutions, as well as private firms such as General Electric, IBM, Citibank, Chemical Bank, and Morgan Guaranty Trust Company. He has held research grants from the Ford, Rockefeller, National Science, General Electric, and Alcoa foundations.

CLAS WIHLBORG is assistant professor of finance and international business at the Graduate School of Business Administration of New York University. He received his Ph.D. in economics from Princeton University in 1977. Dr. Wihlborg's principal areas of research include international finance and monetary economics, and the economics of common property resources. He has published papers in professional journals in these fields, and is coeditor (with Richard M. Levich) of *Exchange Risk and Exposure* (Lexington Books/D. C. Heath, 1980). At the present time his research interests focus on the transmission of disturbances between the real and financial sectors via the exchange rate, and on the economics of exposure management for multinational corporations.